P.E. Teacher's Pre-Sport Skill Lessons, Activities & Games
for Grades 4-6

JOANNE M. LANDY

illustrations by Joanne M. Landy

PARKER PUBLISHING COMPANY
Paramus, New Jersey 07652

Library of Congress Cataloging-in-Publication Data
Landy, Joanne M.
   P.E. teacher's pre-sport skill lessons, activities & games for grades 4-6/
Joanne M. Landy.
     p. cm.
  ISBN 0-13-042751-9
   1. Physical education for children—Curricula.   2. Physical education for
children—Planning.   I. Title: Physical education teacher's pre-sport skill lessons,
activities & games for grades 4-6. II. Title.

GV443 .L333   2002
372.86—dc21   2001059349

Acquisitions Editor: *Susan Kolwicz*
Production Editor: *Tom Curtin*
Interior Design/Formatter: *Inkwell Publishing Services*

© 2002 *by* Joanne M. Landy

Printed in the United States of America

10 9 8 7 6 5 4 3 2

ISBN 0-13-042751-9

Parker Publishing Company
Paramus, NJ 07652

www.phdirect.com/education

DEDICATION

To my dear children, Max and Nikki, and their
children to be—thank you for your constant love,
support, and friendship through the years.

And to the educators of young children who through their
love, compassion, and dedication bring quality, enjoyable
movement experiences to enhance lifelong quality lifestyle!

ABOUT THE AUTHOR

Joanne earned a BED degree, graduating with Great Distinction from the University of Regina, Saskatchewan, Canada in 1974. She also completed a postgraduate international P.E. study course through Concordia University in Montreal, Quebec, and in 1999 a Personal Trainer course through Renouf Fitness Academy in Perth, Western Australia.

Joanne's professional background includes 10 years of secondary teaching in Physical Education/Health and Mathematics; 10 years of specialist teaching in primary Physical Education and Health, as well as several years of University Demonstration teaching in P.E. methodology and pedagogy programs in the Canadian school system. In 1988 Joanne and her late husband, Professor Max Landy, were part of the leadership team for the National Youth Foundation Fitness Camp, held over a 2-month period in Los Angeles, California.

Joanne has presented at major HPERD conferences in the U.S.A., ACHPER conferences in Australia, and PENZ conferences in New Zealand. She also has facilitated many P.E. workshops for primary/secondary teachers in the field and for teacher training programs in P.E. at the University of Western Australia and Notre Dame College of Education in Perth; Western Washington University, Washington, U.S.A.; University of Regina, Saskatchewan, Canada; and major University centers throughout New Zealand. For the past 3 years Joanne has been lecturing at Murdoch University, Faculty of Education, in primary Physical Education teacher training programs in Perth.

She has co-authored several elementary and lower secondary P.E. resources in the areas of movement, dance, fitness, gross and fine motor skills development, teaching strategies and methods, including the *Ready-to-Use PE Activities Program (K–9)* (co-authored with Max Landy, Parker Publishing, 1993) and *Complete Motor Skills Activities Program* (co-authored with Keith Burridge, The Center for Applied Research in Education, 2000), a teaching, assessing, and remediation program. Currently Joanne is developing "Innovative and Manipulative Educational Equipment" handbooks, plus a Fitness book for young children (ages 3-12).

Joanne now resides with her children, Max, Jr. and Nikki, in Perth and operates a Lifestyle Education Consulting business which provide in-depth workshops and inservicing in Physical Education at all levels, including University P.E. teacher-training programs. Joanne has been instrumental in developing and coordinating Youth Activity-Based programs at the recreation centers including "Tune-up Kids" program for young children ages 5–12 years, focusing on development of fundamental movement skills and fitness, basketball development program for 6–12-year-olds, and a program of motivation and self-esteem for teenage girls (13–18 years of age) called "On the Move." She also has initiated several "Tune Up" programs for adults including Tune-Up Basketball; Tune-Up Volleyball; Tune-Up Shape Up (Fitness), and provided team-building and motivational sessions for school staffs, corporate business groups, and other community interest groups. She maintains an active lifestyle in Perth centering on her own personal fitness, tennis, golfing, dancing, jogging, wave skiing, gardening, playing guitar, and writing.

ACKNOWLEDGMENTS

I take this opportunity to once again thank my publisher and editor, Win Huppuch and Susan Kolwicz, and also my production editor, Tom Curtin, at Parker Publishing, for their editorial and production expertise and wonderful support in the making of this book.

I also express a special thank-you to Keith Burridge, my co-writer of other resources, for his advice and guidance in developing the Pre-sport Skill Program.

Finally, my thanks go out to the field teachers, teachers-in-training at tertiary institutes, sports coaches, recreation instructors, and special group leaders of young children, and the hundreds of children who have contributed with their enthusiastic involvement and valuable feedback over the years to the direction and development of this comprehensive resource.

CONTENTS

SECTION 1: TO THE TEACHER 1

ABOUT THIS RESOURCE 1
Bridging the Gap 1
How to Use This Resource 2
The Format 2
Lesson Format Components 2
Teaching Pre-sports Skills 4
Skill Builder Stations 4
The Game 5
The Appendix 6
Tune-up Kids Activity Journal 7

TEACHING POINTERS 7
Sport Skills Acquisition Model 7
Guidelines for Teaching FMS 8
Guidelines for Teaching Games 10
Guidelines for Modifying Games 11
Effective Teaching Methods and Strategies 11
Characteristics of a Pre-adolescent Child 13
Strategies to Encourage the Reluctant Child 14
Components of a Quality Physical Education Program 15
Key Focus Areas of a Balanced Physical Education Program (K–12) 15
Progressive Lesson Model for Teaching Pre-sport Skills 15
Components of a Progressive Lesson. 17

ORGANIZATION AND MANAGEMENT TOOLS 18
Signals as Management Tools 18
The Teamness Concept 18
Organization Signals 19
Formation Signals 21
Starting Positions 23
The Break Concept 24

THE IMPORTANCE OF FITNESS 25
The Preventive Approach. 25
Essential Understandings 27
◆ The "Feel Good Model" of Total Well-being 27
◆ Definition of Fitness 28

◆ Benefits of Fitness 28
◆ Components of Physical Fitness 28
◆ The F.I.T.T. Principle 29
◆ Target Heart Rate 29
◆ Guidelines for Teaching Fitness 30
◆ Twenty Exercise Recommendations 31

SECTION 2: FOUNDATION MOVEMENT REVISION/EXTENSION . 33

KEY FOCUS AREAS: Locomotion, Body Management, and Fitness

Lesson 1:   Organization Signals 35
Lesson 2:   Formation and Grouping Signals—Partner Play 39
Lesson 3:   Grouping Signals—Small Group Play 43
Lesson 4:   Large Group Signals—Teamness 47
Lesson 5:   Aerobic Fitness-builder Stations 51
Lesson 6:   Large Group Signals—Islands, Jumping, and Landings 53
Lesson 7:   Individual Rhythm Rope Jumping, Cooperation Jumping 56
Lesson 8:   Partner Rope Jumping, Aerobic Fitness 61
Lesson 9:   Static and Dynamic Balancing 64
Lesson 10: Aerobic Fitness and Strengtheners 68
Lesson 11: Fit-kid Circuit—Fitness Builder Stations 72

SECTION 3: OBJECT-CONTROL SKILLS USING INNOVATIVE AND MANIPULATIVE EQUIPMENT 77

KEY FOCUS AREAS: Sending and Receiving Revision/Extension

Lesson 12: Underhand Throwing and Catching Using Beanbags/Deck Rings . . . 79
Lesson 13: Low-organized and Lead-up Games Using Beanbags/Deck Rings . . 84
Lesson 14: Tracking and Catching Using Catchballs™ 87
Lesson 15: Overhand Throwing and Catching Using Beanbags/Foxtails™/
Small Balls 93
Lesson 16: Low-organized Games Using Overhand Throwing 97
Lesson 17: More Low-organized and Lead-up Games Using Catchballs™
and Foxtails™ 100
Lesson 18: Rolling and Fielding a Small Ball 103
Lesson 19: Frisbee™ Throwing Using Deck Rings/Frisbees™/Woosh Rings™ . 106
Lesson 20: Frisbee™ Throwing Games 110
Lesson 21: Sending and Receiving Skill Builder Stations 112
Lesson 22: Scoop Play 114
Lesson 23: Scoop and Whiffle Ball 118
Lesson 24: Sending and Receiving an Oval Object 120
Lesson 25: More Sending and Receiving Skill Builder Stations 124

SECTION 4: PRE-SPORT SKILLS . . 127

KEY FOCUS AREA: Basketball Play

Lesson 26: Ball Handling/Chest and Bounce Pass 129
Lesson 27: Footwork/Control Dribbling/Passing. 135
Lesson 28: Footwork/Crossover/Speed Dribbling 139
Lesson 29: Dribbling/Shooting/Passing 143
Lesson 30: Shooting/Layup 148
Lesson 31: Overhead and Sidearm Passing/Layup Shooting 151
Lesson 32: Baseball Pass/Passing Plays 155
Lesson 33: Defense/Offense 159
Lesson 34: Rebounding/Blocking Out. 164
Lesson 35: Skill Builder Stations 168
Lesson 36: Lead-up and Modified Games 171

KEY FOCUS AREA: Floor Hockey Play

Lesson 37: Stick-handling Skills 175
Lesson 38: Shooting and Goalkeeping. 178
Lesson 39: Passing 181
Lesson 40: Facing-off/Offense and Defense. 184
Lesson 41: Skill Builder Stations 187
Lesson 42: Lead-up and Modified Games 190

KEY FOCUS AREA: Volleyball Play

Lesson 43: Underhand Serving. 194
Lesson 44: Setting (Overhead Pass) 197
Lesson 45: Bumping (Forearm Pass) 200
Lesson 46: Overhand Serving. 203
Lesson 47: Digging and Serve Reception. 206
Lesson 48: Introduction to Spiking and Tipping 209
Lesson 49: Introduction to Blocking. 212
Lesson 50: Skill Builder Stations 214
Lesson 51: Lead-up and Modified Games 216

KEY FOCUS AREA: Soccer Play

Lesson 52: Dribbling 221
Lesson 53: Passing and Receiving the Pass 224
Lesson 54: Goal-kicking 228
Lesson 55: Trapping 231
Lesson 56: Tackling 234
Lesson 57: Goalkeeping 236
Lesson 58: Heading the Ball/Throw-in 239
Lesson 59: Skill Builder Stations 243
Lesson 60: Lead-up and Modified Games 245

KEY FOCUS AREA: Softball Play

Lesson 61: Throwing and Catching. 248
Lesson 62: Fielding Grounders/Sidearm Throw 251
Lesson 63: Fielding Fly Balls. 254
Lesson 64: Pitching and Back-catching 257
Lesson 65: Batting 260
Lesson 66: Base Running. 263

Lesson 67:   Skill Builder Stations 266
Lesson 68:   Lead-up and Modified Games 268

KEY FOCUS AREA: Cricket Play
Lesson 69:   Bowling. 273
Lesson 70:   Batting/Fielding 276
Lesson 71:   Lead-up and Modified Games 280

KEY FOCUS AREA: Netball Play
Lesson 72:   Passing and Catching/Footwork 284
Lesson 73:   Goal-scoring 288
Lesson 74:   Lead-up and Modified Games 291

KEY FOCUS AREA: Racquet and Ball Play
Lesson 75:   Handball Play/Forehand Stroking/Footwork. 293
Lesson 76:   Paddle Ball Play/Forehand Stroking/Footwork 296
Lesson 77:   Backhand Stroke/Footwork. 299
Lesson 78:   Ground Strokes and Volleys 302
Lesson 79:   Serving 305
Lesson 80:   Skill Builder Stations 308
Lesson 81:   Lead-up and Modified Games 310

KEY FOCUS AREA: Flag Football Play
Lesson 82:   Passing and Catching 313
Lesson 83:   Ball Snap and Lateral Pass 316
Lesson 84:   Pattern Running and Defensive Guarding 318
Lesson 85:   Ball Carrying and Handing-off 321
Lesson 86:   Punting and Place-kicking. 324
Lesson 87:   Blocking and Tackling. 327
Lesson 88:   Skill Builder Stations 331
Lesson 89:   Lead-up and Modified Games 333

KEY FOCUS AREA: Rhythm and Dance
Lesson 90:   The Bird Dance/Balance Feathers. 337
Lesson 91:   The Bunny Hop/The Stepping Routine 340
Lesson 92:   The Twist/The Schottische 343
Lesson 93:   The Hustle/Rhythmic Ribbons 347
Lesson 94:   Aerobic Ropes/La Raspa/The Limbo 351
Lesson 95:   Barn Dance/Mayim/Rhythm Sticks 354
Lesson 96:   Parachute Dance/Virginia Reel 358
Lesson 97:   Grand March/Cha-cha 362
Lesson 98:   Square Dancing 366
Lesson 99:   The Butterfly/The Troika 369
Lesson 100: The Madison/Progressive Jiving 372

SECTION 5: APPENDIX 377

PRE-SPORT SKILLS TEACHING POINTERS AND RULES

Basketball Pointers, Rules, and Court/Field Diagrams 379
Floor Hockey Pointers, Rules, and Court/Field Diagrams 389
Volleyball Pointers, Rules, and Court/Field Diagrams 394
Soccer Pointers, Rules, and Court/Field Diagrams 400
Softball Pointers, Rules, and Court/Field Diagrams 407

Racquet and Ball, and Tennis Pointers, Rules, and Court/Field Diagrams 415

Cricket Pointers, Rules, and Court/Field Diagrams 421

Netball Pointers, Rules, and Court/Field Diagrams 427

Flag Football Pointers, Rules, and Court/Field Diagrams 433

TOURNAMENT DRAWS **442**

The F.I.T.T. Principle 443

Determining Your Target Heart Rate Range 444

Monitoring Your Resting Heart Rate 445

Busy Muscles & Busy Bones Worksheet 446

Name the Muscles on the Muscle-dude 447

Bone-dude Worksheet 448

Your Activity Pyramid 449

"Math in a Heart Beat" Fitness Activity 450

Your Aerobic Grids 451

Let's Run Around Australia! 452

Your Nutrition Pyramid 453

Nutrition Worksheet #1 454

Nutrition Worksheet #2 455

Fortune Cookie 456

Joker's Wild 457

Exercise Hunt 458

Juggling Scarves Activities 460

Tinikling 462

Boomerang Throwing 464

SECTION 1
TO THE TEACHER

ABOUT THIS RESOURCE

Bridging the Gap

The *P.E. Teacher's Pre-Sport Skills Activities Program* has been developed as a "transition" resource from the teaching of gross and fine motor skills to the teaching of sport-specific skills for a variety of sports. Consisting of 100 sequential and in-depth lesson plans and targeted for grades 4–6, this comprehensive resource provides an immediate extension and "flow-on" from the fundamental movement skills (FMS) developed and learned in the first and third books of the *Complete Motor Skills Activities Program* (The Center, 1999). (The Motor Skills series, developed for the teaching of kindergarten children through grade 3, consists of three books: *Fundamental Motor Skills & Movement Activities for Young Children; Fine Motor Skills & Handwriting Activities for Young Children;* and *Motor Skills & Movement Station Lesson Plans for Young Children.*)

First presented are eleven Foundation lesson plans focusing on locomotor movement skills of running, dodging, stopping, jumping, hopping, skipping, leaping, and sliding; body management skills of static and dynamic balance, body and spatial awareness; and object control skills of rolling, throwing and catching, bouncing, striking and kicking skills using manipulative and innovative equipment. These movement-based lessons provide class organization and management activities; foster and enhance listening skills, alertness and reaction; and promote valuable fitness experiences, while minimizing behavioral problems and creating a positive enjoyable learning environment. The Foundation lessons provide revision and further extension of the FMS through sequential and progressively developed age-appropriate activities that are then applied in low-organized games, lead-up games, and modified games. "Signals," the management and organizational tools used extensively in the *Complete Motor Skills Activities Program,* are further reinforced and extended in these foundation lessons. Thus, the teacher of grades 4 to 6 can "jump in" to the program at this level even if the children have not been exposed to the teachings of the first and third books of the *Complete Motor Skills Activities Program.*

All of the skills introduced in this resource are taught, practiced, reinforced, and extended through using a variety of contemporary innovative and manipulative equipment, as well as standard-based and traditional equipment, taking into consideration school budgets with varied available funding. Cooperative and concentration activities and games, self-esteem builders, along with activities and games that integrate other subject areas, are incorporated into the lesson plans. A wellness approach to teaching children occurs throughout this resource, with a strong focus directed toward fitness enhancement. Fitness should be an *inherent* aspect of all quality movement teaching. Health-related and skill-related fitness builders, activities, and games have been incorporated throughout each and every lesson plan. A special extended Appendix provides further reinforcement and development of the lesson plan focus through Homework Ideas and health-related Fit Think Ideas and In-Class Ideas.

How to Use This Resource

The program is divided into five parts and includes 100 detailed and comprehensive lesson plans:

◆ **Section 1** deals with the teaching guidelines and tools that will provide effective and efficient classroom management and organizational strategies, key teaching methods and strategies that can be used to promote quality teaching, maximize participation, minimize disruptive behavior, and foster an enjoyable shared learning environment.

◆ **Section 2** consists of 11 foundation movement lesson plans focusing on locomotion and body management skills, and fitness builders. You'll find hands-on signals as tools for establishing good listening and response skills, and effective, efficient organization.

◆ **Section 3** includes 14 object control lesson plans that provide revision and extension of previously learned motor skills using a variety of contemporary innovative and manipulative equipment. (This equipment can be readily purchased from a variety of sports catalog companies.)

◆ **Section 4** consists of 75 comprehensive lesson plans for teaching a variety of pre-sports skills, including basketball, floor hockey, volleyball, soccer, softball, cricket, netball, racquet and ball, flag football, as well as rhythm and dance. The content material of each lesson provides a wealth of progressive skill, activity, and game development so that the teacher has the flexibility to teach at the varying ability levels of the children.

◆ **Section 5** is an Appendix consisting of the rules and court/field diagrams for each key focus areas, pre-sports skills teaching pointers, fitness activity worksheets, nutrition worksheets, fit think ideas, in-class and homework ideas, and tournament draws that can be set up.

The Format

The format for each lesson presented in this program is designed for ease of use and practical implementation into day-to-day Physical Education teaching. The flowchart on page 3 shows the format used for developing basketball skills.

Lesson Format Components

◆ **Skill Builders:** provide specific learning areas

◆ **Key Outcomes:** provide 3–4 key achievement goals for that particular lesson

◆ **Teaching Points:** provide specific technique cues or pointers

◆ **Focus Word(s):** key words or phrases, "the movement jargon," which enhance the cognitive aspects of the lesson

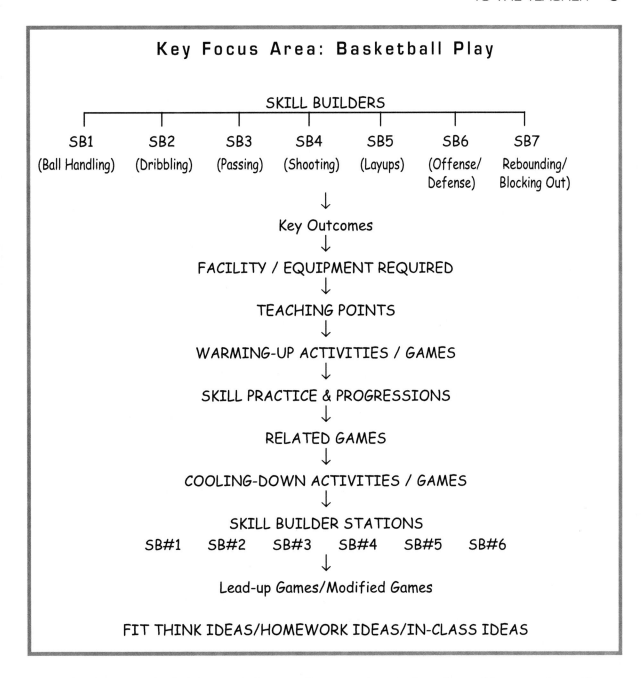

Key Focus Area: Basketball Play

SKILL BUILDERS

SB1 (Ball Handling) SB2 (Dribbling) SB3 (Passing) SB4 (Shooting) SB5 (Layups) SB6 (Offense/Defense) SB7 Rebounding/Blocking Out)

↓

Key Outcomes

↓

FACILITY / EQUIPMENT REQUIRED

↓

TEACHING POINTS

↓

WARMING-UP ACTIVITIES / GAMES

↓

SKILL PRACTICE & PROGRESSIONS

↓

RELATED GAMES

↓

COOLING-DOWN ACTIVITIES / GAMES

↓

SKILL BUILDER STATIONS

SB#1   SB#2   SB#3   SB#4   SB#5   SB#6

↓

Lead-up Games/Modified Games

FIT THINK IDEAS/HOMEWORK IDEAS/IN-CLASS IDEAS

◆ **Warming-up Activities and Games:** fitness orientated and provide warming of large muscle groups, interaction, listening skills, and spatial awareness

◆ **Skill Practice & Progressions:** center on individual, partner, and small group practice tasks and activities, developed through small-step progressions

◆ **Related Game(s)/Lead-up/Modified Games:** further practice to reinforce the skills in a game-like application

◆ **Cooling-down Activities and Games:** provide a cooling-down effect, concentration, and cooperation, and further reinforcement of skills learned in lesson including affective aspects of the lesson

◆ **Skill Builder Stations:** provide further practice, reinforcement, extension of taught skills, as well as cooperative and integrated activities

Teaching Pre-sport Skills

A wide variety of major sports can be modified in terms of the skill content that is taught, the rules, the equipment used, the dimensions of the court or boundaries, the number of participants involved, the scoring procedure, and the time allotment, to help equalize opportunities for all children. Once children have developed and mastered the specific skills of these modified sports, the natural progression is to introduce more adult-based sports where sport-specific skills can be further taught and applied, rules further extended, team strategies developed, and healthy attitudes to competition fostered and encouraged.

Games do not teach sport skills; rather, they provide the means to reinforce skills, and to teach children how and when to use them. The focus should first be to have children **master** the skills involved in playing a particular sport, and to teach these skills through sequential small-step progressions from the fundamentals involved to more specific skills, and at the developmentally appropriate age level so that **all** children will experience successes along the way and feel more competent and confident in participating in the sport. Then the enjoyment element, the "fun-ness," of learning is guaranteed!

Safety is always important! Activities and games need to be played safely, rules abided by, and fair play enforced to ensure good learning experiences. Children need to be warmed up properly (generally and specifically to the demands of the game) and cooled down carefully at the end, through stretching, breathing, and concentration activities. At this time the highlights of the lesson can be recapped and responses solicited from the children. This direct focus on providing quality movement-based experiences will almost guarantee the enjoyment factor and a healthy positive attitude towards learning, minimize behavioral problems, and reduce the risk of "emotional and physical hurts."

To teach games with an **educational purpose,** consider the following variables: skills that are being reinforced; safety considerations; the enjoyable factor for all participants of all skill levels; provision for maximizing participation and minimizing wait time or standing around; social skills reinforced by the game; ease of setting up and executing, collection and dispersal of equipment; and maintaining a gender-friendly environment! Avoid elimination games that tend to provide less practice for the kids who need it most; these can lead to boredom when eliminated and result in misbehavior problems. Provide opportunities for children to have more "ownership" of the game play, allowing them to create their own rules and/or invent game play of their own!

Group games that have a lot in common, such as volleyball, tennis, badminton, and pickle ball which all use a net and require ball-striking skills; and invasion games such as basketball, floor or field hockey, and soccer which all involve dribbling a ball or puck against an opponent. This will help children understand and facilitate their learning of game play and strategies.

Skill Builder Stations

After each component part has been taught for each key focus area and children have practiced the specific skills involved, a lesson plan of SKILL BUILDER STATIONS is introduced for the purpose of further **practicing, mastering, reinforcing, and extending skills,** and includes **fitness builders.** The basic format used for these Skill Builder Tasks Stations is a circuit of 6–8 activity/task stations. Generally 3–4 stations are designed to revise, reinforce, and extend previously learned skills, 1 station to introduce, explore a new skill, and

2–3 stations to allow for free structured play or cooperative play. Fitness is an inherent part of each station activity as well as an integral part of the whole lesson!

The class is divided into teams of 5–6 children; each team rotates through the stations over a certain time period. Each team is assigned to a starting station: Team 1 to Station #1, Team 2 to Station #2, and so forth. A clockwise or counterclockwise order of rotation will then be established; for example, on whistle signal (or music stopped) each group will rotate clockwise to the next station. Rotation will occur about every 5 minutes.

The instructions and demonstrations for each station task should be concise and kept simple in order to maximize participation time. In fact, most of the explanation and set-up organization can be accomplished in the classroom, with each team assigned a station or stations to set up and take down. The diagram or layout of each station can be photocopied from the actual station lesson plan and given to that particular team. The task and/or activities presented at each station are designed to accommodate the different ability levels of children and will include, for example, varying distances, targets, and equipment. They also promote maximum participation. A station or stations can also be set up to allow for ability grouping to occur so that the weaker children can continue to practice and master the skills at their own rate, while the child who has acquired the skills is given more challenge. Buddy or reciprocal teaching could also be incorporated into station work. One or more station could be set up as an assessment station to further monitor mastering of specific skills. Pre-sports skills checklists are provided in the Appendix.

Option 1: The teacher first demonstrates the activity tasks at each station; then circulates, observing performance of children at each station and offering individual feedback as she/he moves around.

Option 2: The teacher has the option of positioning at one station, while still monitoring the other stations. Each team will rotate through to the "teacher" station. The teacher may use this station to focus on a skill or skills being assessed, or provide more instruction for a new skill being introduced or challenging task being explored.

The teacher should provide positive and constructive feedback throughout this session, as well as identify children with difficulties, and then later follow-up with strategies to help these children.

The Game

The culmination of this teaching is to then **apply** the skills in related games, lead-up games, and modified games. Children love to play games and the benefits to them can be many! Participating in games gives each child an opportunity for further learning and practice to occur, fosters teamness and cooperative experiences, enhances social skills, and promotes decision making and fair play, besides just being fun! Each pre-sport skills focus area comes with its own jargon or terminology specific to that sport. For example, in cricket such terms as "boundaries," "wicket," "stumps," "bowler," "wicket keeper," "popping crease," and so forth are used. Gradually, new terminology is introduced, thus further extending children's movement language base. This movement jargon can then be incorporated into specific Signals. For example, in basketball such signals as Triple Threat, Rebound, Pivot, Basketball Key, Jump Ball Circle, Three-Point Circle, etc., could be used: "Lines!"—bounce basketball along lines of Basketball court; "Triple-Threat; Pivot; Rebound!"

> *Note: This program is not "content driven"; it is not a "cookbook" approach per se. The main goal is to teach through **progressive skills development**, not try to teach through every lesson. In fact, each lesson may contain far more content than you may be able to get through in a 30- to 40-minute time allotment. Factors such as the ability levels of the children, the general "mood" of the class, the teaching area, the weather, special events, and so on may have a direct bearing on how much of each lesson is taught. Repetition is a significant principle of quality teaching! You should be prepared to repeat some of the lessons or part(s) of the lesson.*

The Appendix

◆ The Appendix contains a collection of **Wellness "Active" worksheets**—the aim being to give children more awareness and ownership in monitoring their lifestyle activity. These active worksheets include fitness worksheets, nutrition worksheets, and integration activity worksheets with other subject areas such as math skills, geography, history, reading comprehension, music/art, computer literacy, and cultural social aspects.

◆ **Pre-sport Skill Teaching Pointers** are reproducible "cue cards" for teaching each of the specific skills in the key focus areas, as well as providing checklists for assessing each child's ability to perform the specific skills taught in each key focus area.

◆ **Homework Ideas and In-class Ideas** presented throughout the resource as well as in more detailed worksheets provided in the Appendix, have a threefold purpose: to create more awareness and participation in each child's personal wellness on a day-to-day basis out of school time; to further reinforce learning that occurred in school time; and to get the parents more in "the know" and involved in their own child's lifestyle activity.

◆ **Rules for Each Key Focus Area** (for example, Basketball, Volleyball, Soccer, Cricket) as well as reproducible court/field diagrams have been included here as an easily accessible reference.

◆ **Fit Think Ideas** appear throughout the resource at the end of each lesson. Sometimes a *focus word or phrase* is used; at other times certain topics are addressed. These Fit Think sessions can occur at flexible times in the school day when the opportunity arises: perhaps at the end of the school day, ten minutes before children are ready to head home for the day; at the beginning of the day after a morning fitness session; just before a break at lunchtime; following a physical education lesson. Topics (at the appropriate age level) such as the following could be addressed:

What are the different parts (components) of fitness?

What does being physically fit mean to you?

What are the benefits of being fit?

What is good nutrition?

What is the relationship between nutrition and fitness?

How does being fit help us in our everyday living?

Select current articles from newspapers regarding fitness and health issues and discuss or research topics on the Internet.

Tune-up Kids Activity Journal

Children should be given the opportunity to create their own Tune-up Kids Activity Journal in which is entered the activity that they do each day, nutritional habits, resting and active heart rates, general sense of well-being, and other significant information that is relevant to them.

Let each child design his/her own Tune-up Kid cover artwork depicting what good lifestyle means most to each one. Provide time in the classroom for each child to briefly describe and explain the active art cover. Use self-esteem stickers, certificates, etc., to recognize "Legends of the Day" and other goodwill endeavors which children can place in a special section in their Tune-up Kids book. Ensure that every child receives recognition throughout the school year! Have children make recordings of their activities in the form of tables and graphs, thus integrating math skills into their project. From these recordings ask them to make their own evaluations, and help them to determine what goals they need to set to improve or maintain their personal physical fitness status. These journals could be used for parent–teacher interviews, parent visit days at the school, or taken home as part of the reporting procedure.

TEACHING POINTERS

Sport Skills Acquisition Model

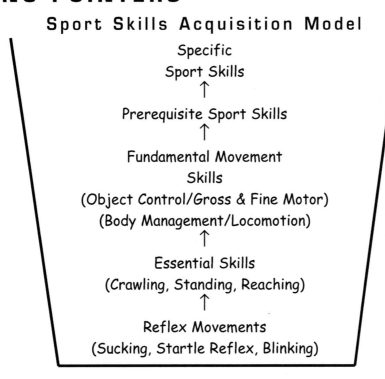

Specific
Sport Skills
↑
Prerequisite Sport Skills
↑
Fundamental Movement
Skills
(Object Control/Gross & Fine Motor)
(Body Management/Locomotion)
↑
Essential Skills
(Crawling, Standing, Reaching)
↑
Reflex Movements
(Sucking, Startle Reflex, Blinking)

◆ Fundamental motor skills are part of a movement continuum that begins before birth and continues for the rest of our lives. Soon after birth, an infant displays reflexes that gradually give way to essential voluntary movements that will allow the infant to socialize, explore the environment, and to literally stand on his/her own two feet. With exposure to movement experiences, the young child begins to learn rudimentary fundamental movement skills that, ideally, will be refined through good modeling, quality instruction, and opportunity to practice. Although children will reach different levels of competence, they move through similar phases.

◆ If children are not taught and then practice and master the "small step" progressions from fundamental motor skills to sport-specific skills, they could experience frustration and even failure, which could have detrimental effects on their pursuing activity on a regular basis as a teenager, and later on as an adult. For example, a young girl learning to play tee ball for the first time, who has not developed good catching, throwing, and striking skills, could become very discouraged by her lack of ability, and simply quit. This becomes a negative experience for her.

◆ Thus, the importance of children acquiring competence and confidence in mastering fundamental motor skills at an early age onwards cannot be emphasized enough! Research tells us that unless a child develops competence and confidence in FMS by the sixth grade, he or she will not pursue activity as an adult on a regular basis. However, children who do consolidate these fundamental motor skills in early life will be more likely to pursue and experience success at a multitude of recreational activities and sport-specific avenues. This will open the door to a lifetime of active lifestyle that will be both habitual and enjoyable!

◆ **Competence** in body management, locomotion skills, object control skills, motor memory, perceptual ability, coordination, skill acquisition, knowledge, fitness, safety, and kinesthetic sense are the desirable outcomes.

◆ **Confidence** has to do with building self-esteem, positive attitude, self-perception, respect, fair play, consideration, tolerance, pride, patience, socially better adjustment, coping ability, and cooperation.

Guidelines for Teaching FMS

◆ Research indicates that it takes 240–600 minutes (or an average of 450 minutes) of quality instruction to teach children to correctly perform a FMS, such as an overhand throw. Therefore, in a 40-week school year based on two 30-minute lessons of P.E. per week, the child would only be able to learn 5–6 skills in one year!

◆ Many teachers underestimate the amount of time it takes to master FMS and try to teach too much too quickly. The result—the teacher ends up teaching for participation or awareness, rather than teaching for mastery of the skills.

◆ How long it takes to learn different FMS depends on such factors as teacher expertise, available equipment (ideally one per child or one for every two children), class size, age of the learner, teaching methodology, and the complexity of the skill being taught.

◆ Keep the purpose of the lesson clear. What FMS component will be learned in this lesson? Continually emphasize the focus of the lesson to the students.

◆ Use the teachable moment in helping children to learn a FMS rather than just participating in the activity. Circulate among the students, observing, offering praise and feedback. Do not passively stand by and observe.

◆ Use demonstrations to help communicate the key components of a FMS to be learned. Link a key word or phrase "cues" to highlight these key components. Before beginning the practice session, use a student or students to demonstrate the skill to further clarify understanding of the instructions.

◆ Keep the time between giving an instruction and allowing the children to practice to an absolute minimum. Be brief and to the point when explaining a related game or activity. Ideally, allow for practice immediately after watching a demonstration. Do not give out any new information until the child has had sufficient opportunity to practice.

Break down the FMS to be learned into small parts. Teach the components of the skill in a progressive manner—"small-step progressions" method. For example, teach the first component of the FMS, practice; teach the second component, practice; then combine the first and second components into a sequence. Continue teaching all the components and incorporating them into the sequence until the entire skill is being performed.

Be patient. Teach one component of the skill at a time, and no more than one or two key teaching points to focus on. Have students self-talk using the cues. For example, link the word "step" to the action of stepping forward during an overhand throw.

Provide ample opportunities to practice each FMS, using a variety of equipment, tasks, and progressions. Repetition and refinement (the two "R's") are the key to mastering each skill.

If games are used to teach FMS, then it is imperative that children are first taught how to perform the component skills of that game.

Provide appropriate, positive feedback; praise often. Feedback of a child's performance works best when it is specific and given immediately. Ensure that the feedback first highlights what is good about the child's performance, and then point out what needs to be improved or corrected.

Ensure that the child achieves success along each step of the way. Plan the practice, drills, and games so that the child has many successful experiences and minimal negative experiences. Success breeds success. No one should be ridiculed for his/her efforts.

Constantly remind children of safety considerations in all their movement and reinforce consistently.

Set group sizes that are as small as is practical to minimize wait time and curb behavior problems. Ideally, have one piece of equipment per child when appropriate, or one piece of equipment between every two for practicing sessions.

Use Signals (hand and voice signal) as efficient and effective management and organization tools. At times use a whistle or a drum to get their attention. Whatever the method, establish early and constantly reinforce.

◆ Children need to be active in P.E.—this is an understatement! Get children moving right away through involvement in moderate to vigorous introductory and fitness activities and games to use up some of their pent-up energy. Then you will find more willing ears to sit and listen to instruction and watch demonstrations.

◆ Use Breaks throughout the FMS lesson teaching to provide changes of pace from passive to active (or vice versa). For example, when using deck rings to teach throwing and catching, break up the instruction/practice phase by playing a game of Team Ring Tag. Select the Red team (those having red rings) to be the IT team who have only a certain time (20–30 seconds) to try to tag all the other players. Each team in turn has a go. This is a vigorous activity and after about two minutes of play, the children will be ready to listen again. In the meantime, aerobic activity, spatial awareness, dodging skills, and fair play have been reinforced!

" KNEE-BOX!"

Guidelines for Teaching Games

1. Be brief when introducing the game. Start with just enough rules to get the game started ("keep it simple principle"), then add on or modify the rules as the game progresses, at the developmental age and ability level of the children participating.

2. Avoid "beehive ball" or "clump ball" (everyone running to the ball) by breaking down the game into small-step progressions. This may mean walking children through a new game before playing at full speed or using floor tape to mark player positions within the court; improving children's spatial awareness and teaching them how "to guard" an opposition player by playing warm-up games such as Artful Dodger, Follow the Leader type games, and 2-on-2 Keep Away.

3. Develop Signals specific to the sport to increase court and spatial awareness. For example, for basketball, develop warm-up signals such as "Listening Circle" (dribble to the listening circle and cross-leg sit), "Sideline" (dribble ball to touch a sideline of court), "End line" (dribble ball to touch an end line of court), "Free Throw" (dribble ball to touch the free-throw line), "In the Paint" (bounce ball only in the key way), "Rebound" (jump in the air and grab the ball bringing it into triple-threat position), "Pivot" (plant on the ball of one foot, using the other foot to push off in different directions), "Jump Stop" (stop by landing on two feet at the same time and bending at the knees), "Shuffle" (slide-step, keeping low, in directions pointed to).

4. Remind children of the safety considerations associated with the game and reinforce constantly.

5. As long as children's performance is at a level that affords safe play, let them play the game, giving them plenty of practice and performance cues.

6. Provide effective demonstrations by showing the correct way first, then errors to avoid, then the correct way again! Use key words or phrases, "cues" that highlight the important part on which the demonstration is focusing.

7. Provide positive constructive feedback and appropriate encouragement. Ensure that the feedback highlights what is good about the child's performance, as well as what can be improved or is wrong. Instead of commenting "Don't stand square on when throwing overhand," say, "You threw the ball quite well, but if you stand side-on and step into your throw, you will throw much better!"

8. Try to provide activities that include several benefits. For example, consider the "Crab-Walk greeting" (in crab-walk position, foot shake by touching the bottom of one foot to another person's foot; use right foot to greet right foot, then the left foot for the next person and so on, and introduce your name to each other) which provides for weight-supporting, balance and coordination, left and right discrimination, social interaction (mingling), and an ice-breaker—all in one activity!

9. Establish an attention signal such as "Iceberg!" (jump stop—look—listen), or use a whistle, drum, or hand clap. Whatever you use, establish this early and constantly reinforce.

10. Use the teachable moment—don't be a "just do it" teacher. Observe them at play, provide feedback, praise in public, remedy in private, strive for success, and minimize negative experiences or failures.

Guidelines for Modifying Games

1. Modify the regulation game by playing small-sided (mini) games such as 2-on-2 or 3-on-3 which can fit into the same space as one regulation game.

2. Set up relays with as few children per group/team as possible to maximize participation. Adjust for uneven numbers by having a selected child go twice, or use a time limit to try to complete a task (how many passes in three minutes) or execute a certain number of times for the task to be completed ("Perform 50 Short Jump Rope turns, then sit down").

3. Modify the equipment: Use a larger softer ball for volleyball; a smaller size-5 ball for basketball-type games; a brighter larger ball for soccer; a larger bat and ball for tee ball or softball; a larger net or target area; lower net or modified net (rope) in volleyball or badminton; lower the height of the basketball ring from the floor or ground.

4. Modify the court boundaries and markings: smaller court than regulation size; several mini-courts marked off; smaller key way or distance from the free-throw line to basketball ring; larger goal-crease area; decreased distance of 3-point semi-circle or soccer zone.

5. Modify the rules: five seconds in the key way; 3–5 traveling steps before passing; three completed passes before attempting to score, no bouncing of the ball just air passing; five bounces allowed before passing; bounce or chest passing only allowed; three seconds to hold ball before shooting or passing; pass to a girl then a boy, then a girl then a boy, etc.; one help on the volleyball serve to get it over; allow three or more hits per side before volleying balloon ball across the net.

6. Provide for more cooperative effort by maximizing involvement.

7. Modify the time required to play the game, such as set up a 3-on-3 tournament of 10-minute games; or play two 15-minute halves instead of 20-minute halves.

8. Modify the scoring procedure; for example, give 2 points for sinking the ball through the basketball net, and 1 point for touching the rim or backboard if the ball does not go through the net; hit the ball, in tee ball and score a point for each base touched before ball is passed in a certain order and batter must then freeze.

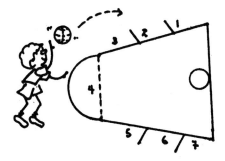

Effective Teaching Methods and Strategies

The most effective teachers are those who not only know **what to teach,** but **how to teach** it. They are not "just do it" teachers; rather they use the teachable moment and are willing to explore different ways of providing quality teaching and creating positive learning experiences.

A number of teaching methods are presented here. The stimulation and motivation provided by using a variety of teaching methods cannot be overlooked. All decisions in a lesson are made by either the teacher or the child, but the amount of decision-making transferred from the teacher to the child is the determining factor in which method is used.

Teaching methods should also be selected to fit the circumstances that exist: the content to be taught, the number of children in the class, the equipment and facilities, the time allotted, the space provided, and the ability levels of the children. Good teachers will use many different methods, often within the same physical education lesson, mixing and matching as the situation dictates The result could be a refreshing sparkle and stimulating challenge for the children and the teacher alike!

DIRECT	← continuum →	**INDIRECT**
Direct Instruction	Problem Solving	Free Play
Task Instruction	Decision Making	Structured Free Play
Guided Discovery	Cooperative	

Teaching Methods

1. **Direct Instruction:** This is the best method for initially teaching fundamental movement skills. The teacher provides step-by-step instruction (small-step progression) and all decisions are made by the teacher. This method provides a good starting point for beginning teachers and acts as a springboard to the use of other methods. Although this method of teaching is economical in the utilization of time available to learn new activities or skills, it should be used sparingly in total class instruction as it tends to discourage creativity and initiative, leads to stereotyped movements, does not allow for individual differences, and restricts the development of decision-making and leadership ability.

2. **Task Instruction:** Task teaching involves the shifting of decision-making from teacher to children, while they work towards the perfection of predetermined skills. Let the children decide at what pace they may work. How the skill is completed remains set and often where the skill is completed is set.

3. **Task Stations:** This method is very useful when teaching large groups of children; when there is insufficient or minimum equipment and apparatus for the entire class, but enough for a small group; when the teacher wishes to be free to give individual attention to children, by rotating to each group; when the teacher wishes to provide children with opportunities for responsibility and leadership; and when skills learned can then be further practiced, reinforced, and extended through station work.

4. **Guided Discovery:** The basic difference between this method and the previous styles mentioned is that in guided discovery, the teacher never tells the children the answer. The teacher solicits certain responses from the children through questions (cues) that are designed to gradually lead the child to the discovery of a predetermined target— hence, success! The teacher presents the tasks and then asks the children to think about how they can best solve these tasks.

5. **Problem Solving:** In the guided discovery method, the child's movement response is prompted by the teacher's cues, but in the problem-solving method, the child is *expected to determine the answer all on his/her own*. This method is open-ended; that is, there is

no predetermined final skill. In fact, there are no right or wrong responses at all. Each child is made to feel that his/her response is acceptable and worthwhile. The assumption is that the children have the prerequisite skills and knowledge to solve the problem. This method is therefore not suitable for younger children.

Usually the teacher using the problem-solving technique will introduce the skill by posing a question as to what has to be accomplished by the skill and the children experiment to find the best alternative. This method thus encourages initiative, self-inquiry, and self-actualization in the child. The child is involved in the thinking, sensing, comprehending, analyzing, and reasoning processes, with the freedom to think, to work alone or in groups, and freedom to work with available apparatus and equipment.

6. **Cooperative Method:** This method has been called cooperative because the teaching–learning–evaluating role is shared between the teacher and all the children in the class in a cooperative effort to assist each other to learn. This method retains the formal style of instruction of the direct and task methods, the informality of the practice session, utilization of task cards as used in the task method, and the self-actualization associated with the guided discovery and problem-solving methods. There is a further shift in decision-making and responsibility in this method that involves the children in the teaching–learning–evaluating processes. The responsibility also extends to handling of equipment and class organization.

7. **Free Play:** This can be considered as a method and is valuable in that time is allowed in the lesson for children to freely and safely explore their new equipment without specific instruction, thus enhancing creative play opportunity.

8. **Structured Free Play:** This method can be used for all years where limitations are put on the responses that can be made and is a prerequisite to problem solving, but is more individual than guided discovery. Limitations may be in the form of spatial demands, time, force, use of body parts, and equipment.

Characteristics of a Pre-adolescent Child

◆   Most active segment of society

◆   Burns more calories than other groups

◆   Skeletal age differences—skeletal age range of 5–11 years

◆   Age/growth causes performance improvements

◆   Not trainable—only small and insignificant changes in aerobic ability

◆   80% of perceived competencies established by age 8

- No muscle fiber differentiation (therefore, the best sprinters are the best distance runners)
- Predictability of sport success impossible
- No major female/male differences in physical performance

Strategies to Encourage the Reluctant Child

- Try to discern *why* the child is reluctant to do activity: Is she or he overweight? Is she or he insecure? Does the child have a low self-esteem? A fear of failure? Does the child feel unsafe? Does not want to get physically or emotionally hurt? Does the child have poor coordination?
- Create a safe, fun positive learning environment—free of any physical threat, ridicule, bullying, put-downs.
- Provide immediate feedback, given out at the "time of doing." Use words of praise and encouragement that are meaningful: "You ran all the way without stopping—that's terrific!"
- Don't be overprotective. Establish consistency and firmness.
- Try to create situations that guarantee success within a short period of time.
- Keep within the limits of the child's abilities. Don't force the child to do the activity; rather, encourage the child to be responsible for her or his own activity involvement.
- From time to time, offer some kind of incentive or reward. The instant reward is praise and encouragement. Set a goal that is followed up by a reward: "If you can try to run for two minutes nonstop, then you can have free play with your favorite piece of equipment at the end!"
- Provide a variety of activity experiences that will sustain children's interest and provide challenge!
- Have the children create activities that the whole class can then do together. Include a description and even a drawing with the "title" of the activity.
- Don't confuse a child's **needs** with the child's **wants**. Young children do not have the knowledge or experience to know what is good for them. We need to impose our knowledge of the importance of exercise on the child and the benefits of regular play activity.

Components of a Quality Physical Education Program

A **quality** Physical Education program:

◆ Is student-centered and based on the developmental needs of the child
◆ Makes movement the basis of the program
◆ Offers opportunity for repetition and refinement of motor skills (the "2 R's" in P.E.)
◆ Is success oriented and creates ongoing positive learning experiences
◆ Is designed for those who need to learn (i.e., the bottom 70% of kids, not elite kids!)
◆ Prepares children for adult activity

The **objectives** of a quality Physical Education program have long-term purposes and include the following:

◆ Personalized physical fitness
◆ Cognitive understanding of health-related fitness and lifestyle activity
◆ Development of motor skills (gross and fine motor)
◆ Development of affective domain skills
◆ Development of life-skill activity and patterns

Key Focus Areas of a Balanced Physical Education Program (K–12)

KEY FOCUS AREA	GRADE/AGE GROUP
Motor Skills	K–7 / 5–12 years
Fitness	K–12 / 5–17 years
Fine Motor	K–10 / 5–15 years
Games	K–12 / 5–17 years
Movement Awareness	K–3 / 5–8 years
Rhythm and Dance	K–12 / 5–17 years
Gymnastics	K–10 / 5–15 years
Pre-Sport/Sport Skills	4–12 / 9–17 years
Outdoor Education	8–12 / 12–17 years
Aquatics	K–12 / 5–17 years

Progressive Lesson Plan Model for Teaching Pre-sport Skills (based on a 30+-minute lesson)

The lesson plan model on page 16 provides a guideline for progressively developing pre-sport skills:

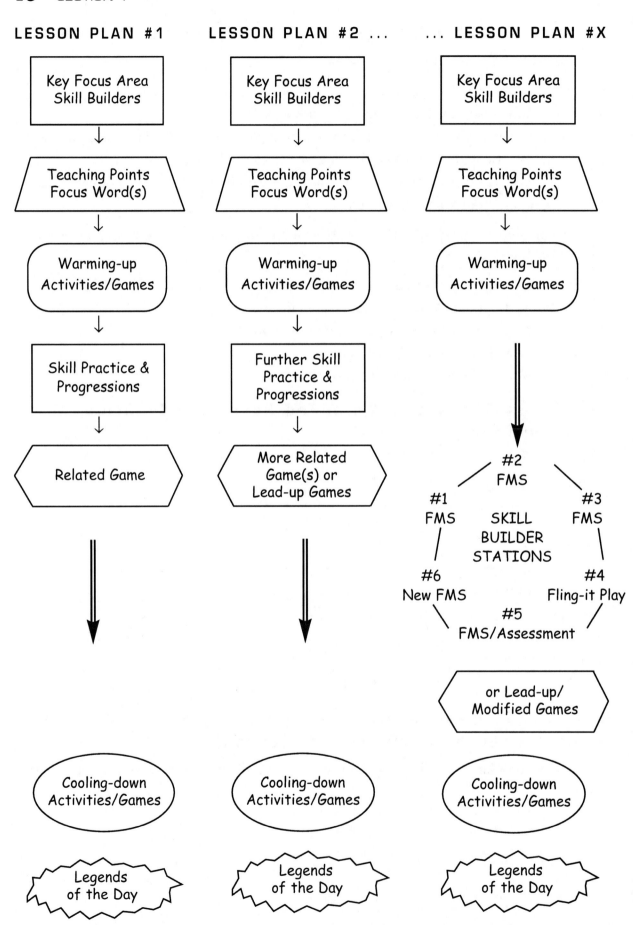

LESSON PLAN #1

Key Focus Area
Skill Builders

↓

Teaching Points
Focus Word(s)

↓

Warming-up
Activities/Games

↓

Skill Practice &
Progressions

↓

Related Game

⇓

Cooling-down
Activities/Games

Legends
of the Day

LESSON PLAN #2 ...

Key Focus Area
Skill Builders

↓

Teaching Points
Focus Word(s)

↓

Warming-up
Activities/Games

↓

Further Skill
Practice &
Progressions

↓

More Related
Game(s) or
Lead-up Games

⇓

Cooling-down
Activities/Games

Legends
of the Day

... LESSON PLAN #X

Key Focus Area
Skill Builders

↓

Teaching Points
Focus Word(s)

↓

Warming-up
Activities/Games

⇓

#2
FMS

#1
FMS

#3
FMS

SKILL
BUILDER
STATIONS

#6
New FMS

#4
Fling-it Play

#5
FMS/Assessment

or Lead-up/
Modified Games

Cooling-down
Activities/Games

Legends
of the Day

Components of a Balanced Lesson (based on a minimum of 30 minutes of activity)

◆ **Warming-up Activities/Games** should be moderate to vigorous in intensity with the intent to produce a general physical warming up of large muscle groups and a "mental warming up" or readiness, lasting about 5–6 minutes. Fitness activities and/or games, emphasizing aerobic endurance and muscular strength and endurance, provide a more specific warm-up related to the skill development of the lesson. The foundation lessons utilize and emphasize **Signals** as an integral part of the warming-up process as well as provide tools to organize and mobilize the children efficiently, to improve listening skills, alertness, spatial awareness, and further develop fitness benefits.

◆ The main purpose of the **Cooling-down Activities/Games** segment of the lesson is to create a cooling-down effect through concentration and cooperation activities, stretching and balancing activities, and more passive related games. This is an ideal time for a general debriefing of the purpose of the lesson and the learning that has taken place. This is also an ideal time for whole class recognition of children's good efforts (Legends of the Day) to occur. Individual child(ren) or a member from each team can be selected to receive this special self-worth recognition. Keep a record of the children selected each lesson so that eventually *all* children will be given recognition throughout the school year! But more important, use every opportunity to provide self-esteem builders and recognition of good effort within each and every lesson! This segment, lasting 5–6 minutes, should never be omitted from a quality balanced lesson.

◆ **Skills Practice & Progressions** is the core teaching segment of the lesson and will focus on one or two skill areas such as Overhand Throwing and revision of Catching. Teaching points need to be taught through small-step progressions to ensure success at each step along the way. Give ample opportunity for children to practice the skills and then apply these learned skills in a related game. The related game may also incorporate previous learned skills as well. As shown in the Lesson Plan Model, subsequent lessons focusing on skill progressions and partner work now provide more opportunity to practice, refine, and master skills. Then the skills can be applied in lead-up games. This Skill Practice & Progressions core segment should last no more than 10–15 minutes.

◆ Once the components of a FMS (or 2–3 FMS) have been learned and consolidated through practice, repetition, and refinement, **Skill Builder Stations** can be introduced to further reinforce and extend skill acquisition. As shown in the Lesson Plan Model, six circuit-type task stations are set up with three of the stations designed for further consolidation of FMS 1, 2, and 3 while Station #4 provides a cooperation activity (such as Fling-It Play); Station #5 is set up for assessing a skill(s) area; and Station #6 is used to introduce and explore a new FMS; for example: FMS 1, Overhand Target Throwing (Accuracy Throwing); FMS 2, Bowling (Target Rolling); FMS 3, Catchball Play (Refined Catching); Station #4, Fling-It Nets (Cooperation, Communication, and Coordination); Station #5, Assessment of Overhand Throw; and Station #6, Paddle Ball Play (introduce forehand stroking with a paddle racquet). Children rotate in groups of 5–6 from one station to the next after a certain period of time (3–5 minutes). Teacher monitors movement, circulates, observes performance, and offers feedback, encouragement, and praise.

◆ Now skills can be applied in **Lead-up and Modified Games.** Refer to "Guidelines for Teaching Games" and "Guidelines for Modifying Games" earlier in this section.

ORGANIZATION AND MANAGEMENT TOOLS

Signals as Management Tools

Signals are "management tools" used to create effective and efficient classroom organization, arrangement, and mobilization of children, maximizing participation time and reducing behavioral problems. Through learning and reacting to these signals, the children develop better listening skills, alertness and reaction; improve in overall spatial and body awareness, and develop good body management and control while moving or stationary; and develop and improve locomotion skills. Through using Signals, cooperation is enhanced, efficient mobilization of children to equipment or equipment to children (collection and dispersal of equipment) is established, and an effective positive learning environment in the P.E. classroom is created.

Signals involve both a verbal and a visual signal and are classified into **Organizational** signals, **Formation** signals, **Starting Positions,** and **Break** signals. These need to be taught early at the beginning of the year and consistently reinforced throughout the school year. The teacher must be both patient and insistent that these signals are responded to immediately by all children and that quality of movement is evident. Consistently and positively reinforce appropriate behavioral responses! Once children have learned to react to the basic signals, then these become the management tools for teaching fundamental movement skills and all other components of the lesson. Furthermore, this concept can be extended to include the development of other signals, thus creating a movement or signals vocabulary—a movement language or jargon—that can be constantly expanded. When the signals are well learned, the verbal signals can be taken away, so that only the visual signal is responded to. It may be necessary under certain conditions—for example, if you are teaching outside or using a lot of music inside the gymnasium—to use a whistle or drum which becomes the immediate attention grabber. Then the Signal can be given, which provides the indicator to do something. Once you become more confident and competent in using these tools, you will find yourself spontaneously creating more signals and usage. Enjoy the challenge!

The Teamness Concept—T.E.A.M. (Together Everyone Achieves More!)

"Teamness" is an important aspect of organizing your classes within the P.E. classroom setting. By placing children into teams, you are creating a sense of belonging for that child, so that social exclusion problems will not occur, and cooperation can be fostered and enhanced in a positive learning environment. Moreover, operating your P.E. classroom through teams will allow for efficient setting up, dispersing, and collecting of equipment; mobilization of children for station work, low organized games, and lead-up and modified game play; and other interactive play experiences.

1. **Creating Teams**

   Children should be placed into teams early into the school year, from kindergarten onwards. Ideally the team size should be confined to 5–6 members, and the number of teams determined by the class size. For example, in a class of 30 children, try to create 5 teams of 6 and balance these teams as best as possible. You may need to readjust the teams from time to time, to "maintain the balance," and after a certain time, may decide to create new teams.

2. **Team Structure**

Within each team, appoint two leaders, a captain who sits at the front of the file, and a co-captain who positions at the end of the file, thus "containing" the team. Strive to have a girl captain and a boy co-captain or vice versa. After a period of two weeks, let the captain and co-captain change roles. After a month has passed, appoint a new captain and co-captain for each team. Continue this pattern until each member has had a turn at being a leader. For each class list the teams on a large paper flip chart using a colored starring (*) system, for example, to record captains and co-captains. These charts then become your "cues" to help you quickly learn the children's names for each class!

3. **Team Leadership**

The duties of the captain and co-captain include such responsibilities as:

◆ Dispersing and collecting equipment

◆ Reporting on team absenteeism

◆ Relaying instructions to team

◆ Providing leadership in different activities and games

◆ Providing "pastoral care" to ensure that everyone on the team is looked after, and receives fair and equal treatment (gender-equity)

◆ Promoting cooperation, communication, and collective decision-making

4. **Team Spirit**

Each team creates a name and a team cheer. Provide opportunity for each team in turn to demonstrate this cheer to the other teams. Team names could be selected on the basis of Rainbow Colors, the Alphabet, special groups such as Animals, Birds, Dinosaurs, Planets, and so on. Several ideas are given throughout this resource to foster leadership skills, respect within the team, responsibilities, equality, team spirit, communication, contribution, and cooperation through team-building activities—all important skills for functioning positively in society and the community at large.

Organization Signals

The following signals provide ways of effectively mobilizing children and of developing their listening skills and spatial awareness. Identify the boundaries of the play area in which children will move around. Use a minimum of 6–8 cone markers or witch's hats spaced evenly apart around the area. Establish the following Signals that children can quickly learn and respond to. Single-out good listeners and praise them!

1. **Homes!** (*Hand Signal*—Make a roof overhead with hands. Mats, hoops, carpet squares, or deck rings could also be used as a Homes space.) Find a free space in the play area. Check that you cannot touch anyone or anything. This is your "Home!" or personal space. Remember it. Now leave your home and touch 6 different markers, with 6 different body parts. Return to "stand tall" in your home space. Go!

2. **Scrambled Eggs!** (*Hand Signal*—Roll hand over hand.) Listen carefully to how I will ask you to move. Then move in this way, in and out of each other, without "touching" anyone. Examples: "Scrambled Eggs—Jogging!" "Scrambled Eggs—Slide-stepping!"

3. **Iceberg!** (*Hand Signal*—Raise one hand in the air with thumb up.) This is your stopping signal. When you hear or see this word, **stop immediately** by jump-stopping (landing on feet at the same time, knees bent, hands out for balance).

4. **Quiet!** (*Hand Signal*—Raise one hand overhead.) This is your stop–look–listen signal. Stop what you are doing and raise your hand overhead, giving me your full attention!

5. **Dead Bug!** (*Hand Signal*—Thumbs down.) Quickly and safely lie on your back, raise your arms and legs in the air, and wiggle them gently.

6. **Hit the Deck!** (*Hand Signal*—Point index fingers of both hands to the ground.) This is your signal to drop carefully to the ground, in front lying position. Stay there until you hear the next signal.

7. **Clear the Deck!** (*Hand Signal*—Raise both hands into the air and out to the sides.) Move quickly to stand outside on one side of the marked play area. Clear the Deck again! Now move to stand outside another side. Continue in this way. (Vary the way children move: slide-step, hop, skip high, walk low, . . .)

8. **Islands!** (*Hand Signal*—Use both hands to draw a square shape in the air.) This is a group/team learning square that can vary in formation, size, and number. Cone markers, ropes, 4 × 6 light carry mats, Station Cards, etc., can be used to indicate each island location and space. Each team or group moves to its designated island taking the necessary equipment along and sets up as instructed. Each islander can still find a Home (individualized learning space) within his or her island. Teacher can designate one square to be the Main Island (the teaching square). Some examples for different teaching skills are illustrated here.

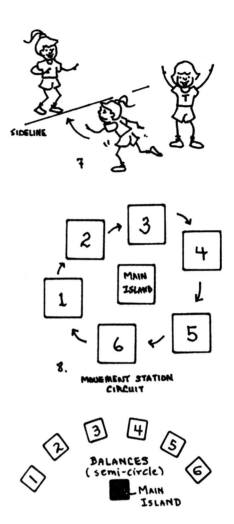

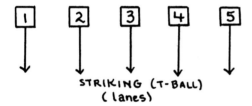

STRIKING (T-BALL)
(lanes)

Formation Signals

Formation signals effectively and efficiently organize the children into location and position. If teaching the P.E. lesson outside, ensure that children are not looking directly into the sun. Use markers to clearly indicate the boundaries of the play area.

1. **Listening Circle.** (*Hand Signal*—Point with index finger to the floor near you while circling the other index finger overhead.) Run quickly and safely to cross-leg sit in the circle that I am pointing to and face me.

2. **Listening Corner.** (*Hand Signal*—Cross your arms, making the letter X, then point to the corner with your index finger.) Run quickly and safely to cross-leg sit in this corner and face me.

3. **Listening Line.** (*Hand Signal*—Arms stretched out sideways as you stand near and facing line. Use the boundaries of the play area.) Immediately run and stand in a long line where I am pointing. Face me and space yourself arm's length apart. Now take giant steps across to the opposite side and stand on a listening line once there. How many giant steps did you take? Return to your listening line, again counting the number of steps.

4. **End Line.** (*Hand Signal*—Arms outstretched to sides, with fingers of hand facing upwards.) Run safely and quickly to stand on the end line that I am pointing to and face me. Check for good spacing.

5. **Groups—"2!", "3!"** . . . (*Hand Signal*—Indicate group size by showing that number of fingers, followed by the Home hand signal.) Children quickly sit in a Home space, in a group indicated by the number of fingers shown.

6. **Teams!** (*Hand Signal*—Both hands held out in front parallel to ground as you stand near a designated line.) Children quickly fall in to their teams, with the captain at the front, and the co-captain at the end of each team. Everyone cross-leg sits in file formation (one behind the other).

7. **Waves!** (Teacher moves from facing the file to position on either side as shown in diagram.) Children, in stand-tall position, space themselves arm's length apart, with each wave on a designated floor line or three giant steps away from the wave in front.

8. **Circle Up!** (*Hand Signal*—Hand raised overhand, circling in a clockwise or counterclockwise direction.) Children run in a clockwise or counterclockwise direction, single file, around the play area.

9. **Snake!** (*Hand Signal*—Listening Line hand signal, then point to line of direction, such as a wall.) Children quickly run to stand on the listening line, then turn to file formation (one behind the other), facing the direction teacher indicates. Children stay in this file order as they move.

10. **Shuttle!** (*Hand Signal*—Use the Team hand signal and then split the team into two groups.) Each team splits into two groups who stand in file formation, each half facing opposite the other, and spaced a designated distance apart.

$$X \quad X \quad X \quad | \quad \text{---} \longrightarrow \longrightarrow \text{---} \longrightarrow \quad | \quad X \quad X \quad X$$
5   3   1   10.   2 4 6

Starting Positions

Starting positions signals provide an efficient way of getting children in the appropriate body position for demands of the skill, activity, or game. Teach these emphasizing good posture.

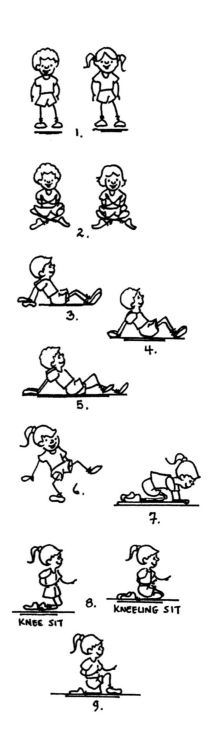

1. **Stand Tall.** Stand with feet comfortably spread apart and toes turned out slightly. Arms are at the sides, hands relaxed, eyes looking forward.

2. **Cross-leg Sit.** Sit with legs crossed and arms resting on the knees.

3. **Long Sit.** Sit with legs outstretched and together. Lean back on your hands for support.

4. **Hook Sit.** Sit with legs together, bending at knees, and feet flat on the floor. Lean back to take weight on the hands.

5. **Half Hook Sit.** Sit with one leg outstretched and the other leg bent. Lean back to support weight on hands.

6. **Wide Sit.** Sit with legs outstretched and comfortably apart. Lean back on hands for support.

7. **All Fours.** Support your weight on hands and knees, facing downwards.

8. **Knee Sit.** Sit upright on your knees, hands resting on your knees. **Kneeling Sit:** Sit back on your knees.

9. **One Knee Up, One Knee Down.** Sit with one knee up and the other knee down as shown. Keep your back straight.

10. **Front Lying Position.** Lie face down with your legs extended backwards and together, arms by your sides at chest level.

11. **Front Support Position.** Support weight on hands and toes, facing downwards. Hold body straight.

12. **Back Lying Position.** Lie facing upwards, legs straight, and arms at sides.

13. **Back Support Position.** From hook sit position, take weight on hands and feet raising body off the floor; keep legs straight and extended, arms slightly bent at elbow.

14. **Hook Lying.** Lie on back with knees bent so that weight is on feet and arms are relaxed at the sides.

15. **Squat.** From standing position, bend knees to raise heels off the floor. Place hands between your legs and rest them on the floor.

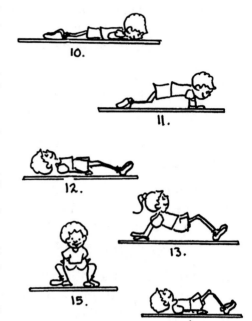

The Break Concept

A "Break" is a short informal activity that, when introduced spontaneously throughout the lesson, can provide a further benefit and extension of signals in the following ways:

◆ Provide a change of pace from the current activity being performed—from passive to active involvement, or from active to passive activity to provide a rest.

◆ Provide a variety of ways for children to interact and respond to different signals and enhance their alertness training.

◆ Provide extra fitness, challenge, and fun—and even the element of surprise.

◆ Mobilize children to equipment or equipment to children and assist in dispersing and collecting equipment.

◆ Create transitional flow between lesson segments.

In the lesson plans that follow, several examples of breaks are presented so that you can get the idea of how to effectively implement them in your daily lesson plan:

1. **Equipment Break:**
   ◆ On signal "Bounce!," bounce your basketball counterclockwise around the play area. Then place the ball in your team container and fall into teams.
   ◆ On signal "Sticky Ball," place the ball between yourself and your partner, and, without using your hands, carry the ball to a designated area.

2. **Organizational Breaks:**
   ◆ Touch a mat, a bench, a rope, and a hoop with a different body part each time, then find a partner and cross-leg sit side-by-side.
   ◆ On signal "Sticky Popcorn!," jump up and down ("pop" as you jump into a large [circle] "popcorn ball"). How quickly can this be done? I am counting, 1-2-3- . . . !

3.   **Tempo Change Break.** On signal "Cocoon!," sink to the ground, then slowly—ever so s-l-o-w-l-y—uncurl to stand in tall position, stretching high into the air.

4.   **Partner Break.** When you hear the signal "Leapfrog!" find a partner and leapfrog from sideline to sideline. (Leapfrog by placing hands on partner's back and straddle-jumping over partner.)

5.   **Stunt Break.** "Thread the Needle"—From stand tall position and fingers interlocked in front of you, lean over and try to put one leg through, then the other leg. Now reverse to your start position. Remember to keep your hand-hold throughout this activity!

"COCOON!" " STICKY POPCORN!" "LEAPFROG" "THREAD THE NEEDLE"

THE IMPORTANCE OF FITNESS

The Preventive Approach

The dual purpose of this resource is to get children involved in enjoyable, meaningful, developmentally appropriate fitness-type activities, and consequently to create an awareness of the benefits to their overall lifestyle, and to instill in children from an early age the "want," the "habit" to be physically active. Research strongly indicates that unless a child becomes a confident and competent mover by the sixth grade, he or she will not pursue activity on a regular basis as an adult.

This approach is preventive rather than being a treatment of the consequence of inactivity. However, as idealistic as this approach may be, in reality an extensive research base gives us a disturbing "gloom and doom" picture—we are increasingly becoming a world of unhealthy children and adults! The problem translates into a huge health bill for each nation and thus this issue has become a universal concern.

Through the past decade an overabundance of research into poor lifestyle habits of young people accusingly points to TV as one of the major culprits and has been so for some time. The Educational Testing Service 1990 study reported that 62% of fourth graders say they spend more than three hours per day watching TV; 64% of eighth graders report watching more than three hours of TV per day. A 1990 AC Nielsen Co. study reported that children aged 2–5 averaged 25 hours per week watching TV; children aged 6–11 averaged more than 22 hours per week watching TV.

There is a direct correlation between the amount of time children spend watching TV and their scores on standardized achievements tests—the more TV watched, the lower the scores! "We suspect that television deters the development of imaginative capacity insofar as it preempts time for spontaneous play." Moreover, research has indicated that body metabolism (and calorie-burning) is an average of 14.5% lower when watching TV than when simply lying in bed (study by Robert Klesges at Memphis State University, 1990).

"By first grade, most children have spent the equivalent of three school years in front of the TV set." ... "By the time most Americans are 18 years old, they have spent more time in front of the television set than they have spent in school, and far more than they have spent talking with their teachers, their friends or even their parents" (*Abandoned in the Wasteland: Children, Television and the First Amendment* by Newton Minnow, former Chairman of the FCC, and Craig LaMay, 1995).

As society is now almost globally immersed in a "digital revolution" as technology continues to evolve at an astounding pace, the sedentary inactive lifestyle of our young people sitting for hours on end at computers is of paramount concern.

In June of 1996 The Surgeon General's Report of Physical Activity and Health was released in the United States, which was summarized in the impactive message: "Americans' love affair with lethargy is killing us!" Over 250,000 Americans die each year as a result of inactivity, placing this sedentary lifestyle in the same risky behavior category as smoking cigarettes, driving drunk, or having unprotected sex. Further to this, research released by the NIH (National Institute of Health) and the National Heart, Lung & Blood Institute in June of 1998 indicated that approximately 55% of American adults (estimated at 97 million people) are medically overweight; and 33% are obese. "Overweightness" or "overfatness" in young children had been steadily increasing throughout the 1990s so that America is experiencing an epidemic in childhood obesity; a significant increase in the early onset of adult Type II diabetes associated with overweightness, as well as hypertension, arthritis, and high blood cholesterol levels. It is estimated that obesity drains $100 billion from the economy each year as a result of missed days at work, decreased productivity, increased costs of providing healthcare to these people, and premature deaths (A.M. Wolf and G.A. Colditz, 1998). Facts do not cease to exist because they are ignored!

The problem is further complicated by the fact that expertise is lacking in terms of specialized physical education/movement-based teachers at the elementary (primary) school levels. An overcrowded curriculum does not provide a priority of balancing quality activity with academic learning experiences, so that P.E. has become a fringe, not a core subject. (Yet a significant correlation exists between learning difficulties and movement difficulties.) There is an aging female population of teachers at the lower elementary level who have little or no background in physical education teaching (or for that matter have little interest or passion for providing quality movement-based experiences from as early an age as possible), as well as a lack of funding for professional inservicing experiences for teachers in the field and inadequate P.E. pedagogy programs for teachers in training at tertiary institutions. These are all compounded by an unfit role model responsible for teaching healthy lifestyle principles to young children.

> *The need now is to structure activity for children within the school timeframe; otherwise, many children will simply miss out experiencing quality movement experiences that create a healthy lifestyle attitude and habit!*

What direction needs to be taken? Governments need to recognize the importance of early intervention as the key to effective prevention of health problems directly related to inactivity. How can this happen? By providing funding for ongoing professional inservicing of teachers in the system which includes quality "hands-on" resources for the teaching, assessing, and remediating of young children; implementing ongoing fundamental movement skills assessment for early recognition of children at movement risk, and ongoing remediation that links the child with the teacher, parents, and field resource specialists; providing quality wellness-based physical education/movement courses for teachers in training; and providing for interpersonal skills/wellness courses for teachers to center on their own personal development.

Essential Understandings

We need to view fitness as the "big" picture—that is, as a holistic experience. Within this total well-being experience are "life keys" that include nutrition, "play" fitness, emotional and mental health, quality sleep and relaxation, productive work, and social interaction. What creates an optimal well-being is to keep all these life keys in balance.

The "Feel Good Model" of Total Well-being

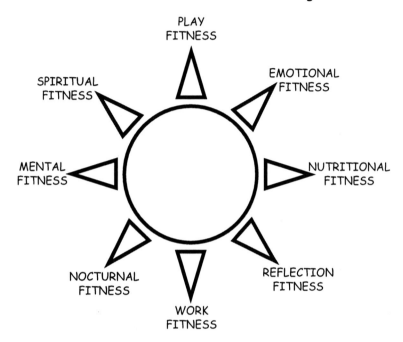

Physical fitness is developed from activity and quality exercising, but must go hand-in-hand with good nutrition to contribute to overall health. One without the other creates an imbalance. The importance lies in teaching children how to establish and maintain this balance; to develop in children a "knowing attitude," not necessarily a fitness attitude, which instills the "want" to be active, the habit of doing exercise and activity on a daily basis, and "in the know" why exercise with nutrition is so beneficial for them. Children need to understand that fitness cannot be stored like you store food in a pantry or fridge—rather being active must be a regular occurrence in their lives from as early on as possible. Children who are active at three or four years of age are more active as adults (Pate, Dowda & Ross, 1996). Children perceive "fitness" much differently from adults. They simply obtain their fitness by doing enjoyable movement experiences. Activity should be fun, interesting, and stimulating. Play should be the central focus of movement experiences. It is really the means by which the child explores, expresses, and discovers many aspects of life from learning skills and rules, to social interaction, fair play, and emotional and psychological growth.

> *Play is the fundamental "key" to life and contributes to the overall development of your children. Through "playful" experiences children can explore, create, express, discover, interact, and learn about their environment around them and about themselves. Play is about "promoting lifestyle activity for youth."*

Definition of Fitness

Physical fitness is defined as one's ability to work efficiently and effectively, to be healthy and to resist hypokinetic diseases, to enjoy leisure-time pursuits, and to meet emergencies successfully.

Benefits of Fitness

Research indicates that physical activity brings some health benefits for children including:

- improving aerobic endurance
- making the heart pump more strongly
- strengthening bones and muscles
- reducing the risk of heart disease
- helping to lower blood pressure and resting heart rate
- providing more energy for play, school work, daily chores
- helping to maintain healthy body weight
- reducing stress

Components of Physical Fitness—Physical fitness is comprised of two components:

- **Health-related** components develop good health and help to prevent hypokinetic diseases such as heart disease, early onset of adult diabetes, hypertension, emphysema resulting from inactivity. These are: cardiovascular, muscular strength, muscular endurance, flexibility, and body composition.

- **Skill-related** components focus on the learning of skills and on developing the ability to perform overall movement, sport skills, dance, and gymnastics. These are: agility, coordination, balance, power, speed, and alertness/reaction.

Physical educators need to realize that in teaching children to be quality and efficient movers, several if not all of these health- and skill-related components are involved in generating a successful outcome. For example, to run efficiently involves coordination and balance, cardiovascular and muscular endurance; to dodge involves these components as well as agility, spurts of speed, and alertness/reaction. Certain technique is involved in developing an overhand throw, but equally important is to develop good arm, wrist, and finger strength to execute it. Young children should use their own body weight to develop muscular strength.

Large muscle groups should be warmed up through low to moderate gentle and rhythmical activity first, before gradually increasing the intensity. Stretching should be smooth and rhythmical, through the full range of motion of "warmed" large group muscles. Muscles should never be stretched "cold" or with ballistic movements and hyperextending any joint areas. Emphasis needs to be placed on the importance of teaching and having children maintain good posture or form while doing the exercise. Proper breathing needs to be taught—when to exhale and when to inhale. The point that needs to be emphasized is that the physical educator teach *total* fitness that involves both skill- and health-related aspects, and in a safe, clean, and appropriate learning environment.

The F. I. T. T. Principle—F.I.T.T. stands for: "F"—frequency or how often activity is done at the target heart rate; "I"—intensity or how hard we do the activity to maintain and improve cardio-respiratory fitness; "T"—time or how long we are active at the target heart rate; and "T"—what types of activity we do.

> *The F.I.T.T. principle states that we need to engage in aerobic-type activity at least 3 days and up to 6 days per week, and that is ongoing continuous activity for at least 20–30 minutes in duration in our target heart rate range.*

A variety of activities such as walking, jogging, inline skating, ice skating, swimming and water exercises, cycling, cross-country skiing, hiking, gardening, dancing, rope jumping, canoeing or kayaking or surf skiing, and different sporting activities (basketball, net ball, soccer, tennis, and so on) is recommended instead of sticking to just one type of activity. Variety of activity allows different muscle groups to be used without creating an overuse of any one muscle group as well as sustaining interest in pursuing activity on a regular basis.

Aerobic fitness is produced through the efficient working of the heart–lung system to supply fuel or oxygen to the working muscles to sustain activity for a long time. This is called cardiovascular endurance. Regular aerobic activity helps to reduce the risk of heart disease by building cardiovascular fitness, burning off calories to keep body fatness in balance, and developing muscular endurance.

Target Heart Rate

A pulse results from a rush of blood through the arteries after each heartbeat. This pulse can be felt on the radial artery in the wrist or on the carotid artery of the neck. The index finger, middle finger, or both are used to take your pulse. Do not use the thumb because it has a pulse of its own. **Heart rate** (HR) is the number of times the heart will beat in one minute. **Resting heart rate** (RHR) is the number of times the heart beats in a 1-minute count when the body is completely relaxed. **Maximum heart rate** (MHR) is the maximum number of times the heart can beat in one minute. MHR is estimated to be 220 minus a person's age in years. For a person to exercise for very long at MHR would be too difficult; it is more beneficial to exercise in the **Target heart rate range** (THR) which is 60% to 80% of the MHR. Exercising in your target heart rate range ("threshold of training") is the minimum amount of exercise necessary to cause improvements in cardio-respiratory fitness. Refer to the example following.

To Find Your Target Heart Rate Range

Maximum Heart Rate (MHR): (220 – Age) beats per minute (bpm)

Target Heart Rate (THR): 60% to 80% of MHR

For a 10-second count rate: Divide THR number by 6

Example: For a 10-year-old:
   MHR = 220 – 10 = 210 bpm
   THR range = 210 × .6 to 210 × .8
                    126   to   168 bpm

10-second count: 13 to 17 bpm

Guidelines for Teaching Fitness

◆ **Reinforce the values and benefits of being active** in an age-appropriate and enjoyable way to the children we teach. Through our daily interaction with children, we as physical educators are in an ideal position to promote and foster desirable positive attitudinal changes in children. You need to ask yourself, "Am I being an effective role model?"

◆ **Strive to maximize quality activity levels** within each physical education lesson, while minimizing wait or standing-around time and behavioral problems.

◆ **Keep the transition, the "flow" of the lesson moving** from one teaching segment to the next.

◆ **Provide variety of tempo.** Change the pace of the lesson from very active, to moderately active, to passive active.

◆ **Observe children at play.** Take a "mental snapshot" of their activity level. Are they generally active throughout the physical education session? Are they sweating? Get them to check their heart rates. Do they express verbally the excitement and fun for what they are doing? Do they show through body language enjoyment and positive response? Are they energetic? enthusiastic? receptive? Are they responding positively to challenges? Are they interacting with you and with others?

◆ **Children do activity intermittently.** Remember, they tire easily, but recover quickly.

◆ From an early age, **educate children about what it means to be "FITT":**
   "F"—How often should we do activity? (frequency)
   "I"—How much effort should be put into it? (intensity)
   "T"—How long should we do the activity? (time)
   "T"—What types of activity can we do? (type)

◆ **Moderate activity is valuable and beneficial.** Active children become active adults. Any activity is better than no activity. Experts recommend that primary school-aged children accumulate at least 30–60 minutes of age and developmentally appropriate physical activity—daily! More than 30–60 minutes should be encouraged; extended periods of inactivity for children, discouraged!

◆ **Keep fitness inherent** throughout the physical education lesson rather than taught as a training regime. Exposure to a variety of interesting, enjoyable, and beneficial activity at the developmentally appropriate age level is highly recommended!

◆ **Make fitness fun!** Children are not mini-adults! They simply obtain their fitness by doing activities that they enjoy. Imposing "training" on them will only create an uphill battle of resistance. Obtaining a love for fitness will result in maintaining fitness for life. It is the process of exercising on a regular basis—so that it becomes a habitual and permanent part of one's lifestyle—that is important; the product, physical fitness, will follow!

◆ **Fitness is for everyone,** regardless of gender, cultural and ethnic background, physical competence, and disabilities. The true "mission" for physical educators is to help children from an early age to enjoy and learn about the benefits of physical activity so that they will develop personal habits of doing exercise regularly and thus continue to be active for the rest of their lives!

Twenty Exercise Recommendations

1. Establish boundaries and mark them clearly for each activity session. Use such markers as witch's hats, domes, or throwing rings.

2. Establish a set of SIGNALS for starting, stopping, and movement. These signals will enhance children's listening skills, alertness and reaction, and spatial awareness. Practice these until the children can respond immediately.

3. Give instructions clearly and concisely. Demonstrate whenever possible.

4. Warm up gently and rhythmically, using as many of the major muscle groups involved in the main activity as possible. Begin in a slow, controlled manner, gradually increasing intensity.

5. Keep the warm-up simple. Use easy, "catchy" names that children will remember.

6. Identify the activities with names that children can easily remember and associate the movement with the name; for example, "Dead Ants"—children quickly and carefully drop to the floor on their backsides with limbs waving in the air.

7. Include specific stretching and movements that are used in the activities to follow.

8. Avoid tag-type games in the early part of the warm-up.

9. Modify and adapt according to age level, space available, and weather conditions.

10. Use music with a moderate, steady beat to enhance the enjoyment and rhythm of the movements.

11. Stretching activities generally can occur during the warm-up and then in the cool-down, but stretching activities should always be performed while the muscles are still warm.

12. Cooling-down time is necessary to help the body return to its normal resting state and should be part of the overall fitness package. The activity is continued, but at a lower intensity.

13. Quiet, gentle background music could be used to help the children "unwind" and relax. Have children concentrate on their breathing.

14. Be aware of children's growth and development. Movement is needed for the development of bones and muscles; therefore, it is important that children experience developmentally appropriate activities for their age group.

15. Be a positive role model by being enthusiastic and joining in whenever and wherever possible. Children learn by example. Encourage, praise, and provide constructive feedback; don't push or be overbearing.

16. Provide a variety of activities. Make the activity fun, challenging, interesting, and motivating. Vary the intensity so that children do not become fatigued.

17. Be aware of exercise "do's" and "don'ts." Never stretch "cold" muscles. Avoid ballistic movements when stretching. Avoid exercises that hyperextend any joint areas. Children should be encouraged to use their own body weight to develop strength. (See the Appendix for a description of the more common stretches that are no longer recognized as suitable for children, why they should be excluded, and what are alternative suggestions.)

18. See fitness as the BIG picture; that is, physical fitness is only one integral part of the total health and well-being package that also includes good nutrition, mental health (thinking), emotional health (attitude), quality sleep, relaxation, and "play" time. The key is to achieve a "balance" of all these health-related components!

19. Establish exercise/activity as a "habit." That is, establish an activity routine schedule, but within this schedule be flexible and realistic as you may not have the time or opportunity to do activity with your child at the same time each day.

20. Develop in your child a "knowing attitude." Get your child used to being active, used to doing exercises, and in the know of WHY exercise is so good for you!

SECTION 2
FOUNDATION MOVEMENT REVISION/EXTENSION

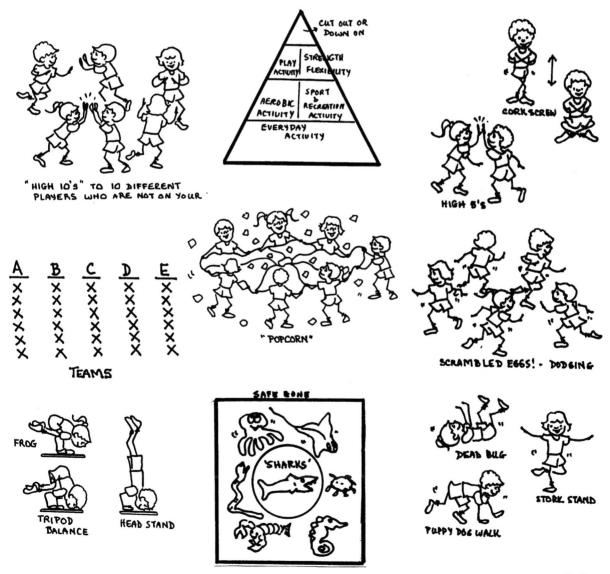

CUT OUT OR DOWN ON

PLAY ACTIVITY | STRENGTH FLEXIBILITY

AEROBIC ACTIVITY | SPORT & RECREATION ACTIVITY

EVERYDAY ACTIVITY

CORK SCREW

"HIGH 10's" TO 10 DIFFERENT PLAYERS WHO ARE NOT ON YOUR

HIGH 5's

A B C D E

TEAMS

"POPCORN"

SCRAMBLED EGGS! - DODGING

FROG

TRIPOD BALANCE

HEAD STAND

SAFE ZONE

'SHARKS'

DEAD BUG

STORK STAND

PUPPY DOG WALK

Lesson 1:
Organization Signals

Skill Builders: organization signals, spatial and body awareness, listening and alertness, dodging, stretching

Expected Student Performance:

◆ Demonstrates good listening skills and quick response to directions.

◆ Demonstrates ability to move in general and personal space with agility and alertness.

◆ Willingly participates in activities and socially interacts with other members of class.

Facility/Equipment Needed:

◆ Outdoor grass area, gymnasium, undercover area, or large multipurpose area

◆ Cones to mark out boundaries of the play area to provide visual guidelines for the children

◆ Music to help establish a sense of rhythm

Warming-up Activities/Games:

Give high 5's to greet 10 different classmates, then find a Home space and "Corkscrew" (stand tall, crossing arms and legs, right over left). Sink down to the floor into cross-leg sit position, hold for 3 seconds, then return to "Standing Tall" without undoing the Corkscrew.

Remember that walking and jogging are heel–toe actions. As you move quicker, you are sprinting on the ball of your foot.

◆ "Scrambled Eggs—Dodging!" "Iceberg!" "Dead Bug!"

◆ "Scrambled Eggs—Skipping." "Iceberg!" Stork Stand on right foot, eyes closed for a 5-second count.

◆ "Scrambled Eggs—Slide Stepping." Pitter-patter in place by jogging as quickly as you can on the spot.

◆ "Iceberg!" "Stork Stand" on left foot, eyes closed, 5 seconds.

◆ "Scrambled Eggs—Power Walking! (walk vigorously, pumping with arms)" "Hit the Deck!"

◆ "Pencil Stretch." "Clear the Deck!"

◆ Touch the 4 boundary lines of the play area with opposite body part (e.g., right knee, left hand; right

elbow, left foot). Then return to a Home space and Corkscrew, crossing arms and legs left over right. Return to standing tall position again without uncrossing body parts.

◆ "Scrambled Eggs—Power Walking!" "Iceberg!"

◆ "Five!" (touch 5 body parts to the ground)

◆ "Crab Walk" to an end line and do a reverse "Compass Walk."

◆ "Puppy Dog Walk" to touch a corner with left elbow, right knee.

◆ "Kangaroo Hop" (change hopping foot every 4 hops) to a sideline, and then "Ski Jump" back and forth over this line.

Games:

1. **Two-way/Four-way Traffic:** Have class number off 1, 2, 3, 4; 1, 2, 3, 4; etc. Then designate one side of a large square (30' by 30' [10m by 10m]) for each group as shown. Signal teams to move across the square in different ways and from a variety of starting positions:

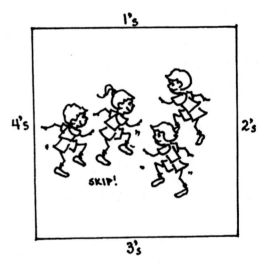

   • 1 and 3's Power Walk; 2 and 4's, Power Walk!

   • 4 and 2's, Skip; 3 and 1's Skip

   • 1 and 3's, Crab Walk; 2 and 4's, Crab Walk

   • 2 and 4's, Backwards Walk; 1 and 3's, Backward Walk

   • 1 . . . 2 . . . 3 . . . 4's, Slide-Step

   • 4 . . . 3 . . . 2 . . . 1's, Jog! Watch where you are going!

   • Front lying position, head on line: 1 and 3's Bear Walk, 2 and 4's, Bear Walk

   • Cross-leg sit position, with backs to the center of square: 4 and 2's, Kangaroo Jump; 3 and 1's, Kangaroo Jump.

   • *Challenge:* Emphasizing safety, challenge which group can reach the opposite side first and knee sit facing center.

2. **Blob Attack!** Designate 3 players to be "baby blobs" who start in the middle of the play area. On signal Blob Attack! baby blobs give chase to the free players. A player tagged by one of these blobs must join hands with that blob. Only the blob can make the tag. Once a blob has grown to a 5-player blob, the second player to be caught is set free and becomes yet another baby blob! Game continues until there are no more free players left. Designate 3 new baby blobs and play again. Emphasize that players watch where they are going at all times. *Variations:*

- Baby blobs have the option of joining together to form "parent blobs."
- Allow players on either end of the blob to tag free players.
- Use deck rings for players to join up rather than hand holds.

Cooling-down Activities/Games:

1. **Foot Artist.** In hook sitting position, lift one leg and draw circles in the air with your pointed toes. Now draw circles in the opposite direction. Repeat using the other foot. Now use your foot to trace your initials, your birth date.

2. **Periscope!** Lie on your back, arms at your sides, and legs straight. Bring one leg straight upwards using both hands, holding gently at the ankle, and gently press it for 10 seconds. Repeat with the other leg. Feel the stretch in your hamstrings (back of upper leg). *Variations:*

   ◆ **Double Periscope.** Bring both legs straight up and hold with hands at the ankles, gently pressing towards you.

   ◆ **Cross-Periscope.** Bring right leg straight up and hold it at the ankle with your left hand. Stretch for 10 seconds. Then repeat with left leg and right hand hold.

3. **Finger Stretcher.** In stand tall position, interlock your fingers of both hands, then gently straighten your arms, pushing the palms of your fingers outwards in front of you. Hold this stretch for 5–10 seconds; relax. Now stretch in this position with arms overhead. Interlock fingers behind you and stretch through your shoulders.

4. **Legend(s) of the Day!** Use this self-esteem builder at the end of every lesson. Have class gather in a listening circle or in teams. Recognize a child (children) from the class or each team as the legend(s) of the day and have them stand in front of the class. Tell the class why you think each "legend" is so special: cooperates so well with others, plays fairly throughout the activity or game, shares equipment, is kind and cheerful, helps others, helps you, or tries hard to improve skill ability.

The class responds by giving these legends a big round of applause (clapping hands while moving them clockwise in a big circle). Ensure that each child in the class eventually receives a "legend of the day" award throughout the school year. You may wish to give each legend a certificate or sticker.

Homework Idea:

Alphabet Scramble/Ramble. (On a large piece of paper write the letters of the alphabet in random order using uppercase letters. Underneath each alphabet letter put a movement letter, C or F or S. Choose one color for the alphabet letters and another color for the movement letters. For C, clap hands together; for F, click fingers of both hands in the air; for S, slap knees with hands.)

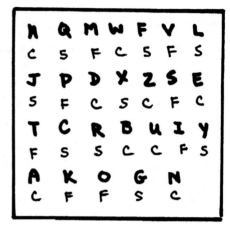

Children on "start cue" say the letter and do the associated movement with that letter. Encourage each child to progress at his/her own rate. Practice row by row (part by part), slowly, until children have mastered each part. Challenge by reading a row from right to left. Further challenge by saying the alphabet backwards. Observe coordination of actions. *Variations:*

- Create more Alphabet Scramble/Rambles by changing the actions. (Suggestions: R—right arm out to right side; L—left arm out to left side; B—both arms out in front.) Scramble the letters.

- Have each child create his/her own Alphabet Scramble/Ramble, then bring to class for each other to try to do.

Fit Think Ideas:

- What are large muscle groups?
- Why is it important to warm up large muscle groups before doing moderate to very active (intense) workouts?
- How can muscles be warmed up? cooled down?
- When do muscles gets injured?
- Why it is important to stretch every day?

Lesson 2:
Formation and Grouping Signals—Partner Play

Skill Builders: formation signals, spatial and body awareness, partner play

Expected Student Performance:

◆ Demonstrates good listening skills and keen response, safety awareness.

◆ Willingly interacts and cooperates with peers in partner activities.

◆ Is learning to identify and name major muscles and bones, and general function of each.

◆ Engages in physical activity demands and cognitive learning of muscles/bones.

Facility/Equipment Needed:

◆ Outdoor grass area, gymnasium, or undercover area

◆ Cones to mark out boundaries of the play area to provide visual guidelines for the children

◆ Music to help establish a sense of rhythm

◆ Circuit signs to show movements

Teaching Points:

'HELP' SPOT

> Remember the three simple rules:
> ◆ Don't hurt yourself!
> ◆ Don't hurt anyone else!
> ◆ And don't hurt the equipment!

1. **Help Spot.** Designate a spot just outside the play area. Suggest using a hoop or carpet square to mark the spot. Anyone who cannot find a partner or is simply unhappy in any way can come to this place and get help. (In this way we can avoid children being socially excluded!)

2. **Mingle.** Whenever you hear this word, this will be the signal to find a new partner/group to work with. It encourages children to interact more with each other!

Warming-up Activities/Games:

1. **Lengths and Widths Circuit.** Mark out a large rectangular area. Children are evenly spread on each side of the rectangle. **Circuit 1:** Traveling (counterclockwise), sprint the lengths; power-walk the widths. Then Pencil Stretch (standing tall) for 10 seconds.

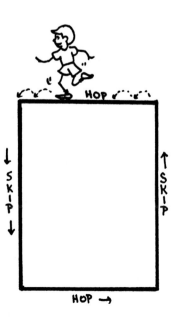

HOP

SKIP   SKIP

HOP →

Circuit 2: Slide-step the widths, grapevine step the lengths (Traveling clockwise—sideways movement, step right over left, step right behind left; reverse footwork for travelling counterclockwise.) Then Periscope Stretch for 10 seconds, each leg.

Circuit 3: Skip the lengths; hop the widths. Then do 10-second side stretches, each side. Giant strides along the lengths; ski jumps along the widths. Then do calf stretch, 10 seconds each leg.

Circuit 4: Touch opposite sidelines with your right hand, left foot. Touch opposite end lines with left hand, right foot. Then run to my Listening Circle, corkscrew, and cross-leg sit. When you see my hand raised overhead, this is your Quiet Signal to stop what you are doing, raise your hand overhead as well, and give me your full attention!

2.

2. Let's pretend you are: (Remember to watch where you are going!)

   - Jet ski slicing through the water.
   - Shadow boxer dancing with your feet while arms punch through the air.
   - F-18 jet taking off down the runway, lift off, then fly into the clouds.
   - Figure skater spinning, balancing on one leg, jump-turning, and doing other tricks.
   - Hurdler jumping over low hurdles or lines on the floor, then coming through the finish line.
   - Karate kid kicking with your feet and slashing with your hands.
   - Shake-shake-shake like a wet dog coming out of water.
   - Crocodile creeping up on its prey.

3.

"KNEE BOX"

4.

"TICK-TOCK"

"BUSY MUSCLES-TRICEPS"

5.

"BUSY BONES-PATELLA"

3. **2's!** Find a partner and stand face-to-face, about one giant step apart and hands resting lightly on knees, knees bent. On signal "Knee Box!" try to touch your partner's knee(s) without letting your partner touch yours. Remember to stay in your Home space. When you hear "Knee Box" again, find a new partner to challenge!

4. **Tick-tock!** Stand back-to-back with new partner. Take half a step away from each other and interlock fingers with your partner. Together lean to one side to touch pointer fingers to floor ("Tick"); then lean to the other side and touch ("Tock"). Remember to bend your knees as you side-stretch together. Can you do 3 "Tick-Tocks" on each side in this way?

5. **Busy muscles/busy bones.** Everyone has a beanbag. Give the signal "Busy Muscles" and call out the name of a muscle; for example, "right biceps." Each player uses his/her beanbag to touch the right bicep muscle of another player. Signal "Busy Muscles" again, and call out another muscle, for example, "left hamstrings." Everyone must now mingle and find a new player to touch beanbag to that player's left hamstring. [*Muscles:* Biceps, Triceps, Quadriceps, Hamstrings, Gastrocnemius, Rectus Abdominus, Gluteus Maximum, Deltoids] Signal "Busy Bones" and call out the name of a bone such as "femur." [*Bones:* Cranium, Mandible, Clavicle, Scapula, Sternum, Humerus, Ulna, Radius, Carpal bones, Phalanges, Metacarpal, Femur, Patella, Fibula, Tibia, Tarsal bones, Coccyx, Ilium, Ribs]

Games:

1. **Artful Dodger.** Children pair off and stand one behind the other. Music is used to start and stop the action. Front partner is the "Dodger" who moves in general space, making quick changes of direction. The other partner is the "Shadow" who tries to follow as closely as possible to the Dodger without touching him or her. When music stops, everyone does an "Iceberg" (jump stops immediately). If the "Shadow" can take one step forward and touch the Dodger, then the two partners change roles. Continue in this way, each time calling out a different locomotor movement such as jogging, power walking, skipping, slide stepping, giant strides, moving backward, puppy walks, crab walks.

SHADOW   DODGER

2. **Just-beat-it Challenges:** Mingle and find a new partner. Stand side-by side in a Home spot. Listen to the challenge, then on the signal "Just Beat It!" try to perform the task and get back to Home space before your partner can. Partner arriving "second" must do 3 push-ups or 3 tummy crunches, or . . . *Challenges:*

RIGHT HAND, LEFT FOOT

   - Touch two sidelines with right foot, left hand; return Home.
   - Touch two end lines with left knee, right elbow; return Home.
   - Touch each corner with a hand and foot, then return Home.
   - Touch each corner, but touch the center jump circle before going to the next corner.

Cooling-down Activities/Games:

1. **Mirrors.** With a partner, facing each other, mirror each other's movements in slow motion. Change from leading to copying roles on my drumbeat. On signal "Mirrors," find a new partner.

2. **Legend(s) of the Day!**

In Class Idea:

For the next few weeks, have a chart that names the "Muscle of the Week" and the "Bone of the Week."

Homework Idea:

"The Muscle-dude" Worksheet. (See the Appendix.) Identify the muscles and locate them on your Muscle-Dude. Learn to spell and say the names and become familiar with their location and function.

Lesson 3:
Grouping Signals—Small Group Play

Skill Builders: grouping signals, spatial and body awareness, small group play, alertness and agility

Expected Student Performance:

Demonstrates fair play and safety at all times.

Willingly interacts and cooperates with peers in group.

Engages in physical activity demands of the activity or game.

Becomes more aware of activity levels on a day-to-day basis.

Facility/Equipment Needed:

Outdoor grass area, gymnasium, undercover area, large multipurpose room

Cone markers to identify boundaries to provide visual guidelines for the children

1 tag belt or flag per player

Focus Words:

● *Muscles of the Week: Quadriceps (thigh muscles)*

● *Bones of the Week: Patella (knee cap)*

Warming-up Activities/Games:

1. **Tail Snatch Tag.** Each player has a flag (tail) tucked in at the back of the shorts except for 3–4 players who are IT. If an IT successfully snatches a tail, then that player becomes the new IT. Continue to play in this way. Remind players to always watch where they are going to avoid collisions. Emphasize that at least two-thirds of the flag must be showing.

2. **Tail Snatch Break.** As for Knee Boxing (Lesson 2), but partners try to snatch away each other's flags that are tucked into the back of their shorts. On each signal "Tail Snatch" find a new partner to play the game.

3. **Hoppo Bumpo.** Partners about the same size take up a position of left hand holding the right foot behind, while the right hand is used to gently push the other partner off balance. On signal "Hoppo Bumpo" challenge a new partner, and reverse hand-hold. Continue in this way.

4. **Transformation Tag:** Form groups of 3. In each group designate one person to be a "Head" (place preferred hand on head); a "Tail" (place preferred hand on bottom); and a "Pocket" (place preferred hand in pocket). On signal "Transform!" Heads, Tails, and Pockets try to tag each other, transforming the tagged player to look like the tagger. In the beginning there is one-third of each tagging group. On signal "Iceberg!" game stops. Now count the numbers in each group and make a comparison of numbers. Play game again! *Variations:* Use different locomotion movements: power walking, slide-stepping, skipping, jogging. Use music to start and stop the game.

5. **Ike, Spike, Squeak, and Wilber.** Form groups of 4, join hands, facing center of circle. To begin game, have all "Squeaks" step out of the group. Squeak then designates one of the circle players to be the "target" and tries to tag ("Ike") within a 20-second time limit. Spike and Wilber try to protect Ike from being tagged. Squeak cannot reach through the circle to make the tag. After time is up or the tag is made, Squeak joins the circle players and Ike becomes the new tagger. Play until all have had a turn at being tagger and target.

Games:

1. **Bone Collectors.** Split the class into groups of 5. Each player in group number off 1, 2, 3, 4, 5. Enough beanbags (bones) are placed in a center circle for each group to have one per person. Each group is designated a Home corner with a hoop placed in this space. On signal "Collect!" the first player from each group leaves Home corner and runs to the center hoop to grab only one bone and take it back to corner hoop. Player #1 gives high 5 to the second player who repeats the task, and so on. Insist that only one player from each group be collecting a bone at any one time. When all the bones have been removed from the center hoop, players are now allowed to remove a bone, one at a time, from each other's hoops. Emphasize that a group is not allowed to prevent other group players from taking a bone from their hoop. Play for a certain time, then have each group count the number of bones collected. *Variation:* Allow players the option of collecting a bone from another group's hoop or from the center hoop.

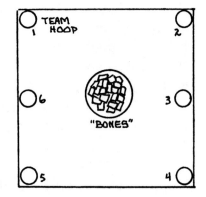

2. **Six Corners:** Use markers positioned at 6 locations in a large rectangular area or hexagonal shape. With a marking pen, number the markers 1 through 6 as shown. On signal "Corner," players must run as quickly and carefully as they can to stand in one of the 6 corners and stay there jogging in place. Throw a large die and see which number comes up. Players caught in the corner with that number must come to the center of the play area and do stretches; the other players continue the game. When only 6 players remain, each player must run to a different corner! Who will be the last 2 players left?

SIX CORNERS

Cooling-down Activities/Games:

"Sticky Popcorn" signals children to start popping into a large circle shoulder to shoulder, then corkscrew and cross-leg sit.

1. **Gotcha.** Each player puts right thumb up and left hand over the thumb of the player on the left. Eyes are closed. Players wait intently for the signal "Gotcha" to be called. Then the challenge is to try to grab the left player's thumb while pulling away their right thumb to stop from being grabbed by the player on their right. Watch the fun! Reverse hand positions and repeat game.

2. **Socket Stretcher.** Standing tall, slowly reach one arm overhead to the opposite side. Let the opposite hand gently grab this arm and **pretend** to pull it out of its socket! Hold for 5 seconds, reverse arm positions, and repeat.

3. **Rhythm Breathing.** Slowly breathe in (inhaling) while circling your arms outward to cross in front. Slowly breathe out (exhale) while circling your arms in the opposite direction.

4. **Heavy Head.** All fours, with head touching the floor, pretend that your head weighs 2,000 pounds (a ton). Slowly move to stand tall with your head being the last to rise.

5. **Legend(s) of the Day!**

Homework Idea:

Fill out what activity you do each day using your Active Fit Kid Pyramid. (See the Appendix.) Keep in your Tune-up Kids Activity Journal.

Fit Think Ideas:

◆ Discuss how strong thigh muscles can help knee area strong.

◆ What does "aerobic fitness" mean? Give examples of aerobic activities.

◆ Choose 4–5 of these activities you have listed that you would enjoy doing.

◆ Choose 2 activities that you would like to try that are new to you.

◆ Discuss the benefits of doing a variety of aerobic activities rather than sticking with one specific aerobic activity.

Lesson 4:
Large Group Signals—Teamness

Skill Builders: large group formation signals, introduction of teams and team building; aerobic fitness, arm strengtheners, cooperation

Expected Student Performance:

◆   Willingly interacts and cooperates in small and large group activities.

◆   Participates enthusiastically in the demands of the physical fitness activities.

◆   Willingly contributes to developing team spirit and engaging in team-building activities.

Facility/Equipment Needed:

◆   Gymnasium or large undercover area

◆   Appropriate lively and popular music with a steady 4/4 beat

◆   CD player or tape recorder

◆   Large parachute (20- to 24-foot diameter), several beanbags, rubber chicken

◆   1 large balloon or balloon ball per team

◆   5–6 large cone markers labeled A, B, C, D, E, F

Focus Words:

●   *Muscles of the Week: Biceps (front of upper arm muscles)*

●   *Bones of the Week: Phalanges (finger and toe bones)*

Warming-up Activities/Games:

1.   **Aerobic Snake.** On signal "Snake," children run to stand one behind the other on a designated line, forming a long snake with a "head" and "tail." Teacher leads the snake in a variety of movement patterns throughout the play area using different locomotor movements. (See example provided.) Emphasize that children stay in order in the file as they move. Use popular music with a steady 4/4 beat. *Challenge:* Keep the Snake moving for the length of one song; two songs!

2.   **Aerobic Circle.** Aerobic Snake coils up in one direction, then coils in the opposite direction and opens up into a large circle as jogging players change to slide-stepping

around the large circle. On signal "In Place," players jog in place keeping feet moving. Now add arm movements such as:

- ◆ Reaches—alternating hands reaching upward every 4 counts
- ◆ Punches—fisted hands, alternating punching arms every 4 counts
- ◆ Slashes—alternating slashing hands diagonally downwards across the body for 4 counts

Continue this pattern; then double the time. Use cue words: "Reach-Reach"; Punch-Punch"; "Slash-Slash." Continue with these:

- ◆ Corkscrew down to a Hook-sit position. Lean back and mime climbing a rope with hands for 20 seconds (stomach muscles).

- ◆ Leg Lifts: Long sit position; right leg 8 times; left leg 8 times.

- ◆ Finger-Walkers: Cross legs left or right in long-leg sit position. Walk fingers down each leg to reach for shoelaces or toes. Hold for 10 seconds. Uncross legs in the air to cross right over left. Repeat Finger Walkers.

ROPE CLIMBERS   LEG LIFTS

- ◆ Finger Stretchers: Interlock fingers and stretch overhead, in front, and behind; slowly breathe in; slowly breathe out.

3. **Parachute Play** (Arm Strengtheners).

- ◆ **Firemen's Rescue.** Using a palms-down grip of the seam of the parachute, lean away from the chute, keeping feet "glued" to the ground.

- ◆ **Wild Horse's Pull.** Turn so back is to parachute and, using a palms-up grip, pull away from the center.

- ◆ **Body Wave.** With one knee up and one knee down, palms-down grip, seal the parachute to the ground, On signal "1-2-3 Up," create a whole body wave lifting the parachute overhead, then bringing back down. Repeat several times. (Call out names of sports teams to cheer!)

- ◆ **Mushroom.** Inflate the parachute on signal "1-2-3, Up!" walk into center 3 steps, then on signal "Down," lower chute sealing seam to the ground and making a mushroom shape.

FIREMEN'S RESCUE

BODY WAVE

◆ **Igloo.** Grip the parachute with right hand over left. Inflate the chute again, take 3 steps towards center of chute, then pull the parachute behind you, uncrossing your arms and cross-leg sit on it to seal in the air. Who lives in igloos?

◆ **Merry-go-round.** Hold parachute with palms-down grip, right hands, and jog in a clockwise direction. Gently lower and raise the chute on signal. On signal "Switch," reverse hand hold and travel in the opposite direction.

◆ **Popcorn.** Place several beanbags in the center of the parachute, held at waist height. See how quickly beanbags can be "popped" or shaken off the parachute.

" POPCORN "

◆ **Wrist Roll.** Holding parachute at waist level, palms-down grip, players gently roll the parachute towards the center. Emphasize keeping the parachute taunt. Ask students if they can feel their wrists. When the parachute is almost completely rolled up, have players gently drop the chute to the ground, step away, and file into their teams in the designated spot.

◆ **Teams.** Have children file into their teams according to the teams you have created. Teach class the Team signal (hands held horizontally out in front, palms facing). Point to 5 or 6 cone markers, labeled A, B, C, D, E, F where teams will sit. Captain is at the front; co-captain at the back, alternating boy–girl. Now allow a certain time for teams to create a team name and team cheer that begin with the designated letter.

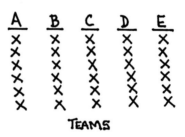

Cooling-down Activities/Games:

These are team-building activities.

1. **Balloon Ball Rally.** Have each team position in a circle in a designated corner of the play area. Each captain collects a large balloon ball for his/her team. *Challenges:* Keep it afloat using different body parts. No one can hit the balloon twice in a row. Given a certain time limit, count the number of successful hits made without the ball touching the floor. If right hand is used to make the hit, then left hand has to be used next time.

2. **Balloon Ball Lift.** Have captain place ball in center of team circle. Teams then "Hit the Deck" and lie with heads gently pressing against balloon ball. Challenge is to raise the balloon to stand tall position without the use of hands!

3. **Legend(s) of the Day.**

In Class Idea:

Create an Aerobic Snake Collage using movement patterns of the "Aerobic Snake" warm-up: zigzags, curves, spirals, waves, diagonals, verticals, horizontal patterns.

Fit Think Idea: (Refer to the Appendix.)

◆   What is the strongest muscle in your body?

◆   How many muscles do you have altogether?

◆   Why do you need strong muscles in day-to-day living?

◆   What muscles are you using in the Parachute Play?

◆   What do you think F.I.T.T. stands for?

HAPPY HEALTHY
HEART

Lesson 5:
Aerobic Fitness-builder Stations

Skill Builders: aerobic fitness, sprint running, agility, pattern running, stretching and strengtheners, coordination, and cooperation

Expected Student Performance:

◆ Demonstrates competency in sprint and pattern running, and agility abilities.

◆ Demonstrates proficiency in aerobic demands, stretching, and strengthening exercises.

◆ Willingly cooperates and integrates with team members.

Facility/Equipment Needed:

◆ Outdoor grass area, gymnasium, or undercover area

◆ Station #1—1 tape recorder and set music

◆ Station #2—obstacles for obstacle course (hoops, cones, mats, ropes, chairs, benches, box horse, and other equipment)

◆ Station #3—large cone markers, measuring tape

◆ Station #4—8 large cone markers

◆ Station #5—8 bases, directional arrows or signs

◆ Station #6—stretching/strengthening poster

◆ Activity Station signs

Skill Builder Station Ideas:

Station #1: Tempo Change Warm-up. (Create a tape using popular music, with varying tempos. Change the tempo every 30 seconds. Intersperse "rest breaks" such as stretch breaks, "reaching for the sky," or "breathing breaks" before picking up the tempo again. Suggest 4–5 minutes of activity.) Keep in time to the music as it changes tempo from quick to slow as you jog, walk, march, skip, slide. Move in general space, watching where you are going. When the music stops, you stop, by jump-stopping; then do the stretch break in your Home space.

MARCH IN PLACE   PENCIL STRETCH   JOG   #1

Station #2: Steeplechase. Create a steeplechase course using hoops, low hurdles, cones, mats, ropes, chairs, benches, box horse, and so on. Complete the course as quickly and safely as possible. Time each other.

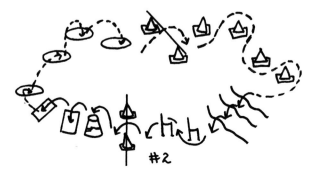

#2

Station #3: Friendly Races. Mark off a 60-yard (meter) distance. Children pair off and race each other to the finish line. Challenge a new runner for the next race.

Station #4: Figure-8 Run. Set up 4 markers in a "fan" pattern, spaced 20 feet (6 meters) apart, marking them 1, 2, 3, and 4 as shown. Set up two identical patterns. Each child in turn starts at the first marker, runs around the second, back around the first, then around the third, and back around the first marker, and finally the fourth marker to the first. Time each other. Strive for a best time in two tries.

Station #5: Baseball Diamond Run. Set up 4 bases in the shape of a diamond as shown. Start with bases spaced 20 feet (6 meters) apart. Set up two identical courses. Use arrows to show direction of movement (one course, run clockwise; other course, counterclockwise). Children take turns running the bases with a foot tag at each base. Designate different locomotor movements each time course is done.

Station #6: Stretching/Strengthening Station. (See the Appendix.)

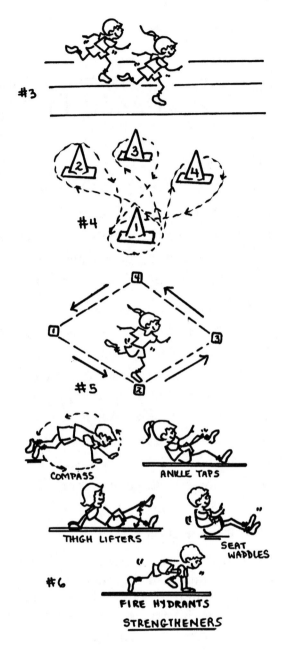

Stretching	*Strengtheners*
Foot Artist	Compass
Periscope Stretch	Ankle Taps
Side Stretcher	Thigh Lifters
Calf Stretch	Seat Waddles
Quad Stretch	Fire Hydrants

Gently stretch, holding for a 10-second count. Display Stretches and Strengtheners poster on a wall.

Legend(s) of the Day!

Lesson 6:
Large Group Signals—Islands, Jumping, and Landings

Skill Builders: large group formation signal "Islands," jumping and landings, cooperation, balance, coordination, aerobic fitness, team-building, relaxation

Expected Student Performance:

◆ Demonstrates competency in jumping for height and distance, and power jumping, and landing skills.

◆ Cooperates in performing jumping group tasks with other team members.

◆ Performs proficiently in fitness demands and imagery focus.

Facility/Equipment Needed:

◆ Outdoor grass area, gymnasium, or undercover area

◆ Exercise Hunt cards for indoor, outdoor use; stretch poster

◆ 30 small cone or dome markers

◆ Island sign and task card

◆ 2 long jump ropes

◆ 10 hoops, low box horse, gym mat, low hurdles, and ball in sock suspended

◆ 1 deck ring and long rope

◆ 4 cone markers and 6 beanbags

◆ Different hopscotch patterns or squares

◆ Wall tape to set different jumping heights (or jump flags)

Focus Words:

◆ Muscles of the Week: Gastrocnemius (calf muscles)

◆ Bones of the Week: Femur (upper leg)

"HIGH IO's" TO IO DIFFERENT PLAYERS WHO ARE NOT ON YOUR TEAM.

Warming-up Activities/Games:

1. **Exercise Hunt.** This is an aerobic fitness and team-building activity. A series of 10 activities are created and listed on a card. Exercise Hunts can be created for indoor, outdoor, multipurpose area, undercover area, or for a certain focus and further reinforce the teamness concept. Some sample Exercise Hunts are given in the Appendix.

STRETCH TREE

- Each captain is given an Exercise Hunt card.

- Each team must complete the exercise hunt, then gather at the Stretch Tree to do a series of stretches.

- Every activity or exercise would have been taught before being placed in an Exercise Hunt. Quality of movement is constantly stressed and reinforced.

- A team cannot move onto the next activity until every one in the team has completed the prior activity.

- Captains and co-captains are responsible for keeping their team members together.

- Observe teams in motion and offer feedback at the end.

- Participate yourself by joining in with each group to do some of the activity with them! In this way the children observe you as an active role model.

Variation: Have each team design its own Exercise Hunt. Use these as future warm-ups!

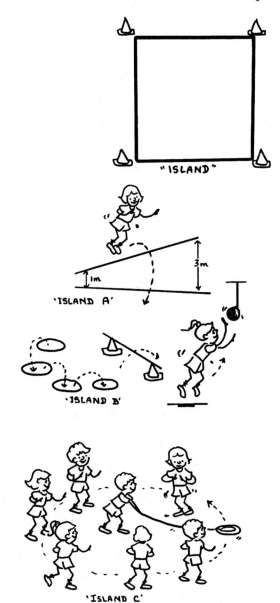

2. **Jumping Islands.** Use small cones to mark out an "island" (3m × 3m) for each team. Assign each team to an island and give their island a name. Teams perform the jumping tasks at that island, then on signal rotate to the next island, until all islands have been visited. Emphasize and practice good landings with knees bending to give with the impact, feet shoulder-width apart, and arms extended to sides to ensure balance.

- ◆ **Island A: Jump the Stream.** Place two long ropes as shown in the diagram. Take turns jumping across the "stream" from its narrowest point to its widest.

- ◆ **Island B: Jumping Circuit.** Set up 10 hoops, low box horse, gym mat, low hurdles, and suspend a ball in a sock from a fixed structure. Players jump through a hoop pattern, over low hurdles, off a low box horse, at a suspended object as shown.

- ◆ **Island C: Jump the Ring.** One team member swings a deck ring attached to a long rope in a large circle along the ground. Other team members must try to jump the ring each time it passes under the feet.

- ◆ **Island D: Jumping for Distance.** Take turns jumping from a marked line to land on a mat. Use beanbags to mark your jumping distance. Remember to use arms to help you jump forward.

- ◆ **Island E: Jumping for Height.** Stand near a wall, side on, and jump upwards as high as possible to touch a mark on the wall. Set marks at different heights.
- ◆ **Island F: Hopscotch.** Introduce different hopscotch patterns. Players decide the rules, then play the game.

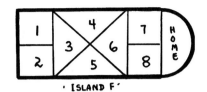
· ISLAND F ·

Variations:

- ◆ **Skip-n-hop.** Twirl a ball tethered to one leg while hopping over it.
- ◆ **Jump-a-hoop.** Use specially designed jump hoops which players use to go through a zigzag course.

Cooling-down Activities/Games:

Use relaxing music softly played in the background.

1. **Imagery—R-E-L-A-X!** Lie on a mat in back lying position and relax. Think of something that is very pleasant and will bring a smile to your face. Listen to the quiet background music. Breathe slowly.

   - Relax—let yourself just go.
   - Tense your legs and feet. Relax.
   - Tense your seat muscles. Relax.
   - Tense your stomach muscles. Relax.
   - Tense your shoulders. Relax.
   - Tense just your hands. Relax.
   - Tense your face. Relax.
   - Tense all over! Relax—breathe slowly in; slowly out.

TENSE LEGS & FEET

TENSE HANDS

2. **Legends of the Day.**

Homework Ideas:

Monitoring Your Resting Heart Rate (See the Appendix.)

Fit Think Idea:

- ◆ Discuss the major muscles used in jumping and landing.
- ◆ Discuss landing properly and "breaking a fall" to avoid injury.
- ◆ Discuss ways of warming-up and stretching out leg muscles.

Lesson 7:
Individual Rhythm Rope
Jumping, Cooperation Jumping

Skill Builders: rhythm rope jumping, aerobic fitness, overall coordination, cooperation

Expected Student Performance:

- ◆ Demonstrates competency in jumping with a short rope.
- ◆ Performs proficiency in aerobic fitness and flexibility demands.
- ◆ Demonstrates good overall coordination.
- ◆ Displays a willingness to cooperate in team activity.

Facility/Equipment Needed:

- ◆ Outdoor flat surface area, gymnasium, or undercover area
- ◆ Music with a steady 4/4 beat
- ◆ CD player or tape recorder
- ◆ 1 short jump rope per person
- ◆ 1 set of jump bands per team

Teaching Points:

Rope jumping should be taught throughout the school year as a fitness activity or as the main focus of the lesson. Rope jumping contributes significantly to the development of coordination, rhythm, aerobic endurance, timing, and leg and wrist strength and enjoyment!

STORAGE   SIZING

- ◆ Color-code the handles for different lengths.
- ◆ Store jump ropes by hanging them on hooks or a storage rack that can be easily accessed.
- ◆ To check for proper length, have jumpers "size" the rope by holding a handle in each hand and placing a foot in the middle of the rope. The rope should reach at least to the armpits, but no higher than the tops of the shoulders for ease of turning.
- ◆ Hold each handle of the rope with thumbs along the handles.
- ◆ Keep elbows close to side, point forearms and hands slightly forward, and away from body, head up, knees slightly bent.

◆ Turn rope with small circular wrist movements.

◆ Emphasize smooth rhythmical rope turning and jumping.

◆ Use music with a lively beat to enhance rhythm jumping.

◆ Ensure that rope jumpers have enough space to turn the ropes through the air or to the ground easily and safely.

Warming-up Activities/Games:

Aerobic Ropes

Have jumpers double rope and hold both handles in one hand. Swing rope gently overhead and check for good spacing.

1. **Helicopters.** Swing rope counterclockwise overhead for 8 counts in right hand; repeat with left hand.

2. **Propellers.** Swing rope clockwise in front with right hand, then with left hand.

3. **Wheelers.** Swing rope counterclockwise with right hand to right side; swing rope with left hand to left side.

4. **Figure 8's.** Swing rope in front in a figure-8 pattern.

5. **Fancy Footwork:**

 ◆ Helicopters while jogging in place

 ◆ Propellers while jumping feet apart, together

 ◆ Wheelers while doing Pogo Springs (jump one foot forward, then the other)

 ◆ Figure-8's while twist jumping (jump and twist upper body to one side, while lower body twists to the other side)

6. **Levels.** Helicopter swings while moving from stand tall to knee sit, kneeling sit, long sit, lying back, and back to kneel sit, one knee up, one knee down, and stand.

7. **Double Side Swings.** Hold a rope handle in each hand. Keeping hands together, swing rope to one side, then the other side, open hands, and jump over rope. Repeat 4 times. **Single Side Swings:** Swing rope to one side, jump over; swing rope to other side, jump over. Repeat sequence through 4 times.

8. **Rope Stretchers.** Hold a folded rope overhead and taut in both hands. Gently stretch from side-to-side; stretch overhead; stretch holding rope behind you. In back lying position, Periscope position, place folded rope over raised foot and gently pull on rope to stretch leg toward you. Hold for 5 seconds. Stretch other leg. Stretch both legs together.

Rope Stunts

1. **Rope Yank.** Hold folded rope at chest level and try to pull it apart!

2. **Thread the Needle.** Hold folded rope low and in front with both hands apart. Thread the needle by stepping over it, one foot at a time, then reverse. Fold rope again in half and repeat.

3. **Rope Tugs.** With a partner about your size, fold rope in half. Grip rope with right hands, and try to pull partner over a line. Repeat with left hands; two hands.

4. **Skiers.** Stretch rope out along the floor/ground. Stand at one end of the rope, side-on to it. Jump back and forth over rope from one end to the other end. Hop on one foot back and forth over rope. Change hopping foot and repeat.

5. **Bells.** Face rope, and jump forward and backward over the rope.

6. **Bunny Jumps.** Keep hands on floor and jump back and forth as you move along the rope. Explore other ways of moving along rope.

7. **Limbo the Rope.** In your teams, while 2 members hold the rope at waist level taut between them, the other members try to move under the rope with body facing upwards and feet leading. Challenge is to go as low as possible. Take turns.

Jump Rope Tricks

1. **Rocker.** Place one foot ahead of the other. Jump taking weight on front foot, leaning forward slightly. Jump, shifting weight to back foot and leaning on it. Repeat this pattern.

2. **Boxer.** Jump twice with your right foot and then twice with left foot. Continue this pattern.

3. **Jogger.** Using a running step, step over rope with one foot, then the other. Continue to alternate footwork, taking a jump for each step.

1. ROPE YANK

2. "THREAD THE NEEDLE"

3. ROPE TUGS

4. SKIERS

6. BUNNY JUMPS

7. 'LIMBO'

1. ROCKER

2. BOXER

3. JOGGER

4. SKIERS

4. **Skier.** Jump feet together, from side to side as you turn the rope.

5. **Bells.** Jump forward and backward, feet together, over the rope.

6. **Side Straddles.** Jump feet together, jump feet apart. **Forward Straddles:** Jump alternating front and back foot forward.

7. **The "X."** Jump feet apart, jump crossing feet, jump feet apart, jump crossing feet. Repeat.

8. **Twister.** Jump feet together, twisting body a quarter turn from one side to the other with each jump.

9. **Criss-cross.** Jump the rope, crossing your arms in front.

10. **Backwards Jump.** Swing the rope backward as you jump. Try to do some of these tricks while swinging rope backward.

11. **Jumping Routine.** Create a jumping routine by combining 3–4 tricks.

6. SIDE STRADDLE   7. THE "X"

8. TWISTER   9. CRISS-CROSS

10. BACKWARDS JUMP

Cooling-down Activities/Games:

1. **Jump Bands.** (Colorful 1-inch wide elastic bands that attach to the jumpers' legs as shown. Jump band kits are available from sport catalog companies. Each kit includes six pair of bands, a video, a set of activity cards, and an audio cassette.) Each team positions in its Island in groups of 3–4. Two jumpers attach a jump band to each leg and stretch it out until it is taut between them. One or two jumpers in the middle move in and out of the bands as the jumpers jump feet apart, then feet together in rhythm.

JUMP BANDS

'TINIKLING'

2. **Tinikling Sticks.** This traditional Philippine folk dance is used to develop excellent eye–foot coordination, improve both rhythm and auditory response, and provide excellent cooperation experience. The sticks consist of two 8-foot PVC pipes and slide boards as shown. Also available from sports catalog companies are Tinikling Sticks filled with plastic-filled pellets so that the sticks sound like maracas, further enhancing rhythm and sensory perception. (See the Appendix for a description of the different types of footwork patterns.)

3. **Legends of the Day!**

Homework Idea:

Training Heart Rate Range worksheet (See the Appendix.)

Fit Think Idea:

Discuss the effects of having a resting heart rate of 82 (mostly an inactive person), and a resting heart rate of 56 (athletic—fit person) based on what you learned by doing the Maths in a Heart Beat worksheet. (See the Appendix.)

Lesson 8:
Partner Rope Jumping, Aerobic Fitness

Skill Builders: partner rope jumping, coordination, cooperation, communication, balancing, aerobic fitness

Expected Student Performance:

◆ Demonstrates competency and confidence in performing one-point balances without equipment.

◆ Cooperates and coordinates with partner in partner jumping tasks.

◆ Performs proficiently in aerobic fitness and flexibility demands.

◆ Willingly interacts socially and plays fairly.

Facility/Equipment Needed:

◆ Outdoor flat surface area, gymnasium, or undercover area

◆ Orienteering maps—1 per team

◆ Stretch poster

◆ Cones to mark out Islands

◆ 1 short rope per jumper

◆ CD player and "Pink Panther" music

◆ One-point, two-point, three-point balance cards

Focus Words:

● *Muscles of the Week: Triceps (back of upper arm)*

● *Bones of the Week: Carpals (wrist bones); Tarsals (ankle bones)*

Warming-up Activities/Games:

1. **Orienteering Circuit.** Set up an orienteering course and give each team a map that provides directions for completing the course. Each team has a slightly different course to run. At each designated location is a colored clue to collect. After all the clues have been collected, the teams go to the Stretch Tree to do 3 cooling-down stretches, then each team meets in an Island to unravel the clues and create a message.

    Sample: Team One Course: Run to the large tree at the end of the oval and collect a Red Clue; next to the basketball courts and collect a Blue Clue; then to the flag pole and collect a Green Clue, and so on.

2. **Partner Rope Jumping.** Pair up with a partner about the same size and collect a rope to share. Check that the rope is the correct length. Find a Home space.

♦ **Side-by-side.** Each partner holds one handle of the rope. Inside hands are joined or inside arms are placed around partner's waist. In union, rope is turned with free hands.

— Jump in place together.

— Skip forward; skip backward.

— One partner moves out and back into position while continuing to turn rope. Other partner does the same.

— Then both partners move out together and back into position again.

— One partner circles the other partner while both continue to turn the rope.

SIDE-BY-SIDE
(ONE ROPE)

♦ **Face-to-face.** Stand face to face. One partner turns the rope and both jump in union. Take turns being the rope turner.

— Free partner jump turns in place.

— Run out and jump back in place.

— Jump behind the rope turner.

— Free partner tries to take over the rope turning.

FACE-TO-FACE

♦ **Two Ropes, Side-by-side.** Stand beside partner, facing the same direction. Each partner's inside hand turns the other partner's rope, while outer hands turn own rope.

— Practice forward turning both ropes at same time.

— Jump basic rope tricks in this position.

— Turn the ropes backward and jump in union.

— Skip around the play area in this way.

SIDE-BY-SIDES

♦ **Rope Combatives.** Partners facing, each grips a folded rope and tries to pull the other across a line.

♦ **One-point Balances** (Each balancer has a small carry mat.)

— Stork Stand

— Front Scale

— Jump and balance on one foot

— Leap and balance on one foot

— V-Sit

STORK STAND   FRONT SCALE   V-SIT

JUMP-BALANCE   LEAP-BALANCE

Cooling-down Activities/Games:

1. **Pink Panther.** Use the theme music, if possible, from the "Pink Panther" movies. Select three players to be the Pink Panthers, the rest are "Sleepers" who find a Home space in the play area and get into a back lying position, arms folded across chest and eyes closed. When the music starts, the Pink Panthers go on the prowl! Keeping hands behind their backs, they approach a sleeping player, lean over, and try to wake up this Sleeper by saying funny, clever things. If the Sleeper stirs in any way, she/he is caught and must become a Pink Panther helper. The aim of the Panthers is to wake up all Sleepers before the music stops; the challenge for the Sleepers is to last the length of the music to become the best concentrator(s) of the day!

2. **Legends of the Day!**

Homework Ideas:

◆ **"Dem-bones" Worksheet.** (See the Appendix.) Identify the major bones of your body and locate them on your Bones-dude. Learn to spell and say each bone name and become familiar with their location.

◆ **Active Fit Kid Pyramid.** Fill in your activities for each day by writing them on your Active Fit Kid Pyramid sheet.

Lesson 9:
Static and Dynamic Balancing

Skill Builders: aerobic fitness, static balancing, dynamic balancing, cooperation, concentration, overall body coordination

Expected Student Performance:

◆ Demonstrates competence and confidence in performing static balances without equipment; dynamic balances with equipment; overall body coordination.

◆ Cooperates and communicates in group balances and group work.

◆ Performs proficiently in aerobic fitness, strength, and flexibility demands.

Facility/Equipment Needed:

◆ Outdoor grass area, gymnasium, undercover area

◆ Numbered cones, stopwatch, lap recording sheet, small mats, whistle, coffee can stilts, Duck Walkers™, tilt walkers, lo-lo bouncers, one bench per group

◆ Large drawing sheets and 3 different marking pens per group

Warming-up Activities/Games:

Grand Prix Circuit. Mark out a large oval area using numbered cone markers as shown. Ideally have one cone marker for each participant. Each person is given a Formula I number and takes up a position on the outside of the corresponding cone number, facing clockwise. A time limit is set: beginner's time: 3 minutes; intermediate: 4 minutes; advanced: 5 minutes. Encourage drivers to equal or better their time with each circuit run.

Drivers try to cover as many laps of the track as they can in the given time. They can walk and/or jog at any time. When time is up, each driver takes a 10-second Heart Rate Count, then walks one extra lap around the track to cool off; followed by a 30-second Calf Stretch. They then record their laps and date the event.

Variations: Whistle signal indicates a change of direction from clockwise to counterclockwise. Increase the time limit as ability level improves. If indoors, use popular music as a motivator!

Pit Stop. Drivers find a home mat and do the following tasks:

- 30 seconds: Sit-ups
- 30 seconds: Push-ups
- 30 seconds: Hip Flexors
- 30 seconds: Sprinters

- 10-second Pencil Stretch
- 10-second Overhead Finger Stretch
- 10-second Periscope Stretch
- 10-second Butterfly Stretch

Static Balances

Two-/Three-point Balances (spotting as needed):

- ◆ Tripod Balance
- ◆ Frog Balance
- ◆ Head Stand

Partner Balancing Challenges:

Balances in 2's:

Dynamic Balances

Two-Point Balances:

- Coffee Can Stilts
- Duck Walker™
- Tilt Walker
- Lo-lo Bouncer

Bench or Balance Beam Challenges: One bench per group of 4–5 if possible. Each group carefully carries bench to Island. Place mats on either side of bench and at one end. Take turns to do the following tasks:

- Walk heel–toe along bench to opposite end.
- Walk backwards along bench to the start.
- Run carefully forward along bench and jump off, gently landing.
- Jump your way along the bench.
- Walk along the bench with one leg on the bench and the opposite leg moving at ground level.
- Throw and catch a beanbag or deck ring as you walk along the bench.
- Create your own stunt as you move along the bench.

Be careful at all times!

WALK · TOSS · CATCH

Cooling-down Activities/Games:

1. **Create a Being.** Mark out several team Islands as shown. Assign each team to a starting Island. Each group has a large sheet of drawing paper and 3 different colored marking pens. One team member lies down in back-lying position on the large sheet of paper. Another member(s), using the black marking pen, traces an outline of the team member onto the paper. Each member, using the green marking pen, then takes a turn to write a positive attribute inside the body shape. Repeat this task, but now members write negatives (emotional hurts). After each member has had a turn, let members volunteer to contribute other positives or negatives that have not been mentioned. Have each team captain/co-captain place their "Being" on the display board for the whole class to view.

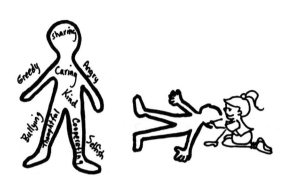

2. **Legend(s) of the Day!**

Homework Idea:

Tune-up Kids Journal. Be a "Positive Being" for the whole day. At the end of your day, record in your journal how you did this.

Lesson 10:
Aerobic Fitness and Strengtheners

Skill Builders: aerobic fitness, partner/group strengtheners, agility, cooperation, concentration, overall body coordination

Expected Student Performance:

◆ Demonstrates competency in moving to music and following a pattern of actions.

◆ Willingly cooperates and integrates with other class and team members.

◆ Performs proficiently in aerobic fitness, agility, and strength demands.

Facility/Equipment Needed:

◆ Gymnasium, undercover area, or large multipurpose room

◆ Cassette or CD player, popular music

◆ 10 large mats, cone markers, tagging objects or flags

◆ Relay equipment such as jump-a-hoops or hoops, short jump ropes, basketballs, lo-lo balls, scooter boards

Focus Words:

● *Muscles of the Week: Rectus Abdominus (stomach muscles)*

● *Bones of the Week: Fibula (outer bone of lower leg); Tibia (inner bone of lower leg)*

Warming-up Activities/Games:

'Scrambled-Eggs' Jog!

Front Crawl

Back-stroke

Breast Stroke

Sidestroke

Butterfly

Treading

1. **Splash Routine.** Choose popular music with a steady 4/4 beat.

   16 counts: "Scramble eggs—jog." Jog in general space, in and out of each other.

   8 counts: Front-crawl while jogging in place.

   8 counts: Back-stroke while jogging in place.

   Pause Break: Hands on hips, feet together, push seat out to one side for two counts; repeat to other side. Say "Splash" (raise hands in air) for two counts, and "Clap!" (two counts).

   16 counts: Jog to the music in "Scrambled Eggs" pattern.

   8 counts: Breaststroke while jogging in place.

   8 counts: Back-stroke while jogging in place.

   Pause Break

   16 counts: Jog to the music in "Scrambled Eggs" pattern.

   8 counts: Sidestroke while jogging in place.

8 counts: Back-stroke while jogging in place.

Pause Break

16 counts: Jog to the music in "Scrambled Eggs" pattern.

8 counts: Butterfly while lightly bouncing in place.

8 counts: Back-stroke while jogging in place.

Pause Break

16 counts: "Tread water" by swaying arms in air, and swaying legs in place. Breathe gently to catch your breath—slow down!

2. **"Sea-ercise"**

- **Crab Walk Greeting:** In Crab Walk position, greet 6 different Crabs by "shaking feet" (touching bottom of foot to another player's.) Alternate feet each time you greet another crab.

LEFT FOOT SHAKE!

- **Shark-a-tugs:** Partners facing, use a right wrist grip and try to pull the other over a line. Repeat using left wrist grip. Challenge another player.

SHARK-A-TUGS

- **Porpoise Roll:** Groups of 3 on a large mat in Pencil Stretch position, spaced 3 feet (1 m) apart. Number off 1, 2, 3 as shown. Number 2 in middle rolls towards outside (either 1 or 3). As soon as number 2 comes close to outside player, that player does a "porpoise flip" over middle player and continues to roll to outside. Continue rotation in this way and watch the fun. Emphasize safety in springing over each other!

PORPOISE ROLL

3. **Sea Shapes**

Partners:

Make the letter "D," "F," "Y," "X," "Z"

Make the following numbers: 2, 5, 17, 36

Make up two-letter words.

In three's:

Make shapes: circle, triangle, square, diamond.

"Y"   "d"   "17"

"TRIANGLE"

Make different letters.

Make triple-digit numbers.

Make simple 3-letter words.

Games:

The Underwater Cave: Give each team a sea creature name such as Sharks, Eels, Stingrays, Octopuses, Lobsters, Crabs, Seahorses. Select one team to be the IT team (for example, the Sharks) and have them stand in the middle of a large circular area (the underwater cave). The other teams "swim" around the outside of this cave (using different locomotor movements that teacher designates), and call out, "What underwater monster are you?" Leader Shark can give several answers, but when the Leader Shark says "YOURS!" the chase is on. Outside sea creatures must then swim to the safe zones (outside boundary lines of a large square play area). Any captured (tagged) creature must join the Shark team. IT team uses soft tagging objects such as beanbags or small sponge balls. Next time you play the game, let another team be IT.

Variation: Sea creatures have a flag tucked in the back of gym shorts which is pulled to make the tag.

Cooling-down Activities/Games:

1. **Shuttle Relays.** Groups of 6 in shuttle formation.

   - Animal Walks: Puppy dog walk, bunny hop, seal walk, crab walk, chicken walk, etc.
   - Zigzag ball dribble through the markers
   - Lo-lo bouncer or pogo-bouncer
   - Jump-a-hoop
   - Short Rope jumping
   - Scooter boards

2. **Legends of the Day!**

Classroom Idea:

The Eye Box. On a whiteboard draw a large rectangle box and write the following locations in the box: Top Right (TR); Top Middle (TM); Top Left (TL); Bottom Right (BR); Bottom Middle (BM); Bottom Left (BL). Make sure students can all see the Eye Box. Call out the different locations. Each student moves only his/her eyes to those places. Observe their actions and comment. Now have them imagine an Eye Box in front of them. Again call out the different locations. Draw an Eye Box in your Tune-up Kid Activity Journal and practice eye focusing.

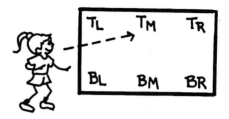

Lesson 11:
Fit-kid Circuit—Fitness Builder Stations

Expected Student Performance:

◆ Demonstrates competency in performing balance/stretching movements.

◆ Demonstrates proficiency in running, dodging/agility movements.

◆ Demonstrates proficiency in strength, power, and speed.

◆ Willingly cooperates and integrates with team members.

Facility/Equipment Needed:

◆ Gymnasium, undercover area, or large multipurpose room

◆ CD or tape recorder and motivating popular 'energy' music with a steady 4/4 count

◆ Fit-Kid Circuit Recording form (see sample)

◆ 1 pencil per participant

◆ Station#1: 2 sets of numbered cones 1–10

◆ Station #2: 1 mat per person

◆ Station #3: 2 benches

◆ Station #4: 1 mat per person

◆ Station #5: 1 jump rope per person

◆ Station #6: 2 Duck Walkers™; 1 lo-lo ball; 1 safe pogo bouncer

◆ Station #7: 10 cone markers

◆ Station #8: low hurdles, several hoops

FIT-KID CIRCUIT:

This sample circuit involves 8 stations of aerobic, agility, speed, power, reaction, and strength tasks. Suggest that class be divided into groups of 4 and each group assigned a station at which to begin. Before circuit is started, a 3-minute warm-up takes place, and, at the end, a 3-minute cool-down occurs. After the designated time is up, participants rotate clockwise to next station. At the completion of each station, participants quickly, but accurately, record their score. Emphasize and encourage good form.

Four progressive achievement levels are suggested:

Level	Time Allotment per Station Task	Circuit Completion Time
Green	30 seconds	10 minutes
Yellow	1 minute	15 minutes
Blue	1½ minutes	20 minutes
Red	2 minutes	25 minutes

At the completion of the Fit-Kid Circuit, everyone must cool down by walking once around the circuit area, focusing on breathing, and then finish up at the Stretch Tree to do a set of upper body and lower body stretches.

Fit-kid Warm-Up: (3 minutes)

- Jog once around the outside of the Fit-Kid Circuit area.

- Return to start to jog in place while circling arms gently forward.

- Alternate arm reaches with leg side lunges.

- Do calf stretches.

Fit-kid Circuit Stations:

Station #1: Loop Agility Run. (Use numbered cones to mark out the loop courses as shown in the diagram. If possible, set up two courses—with one course being easier than the other.) Three runners at each station, in turn, try to complete the course as quickly as possible; each runner gets two chances and runners take turns to time each other. Record times. At completion do a 10-second calf stretch of each leg.

Station #2: Tummy Crunchers. Each participant begins in hook lying position on a mat as shown. Weight rests on heel of feet and hands on upper thighs. A gentle cadence or rhythm is set to the count of 4:

- On "1–2" participants breathe out as they gently curl torso upwards so that wrists slide just past knees.

- On "3–4" participants breathe in as they curl back down, with hands sliding back to upper thighs. Continue in this way for the allotted time. Count number and record. At completion do a 10-second pencil stretch on front; then repeat on back.

- **Station #3: Bench Step-ups.** Position 2 benches as shown with 2 participants facing each bench. Offer two different height levels; participants choose the height level to suit their ability level. Again a cadence is set to 4 counts as follows for one beach step-up set:

Warm-Up

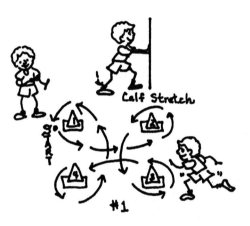

Calf Stretch

#1

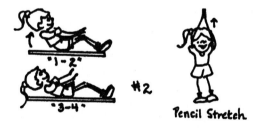

#2

Pencil Stretch

#3

Hamstring Stretch

- On "1" step right foot onto bench.
- On "2" step left foot onto bench.
- On "3" step right foot to floor.
- On "4" step left foot to floor.

Count the number of bench step-up sets and record. At completion do a hamstring stretch for 10 seconds, each leg.

Station #4: Upper-body Push-ups. Each participant positions on all-fours on a mat as shown. Keeping back straight, participant leans forward from the knees, taking weight on hands, and slowly lowers to a "1–2" count to mat, then straightens arms to a "3–4" count. If participants tire, they are allowed to rest, then continue. Continue in this way, counting the number of upper-body push-ups in the given time, and record. At completion do a 10-second upper arm stretch for each arm.

Station #5: Power Rope Jumping. Each participant has a designated spot and jumps rope for the designated time. Count the number of jumps and record. At the completion do a 10-second thigh stretch, each leg.

Station #6: Balancing Station. (This is a body management station and needs just a tick [✓] to show that it was completed.) Include Duck Walkers™ or homemade balance boards, lo-lo balls, or pogo bouncers. Challenge is to try to stay on the equipment without losing balance for the time allotment.

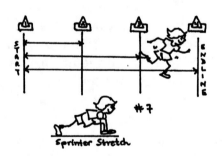

Station #7: Agility Lines. Use cones to mark off a series of lines as shown in the diagram. Each participant must run to each line, in turn, touch it with one hand and return to the Home line, before continuing to the next line. When all lines in the set have been touched, start over again. Count the number of lines touched in the allotted time. Record score. At the completion, do a 10-second sprinter stretch, each leg.

Station #8: Hurdle Jump Circuit. Using hoops placed flat on the ground and low hurdles, have participants complete the course in as many times as possible in the given time allotment. Set up an easier course and a more challenging course. Participants decide which course to do, but only 2 per course. An example course is illustrated. At the completion, do a 10-second Periscope Stretch, each leg.

Legends of the Day.

SECTION 3

OBJECT-CONTROL SKILLS USING INNOVATIVE AND MANIPULATIVE EQUIPMENT

Lesson 12:
Underhand Throwing and Catching Using Beanbags and Deck Rings

Skill Builders: catching technique, underhand throwing technique, hand–eye coordination, eye tracking, partner work

Expected Student Performance:

◆ Demonstrates competency and confidence in executing an underhand throw and catching.

◆ Willingly cooperates and integrates with other class and team members.

◆ Performs proficiently in aerobic fitness, agility, and strength demands.

Facility/Equipment Needed:

◆ Outdoor grass area, gymnasium, or undercover area

◆ Cassette or CD player, popular music

◆ Small playground balls

◆ 1 beanbag and 1 deck ring per person

Teaching Points:

1. **Underhand Throwing**

    ◆ Stand square-on to target, balanced, feet comfortably spread.

    ◆ Hold ball in fingers, not in hand.

    ◆ Extend throwing arm down and back, taking weight on back foot.

    ◆ Step forward with foot opposite to throwing arm to transfer weight from back foot to front foot as throwing arm swings through.

    ◆ Release ball in front of body.

    ◆ Follow-through up and out in line of direction.

    ◆ Keep eyes focused on target.

2. **Catching**

    ◆ Keep balanced, body positioned behind the ball.

    ◆ Reach with hands, fingers spread and slightly curved.

    ◆ Adjust hand distance to the size of the ball.

SQUARE-ON   FINGER GRIP

◆ Bend arms at the elbows to give with the ball as it meets hands.

◆ Keep eyes focused on the ball, tracking it into the hands.

◆ Let fingers wrap around the ball, do not clap it.

◆ For a high ball, position thumbs close together, fingers pointing upwards.

◆ For a low ball, position little fingers together, fingers facing downwards.

Focus Words:

● *Muscles of the Week: Deltoids (shoulder muscles)*

● *Bones of the Week: Humerus (upper arm bone)*

Warming-up Activities/Games:

Whistle Blower. Find a partner and a Home space. One partner has a beanbag or small ball. On signal "Toss" (or music played), move around the play area tossing a ball back and forth to each other. On "whistle" signal (or music stops), partner with the ball is IT and gives chase to the other partner, trying to tag him/her with the beanbag. On signal "Toss," partners stop the chase and continue tossing the ball back and forth to each other as they jog along. On "whistle" signal, the chase is on again. Continue in this way. On signal "Mingle," find a new partner and continue the activity.

Skills Practice & Progressions:

Partner Tasks Using Beanbags

1. Stand facing each other about 3 giant steps away. Toss 1 beanbag back and forth, using your favorite hand to toss and catch. Remember to step forward with the opposite foot to throwing hand. Gradually increase the underhand throwing distance.

   ◆ Toss beanbag high, to right side, to left side; toss it short; toss it long. Use one or both hands to catch it.

   ◆ Repeat tasks using your other hand.

   ◆ Toss beanbag with one hand, catch with the other.

2. **Beanbag Wasps.** Partner with the beanbag is the "Wasp" and gives chase to the other partner, trying to "sting" him/her by underhand tossing the beanbag to try to hit partner below the knee. If Wasp does sting the other Partner, then that partner becomes the Wasp. Emphasize watching where you are going!

3. **Challenge Toss.** Partners toss a beanbag to each other at the same time. Watch the fun! Toss with one hand, catch with the other. Remember to step the opposite foot forward to throwing hand. *Challenge:* Complete the most number of passes in a certain time; or complete 50 passes the quickest!

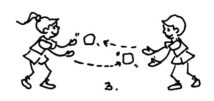

4. **Reaction Toss.** One partner (#1) stands with back to other partner (#2). Partner #2 underhand tosses beanbag to #1 and at the same time calls out his/her name. Partner #1 quickly turns around, hands in ready position to catch the oncoming beanbag. Switch roles and repeat the task. Emphasize good spacing between pairs.

Individual Activities Using Deck Rings:

1. Hold the deck ring vertically on the ground. Spin it and run to touch an object (line). Grab the ring before it stops spinning. Repeat trying to touch two objects (lines), etc.

2. Roll the deck ring along the ground by holding it vertically with palm facing the direction of the roll and pointer finger positioned down on the back of the ring. Let your pointer finger push the ring forward and snap wrist through.

   - Roll ring, run along side of it, and try to hook it through one foot.
   - Hold balance. Do this again. Now repeat task trying to hook ring with other foot.
   - Roll ring along the ground and jump back and forth over it.
   - Roll ring along the ground, chase it to get in front, and field it.

3. Pick up ring with your feet and flick it into your hands.

4. Hold the ring horizontally and flip it into the air so that it air spins. Try to ring it through your hand as it comes down. Try this stunt with the other hand.

5. Hold ring vertically with favorite hand and flick it into the air. Catch it in that hand. Flick and catch with other hand. Flick ring into air with one hand and catch with other.

6. Use your feet, inside of the foot, outside of the foot—like a soccer player—to dribble the deck ring around the play area. Don't let your ring touch any other rings!

7. Invent a deck ring stunt of your own!

Partner Activities Using Deck Rings:

1. Holding the ring vertically, toss it back and forth to each other with favorite hand. Catch with 2 hands. Gradually increase the throwing distance.

2. Repeat task #1, throwing and catching with favorite hand.

3. Repeat task #1, throwing and catching with other hand.

4. Vertically toss a ring at the same time to your partner: toss with right hand, catch left. Toss with left hand, catch right. Remember to step the opposite foot to the throwing hand forward.

5. Reaction Toss—Perform activity as for #4, Beanbags.

6. How many passes can be made in a certain time limit?

Deck Ring Team Tag

Everyone has a deck ring and starts in a Home space. Designate one color, red, as the tagging color. Players with that colored deck ring are the IT team and have a certain time limit (30 seconds) to use their ring to tag as many opposition players as they can before time is up. A tagged player must put the ring on his/her head, and gently jog in place. On "Stop" signal, count the number of tagged players. This becomes the Red Team's score. Then start a new game, designating another tagging color (yellow) and continue in this way. Which team will have the better tagging score? Remind players to watch where they are going at all times and to stay within the defined boundaries of a large play area.

IT

Cooling-down Activity/Game:

1. **Deck Ring Yoga (Beanbag Yoga).** (Suggest using relaxing music for these movements.) Keeping deck ring on your head, lower from stand tall, to knee sit, to kneeling sit, to hook sit. Slowly rise up to standing tall position. Turn slowly around—one way, the other way.

   - Lunge foot in one direction, then in the other direction.

   - Place a beanbag in each palm of hand, and slowly and gently move arms in an in-and-out motion.

'Stretch!'

- Let your eyes track the deck ring or beanbag as you move your arms in a large circle clockwise; counterclockwise.
- Place beanbag on the back of each hand and move arms gently.
- Explore stretching body using your beanbag or deck ring.
- Explore using your deck ring to stretch with a partner, breathing gently in; breathing gently out.

2. **Legends of the Day!**

Homework Ideas:

Monitoring Your Resting Heart Rate Graph. Take your resting heart rate each morning and before you go to sleep for one week. Record on the graph sheets provided. (See the Appendix.)

Fit Think Idea:

Active Fit-kid Pyramid. Fill in your activities for each day on your Active Fit-kid Pyramid sheet.

Lesson 13:
Low-organized and Lead-up Games Using Beanbags and Deck Rings

Skill Builders: Foot–eye and hand–eye coordination, tracking, cooperation

Expected Student Performance:

◆ Demonstrates throwing with accuracy and catching competency.

◆ Is developing court awareness and positional play (guarding an opponent).

◆ Willingly cooperates and integrates with other class and team members.

◆ Performs proficiently in aerobic fitness, agility, and strength demands.

Facility/Equipment Needed:

◆ Outdoor grass area, gymnasium, or undercover area

◆ Cassette or CD player, popular music

◆ 1 long rope, 1 deck ring

◆ 1 deck ring per mini-soccer game, large cone markers for goals

◆ 1 deck ring per mini-hockey game and 2 small nets or cone markers

◆ Several sets of colored bibs

Deck Ring Games:

1. **Jump the Ring.** Tie a long rope to a deck ring. Players in groups of 8 form a large circle with one rope turner in the center. Turner swings the rope clockwise or counterclockwise along the ground, while circle players try to jump over the rope. A player caught on the rope must run once around the play area before rejoining the game. Change the turner after every 5 chances. Play until everyone has had a turn as rope turner.

2. **Deck Ring Soccer.** Mark out several mini-soccer areas and use large cone markers spaced 2 yards apart as the goals. Play 3-a-side soccer plus one goalie each for each team. Each team wears a set of bibs. Surfaces such as gym floors, tiled multipurpose areas, undercover areas, or durable commercial-grade carpet are ideal for the ring to slide along.

3. **Deck Ring Hockey.** Set up mini-hockey courts. Play 4-on-4 games, with one player from each team being a goalie who protects a small net (or cone markers) and stands in a creased area. Use doweling sticks of 3-foot (90-cm) lengths, taped at both ends with floor

tape. Enforce the rules of 3: Allow 3 traveling steps before passing, 3 seconds before the opposition player can try to take possession of the ring from the player he/she is guarding, and 3 passes before trying to score a goal. Strictly enforce that sticks are not to be raised any higher than knee level. Start the game with a face-off in the middle of the play area. Each team wears a set of bibs.

4.   Create a deck ring game with your partner or teammates!

Beanbag/Deck Ring Play:

1.   **Beanbag Horseshoes.** Each partner has a bean-bag critter and a deck ring. The deck ring is positioned 3 yards from a throwing line. Partners, in turn, toss beanbag towards ring. Partner closer to ring scores a point; 2 points for landing in ring. After five throws, tally scores. Then challenge another partner. Gradually increase the throwing accuracy distance.

2.   **Beanbag/Deck Ring Basketball.** Partners stand facing each other 3 yards apart. One partner is the Shooter and holds a beanbag. Other partner is the "Hoop" and holds a deck ring horizontally in front. Shooter underhand tosses beanbag towards the hoop while the other partner tracks the beanbag to land in the hoop. After every 3 throws, switch roles and continue in this way. *Variation:* Shooter tosses beanbag to the left, to the right, higher in the air, slightly short of the partner. Hoop partner must adjust to make the "basket."

3.   **Knock 'Em Over.** One partner rolls the deck ring while the other gives chase and tries to throw beanbag at rolling ring to knock it over. After 3 tries, switch roles.

4.   **Garbage Collector.** Set up teams of 4 in relay formation, with each team standing behind a large hoop and facing a row of 4 deck rings spaced 2 yards apart and a beanbag in each ring. First player must "collect the garbage" by running to the first ring, picking up the beanbag and placing it in the hoop, then running to the second ring to pick up the beanbag and place it in the hoop, until all 4 beanbags are in hoop. The second player "puts out the garbage" by returning each beanbag to a deck ring, one at a time. The third player collects them, and the fourth player puts them back. First team to complete the task wins. Increase the challenge level by spacing rings farther apart and adding another ring.

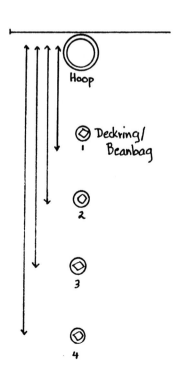

5.   Invent a beanbag/deck ring game with your partner or teammates!

6.   **Legends of the Day!**

Homework Idea:

◆   **Resting Heart Rate Graph.** Continue to take your resting heart rate each morning and before you go to sleep and record on graph.

◆   **Active Fit-kid Pyramid.** Fill in your activities for this day on your Active Fit-kid Pyramid sheet.

Fit Think Idea:

Nutrition Activity Sheet. (See the Appendix.)

Lesson 14:
Tracking and Catching Using Catchballs™

Skill Builders: eye tracking and catching, accuracy in underhand throwing, hand–eye coordination, manual dexterity, arm/wrist strengtheners, and cooperation

Expected Student Performance:

> Demonstrates competence and confidence in tracking the object and catching.
>
> Demonstrates proficiency in using either hand to throw and catch.
>
> Willingly cooperates and integrates with other class and team members.
>
> Performs proficiently in strength demands using a parachute.

Facility/Equipment Needed:

> Outdoor grass area, gymnasium, or undercover area
>
> Cassette or CD player, popular music
>
> 1 Catchball™ for each pair
>
> Parachute, rubber chook, beanbags

Teaching Points:

Parachute Play

Besides the fun element, the parachute is a valuable piece of equipment for developing arm/wrist strength and cooperation. The parachute comes in 4 different sizes: 6′, 12′, 20′, and 24′. The 24′ diameter parachute is ideal for grades 4–6.

> Hold handles of the chute or grip the seam of the chute with either a palms-up or palms-down grip.
>
> Establish definite signals or cue words for inflating chute, starting, and stopping activity.
>
> Emphasize that children carefully listen to signals or cue words to create a cooperative effort.
>
> Use parachute indoors or on grass outdoors; avoid hard surfaces and windy days.

Catchball Play

A Catchball™ is a soft-vinyl, air-inflatable, star-shaped object with 6 tip-numbered handles, coordinated by color: yellow = 0; blue = 1; green = 2; orange = 3, red = 4. Catchballs™ can be used indoors, outdoors, confined areas, playgrounds and fields, tennis courts, swimming pools, parks, and at the beach. If equipment budget is limited, set up a Catchball™ Skill Builder station using only 3 Catchballs™ (one Catchball per pair).

Throwing:

◆ Hold one of the handles (softspokes) with fingers of favorite hand.

◆ Swing Catchball™ downwards and back.

◆ Step forward with opposite foot to throwing hand.

◆ At the same time, swing arm forward, releasing Catchball™ upwards and outwards from fingers.

Receiving:

◆ Place hands in the ready position to make the catch.

◆ Let eyes track Catchball™ into the receiving hand.

◆ Reach out and gently grab a handle.

Focus Words:

◆ Muscles of the Week: Hamstrings (back thigh muscles)

◆ Bones of the Week: Metacarpals (bones of the hand); Metatarsals (bones of foot)

Warming-up Activities/Games:

"Sticky Popcorn" signals children to start popping into a large circle shoulder to shoulder, then corkscrew and cross-leg sit.

Parachute Play:

1. **Shake, Shake, Shake.** Children space evenly around the parachute, gripping handles or the seam with an underhand grip. Spread the parachute out and at waist height and slowly, gently, quietly begin to shake the chute. Gradually increase from ripples, to mini-waves, to rolling waves, to surfs up, to king waves!

2. **Body Waves.** Lower the chute to the ground and on signal "Up!" raise the chute overhead, letting it billow with air, then slowly bring it all the way down. Repeat 2–3 times.

3.

3. **Merry-go-round (Carousel).** Hold onto the parachute with right hand, everyone facing in a clockwise direction. Use cue words such as "walk," "power walk," "jog." On whistle, players quickly switch to travel in the opposite direction. Keep chute stretched out and have players gently raise and lower chute as they travel. Hold chute with both hands, and slide-step clockwise/counterclockwise, gently shaking the chute.

4. **Fireman's Pull.** Face parachute and stretch it out using the overhand grip. Glue feet to the floor and carefully lean back keeping parachute taut. Hold for 10 seconds. **Wild Horses Pull:** Turn back to chute and grip with underhand grip. Try to pull parachute away from its center. Feel the stretch in your arms and legs.

5. **Chook and Critter Tag.** Place a chook (rubber chicken) and a beanbag critter in the middle of the chute. Children use an overhand grip to shake the chute. Challenge is to see which critter will tag the other first! Watch the fun as the children will shake until their arms are ready to drop off!

5.

6. **Mission Impossible.** Number the players 1, 2, 1, 2 around the parachute. Place several beanbag critters in the center of the chute. Have the 1's take one giant step away from the parachute. On signal "Shake," the 2's challenge is to try to shake all the critters off the chute. The 1's challenge is to catch, or fetch, the beanbag critters and toss them back on the chute. Watch the fun! Switch roles and play again.

7. **Wrist Roll.** Keeping parachute stretched at waist level with overhand grip, begin to roll the parachute towards the middle. When the parachute is completely rolled, it is now ready to be put away.

6.

Skill Practice & Progressions:

Individual Activities Using a Catchball™

1. Toss Catchball™ into air and catch it with both hands. Repeat.

2. Toss Catchball™ into air and catch any handle with one hand.

3. Toss Catchball™ into air. Each time try to catch a different colored handle. Add up the points you have earned after 6 tosses.

4. Flip the Catchball™ so that it quickly rotates, then try to catch it with one hand.

5. Toss, clap, catch; toss, 2 claps, catch; continue this pattern.

6. Toss from one hand to the other hand.

7. Toss into air, and jump up and grab it.

8. Invent a Catchball™ stunt of your own!

Partner Activities

1. Stand about 3 giant steps apart. Underhand throw Catchball™ to partner in a slow arch so that partner has enough time and opportunity to make the catch. Partner catches with two hands at first, then just one hand. Throw with the other hand and catch with that hand.

2. For every successful catch each partner makes, take a step backwards. Use 2 hands to make the catch; use only 1 hand to make catch.

3. Toss Catchball™ to partner to the right, to the left, short, high, low. Partner must move to get into position to front the throw and make the catch.

4. Repeat, but partner must now grab a specific colored handle as called out by throwing partner ("Red!").

5. Repeat tasks above using nondominant to throw and catch.

Catchball™ Games

1. **"21."** Each player tosses the Catchball™ into the air and catches it, trying to accumulate points to reach a score of 21 the quickest. If the catch is missed, 1 point is deducted from the total score. *Variation:* Play game setting a different target score.

2. **Colors.** Players toss the Catchball™ back and forth from varying distances. The catcher has to catch the handle of the same color that the thrower used. Each throw has to be made with a different colored handle than the previous two throws.

3. **Catchball™ Horseshoes.** One Catchball™ per player. Place 2 small hoops about 10 yards apart from each other. Partners in turn challenge another pair by tossing the Catchballs™ to get them to land inside the hoop or closest to it. Score 1 point for closest to outside of ring. If Catchball™ lands inside, score the sum of the 3 spokes pointed in the air.

4. **Catchball™ Shuttle Relay.** Mark out two shuttle lines, spaced about 4–5 yards apart from each other. Each team positions in shuttle formation as shown. Catchball™ is tossed across to the opposite shuttle line player to score a point. Player making the toss then runs to join the opposite shuttle line. Which team can make more Catchball™ passes in a certain time limit or complete a certain number of passes quicker?

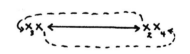

5. Invent a Catchball™ game with your partner or teammates!

Cooling-down Activities/Games:

1. **"Sticky Popcorn" signal.**

2. **Gotcha!** Each player puts right thumb up and left hand over the thumb of the player on the left. Eyes are closed. Players wait intently for the signal "Gotcha" to be called. Then the challenge is to try to grab the left player's thumb while pulling away their right thumb from being grabbed by the player on their right. Watch the fun!

   • Reverse hand positions and repeat game.
   • "Mingle" and play the game again.

3. **Legend(s) of the Day!**

Fit Think Idea:

1. What is cholesterol? What is the difference between bad and good cholesterol? What foods should you eat to help keep your cholesterol levels healthy?

2. **Active Fit-kid Pyramid.** Fill in your activities for this day on your Active Fit-kid Pyramid sheet. Don't forget to do this!

Lesson 15:
Overhand Throwing and Catching Using
Beanbags/Foxtails™/Small Balls

Skill Builders: overhand throwing technique and accuracy, catching technique, hand–eye coordination, accuracy, tracking and follow-through, cooperation

Expected Student Performance:

Demonstrates competence and confidence in overhand throwing and catching technique.

Demonstrates ability to perform a windmill throw and catch.

Willingly cooperates and integrates with other class and team members.

Performs proficiently in aerobic fitness, agility, and strength demands.

Facility/Equipment Needed:

Outdoor grass area, gymnasium, or undercover area

Cassette or CD player, popular music

Cone markers

30–40 beanbags, small balls such as tennis balls

Foxtails™ or Poco Balls™

1 flag per player

Teaching Points:

A Foxtail™ is a baseball-sized leather-covered foam ball sewn into a 3-foot (1-meter) tri-color nylon sock. It can be used indoors in a large, open area with high ceilings, or outdoors just about anywhere. A Poco Ball™ is a small vinyl ball with a colorful multi-ribbon tail that will soar gracefully through the air like a little comet. It can be thrown, caught, bounced, or juggled. Both are ideal pieces of equipment for teaching follow-through and enhancing eye tracking. The colorful tails makes it easy to see and serve as an aid to catching for the physically challenged.

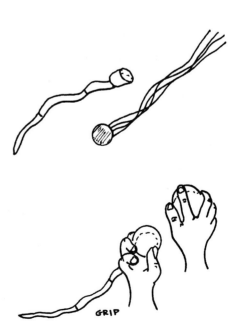

GRIP

This equipment is ideal for providing a visual follow-through trailer to help develop line of direction.

If equipment budget is limited, use 3 Foxtails™ or Poco Balls™ in skill builder stations.

Underhand Throwing Revision with a Foxtail™:

- Stand square-on to your target or receiver, eyes on target.
- Hold the Foxtail™ head/Poco Ball™ in the fingers of your throwing hand.
- Swing throwing hand downwards and back.
- Step forward with opposite foot to throwing hand.
- At the same time, swing throwing hand through, releasing Foxtail™/Poco Ball™ upwards and out-wards in line of direction to target.

Windmill Throwing:

- Stand square-on to target, eyes on target.
- Hold Foxtail™/Poco Ball™ by the end or middle section and swing it full circle towards the receiver.
- Release the tail as throwing hand extends out and up.

Overhand Throwing:

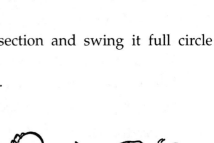

- Stand side-on to target or receiver, eyes on target.
- Grip object ball in your fingers, wrist cocked.
- Pointer finger of nonthrowing hand points at target.
- Throwing hand swings in a downward and back-ward arc. Weight transfers onto back foot.
- Elbow bends as throwing hand moves behind head, wrist cocked.
- Front foot steps forward as weight trans-fers from back foot.
- Hips, then shoulders, rotate forward.
- Lead the arm motion with the elbow.
- Release with a wrist snap.
- Follow-through in the intended direction of flight.

Catching:

- Keep eyes tracking object ball all the way to your hands.
- Hands are cupped and in ready position.
- Reach and absorb impact of throw by bending elbows.
- Catch may be made with one hand grabbing part of the tail.

Warming-up Activities/Games:

1. **Mission Possible.** Mark off a large rectangular play area with an end zone for each half as shown. Scatter at least 20 beanbags in each end zone. These are precious "gems."

(Use deck rings if not enough beanbags.) Game starts with two teams each standing in their half of the play area. Each team's mission is to try to collect as many gems as possible in their respective end zone in a certain time limit. On signal "Gems!" players cross into the other team's territory to pick up gems and carry them back to their end zone. *Strict rules must be enforced:*

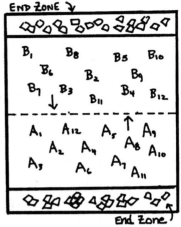

- A player must carry only one gem at a time.
- Gems must be placed gently into end zone, not thrown!
- Everyone must contribute to the task!
- A player breaking any rule will be penalized by jogging on the spot for 10 seconds (and deducting a point from total score). [Use music if indoors to spur teams on. Adjust time to suit the ability level of the group. Encourage fair play at all times.]

2. **Partner Combatives.** On signal "Mingle," find a new partner.

- **Partner Tail Snatch:** Must stay in Home space; try to snatch other partner's tail.

'TAIL SNATCH'

- **Partner Wrist Pulls:** Right wrist hold; left wrist hold.

- **Partner Hoppo Bumpo:** Grab right leg with left hand and hold left elbow with right hand behind your back. Gently push against each other's shoulders to get the other partner off balance.

'HOPPO BUMPO'

Skill Practice & Progressions:

1. **Beanbag Overhand Throwing.** Revise overhand throwing and catching using beanbags. Partners stand 6 yards apart from each other. Gradually increase the throwing distance. Throw to the right, to the left, high, low. Track the beanbag into your hands to make the catch. *Variation:* Repeat tasks using a small ball such as a tennis ball.

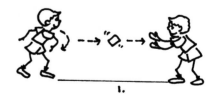

1.

2. **Foxtail™ Underhand Throwing**

- Partners, spaced 3 giant steps apart, underhand throw and catch Foxtail™/Poco Ball™ by the head. After every two successful throws and catches, take a step away from each other. Focus on your follow-through, which should send the Foxtail™ "up and out" in line of direction.

2.

- Repeat activity #1, but catch the Foxtail™ by a tail section. Earn points as follows: 1 point for section nearest head; 2 points for middle section; and 3 points for end section of tail.

- Explore underhand tossing Foxtail™/Poco Ball™: high, low, to the right, to the left of receiver.

3. **Foxtail™ Windmill Throwing**

- Send the Foxtail™/Poco Ball™ back and forth to each other using the windmill underhand throw. Try to catch it with either hand by the tail. Watch your follow-through—will indicate to you at what point you let the Foxtail™ go.

- Take turns slinging the Foxtail™/Poco Ball™, using the windmill throw, as high as you can into the air then try to catch it by the tail alone.

4. **Foxtail™ Overhand Throwing**

- Overhand throw the Foxtail™/Poco Ball™ back and forth to each other. Practice catching using both hands at first, then just one hand grabbing the tail. Observe your follow-through and adjust as needed.

- **Foxtail™/Poco Ball™ Scoring Challenge:** Set up a throwing distance using cone markers. Adjust distance according to the ability level of the children. Throw Foxtail™/Poco Ball™ back and forth to a partner. Catch and score points: 3 points for the end section of tail; 2 points for middle section; 1 point for section nearest head.

- **Foxtail™ Distance Throwing Challenge:** Who can throw the Foxtail™ the highest? the farthest?

- Overhand throw the Foxtail™/Poco Ball™ at, through, or into targets. Take turns throwing with your partner and vary the throwing distance.

DISTANCE THROWING

Cooling-down Activities/Games:

- **Partner Stretchers:** See illustrations for shoulder stretcher and hamstring stretcher.

- **Legends of the Day!**

Fit Think Idea:

Active Fit-kid Pyramid: Fill in your activities for this day on your Active Fit-kid Pyramid. (See the Appendix.)

SHOULDER STRETCHER

HAMSTRING STRETCHER

Lesson 16:
Low-organized Games Using Overhand Throwing

Skill Builders: overhand throwing at moving targets, catching skills, dodging, team work, spatial awareness, and fair play

Expected Student Performance:

◆ Demonstrates competency in overhand throwing at moving targets and catching.

◆ Willingly cooperates and integrates with team members and demonstrates fair play.

◆ Performs proficiently in dodging, agility, and alertness demands.

Facility/Equipment Needed:

◆ Outdoor grass area, gymnasium, or undercover area

◆ Cassette or CD player, popular music

◆ Cone markers

◆ 30–40 beanbags, deck rings, small balls such as foam balls, dodge balls

◆ Foxtails™ or Poco Balls™

Activities/Games:

1. **Everyone for Yourself.** Mark out a large rectangular play area. Everyone scatters inside the play area. To start the game, toss out 1 foam dodge ball, then another, and then another, up to 5 balls! The ball is up for grabs by anyone and everyone. Once a player has a ball, he/she attempts to throw it at another player and hit that player below the knees, but is only allowed pivot steps (cannot travel with the ball). If the targeted player is hit, he/she must stand outside the boundary area, on a sideline closest to where the player was hit. The hit player must remember which player made the hit. If this player gets hit out, then all the players that were sidelined by this player can now return to the game. Sideline players can field balls and try to hit an inside player as well. This provides another option to return to the inside court. If a player catches a thrown ball, then the thrower is automatically sidelined. *Variations:*

   ● Ball can hit the floor first, then the player, but only the nondominant hand can be used to throw.

   ● Sideline player is allowed only to hit the player who initially hit him/her out.

   ● Player with the ball is allowed up to 3 traveling steps.

2. **Beanbag Conspiracy.** This low-organized game starts out with one player being IT who holds a beanbag or small foam dodge ball. IT is allowed to run with the ball until IT hits a free player below the knees. A hit player must then put on a bib and join the IT team. From now on IT players are NOT allowed to run with the ball, but may only pass to each other until they "corner" a free player and hit that player below the knees with the ball. Gradually the IT team begins to build in numbers while the free players become fewer and fewer. Encourage IT players to pass to everyone in the IT team, so that not just a few players are controlling the game. Challenge is to capture all free players within a certain time limit. *Variations:*

   - Allow up to 3 traveling steps before making the pass or trying to hit a free player.
   - Allow bounce passes as well as air passes.
   - Enforce 3 passes being made before a "hit" can be made.
   - Allow no throwing to capture a player. Must tag a free player below the waist with the ball.

3. **Star Wars.** Mark out a large rectangular area "black hole" with safety end zones as shown in diagram. Give each team a "Star Wars™" name such as Hans Solo, Luke Skywalker, Chewbacca, C3P0, R2D2, Princess Leia, or Ewoks. Select one team to be the IT team (Darth Vader and his Storm Troopers) who each stand in a hoop positioned through the middle of the rectangular area as shown. Each IT player holds a small foam ball or dodge ball. Darth Vader gives the signal for at least 2 groups to fly their spaceships across the black hole. The IT team uses an overhand throw below the knees to try to hit the flying spaceships. If Darth Vader signals "Jedi," then all groups must go. A hit spaceship must sink to the ground and stay in a knee-sit position. If a grounded spaceship touches a passing spaceship, the two change roles. *Variations:* Let each group take a turn at being the IT team.

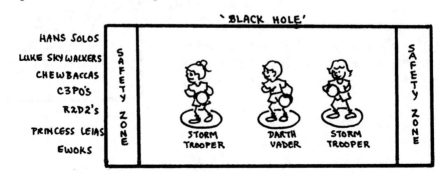

4. **Space Attack.** Divide the class into 2 teams: the Spaceship Team and the Asteroid Team. The Asteroid players space themselves arm's length apart on either of two side-

lines that are marked off 10 yards (meters) apart as shown in the diagram. The Spaceship players equally divide themselves and position half behind each end line as shown. Asteroid players are given 3 foam balls for each sideline. These balls can be rolled or thrown underhand or overhand at the spaceships as they fly through the field from one end to the other. A Spaceship can only be hit below the knees. A hit Spaceship must become an Asteroid clone and help field balls for the Asteroid players to throw. After two fly-throughs, the Asteroid and Spaceship teams change roles and a new game begins. *Variations:*

- Allow only a certain type of throw to be made.
- Spaceships must wait for the signal "Fly Through" to move from one end line to the other.

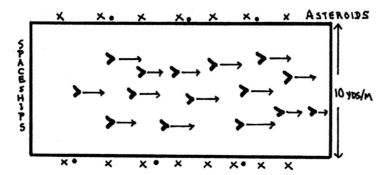

5. **Surf Rescue.** Divide the class into two teams who position in each half of a large rectangular play area ("the ocean"). Mark off an end zone ("the beach") for each half. Give each team 2 soft dodge balls. Team players throw dodge balls at each other from their own court only, trying to hit a player below the knees. Each team selects one player to be the "Rescuer" whose job is to rescue hit players by dragging them into the end zone (beach) where they are resuscitated and can then return to the game. If a Rescuer gets hit, then the opposing team can invade the other team's court only on a certain designated line. Game finishes when a certain time limit is up or one team has no more "mobile" players. *Variations:*

- A player is "resuscitated" by doing a certain task: 5 push-ups; touching one sideline to the opposite sideline of the beach, and so on.
- Allow the invading team to position on the outside of any of the other 3 sidelines of the opposition's court.

Cooling-down Activity:

Legends of the Day!

Lesson 17:
More Low-organized and Lead-up Games Using Catchballs™ and Foxtails™

Skill Builders: underhand/overhand accuracy throwing and catching with dominant and nondominant hand, hand–eye coordination, tracking, 3-on-3 team play, cooperation, math concepts

Expected Student Performance:

◆ Demonstrates throwing with accuracy and catching competency.

◆ Is developing court awareness and positional play (guarding an opponent) and demonstrates fair play.

◆ Willingly cooperates and integrates with other class and team members.

◆ Performs proficiently in aerobic fitness, agility, and strength demands.

Facility/Equipment Needed:

◆ Outdoor grass area, gymnasium, or undercover area

◆ Cassette or CD player, popular music

◆ Catchballs™

◆ Foxtails™

◆ 2 Skore Nets™, floor tape, or dome markers

Catchball™ Games:

1. **Catchball™ Volleyball.** Play 6–8 a side. Throw and catch over a high net. **Catchball™ Badminton:** Play 4 a side. Throw and catch over a low net. *Variation:* Throw and catch with nondominant hand.

2. **Catchball™ Score.** Partners stand facing 3 yards apart. Partners throw a Catchball™ to each other. Points are added or subtracted according to the softspoke number caught: yellow—0 points; blue—1 point; orange—2 points; green—3 points; and red—4 points. A Catchball™ thrown poorly (too short, too far to the right or left, or too high over the player's head) will result in the thrower losing 1 point from his/her score. *Variation:* A player can double his/her points earned by calling out the color he/she will catch before the thrower makes the throw. However, if the player does not catch the Catchball™ by that color, the player will lose *double* those points!

3. **Shuttle Catchball™.** Teams of 6 set up in shuttle formation and pass the Catchball™ from one side to the other, trying to accumulate the highest score in a given time limit (3 minutes). Score one point for each successful catch; subtract 1 point for each unsuccessful catch.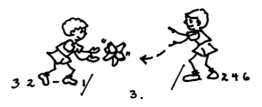
Variation: Each player must catch a handle and call out the number on the end of the handle. This score is added (subtracted for dropped ball) to the previous score. First team to reach 32 wins.

4. **Catchball™ Math.** For each game have 6 players numbered off from 1 to 6. Start with number 1 as the thrower. He/she throws the Catchball™ out into the field of players calling out a number; for example, "6." That player tries to make the catch. If unsuccessful, he/she is given a letter "I." A second time unsuccessful earns him/her the letter "T" and he/she is now IT. Now IT must go to the math table (30 index cards, with each card containing an addition, subtraction, multiplication, or  division question), and answer 4 math questions correctly before getting back into the game. After 4 throws, player #2 becomes the new thrower. Continue in this way.

5. **Catchball™ Water Polo.** Play keep-away in teams of 4–6 and watch the fun!

Foxtail™/Poco Ball™ Games:

1. **Foxtail™/Poco Ball™ Volleyball.** Play 6 a side as for volleyball. Throw Foxtail™/Poco Ball™ over a high net. Score a point if object hits opposition's floor. Emphasize that players take equal turns throwing and catching object.

2. **Foxtail™/Poco Ball™ Badminton.** Play 4 a side and throw Foxtail™/Poco Ball™ back and forth over a low net. Score a point if Foxtail™/Poco Ball™ lands in the opposition's court without being caught. Emphasize fair play and that players take equal turns to throw. Vary the size of the court, according to the ability level of the players. *Variation:* Catch Foxtail™ only with nondominant hand.

3. **Three Passes Foxtail™/Poco Ball™.** Ideally play rules of 3: 3-on-3 players, one group with bibs; allow 3 traveling steps; 3-second count to be in possession of the Foxtail™ before passing; 3 uninterrupted passes must be made by a team to score a point. Vary the size of the court according to the ability level of the players.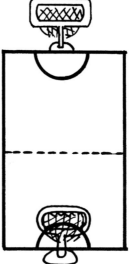

4. **Foxtail™ Skore™-Away.** Set up two Skore Nets™ on the middle of the end lines of a large rectangular play area. Mark out a goal crease

that no player can step into, except for the goalie. Vary the depth of this crease area according to the ability level of the players; that is, small area for younger players. Play rule of 3's: 3–4 a side with one team wearing bibs; allow 3 traveling steps; 3 passes must be made before attempting to score; have ball in possession for a 3-second count, then must pass or try to score a goal by successfully throwing the Foxtail™ into the Skore Net™.

5. Invent a Foxtail™/Poco Ball™ game with your partner or teammates!

Cooling-down Activity:

Legends of the Day!

Lesson 18:
Rolling and Fielding a Small Ball

Skill Builders: rolling with dominant and nondominant hand, fielding skills, hand–eye coordination, tracking, agility, cooperation, fair play

Expected Student Performance:

Demonstrates competence in rolling and fielding a low moving ball.

Willingly cooperates and integrates with other class and team members.

Performs proficiently in aerobic fitness and agility demands.

Facility/Equipment Needed:

Outdoor grass area, gymnasium, or undercover area

Small playground balls, tennis balls

1 pin per group of 4–5

Targets such as boxes, bins, cone markers

Teaching Points:

1. **Receiving the Rolling Object**

    ◆ Keep eyes focused on the object, tracking it along the ground.

    ◆ Position body directly in line with the oncoming object.

    ◆ Spread fingers and face downwards, hands reaching for object.

    ◆ Bend knees to get down to the ball, with preferred leg in front.

    ◆ Receive object in both hands, giving with the impact.

2. **Rolling an Object Along the Ground**

    ◆ Hold ball in both hands, feet shoulder-width apart.

    ◆ Bring arms back on your favorite side.

    ◆ Step forward with opposite foot and swing rolling hand forward and through.

    ◆ Release the ball downward with favorite hand.

    ◆ Follow-through in line of direction.

Focus Words:

● *Muscles of the Week: Gluteus Maximus (buttocks)*

● *Bones of the Week: Cranium (bones of the head); Mandible (jaw bone—strongest bone!)*

Warming-up Activities/Games

Indi-500 Run. Mark out a large oval and position 10 cone markers every 10 meters (30 feet) apart as shown. Perimeter will be about 100 meters in length. To start, have 2–3 runners stand on the outside of each cone marker. On "Go" signal, runners begin the circuit of sprinting to a cone marker, then power-walking to the next; sprinting to the next cone marker, power-walking to the next, and so on. Each runner progresses at his/her own rate, counting one each time the starting cone marker is passed. The number of laps completed is recorded at the end. *Variations:*

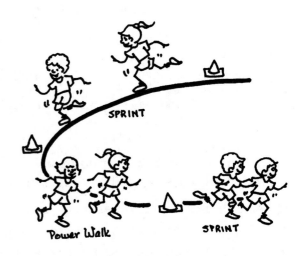

- Set a certain time limit (3 minutes) and gradually increase the time.
- Set a certain task: "Today you must try to do five laps." Next time increase the number of laps.
- Count the laps in 5 minutes.

Skill Practice & Progressions:

1. **Partner Rolling.** Roll a ball back and forth to each other. Start 5 giant steps apart and gradually increase the distance. Roll the ball to one side or to the other side. Partner must react and position to get in front of the oncoming ball. Use the dominant hand; use the nondominant hand; alternate rolling hand; field in two hands; field in one hand.

2. **Roller Ball Derby.** Partners position 5 giant steps away from each other on opposite sides of a line as shown. At the same time, each partner rolls a ball straight ahead toward the other partner's line. Each partner quickly moves to get in front of the oncoming ball and receive it. Ball is then rolled straight back. As ability level improves, increase the distance between the two lines and watch the fun!

3. **Target Rolling.** Set up different targets, such as an open box or bin on its side, or 2 large cone markers. Gradually increase the rolling distance to add more challenge!

4. **Guard the Pin.** In groups of 5–6, one player guards a large pin or cone marker while the other players stand in a circle around the pin, rolling the ball at the target and trying to knock over the protected pin. Everyone must take turns at being in the middle and take turns at rolling the ball at the pin. Players may quickly pass the ball to each other to try to catch the middle player off-guard.

5. Create a rolling stunt of your own!

Cooling-down Activities/Games:

1. **Circle Pattern Roll.** Each team is assigned an area where members knee-sit in a circle, facing the center. Leader begins the rolling pattern and rolls the ball across the circle to a member who is not on either side of him/her. Each member does the same, in turn. When the ball returns to the leader, the pattern begins again. *Variations:*

   - Which team can complete the most number of patterns in a certain time limit?

   - Which team can complete 10 patterns the quickest?

   - Introduce a second ball to increase the challenge.

   - Use the nondominant hand to roll the ball.

2. **Legend(s) of the Day!**

Fit Think Idea:

Active Fit-kid Pyramid. Fill in your activities for this day on your Active Fit-kid Pyramid sheet. Discuss the benefits of "Interval Running" in the Indi-500 Run (creates a "conditioning" effect).

Lesson 19:
Frisbee™ Throwing Using Deck Rings/Frisbees™/Woosh Rings™

Skill Builders: Frisbee™ throws, catching technique, hand–eye coordination, eye tracking, fitness, cooperation and communication skills

Expected Student Performance:

◆ Demonstrates competency in Frisbee™ throwing techniques and catching.

◆ Willingly cooperates and integrates with other class and team members.

◆ Performs proficiently in fitness demands and communicating.

Facility/Equipment Needed:

◆ Large playground area or grass oval

◆ Cassette or CD player, popular music

◆ 1 deck ring per pair; 1 Frisbee™ per pair

◆ Several Woosh Rings™

Teaching Points:

Frisbee™ Throwing

◆ Grip the Frisbee™ (deck ring) by placing the thumb on top of it and the index finger just underneath the rim; middle finger is extended toward the center; fourth and fifth fingers are curled back against the rim. Relax the grip as if you were going to use it like a fan.

Thumbs-Up
- Below Chest

◆ Stand side-on to target or partner.

◆ Step toward target with the leading leg.

◆ For a backhand throw, bring Frisbee™ across to the other side of the body and fling it forward.

◆ Wrist and forearm are coiled like a spring. Uncoil and extend arm towards the target, releasing Frisbee™ with a snap of the wrist.

Thumbs-Down
- Above Chest

◆ For a sidearm throw, swing arm back, and then rotate it outward so that the forearm is almost parallel with the ground and flick it forward on the same side of body.

◆ For an underhand throw, take Frisbee™ back in an underhand motion, then on the upward swing, about waist level, release the Frisbee™ with a snap of the wrist.

Frisbee™ Catching:

◆ Keep your eyes on the Frisbee™, following it to your hands.

◆ Using both hands catch the Frisbee™ on its outside rim, with thumbs down and fingers up and relaxed.

◆ Reach for the Frisbee™ and close the thumbs and fingers over it.

◆ Catch the Frisbee™ with one hand with thumb down if Frisbee™ is above the chest; and thumb up if Frisbee™ falls below the chest.

Focus Words:

● *Muscles of the Week: Trapezius (shoulder-blade muscles)*

● *Bones of the Week: Scapula (shoulder blade)*

Other Throws:

1. **Overhand.** Hold Frisbee™ with thumb underneath rim and fingers on top. Cock wrist backwards. Bring extended arm around at shoulder level and snap wrist forward at point of release.

2. **Sidearm.** Stand side-on to target. Hold Frisbee™ with thumb on top, and index and middle fingers on the underside. Extend upper throwing arm out diagonally and down from your shoulder and the forearm straight up from the elbow. Cock wrist backwards, and swing arm forward with forearm parallel to the ground. Snap wrist forward at point of release and follow through with arm across the body.

Overhand

Sidearm

3. **The Curve.** As for the backswing throw, but tilt Frisbee™ in the direction of the desired curve.

4. **Skip.** Use the same motion as for a curve left throw. Frisbee™ should hit the ground on the forward edge (not flat) about midway to the target, skip along the ground, and fly up to the catcher.

Warming-up Activities/Games:

1. **Exercise Hunt (Out-of-doors).** (See Lesson 6.) Teams are each given an Exercise Hunt (out-of-doors). See the Appendix for Exercise Hunts. At the completion of the activity, teams go to the Stretch Tree to stretch. Join the Exercise Hunt by doing an activity with each group. Observe and offer comments about quality of movement, teamness and cooperation, fair play, and exemplary behavior.

2. **Partner Wheelbarrows.** Partners should be about same size. Excellent activity for upper body strength.

   - **Stubborn Donkey:** Driver gently tries to move forward, but Donkey resists.
   - **Stubborn Driver:** Donkey tries to move forward, but Driver resists.

Skill Practice & Progressions:

1. **Deck Ring Frisbee™ Throw.** Partners use a deck ring to throw back and forth to each other using a Frisbee™ backswing throw. Gradually increase the throwing distance. *Challenge:* Each partner throws a deck ring at the same time.

2. **Deck Ring Badminton.** Play 3 a side, one deck ring per side. Toss back and forth over a low net. Score 1 point for each deck ring that lands in the opposition's side.

3. **Frisbee™ Throw.** Repeat task #1 using a Frisbee™. Explore using other throws with the Frisbee™: high, low, curves, sidearm, overarm, skips.

4. Explore catching the Frisbee™: high, low, finger catch, between the legs, behind the back, tipping it. Create a catching stunt of your own!

5. Explore throwing and catching with a Woosh Ring™. Try bouncing the Woosh Ring™ to your partner with an overarm throw.

6. **Longest Throw.** In partners, one at the throwing line with deck ring or Frisbee™; other partner with a beanbag marker. Each partner take two throws to see if they can equal or better the first throw.

7. **Accuracy Throw.** Throw Frisbee™ or deck ring into a suspended hoop, hoop in a hoop stand, or Skore Net™. Vary the throwing distances.

8. **Boomerang Throw.** Take turns throwing a curve throw into the wind. Track the Frisbee™, trying to catch it before it touches the ground.

9. **Frisbee™ Volleyball™.** Play each game on a rectangular court with a neutral zone of 10–15 meters marked out in the center. (Adjust this according to the ability level of the players.) Each team of 6 players positions in one half of the play area. Each team has two Frisbees™ or Woosh Rings™. The Frisbee™ is thrown across the neutral zone ("net") to land in the opposition's court to score a point.

Cooling-down Activities/Games:

1.   **Blinders.** Each team puts on blindfolds and, on signal, team members cooperate and communicate to arrange the team in "tallest to smallest" order. Do the challenge again. But this time, "smallest to tallest."

2.   **Legends of the Day!**

Fit Think Idea:

Active Fit-kid Pyramid. Fill in your activities for this day on your Active Fit-kid Pyramid sheet.

Lesson 20:
Frisbee™ Throwing Games

Skill Builders: Frisbee™ throwing and catching, tracking and hand–eye coordination, team work, positional play, court awareness, guarding, fair play

Expected Student Performance:

◆ Demonstrates competency in Frisbee™ throwing and catching in game situations.

◆ Willingly cooperates and integrates with other class and team members.

◆ Performs proficiently in a game situation, demonstrating good game sense, court awareness, and positional play.

Facility/Equipment Needed:

◆ Large playground and field area

◆ 6 large cone markers, variety of "holes"—garbage bin, hoop in stand, trees, posts, Skore Net™

◆ 1 score card per player, 1 Frisbee™ per player

◆ 1 set of flags per each team

◆ Several cone markers

Activities/Games:

1. **Frisbee™ Golf.** Set up a golf course of about 6 fairways. Players pair off, each with a Frisbee™ and a score card. Assign each pair a starting hole, and have pairs rotate in order until all the holes have been played. Use garbage bins, trees, poles, Skore Nets™, hoops in hoop stands as the "holes." Use large numbered markers at the tee-off marker. Make the course challenging by having some holes "out of sight" (use the corner of the school building) or use obstacles on the pathway to the hole (such as playground equipment). Establish a "par" for each hole (par 3's, par 4's, par 5's) and explain that "to par a hole" means that you have taken exactly that number of throws as the par indicated; a "birdie" means one under par; an "eagle," two under par; a "bogie," one over par; "double bogie," two over par. Emphasize correct technique rather than forcing a throw for extra distance.

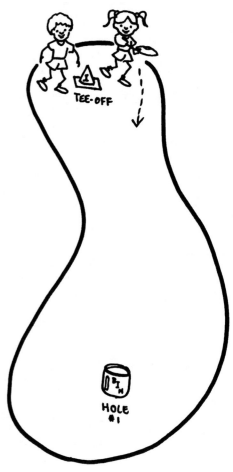

Rules of Etiquette:

- Toss a coin to see which partner will tee-off first. Thereafter, determine the order of throwing by the player whose Frisbee™ is farthest from the hole.
- Take turns teeing-off at each hole until completed.
- NO cheating—play fairly.
- To take the next throw, place your front foot on the spot where the Frisbee™ landed and throw from there.
- Record your score for each hole. At the end determine your total score and date it.
- Have FUN!!!

2. **Frisbee™ Football.** Mark out a rectangular play area using cone markers on a grassy field. Set up each mini-game of 2 teams of 3-on-3 players: Team A vs. Team B; Team C vs. Team D; and so forth. For each game, each team wears flags tucked into back of shorts. A toss of the coin will determine which team will get possession of the Frisbee™ to start the game. Each player then shakes hands with an opposition player about his/her size. These two players will guard each other. Each team then takes up court position in its own half. Object of the game is to pass the Frisbee™ among your teammates to try to score a goal by finally passing the Frisbee™ to one of your own players across the opponent's goal line. Allow 3 traveling steps when in possession of the Frisbee™. If the player with the Frisbee™ has his/her flag pulled, he/she must give the Frisbee™ to that opposing player. But only the player guarding that opposing player may pull the flag! Encourage players to spread out to avoid cluttering!

Variations:

- Play 4-on-4; 5-on-5 mini-games.
- Play 3 (4, or 5) passes to score a point. No goalie area involved.
- Place a goal just behind the opposition's goal line.
- Play 2 active court teams, and 2 teams on the sidelines. Throw to a teammate on the sideline as well as to court teammates.
- Mark off an end zone area at each end of the rectangular area. Score a goal by throwing the Frisbee™ to a team player in the opposition's end zone.

Lesson 21:
Sending and Receiving Skill Builder Stations

Skill Builders: underhand and overhand accuracy throwing, Frisbee™ throwing, catching, hand–eye coordination, tracking, rhythm rope jumping, cooperation

Expected Student Performance:

◆ Demonstrates competence and confidence in underhand and overhand accuracy throwing.

◆ Demonstrates competence in Frisbee™ throwing and rope jumping coordination and rhythm.

◆ Performs proficiently in more challenging tracking and hand–eye coordinated activities.

◆ Willingly cooperates and integrates with other team members.

Facility/Equipment Needed:

◆ Gymnasium or undercover area

◆ Cassette or CD player; station signs

◆ Station #1—2 benches, 10 skittles (pins or cones), cone markers, 4 small balls

◆ Station #2—2–3 Foxtails™, 1 volleyball net or long rope, 2 poles

◆ Station #3—2 long ropes, 1 pogo bouncer, 2 short ropes, 2 large playground balls, 2 large basketballs

◆ Station #4—wall targets, hoops and hoop stands, bins or boxes, 6 dome markers, cone markers

◆ Station #5—3 Z-Balls™ or 3 Saturn™ balls

◆ Station #6—6 Loop-n-Catch™ equipment, 3 Squellets™ or beanbag balls

◆ Station # 7—3 Woosh Rings™ or Frisbees™

◆ Station #8—3 boomerangs

Skill Builder Station Ideas:

Station #1: Overhead Target Toss. Set up 2 stations of skittle (pins) or cones on a bench as shown. Each thrower takes 2 overhand throws to try to knock over as many skittles as possible with a small ball. Challenge each other. Vary the throwing distance.

Station #2: Foxtail™ Volleyball. Use a rope between 2 poles or lower the volleyball net to just above head height. Half of group positions on each side of the net. Each side has a Foxtail™. Object of the game is to get the Foxtail™ to land in the opposition's court to score a point. Encourage players to throw into "holes"—empty spaces in the opposition's court. Insist that everyone get an equal turn at throwing the Foxtail™. *Challenge:* Introduce another Foxtail™!

Station #3: Long Rope Jumping. Children work in groups of 3–4 (2 turners and 1 jumper), taking turns to jump in a long rope. *Challenges:*

◆ Bounce on a pogo bouncer in the middle.

◆ Jump a short rope in the middle.

◆ Bounce a ball in the middle.

◆ Catch a ball thrown to you.

◆ Invent a stunt of your own!

Station #4: Underhand Target Tossing. Set up a variety of targets. Use one hand, then the other hand, to toss a beanbag into the targets: wall targets, vertical or floor hoop targets, bins, or boxes. Each tosser uses a marker to mark his/her throwing spot. Gradually increase throwing distance.

Station #5: Z-ball™/Saturn™ Ball. Partners overhand throw a Z-Ball™ or Saturn Ball™ to each other, making the ball bounce off the floor first or off a wall.

Station #6: Loop-n-catch™/Squellet™ Ball or Beanbag Ball. Partners use a loop to toss and catch a small object such as a Squellet™ Ball or beanbag ball. Start about 2 giant steps apart and gradually increase the distance.

Station #7: Woosh Ring™ Throw. Partners throw a Woosh Ring™ (or Frisbee™) back and forth to each other. Try to catch the ring in different ways. Explore "bouncing" the ring on the ground using an overhand throw.

Station #8: Boomerang Throwing. (See the Appendix.) Partners practice throwing a boomerang. Check for good spacing from other station activities.

Lesson 22:
Scoop Play

Skill Builders: underhand/overhand throwing and catching technique, hand–eye coordination, eye tracking, effort awareness, right–left dexterity, cooperation, rhythmic aerobic stamina

Expected Student Performance:

◆   Demonstrates competency in using a scoop to send and receive an object.

◆   Listens to instructions and moves rhythmically to music.

◆   Willingly cooperates and interacts with team members in relays.

◆   Performs proficiently in applying skill to a game situation.

Facility/Equipment Needed:

◆   Large grass area, gymnasium, or undercover area

◆   Cassette or CD player, popular music

◆   1 scoop per player

◆   1 Cosom Fun Ball® per pair

Teaching Points:

Scoops are plastic molded wide-mouthed manipulative equipment that can be purchased in sets of 6 rainbow colors. They are used with Cosom Fun Balls®, which are plastic molded and holed balls that also come in rainbow sets of 6 and in softball or baseball size.

Sending—Underhand Flick

◆   Stand square-on to the target or receiver.

◆   Hold scoop with tip tilted slightly upward so that ball does not roll out.

◆   Bring scoop back behind the waist, then flick it forward with arm and wrist, keeping throwing arm straight.

◆   At the same time, step forward on opposite foot to throwing hand.

◆   Throw is similar to a softball pitch.

◆   Scoop should not rise higher than the waist as the ball is delivered.

◆   Flick the ball up and outward in line of direction.

Sending—Overhand Flick

◆   Stand square-on to the target or receiver.

◆   Place ball in scoop and hold scoop vertically about head high and slightly forward from the body.

◆   Tilt tip slightly backward, but not so far back that the ball drops out.

◆   Step forward with opposite foot to throwing hand.

◆ Without moving arm, snap the wrist forward to "flick" the ball quickly in line of direction of target.

Receiving

◆ Position in front of the ball, eyes tracking the ball all the way to scoop.

◆ To catch a high ball, hold scoop in the vertical position and let ball enter the tip and roll along the curve.

◆ Cushion the impact and smother the spin to prevent the ball from bouncing out.

◆ To catch a fly ball, hold the scoop parallel to the ground. Allow the ball to drop into the scoop, then "give" with the impact by drawing the scoop towards you as the ball enters the scoop.

Focus Words:

● *Muscles of the Week: Pectorals (chest muscles)*

● *Bones of the Week: Sternum (breast bone)*

Warming-up Activities/Games:

Aerobic Mingler:

● To start everyone jog lightly in place to the music, reaching arms upwards.

● On signal "Scrambled Eggs—Mingle," jog in and out of each other, giving high 5's.

● On signal "Elbow Swing," partner up and do a right-elbow swing for 4 counts; followed by a left-elbow swing for another 4 counts.

● "Scrambled Eggs—Mingle."

● "Full Swing," partner up, join hands, and skip together 4 counts clockwise; 4 counts counterclockwise.

● "Scrambled Eggs—Mingle."

● "Sashay," partner up, join hands and slide step together 8 counts in one direction, 8 counts in the opposite.

● "Scrambled Eggs—Mingle."

● "Inchworm," begin in front support position, walk feet up to hands, then walk hands forward to start position.

● "Twister" in place, by jumping in place, twisting upper body from side to side for 8 counts.

● "Marching" in place, gently swinging arms in full circles away from center for 4 counts; towards center for 4 counts, slowly breathing in and out.

● "Rope Climbers," in hook sit position, lean back, and pantomime climbing up a rope. Feel the tightness in your abs.

● Stretch to the sky! Stretch wide! Stretch from side-to-side.

Skill Practice & Progressions:

Individual Tasks (Each player has a scoop and Cosom Fun Ball™.)

1. Stand facing a wall about 4–5 giant steps away. Practice underhand throwing and catching using your scoop. Flick the ball up and outward. Use either hand.

2. Practice using the overhand flick to send the ball to the wall. Remember to "give" with the impact as the ball lands in the scoop so that it does not bounce out. Use either hand.

3. Practice underhand tossing the ball high into the air. Track the ball and make the catch. Explore varying the effort used to release the ball.

Partner Tasks

1. Stand facing a partner about 4–5 yards away. Practice using scoops to underhand toss the ball to each other. Gradually increase the distance apart from each other. Experiment with the effort required to send the ball farther. Explore using nondominant hand to send and receive the ball.

2. Repeat task above, but send the ball using the overhand flick of the scoop.

3. **Scoop It Up.** Partners roll the ball back and forth to each other. Field the ball in the scoop by fronting its oncoming path and positioning the scoop so that the ball will roll into it.

4. **Sidearm Throw.** Send the ball from the scoop with a sidearm motion; with a wrist flick.

5. **Triangle Scoop Pass.** Groups of 3, triangle formation, spaced 4–5 yards apart, underhand pass ball from one player to the other using scoops. Spread farther apart and use the overhand flick to send ball.

6. **Scoop Pattern Passing.** Form a large circle of 6 players and pass the ball in a certain pattern using scoops.

7. **Scoop in the Middle.** Circle players pass the ball to each other while a middle player tries to intercept the pass. Circle players are not allowed to pass to a player on either side of them.

8. **Passing on the Move.** Pass the ball to each other with your scoops as you move in general space. Keep about 3–4 yards apart from each other as you move. Remember to look out for others.

9. Play **Keep-away** in fours (2-on-2).

Cooling-down Activities/Games:

1. **Circle Relays.** For large class, number off in groups of 6 around the circle as shown. On signal, number 1's run clockwise (or counterclockwise) around the circle, back into place to tag the next player. Continue until everyone has had a turn. First group to cross-leg sit wins. *Variations:*

   - Split class into two circles of 2 groups of 6.
   - Form 2 circles of 2 groups of six. Spread circles so that players are spaced about 1 meter (3 feet apart). Each player must zigzag through the class to return to place.
   - Run with an object (deck ring), which is handed off to the next player.
   - Leapfrog around the circle to place.

   LEAP FROG

   - **Spoke Relay:** Players are in front lying position with heads towards center of circle as shown. Each player must leap over the legs (spokes) of the other players and return to place.

2. **Legend(s) of the Day!**

   SPOKE RELAY

Lesson 23:
Scoop and Whiffle Ball

Skill Builders: sending (passing) and receiving with scoops and whiffle balls in game play, hand–eye coordination, eye tracking, cooperation, court awareness, positional play, team work

Expected Student Performance:

◆ Demonstrates competency in using a scoop to send (pass) and receive a whiffle ball.

◆ Willingly cooperates and interacts with other class and team members.

◆ Performs proficiently in applying skills to a game situation.

Facility/Equipment Needed:

◆ Large grass area, gymnasium, or undercover area

◆ 1 scoop per player

◆ 1 Cosom Fun Ball® (whiffle ball) per pair

◆ 1 scooter per player

◆ Badminton nets and poles or long rope

◆ Volleyball net and poles

◆ 12–15 cone markers

◆ Soccer or hockey nets; floor tape for goal crease

Focus Words:

● *Muscles of the Week: Coccyx (tail bone)*

● *Bones of the Week: Ilium (pelvis)*

Scoop and Whiffle Ball Games:

1. **Scoop Badminton.** Play 3 a side, sending whiffle back and forth over a low net. Object of the game is to not let the ball touch the floor.

2. **Scoop Volleyball.** Play 5–6 a side, sending the whiffle ball back and forth over a high net. Score a point for each time the ball hits the floor on the opposition's side. Each team has a ball to send at the start of the game.

3. **End Zone Scoopball.** Mark out a large rectangular area with an end zone at each end. Play 3-on-3 or 4-on-4. Start the game with a throw-in from the sideline at center. A goalie for each team positions behind the opposite end zone. *Rules of 3:* Allow 3 traveling steps,

2.

3.

3 seconds to hang onto the ball, and 3 uninterrupted passes before attempting to score in the opposition's half. Score a goal by sending the ball to the goalie who must catch it in the scoop. Goalies are allowed to move anywhere in this end zone. Ensure that each player has an opposition player to guard. Change goalies frequently throughout the game.

4. **Scoop Netball.** Play the game as for End Zone Scoopball, but have each goalie position in a goalie area with a goal crease in his/her team's half. Goalie must protect the ball sent by an opposition player (outside of the goalie crease) from landing in their large net as shown. No one is allowed in the goal crease except the goalie.

5. **Scooter Scoop Ball.** Play as for Scoop Netball, but have players sit on scooter boards.

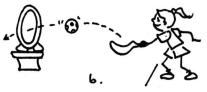

6. **Target Toss.** Set up as a Skill Builder Station activity. Children take turns using scoops to toss fun balls into targets: boxes or bins positioned near a wall, wall targets, or hoops vertically mounted on hoop stands positioned on a bench. Vary the throwing distance. At one target, have them use the nondominant hand.

7. Invent a scoop/ball game with your partner or teammates!

Cooling-down Activity:

Legends of the Day!

Fit Think Idea:

Discuss Competitive Play vs. Play-for-fun. Take a vote (favor or not in favor) to observe overall class reaction.

Lesson 24:
Sending and Receiving an Oval Object

Skill Builders: overhand throwing and catching skills using oval-shaped balls, accuracy and distance throwing, hand–eye coordination, eye tracking, fitness, team work, guarding

Expected Student Performance:

◆   Demonstrates competency in overhand throwing, throwing for accuracy and distance, with a variety of oval balls.

◆   Willingly cooperates and interacts with other class and team members.

◆   Demonstrates good positional play, guarding ability, and team work.

◆   Performs proficiently in aerobic fitness, agility, and strength demands.

Facility/Equipment Needed:

◆   Large grass area, gymnasium, or undercover area

◆   Cassette or CD player; popular music

◆   1 football per pair

Teaching Points:

◆   A Vortex Howler™ is a throwing football with a dart-like tail. If thrown correctly, its 3 howling whistles give off a sensational high-pitched sound effect.

◆   Turbine™ Football, the Vortex Jr., is a hybrid of the adult version. It is ideal for small hands and boasts the furthest flying capacity with its stabilizing plastic fins for perfect spirals on every throw.

◆   Zwirl® Football is molded in one solid piece from rugged, soft, and safe polyurethane. The unique corkscrew design provides grip channels for fingers and serves to stabilize the ball in flight.

◆   Turbojav™, 700 cm long, under 300 grams in weight, was invented by the two-time world-record holder in the Javelin throw, Tom Petranoff, and is a new teaching aid for javelin.

Throwing

◆   Hold the football in throwing hand with hand underneath, fingers pointing upwards (fingers on the lace), thumb on one side.

◆   Turn sideways to the target.

◆   Raise the football back and over your shoulder.

◆   Step forward with leading foot, and snap wrist downward, whipping ball through to target.

◆   Follow-through down and across the body.

Catching

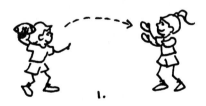

- ◆ Keep eyes tracking football all the way to your hands.
- ◆ Hands are cupped and in ready position; fingers relaxed.
- ◆ Reach for the ball, letting it fall into the cradle of your hands.
- ◆ "Give" with the hands, wrists, elbows, and knees by drawing the ball toward the body to absorb the impact.

Focus Words:

- ● *Muscles of the Week: Obliques (diagonal stomach muscles)*
- ● *Bones of the Week: Ribs (bones of chest); Vertebrae (bones of spine)*

Warming-up Activities/Games:

Artful Dodger (one-on-one checking). Players partner off and each pair stands in a Home space, file position (one behind the other). Front partner is the "Dodger"; other partner is the "Shadow." On signal to move (power walking, slide-stepping, jogging . . .), Dodger tries to lose Shadow. Shadow follows as closely as possible without touching Dodger. On signal to stop, everyone jump stops and freezes. Each Shadow is then allowed to take a giant step toward his/her Dodger to try to touch him/her. If successful, Dodger and Shadow exchange places. Remind everyone to always watch where they are going! *Variation:*

- ● Use music to start and stop action.
- ● Vary the way participants will move.
- ● On signal "Mingle," find new partners and continue activity.

Skill Practice & Progressions:

1. Demonstrate the proper grip and throwing action using teaching cues. Then have players pair off and explore throwing and catching the different types of oval-shaped balls. Start about 8 yards apart, and gradually increase distance. Emphasize tracking the football all the way into hands and "giving" with hands and elbows to cushion the impact.

2. **Oval-ball Throwing Contest.** One partner throws the oval ball; the other partner marks the distance, using a beanbag as a marker. Vary the type of oval ball used. Declare a Boy Champ and a Girl Champ.

3. **Oval-ball Target Throwing.** Use targets such as a suspended hoop or hoops vertically positioned in a hoop stand on a bench, plastic pins, or jugs spaced apart on a bench. Vary the throwing distance. Vary the type of oval ball used. This could be set up as a Skill Builder Station activity, emphasizing overhand throwing accuracy.

4. **Three Passes.** For each game, play 4 a side, with one team wearing bibs. Mark out a play area about half the size of tennis court. Score one point for every 3 successful passes. Emphasize that each player guard an opposition player and encourage players to spread out. Rules of 3 are in effect: Allow 3 traveling steps before passing; 3 seconds to hang onto the ball; and must complete 3 uninterrupted passes to score a point. Players are allowed to pivot on one foot.

5. **Oval-ball.** Designate a mini play area for each game consisting of two teams of 4 players. Players for each team wear a designated color bib: Red vs. Blue; Green vs. Yellow; Orange vs. Purple. Game is played as for "Three Passes," but now a team can score a goal after the completion of three passes, by passing to a teammate who stands anywhere behind the opposition's end line as shown.

Cooling-down Activities/Games:

1. **Sky Ball.** Play in groups of 4–6 players with one thrower; the rest are fielders. Number players from 1 through 6. Number 1 becomes the first thrower, calls out a number from 2–6, then throws the ball high into the air towards that player. The player with that number must make the catch. If successful, that player becomes the new thrower; if not, then the original thrower continues. *Variation:* Change the middle thrower after every 4 throws. If a player is unsuccessful in making the catch, she/he gets a "letter." Once these letters complete the word "F-I-T," that player must go to the Stretch Tree nearby.

2. **Legend(s) of the Day!**

Fit Think Idea:

The Aerobic Fitness Grid. Each time a child is involved in an aerobic activity of a minimum of 15 minutes, a grid square can be colored in. The idea is to heighten awareness of the activity that each child does in day-to-day living: walking or riding bike to school; taking the dog for a walk after school; kicking the football with a friend; attending dance class, gymnastics, soccer, swimming, or basketball training after school; playing tennis; sweeping the patio; mowing the lawn; raking the leaves; skating; cross-country, snow or water skiing; tobogganing; playing hockey; and so on. See the Appendix for a sample Aerobic Fitness Grid.

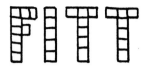

Lesson 25:
More Sending and Receiving
Skill Builder Stations

Skill Builders: underhand and overhand throwing and rolling, catching, hand–eye coordination, tracking, cooperation

Expected Student Performance:

◆   Demonstrates competency in accurate sending and receiving of an object along the ground or through the air.

◆   Performs proficiently in tracking tasks using a small object.

◆   Willingly cooperates and interacts with other team members.

Facility/Equipment Needed:

◆   Large grass area, gymnasium, or undercover area

◆   Cassette or CD player, popular music; station signs

◆   Station #1—12 poly spots or carpet shapes, 6 spider balls/beanbags

◆   Station #2—6 tennis tins, 6 tennis balls

◆   Station #3—15 bowling pins, 8 small play balls

◆   Station #4—3 small footballs or Vortex Howlers™; 3 junior Vortex™ footballs, 3–4 hoops and hoop stands, 1 bench, 1 support for suspending a hoop, rope

◆   Station #5—3 Fling-it™ nets and variety of small tossing objects

◆   Station #6—6 lummi sticks, 3 deck rings

Skill Builder Station Ideas:

Station #1: Spider Ball Shuffleboard. (Each group can create its own shuffleboard formation [see example on right]. If possible, provide enough poly spots [squares] to set up two different formations. Each spot is given a point score.) Each member in turn rolls spider ball to try to land it on a spot to earn points. Keep track of points and try to achieve personal best score for every three throws. *Variations:*

●   Use floor tape to mark out a 4 × 4 grid. Each square in grid has a point value. Roll spider balls into grid squares to earn points.

●   **Beanbag Shuffleboard:** Toss beanbags into grid squares.

#1

2	1	2
1	3	1
2	1	2

BEANBAG SHUFFLEBOARD

Station #2: Tennis Tin Ball. Each member has a tennis tin and a tennis ball. Explore different ways of tossing and catching ball in the tin: one bounce; no bounce; off a wall with one bounce; off a wall with no bounce; tossing back and forth to each other—one ball, two balls.

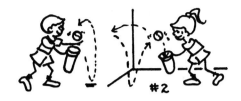

Station #3: Target Bowling. Set up two stations if possible. One could be in a 5-pin formation; the other in a 10-pin formation. Mark off a bowling line at which the ball must be released. Offer two bowling lines, one being more challenging in distance than the other. Each pin is worth a certain number of points as shown. Bowlers are allowed to roll 2 balls each for each game to try to knock over as many pins as possible.

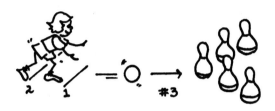

Station #4: Football Hoop Throw. Suspend a hoop from a backboard or suitable frame as one target. Snap a hoop into a hoop stand and position on a bench. If possible, set up 3 of these targets. Mark off 2 different throwing lines. Use small footballs or junior Vortex Howlers™. Throwers take turns trying to throw the football through the hoop and keep track of score. *Variations:*

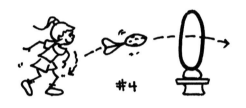

- Throw Frisbees™ into vertical targets.
- Use a Skore Net™ to throw Frisbees™ into.
- Use Foxtails™ or Poco Balls™.

Station #5: Fling-it™ Play. Partners use a Fling-it™ net to toss an object high into the air and catch it in the net. Provide a variety of different objects to toss: tennis balls, whiffle balls, small play balls, Foxtails™, and the like. *Variations:*

- Use lightweight sheets about the size of a towel.
- Partners toss object from their net into another pair's net.
- Toss more than one object at the same time.
- One pair tosses object from their net into another pair's net.
- Each pair tosses object at the same time into the other pair's net.

Station #6: Ring-it. Partners toss a deck ring to each other and try to catch the deck ring with a lummi stick. Vary the throwing distance. *Variations:*

- Use upturned chairs and ring the legs.
- Use Loop-n-Catch™ and a beanbag ball or Squellet™ Ball to toss and catch with.

Cooling-down Activity:

Legend(s) of the Day!

Homework Idea:

The Aerobic Fitness Grid. Color in grid squares based on the aerobic activity for the day.

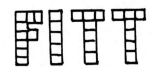

SECTION 4
PRE-SPORT SKILLS

Lesson 26:
Ball Handling/Chest and Bounce Pass

Skill Builders: ball handling, chest and bounce passing, catching techniques, hand–eye coordination, tracking, footwork, cooperation

Expected Student Performance:

Demonstrates competency in chest and bounce passing and catching.

Demonstrates proficiency in ball-handling tasks and executing offensive footwork.

Willingly cooperates and interacts with other class and team members.

Performs proficiently in aerobic fitness, agility, and strength demands.

Facility/Equipment Needed:

Gymnasium, undercover area, or flat surface

Cassette or CD player; popular music

1 basketball ("hands-on"*) per player or large playground ball

Teaching Points:

Chest Passing

Start in a balanced stance.

Hold ball with your fingers (not hand) in front of chest, one hand on each side of the ball. Spread fingers, thumbs up, elbows in. Hands should be slightly behind the ball in a relaxed position.

See your target without looking at it.

In one motion, step in the direction of the pass and force your wrists and fingers "through" the ball.

Release the ball off the first and second fingers of both hands to impart backspin and give the ball direction.

Follow-through with arms fully extended and fingers pointing towards the target with palms facing down.

Aim for the receiver's hand target (chest level).

*The "hands-on" basketball has the hand/finger positions painted on the ball for a right- or left-hander, which is ideal for teaching correct shooting positioning as well as passing. These basketballs are available from major sports catalog companies.

Bounce Passing (Start position is similar to the chest pass.)

◆ Start by holding the ball at your waist with fingers spread on each side of ball; thumbs up, elbows in.

◆ In one motion, step in direction of pass and force wrist and fingers "through" the ball.

◆ Use fingertip release off first and second fingers to impart backspin and accuracy.

◆ Aim for a spot on the floor about two-thirds of the way or a few feet in front of target. Ball should bounce to receiver's waist.

◆ Follow-through by pointing fingers at target with palms of hands facing downwards.

Catching a Pass (away from the scoring area)

◆ See ball and go to meet the pass.

◆ Land with feet shoulder-width apart, knees flexed, balanced stance.

◆ Use hands to set a target, facing your partner, and "asking for the ball."

◆ Keep eyes on the ball, tracking it all the way into your hands.

◆ Catch the ball with both hands, with thumbs and fingers relaxed.

◆ "Give" with the ball on the catch, bringing arms and hands into position in front of chest.

◆ After receiving the pass, land with a one-two stop.

◆ Be ready to make the next pass or shoot.

Warming-up Activities/Games:

Basketball is a team game. To be effective contributing team players, students must master the fundamental skills of shooting, passing, dribbling, rebounding, defending, moving with the ball, and moving without the ball.

Basketball Signals develop footwork, body work, listening skills, court awareness, and general and personal space awareness. Perform without a basketball at first, then with a basketball that is dribbled.

1. **Basketball Scramble:** Run in and out of each other with quick changes of direction and without making contact or losing control of the ball.

2. **Jump Stop** with both feet landing simultaneously, feet shoulder-width apart, knees bent, and hands out to side for balance.

3. **Triple Threat:** Land on two feet at the same time, bending at the knees, hands/arms out to sides for balance, head up. Ball is held in both hands in close to inside of one hip. Makes you a "triple threat" to shoot, pass, or drive.

'TRIPLE THREAT' 'PIVOT' 'REBOUND'

4. **Pivot:** Keep contact with the floor on the ball of one foot (which acts like a swivel). Use the other foot to push off in different directions.

5. **Rebound:** Jump up in the air, stretching high while grabbing an imaginary ball rebounding off the basketball backboard. Land, bending at the knees, and bring the ball to the triple-threat position.

6. **Circles:** Jog quickly, head up to touch all the basketball circles with two hands. When finished jog in place.

7. **Three-point Circle:** Run to 3-point circle and ski-jump back and forth over the circle line.

8. **Sidelines:** Shuffle from one sideline to the other, touching each with one hand.

9. **End Lines:** Sprint from one end line to the other. Watch where you are going to avoid collisions. Touch each end line with opposite foot to dribbling hand.

10. **Free-throw Line:** Touch with right hand, left foot. Reverse for other line.

11. **Keyway:** Run to keyway and use a shuffle step to cut in and out of keyway from high post to low post to mid post.

12. **Switch:** Use the other hand to dribble!

Skill Practice & Progressions:

Ball Handling. Each player has a ball and starts in a Home space. Use music to further reinforce ball-handling rhythm.

1. **Wake-up.** Toss ball up into the air. Catch it in both hands. Slap the ball to wake up your hands. Feel the ball on your fingers.

2. **Flash Fingers.** Pass the ball quickly but in control from hand to hand in front of your body while jogging in place; while marching in place; while lightly jumping in place. Start with hands close together, gradually move them farther apart. Emphasize control. Watch the ball, then close your eyes and repeat task. *Variations:*

    ● Can you pass the ball behind your back?
    ● Pass the ball while one-knee sitting, kneeling, wide sitting, standing up again.

3. **Body Wraps.** Spread your feet and pass the ball around your waist clockwise, then counterclockwise. Try this while jogging in place; side-stepping in place; jogging in general space. Pass the ball around your right knee; left knee; both knees. Try the sequence: around the waist, right knee, left knee, both knees, again around the waist. Repeat! Make up your own body-wrap sequence!

4. **Figure 8's.** Pass the ball in a figure-8 pattern around one leg, between legs, around the other leg. Reverse the pattern. **Gorilla Walk:** Do figure 8's while walking forward in a straight line.

5. **Body Circles.** Holding the ball in both hands, use it to "trace" a large circle in front of you. Do this in slow motion, then reverse direction.

6. **Flip-flops.** Lean over, bending at the knees, and hold the ball between your legs with one hand in front and the other behind. Drop the ball, change hands over to catch it. Let the ball bounce to practice the hand switch, then repeat with no bounce.

7. **Tappers.** Keep the ball bouncing by tapping it with each hand in front, then each hand behind. Be patient—this takes some practice!

8. Make up a ball-handling stunt of your own!

Passing and Catching

1. Demonstrate the chest pass and catch technique. Use the cue words for *passing:* "Chest, thumbs up, elbows in, step and push away, flick and follow-through, thumbs down." *Catching:* "Target, eyes, reach and give."

2. Partners face about 3–5 yards/meters apart. Practice chest passing ball back and forth to each other. Emphasize setting hand targets to receive the ball. Observe each other and give feedback. Make 20 passes.

3. Demonstrate the bounce pass and catch technique. Use the cue words for *passing:* "Chest, thumbs up, elbows in, step and push down, flick and follow-through, thumbs down." Have passers experiment with where the ball should contact the floor on the way to their partner. Make 20 passes.

4. **Hot Pepper Passes.** Which pair can make 20 chest passes the quickest and end in a one-knee sit position? Make 20 bounce passes!

5. **Combination Passing.** Using one ball, one partner bounce passes, while other partner chest passes. Switch roles. Make 20 passes quickly, then get into a one-knee sit position.

6. **Split-vision Passing.** Form groups of 3 in triangle formation. Start with one ball, then introduce two balls to pass and receive a ball at the same time. Heads up! Use chest pass; bounce pass.

Games:

1. **Corner-spry.** Form teams of 5–6 players, with each team lined up in a semi-circle. Leader positions in the center facing the team and holding a basketball. Leader chest passes the ball to each player in turn. Each player receives the pass and chest passes the ball back to the leader. When the last player receives the ball, he/she dribbles to the center to become the new leader while the former leader runs to join the opposite end of the semi-circle. **Corner-Spry Challenge:** Use two balls, with leader and first passer having a ball to start the activity.

2. **Bull in the Ring.** Play with 3–6 players. One player (defensive player) stands in the middle of the ring or jump ball circle. Other players (offensive players) pass ball to each other while ring player tries to intercept, deflect, or touch the pass. If defensive player is successful, then the passer becomes the defender in the middle and the defender goes to offense. Encourage player with the ball to fake the pass in one direction and pass in another direction. Make the rule that the passer may not hold the ball longer than a 3-second count.

Cooling-down Activities/Games:

1. **Shuttle Pass Relays.** Each half of the team positions in a file opposite the other, 10 yards apart. Chest pass to the front player of opposite line, then run to join the end of that file, passing file on the right side. Drill continues with each player catching, passing, and following the pass with quickness and accuracy. Repeat relay using the bounce pass. Remember to pass first, then move feet!

2. **Legend(s) of the Day!**

Homework Idea:

Spinners. Practice spinning the ball on your middle or index finger. Provide opportunity for players to demonstrate their spinning ability!

Fit-think Idea:

Discuss the following focus word: P-R-I-D-E. Let "P.R.I.D.E." be the focus word for the week.

"P" —Be positive within and without.

"R" —Respect yourself and show respect to others.

"I" —Make intelligent decisions (think before you act!).

"D" —Be determined. Have a dream.

"E" —Be enthusiastic. Put in the effort to get results.

Lesson 27:
Footwork/Control Dribbling/Passing

Skill Builders: control ball handling, footwork, chest and bounce passing and catching revision and extension, hand–eye coordination, tracking, cooperation

Expected Student Performance:

Demonstrates proficiency in footwork drills and dribbling the ball with control.

Demonstrates competency in chest and bounce passing and catching tasks.

Demonstrates fair play and interacts with other players in dribbling games.

Performs proficiently in aerobic fitness, agility, and strength demands.

Facility/Equipment Needed:

Gymnasium, undercover area, or flat surface

Cassette or CD player; popular music

1 basketball ("hands-on") per player or large playground ball

Teaching Points:

Control Dribbling. Use the control dribble when closely guarded and to keep the ball protected and under control. Maintain a well-balanced stance, basic to the control dribble, which will allow you to move quickly, change direction or pace, be a "triple threat" to shoot, pass, or drive, and stop under control.

Position in a diagonal stance, feet at least shoulder-width apart, weight evenly distributed on balls of feet, knees flexed, body low, foot opposite dribbling hand slightly forward.

Learn to dribble without looking at the ball.

Keep head over your waist and back straight.

Keep elbow of dribbling hand close to your body.

Relax dribbling hand, thumb relaxed and fingers comfortably spread.

Dribble off finger pads with fingertip control, not the palm of hand, flexing wrist and fingers to impart force to the ball.

Do not pump your arm. Don't pat or slap the ball!

Dribble ball at knee level or lower, keeping the ball close to your body and bouncing it in the "pocket" created by the diagonal stance.

Keep nondribbling hand in a protective position close to the ball.

Position body between your defender and the ball.

Focus Words:

● *P. R. I. D. E. and Control*

Warming-up Activities/Games:

1. **Heads-up Drill.** Teams position in "wave" formation as shown. Use hands signals to indicate flow of direction to right or left; move forward or backward. Players move using a shuffle step. Add other basketball signals:

   ● Pivot

   ● Rebound

   ● Triple Threat

   ● Stutter Step. Take very quick steps in place.

   ● Fall Back. Gently fall backward, rock back and forward onto feet.

   ● Hands. In guarding position, bend knees, one foot slightly forward, one hand up, other hand down. Mirror hand movements of teacher.

2. **Basketball Stretches:**

   ● Take ball in both hands high into air and stretch on tip-toes.

   ● Stretch to one side, to other side for 10-second counts.

   ● Trace large circles in front, clockwise and counterclockwise.

   ● Spread feet, lean over, and roll ball from one foot to the other.

   ● Long sit and roll ball down your legs to rest on the toes.

   ● Periscope stretch with ball between your ankles.

3. **Partner Passing.** Revise chest and bounce passing. Make 20 passes of each. **Individual Wall Passing:** Revise chest and bounce passing.

4. **Combination Two-ball Passing.** Each partner with a ball, one partner chest passes while the other bounce passes. Then switch roles.

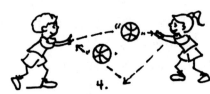

Skill Practice & Progressions:

1. **Ball Bouncing (One-handed) Progressions:**

   ● Get into kneeling position and bounce ball in Home space with your favorite hand. Remember to relax fingers and not slap at the ball. Let your fingers meet the ball and push it downward.

- **Keyboard Dribbling:** Play the "piano" on the ball. Start with pointer finger to bounce the ball, then let each finger in turn bounce the ball: middle, ring, pinky, and thumb. Now use all fingers working together to bounce the ball. Feel the ball—let it be an extension of your hand!

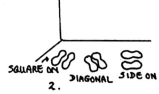

2. **Footwork (Stance).** Stand facing a wall square on; side on (10 toes facing the wall/sideline). Open up stance to face diagonally, toward a corner, creating a "pocket" to bounce the ball into.

3. **Pocket Dribble.** Stand with bent knees and feet shoulder-width apart, diagonal stance. Bounce ball in preferred hand in the "pocket" formed by your body and feet. Can you bounce your ball while looking slightly ahead of the ball?

   - Bounce at waist height; bounce low; bounce high.
   - Close your eyes and listen to the rhythm of the ball bouncing!

4. **Ball Dribble Tasks:**
   - Dribble ball heads-up and call out the number of fingers I am showing.
   - Dribble the ball high, low, lower; high to low; low to high.
   - Dribble the ball while marching in place.
   - Dribble ball in place while you walk (skip) around the ball.

   - Dribble the ball while going from stand tall to one-knee sit, to kneeling to long sitting, back to kneeling, one-knee, to stand tall position. Dribble the ball in a figure-eight through your legs.

5. **Walking Dribble.** Keep the ball bouncing as you walk forward. Concentrate on pushing the ball slightly out in front of your body, and looking slightly ahead of the ball in the direction you are moving.

6. **Sideline Dribble.** Dribble ball from one sideline to the other. Jump stop on that sideline. Pivot to face the opposite direction and bounce ball back to starting sideline. Continue in this way.

7. **Nondominant Hand Dribble.** Repeat tasks 1–5 bounce ball with other hand.

8. **Crossover Dribble.** In a balanced stance, change ball from one hand to the other while dribbling it below the knees. Keep nondribbling hand up as a guard hand for protection. Remember to change the position of your feet and body to protect the ball with your body.

Dribbling Game:

Knock-away. Play game in one half of the basketball court. On signal "Knock-Away!" players use free hand to try to knock each other's ball away. If successful, that player losing the ball must dribble with weak hand once around the play area, and then is allowed to return to the game. After two "life lines" (chances!) have been used up, that player must step outside the playing area and V-dribble in place on the outside. When only a few players are still active, confine the game to a basketball circle. Emphasize fair dribbling—no double dribbles, no running with the ball or kicking it, and no body contact. *Variation:* Play separate girls and guys games, each game played in the 3-point circle area.

Cooling-down Activities/Games:

1. **Figure-8 Scramble.** Mark out a rectangular play area with sidelines spaced about 8 meters/yards apart, a hoop containing two basketballs in the middle of the play area, and a chair (large cone/bin) placed at each end as shown. Set up 2–3 games that can be run at the same time to maximize participation. Teams stand behind the designated sideline. Each team numbers off from 1–6. If uneven numbers, let one player receive two numbers. Call out a number, "3's." This is the signal for players #3 to run to the hoop, grab a basketball, and dribble it around one chair, then the other in a figure-8 pattern, return the basketball to the hoop, and quickly run to stand in their starting spot. First player to accomplish the task earns a point for his/her team. Ensure that all numbers are called.

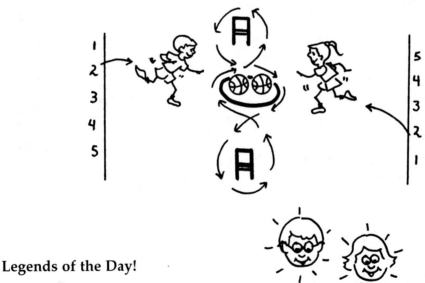

2. **Legends of the Day!**

Homework Ideas:

1. **The Aerobic Fitness Grid.** Color in grid squares based on the aerobic activity for the day.
2. With a partner create a focus word for each letter of the word C. O. N. T. R. O. L.

Fit Think Idea:

Discuss what large muscle groups are used to play basketball and how these muscles are warmed-up for more strenuous activity.

Lesson 28:
Footwork/Crossover/Speed Dribbling

Skill Builders: control dribbling, crossover dribbling, speed dribbling, footwork, aerobic fitness, hand–eye coordination, teamwork

Expected Student Performance:

◆   Demonstrates proficiency in crossover dribbling and speed dribbling.

◆   Demonstrates competence and confidence in dribbling with control and footwork.

◆   Demonstrates fair play and interacts with other players in dribbling games.

◆   Performs proficiently in aerobic fitness, agility, and strength demands.

Facility/Equipment Needed:

◆   Gymnasium, undercover area, or flat surface

◆   Cassette or CD player; popular music

◆   1 basketball ("hands-on") per player or large playground ball

Teaching Points:

Crossover Dribble. Use in the open court on a fast break, to get open on your drive to basket, or to create an opening for a shot. The effectiveness of this dribble depends on how sharply the dribble is changed from one direction to another.

CROSSOVER DRIBBLE

Cross the ball in front at a backward angle.

Switch the dribble from one hand to the other.

Dribble the ball close to you at knee level or lower with a control dribble (waist level for a speed dribble).

When making change of direction, bring nondribbling hand up and change lead foot and body position for protection.

Speed Dribble. Useful when not closely guarded to move ball quickly up court or to open spaces, or to drive to the basket.

SPEED DRIBBLE

Push dribble forward at waist level.

Keep head up and see the entire court and rim of the hoop.

Ball must leave hand before lifting pivot foot.

Dribble ball off finger pads, flexing wrist and fingers to put force on the ball.

Focus Words:

● *Back Court and Front Court*

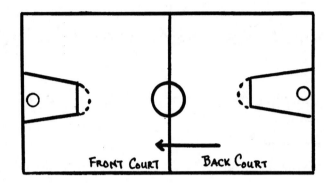

FRONT COURT   BACK COURT

Warming-up Activity/Game:

Aerobic Basketball Snake. Use basketball court and markings to lead players through an aerobic snake warm-up as they dribble their basketballs. If a player loses control, retrieve ball and join the end of the snake. Finish in an aerobic circle: arm reaches; arm punches; arm slashes; knee push-ups; and general stretching with ball.

Skill Practice & Progressions:

1. **Footwork Drill (Pivoting).** Spread out arm's length apart on sideline. Dribble ball forward; on whistle signal, jump stop, ball in "triple threat" position, and pivot. "Right pivot"—keep right foot planted and pivot off ball of foot in a different direction. "Left pivot"—keep left foot planted, pivot off ball of foot. **Reverse Pivot:** Drop step leading foot straight back, moving foot low to floor, while making a reverse pivot with back foot in direction of drop step.

PIVOTING   'TRIPLE THREAT'

2. **More Dribbling**
   - **"V" Dribble:** Stand facing square-on and bend your knees. Bounce ball from one hand to the other in a "V" pathway on the crossover. Remember to stay low, knees bent, keeping ball below the waist.
   - **Yo-Yo Dribble:** Dribble the ball from one side to the other using your right hand only. Use your left hand only. Yo-Yo dribble through one leg; other leg.
   - **Retreat Dribble:** Use short quick retreat steps while dribbling in a backward direction. Keep ball protected. Keep balanced and head up.

'V' DRIBBLE   Yo-Yo DRIBBLE

3. **Crossover Dribble.** In a balanced diagonal stance, change ball from one hand to the other, dribbling it below the knees. Keep nondribbling hand up as a guard hand for protection. Remember to change the position of your feet and body to protect the ball with your body.

CROSS-OVER
DRIBBLE

4. **Dribble Combinations.** (Option: Use music with a steady 4/4 count.)

   - 4 counts Pocket Dribble (best hand), Crossover Dribble
   - 4 counts Pocket Dribble (other hand), Crossover Dribble
   - 8 counts "V" Dribble
   - 4 counts Yo-Yo Dribble (best hand), Crossover Dribble
   - 4 counts Yo-Yo Dribble (other hand), Crossover Dribble
   - Continue in this sequence.

5. **Zigzag Dribble** ball in and out of cone markers spaced 2 yards apart. Set up a zigzag course for each team as shown. After passing a cone, immediately make a crossover dribble and change ball in front to your other hand. Dribble back to start with your nondominant hand.

ZIGZAG DRIBBLE

6. **Speed Dribble.** Partners stand one behind the other at one end line of a basketball court. Each partner, in turn, dribbles with better hand to opposite end line traveling as quickly as possible. Emphasize pushing the ball out in front and eyes focusing slightly ahead. Remind dribblers to travel only as fast as they can keep in control of the ball. Return to starting end line using the other hand. Repeat.

7. **Basketball Pirates.** Everyone has a basketball to dribble except for 4–5 players who are the "Pirates." On Go signal, Pirates run after dribblers, trying to steal their ball away by knocking it or grabbing it from the dribbler and taking possession. This player then becomes a Pirate. Stress that no body contact is allowed. Object is to last the game without becoming a Pirate or being a Pirate the fewest number of times. Remind players to watch where they are going and dribble "heads up!"

Cooling-down Activities/Games:

1. **Relays**
    - **Speed Dribble Relay:** Each team starts in file formation behind the start line and, in turn, dribbles ball from start line to turning line using preferred hand to dribble to turning line; nonpreferred hand to return to start line.
    - **Shuttle Dribble Relay:** In teams of 6, 3 on each side, spaced 10 yards apart, dribble ball from one side to other, until each dribbler has gone twice.
    - **Circle Dribble Relay:** Two teams in circle formation, numbered off. Each dribbler in turn dribbles clockwise (or counterclockwise) around the circle back to place. First team to complete the challenge wins.

2. **Legends of the Day!**

Homework Idea:

The Aerobic Fitness Grid. Color in grid squares based on the aerobic activity for the day.

Lesson 29:
Dribbling/Shooting/Passing

Skill Builders: shooting (one-hand set shot) technique and progressions, partner and team chest/bounce passing and catching extension, hand–eye coordination, partner work, cooperation, and communication

Expected Student Performance:

Demonstrates competency in control dribbling, chest and bounce passing, and catching.

Demonstrates proficiency in performing a one-hand set shot.

Willingly cooperates and integrates with other class members.

Performs proficiently in aerobic fitness, agility, and strength demands.

Facility/Equipment Needed:

Gymnasium, undercover area, or outdoor basketball court

Cassette or CD player; popular music

1 basketball ("hands-on") per player or large playground ball

Dome markers or floor tape

Teaching Points:

Shooting (One-hand Set Shot for Right-hander)

Stand square to target, feet shoulder width apart, with right foot slightly ahead of the other.

Keep eyes on target.

Knees flexed, shoulder relaxed, head over the waist and feet.

Hold basketball in finger pads, *not* the palm of the hand.

SQUARE-ON   HOLD IN FINGERS

Place shooting hand directly behind the ball, index finger directly at its midpoint.

Place nonshooting hand to the side and slightly under the ball for balance. This is sometimes called the "T" position in which the thumbs form the letter "T" on its side. (See illustration.)

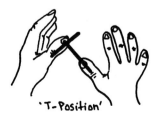

'T-Position'

Hold ball comfortably in front of and above shooting-side shoulder, between ear and shoulder. Keep shooting elbow in and shooting arm bent at a right angle. Check alignment: right knee, right elbow, hand, eye, ball.

Shoot ball with a smooth, rhythmical lifting motion.

- Start with knees slightly flexed, bend knees and then fully extend legs in a down-and-up motion.

- As shot starts, tip ball back from balance hand to shooting hand, dropping wrist back only until there is wrinkle in the skin.

- Release ball off index finger with soft fingertip touch to impart backspin on ball and soften shot.

- Keep balance hand on ball until point of release.

- Follow-through, keeping arm up and fully extended, index finger pointing straight to target.

- Palm of shooting hand should face down; palm of balance hand should face up.

- Hold arm up in this complete follow-through position until ball reaches the hoop.

- Keep in a balanced position throughout the shot.

Focus Word:

- *"B.E.E.F.F." (Balanced, Eyes on target, Elbow bent, Flick, and Follow-through)*

Warming-up Activities/Games:

1. **Ball-handling Warm-up.** See Lesson 26. Set to music.

2. **Basketball Greeting.** Dribble the ball with the left hand. Continue dribbling as you "shake hands" with other players, greeting each player by name, "Hi, Max!" "Hi Nikki!" Don't forget to smile!

3. **Agility Line Dribble.** Partners stand facing a set of lines, spaced 3 yards apart, as shown. Each partner, in turn, speed dribbles with preferred hand to first shuttle line, return dribbles with other hand to start line, then dribbles with best hand to second shuttle line, returns dribble with other hand to start line. Continue until dribbler has completed the course, then partner goes. Waiting partner does different ball-handling skills. (Refer to Lesson 26.) *Variation:* To increase distance, use end line, 3-point line back court, center line, 3-point line front court, opposite end line.

4. **Stretches.** Do 10-second calf stretches; 10-second hamstring stretches.

Skill Practice & Progressions:

1. **Pass and Follow.** Each team sets up in a circular pattern. Pass to a circle player who is not on either side of you and then follow the pass to take the place of that player you have just passed to. Emphasize passing first, then moving feet! Use the chest pass; then the bounce pass. Continue in this way.

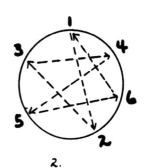

2. **Star Pass & Go.** Similar to activity 1, but establish an order and continue to pass in this order. At first, do not follow pass. Then, once order is established, pass and go.

2.

3. **Dribble–Jump Stop–Pass Drill.** Partners stand facing each other, spaced 3–4 yards apart. Partner with ball chest passes to other partner, then runs to his/her spot, jump-stops and jump-turns, setting a hand target to receive a pass. Partner receiving pass dribbles ball across to partner's line, jump stops, pivots, and passes to partner. Continue in this way. Repeat drill using the bounce pass.

3.

4. **Shooting Progressions**

   • **Demonstrate the correct "T" positioning of the hands on the ball.** Place shooting hand behind the ball and support hand on the side of the ball. Check for "daylight," that is, space between the ball and palm of hand. Check for elbows in.

'T'-Positioning

   • **Demonstrate what is backspin and how/why to create backspin.** Have shooters lie on their backs, hold the ball in finger pads, and position it above shooting shoulder. Shoot the ball up into the air, flicking it off the fingers. Follow through with full arm extension. Ball should return straight back to shooting position without having to move hands on the catch.

'Backspin'

   • **Shooters now stand and try to balance the ball in the shooting hand, in the shooting position:** ball held comfortably in front of and above shooting-side shoulder, between ear and shoulder. Keep shooting elbow in and shooting arm bent at a right angle. Check alignment: right knee, right elbow, hand, eye, ball. Extend shooting arm upward and snap wrist, flicking the ball off the fingertips to give it backspin and send it in a high arc.

- Now **demonstrate the shooting action.** (Make sure you face the same direction as the shooters.) Set up focus word: "B.E.E.F.F." (**B**alanced, **E**yes on target, **E**lbow bent, **F**lick, and **F**ollow-through). Have shooters stand about 2 giant steps away from a wall. Shooters begin with ball in the shooting pocket (in front of chest), square to wall, with one foot slightly ahead of the other. Check for correct hand positioning. Check for correct alignment: right knee, right elbow, hand, eye, ball. Say cue words above as shooters take ball to shooting position, extend shooting arm upward and snap wrist, flicking the ball off the fingertips to give it backspin and send it in a high arc toward target. Emphasize shooting the ball with a smooth, rhythmical lifting motion. Shooters practice.

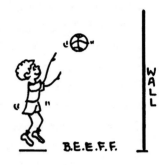

- Shooters now pair up and practice shooting the ball toward each other. Partners start in sitting position about 3 giant steps apart, and practice sending the ball with backspin in a high arc to each other. Partners then practice shooting the ball to each other from standing position. Check each other for correct hand positioning, proper alignment, follow-through, high arc, and backspin on the ball.

- Now stand inside basketball keyway, square to basketball hoop (about 2 giant steps away). Practice shooting. Keep eyes focused on back of rim. If the nonshooting hand tends to interfere with the shot, have shooter do a one-hand shooting drill positioned about 3 yards from hoop: keep the nonshooting hand behind the back; balance the ball in the shooting hand.

- Practice the "bank shot" off the backboard into the basketball hoop. Place a hoop on each side of the rim and have 3–4 shooters stand in a file behind a cone marker as shown. Shooters aim for the top right corner of target square on right side; top left corner on left side. After shooting, collect rebound and dribble to other group's side. Check for backspin.

- Three or four shooters stand behind each cone marker (placed on either side, parallel to free-throw line) as shown. Shooters dribble to floor hoop, jump stop in it, and execute a bank shot. Remove floor hoop and repeat. After shooting, collect ball and join the opposite file.

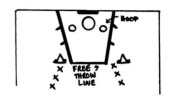

Cooling-down Activities/Games:

1. **"Around-the-world in Seven Shots."** Pair up and collect one basketball per pair, or, if possible, one basketball per shooter. Each pair starts at a designated spot on the keyway. Each partner must make a shot at each of the seven designated spots on the basketball keyway lines before moving to the next spot. Which partner will complete the "around-the-world" trip the quickest?

2. **Legends of the Day!**

Fit Think Ideas:

- Discuss why the ball needs to backspin as it travels to the basketball board/hoop. How is backspin created?

- How many basketballs will go through the hoop at one time? (2)

Lesson 30:
Shooting/Layup

Skill Builders: layup technique, shooting technique, ball dribbling control in low-organized game situation, hand–eye coordination, tracking, footwork, cooperation

Expected Student Performance:

◆ Demonstrates competency in executing a layup, either side of hoop.

◆ Demonstrates proficiency in ball dribbling control in game situation.

◆ Willingly cooperates and integrates with other class and team members.

◆ Performs proficiently in aerobic fitness, agility, and strength demands.

Facility/Equipment Needed:

◆ Gymnasium, undercover area, or outdoor basketball court

◆ Cassette or CD player; popular music

◆ 1 basketball ("hands-on") per player or large playground ball

◆ 1 flag per dribbler

◆ Dome markers

Teaching Points—Layup (Right-hander):

◆ Begin by holding ball in both hands, triple-threat position.

◆ Approach path is at a 45- to 60-degree angle to the basket.

◆ Step forward with the left foot and let ball bounce once near this foot.

◆ Protect ball by keeping it to right side of your body.

◆ Pick ball up in two hands with right hand on top; left hand on side for balance.

◆ Step right foot as you take ball in two hands, then left foot.

◆ Push upward off left foot, driving the right knee up to increase height of jump.

◆ Keep both hands on the ball until you reach the height of your jump, bringing ball into the shooting position.

◆ Cock the right-hand wrist back and release ball off index finger with a soft touch.

◆ Aim for the top right corner of the backboard square.

◆ Keep balance hand on the ball until the release.

◆ Keep eyes focusing on target.

◆ Let fingers follow-through and balance hand come off the ball but stay in the air to protect the shot.

Focus Word:

● *Layup*

Warming-up Activities/Games:

1. **Dribble Tag.** Partners, each with a basketball, stand with backs to each other and number off 1 and 2. Partner 1 (or 2) is IT and gives chase to partner 2 while both dribble their basketballs. If partner 2 is tagged, then he/she becomes IT. Remind players to dribble heads up and to keep ball under control.

2. **Basketball Tails.** Each player has a flag tucked in the back of the shorts. Object is to steal as many tails as possible while dribbling ball. After a certain time, game is stopped and a tail count is taken. Play again! Emphasize that players must dribble ball fairly, no traveling with ball.

3. **Partner Dribble Challenges:**
   - **Double Bounce:** Bounce two balls at the same time in place.
   - **Double Bounce on the Move:** Bounce two balls while traveling in general space.
   - **Alternate Bounce:** Alternate bounce two balls in place (one is going up while the other is going down). Who can do this while traveling?

   Variations: Partners, in hook-sit position and facing, take turns bouncing two basketballs in unison, alternating bounce, then standing.

Skill Practice & Progressions:

1. Revise shooting technique at wall (or to a partner). Take 3–4 dribbles toward wall (partner), jump stop, and shoot. Practice. Add **rebounding** the ball: Reach up high to grab ball in both hands and bring down into triple-threat position and shoot again.

2. Stand in keyway, spin ball away from hoop. Grab it, pivot to square to basketball hoop and shoot. Grab the rebound. Repeat.

3. **Layup Progressions** (right-hander):
   - Demonstrate the sequence "step left and bounce–right–left–up" in a Home space. On "up" take the ball in two hands, reaching high. Shoot the ball into the air towards an imaginary backboard square. Have players "walk" through this sequence several times. Emphasize pushing upward off left foot, driving the right knee up to increase height of jump. Keep both hands on the ball until you reach the height of your jump, bring ball into the shooting position, and release ball off index finger with a soft touch.

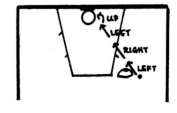

- Demonstrate the layup step sequence towards the hoop from a takeoff cone on the right side of the basketball hoop. Then assign each team to a backboard and have shooters position at the dome marker as shown. Players practice the "step left and bounce–right–left foot" sequence, and execute a layup off the backboard. Emphasize aiming for the top right corner of the backboard square and laying the ball up gently against this target on the backboard. Keep eyes focusing on target. Shooter practices performing a right-hand layup first. Collect the rebound and dribble back to the file.

- Reverse footwork and handwork for left-hand layup: "step right and bounce–step left–step right–up."

4. **Gotcha Basketball.** Partner A shoots anywhere in the key area. If successful, Partner B must make the same shot; otherwise, B missing the shot is given a letter "G," etc. If Partner A misses the shot, B can take a shot of his/her choice. First one to "Gotcha" is out.

5. Design a shooting game with your partner or teammate.

Cooling-down Activities/Games:

1. **Free-throw Shoot-out.** Divide class into groups of 3: one shooter, two ball retrievers. Each shooter takes 10 shots. Keep score. If not enough baskets, use wall targets. Adjust shooting distance according to the age and ability level of the children. Emphasize developing a sound routine each time, which will help shooter to relax, focus, shoot with rhythm, and enhance confidence:

- Set up in a balanced stance, position feet behind the free-throw line, making certain to line up the ball (not head) with the middle of the basket.

- Bounce the ball a certain number of times to help you relax.

- Take a deep breath. Relax your shoulders, arms, hands, and fingers.

- Check for correct hand positioning; elbow-in alignment.

- Before shooting, visualize a successful shot!

- Focus and shoot.

- Exaggerate follow-through, keeping eyes on target and shooting arm up until ball reaches the basket.

FREE THROW LINE

2. **Legends of the Day!**

Fit Think Idea:

Discuss what it means to be a "team player."

Lesson 31:
Overhead and Sidearm Passing/Layup Shooting

Skill Builders: revise and extend layup technique, one-on-one guarding, "faking" movement, overhead and sidearm passing techniques, hand–eye coordination, partner work, team work

Expected Student Performance:

Demonstrates competency in shooting/layup technique.

Demonstrates proficiency in passing using the overhead and sidearm passes.

Willingly cooperates and integrates with other class and team members.

Performs proficiently in agility and dodging to fake and guard a player.

Facility/Equipment Needed:

Gymnasium, undercover area, or outdoor basketball court

Cassette or CD player; popular music

1 basketball ("hands-on") per player or large playground ball

Several sets of colored bibs

Cone or dome markers

Teaching Points:

Overhead Pass. Use when a player is closely guarded and has to pass over the defender, as an outlet pass to start a fast break against pressing defenders, and as a lob pass to a player cutting "backdoor" (behind defender) to the basket.

See target without looking.

Start in a balanced stance, holding ball above forehead with elbows in and flexed about 90 degrees.

Do not bring ball behind your head from where it can be stolen or take longer to execute a pass.

Step in direction of target, extending legs and back to get maximum power.

Pass ball quickly, extending arms and flexing wrists and fingers.

Release ball off first and second fingers of both hands.

Follow-through by pointing your fingers at the target, palms down.

Sidearm Pass. Similar to the overhead pass in execution, use when closely guarded to pass around a defender. A sidearm bounce pass can also be used to feed the ball to a low post player.

◆   See the target without looking.

◆   Using 2 hands as in the overhead pass, start by moving the ball to one side, between shoulder and hip, and step to that side.

◆   Do not bring ball behind the body where it can be stolen.

◆   Follow-through by pointing fingers toward the target, palms to the side.

◆   With one hand, place passing hand behind the ball.

◆   Keep nonpassing hand in front and on the ball until point of release.

Focus Words:

●   *Button-Hook and Jab Step*

Warming-up Activities/Games:

1.   **Change-of-pace Dribble.** Players start at one end line of basketball court or play area in waves of 6 deep. Give a whistle signal for each wave to move forward, dribbling basketball. Dribblers stop at other end line and, while waiting for signal to move again, do ball handling in place. Dribblers change the pace of the ball dribble from control to speed to control to speed, and so on as they dribble down the court. Emphasize pushing the dribble out to change quickly from a slower to a faster speed.

2.   **"Button-hook Fake" Drill.** A button-hook movement is a fake in one direction, then a quick move into another direction. It is used to "free up" from an opposition player who is guarding you. Start in a Home space with partner. One partner is the offensive player; the other, the defensive player. On one whistle signal, offensive players do button-hooks to try to lose the defensive player. On two whistle players, jump-stop and check positions. Switch roles and continue.

3.   **Partner Stretches Using Basketball**
     ●   Overhead, through the legs.
     ●   Side-to-side; reverse direction.
     ●   Right side to right side. Left side to left side.

Skill Practice & Progressions:

1. **Layup Drill.** Revise layup technique learned from previous lesson. Practice strong side and weak side. Then start from the 3-point line (cone marker) and do a layup. *Variation:* Place cone markers and have dribbler weave and layup ball.

1. 45° degree angle

2. **Three-point Power Layup Drill.** Players line up at a cone marker set on the 3-point semi-circle on each side of the basketball hoop as shown. Dribble the ball quickly and under control at a 45-degree angle towards hoop. Jump-stop and softly do a layup against the backboard. Make an aggressive drive step (called a **jab step**) to hoop. Take a quick step with nonpivot foot straight toward hoop. *Variation:*

   • **V-formation Layup Drill:** For each basketball hoop, set up a rebound line and a layup line as shown. Each player in the layup line has a basketball. Each player, in turn, dribbles in to execute a layup, then continues around the outside of the rebounding line to join the end. Each rebound player times the shot to catch the rebound, then dribbles the ball to join the layup line. Continue in this way.

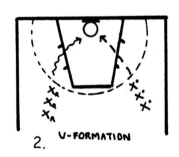

2. V-FORMATION

3. **Wall Passing.** This helps develop quickness, accuracy, and confidence in passing. Execute different passes at the wall. *Variation:*

   • Revise chest pass while slide-stepping and chest passing to wall.

3.

4. **Introduce and demonstrate the overhead pass** using the cues from the teaching points. Emphasize sending ball from above the forehead, not behind it where it can be stolen. Have players pair up and practice.

5. **Introduce and demonstrate the sidearm pass.** Emphasize that the ball is not brought behind the body where it can be stolen. Follow-through by pointing fingers toward the target, palms to the side. With one hand, place passing hand behind the ball. Partners practice. *Variation:* For Skill Builder Station Work, pass into a rebound net if available.

6. **Inbounding Ball Drill.** Have players split up into 3's with 2 offensive players and 1 defensive player. One offensive player uses the overhead or sidearm pass to inbound the ball to offensive player who is being guarded by defensive player. Offensive player

6. 'Button Hook'

uses a button-hook fake to try to lose defensive player and receive the pass. Switch roles after 3 attempts at each position.

7. **Three Passes.** Play 3-on-3, with one team wearing bibs. Mark out a rectangular or square play area. A team scores a point each time 3 uninterrupted passes are made. Allow chest or bounce pass, overhead pass, sidearm passing, pivoting, but no dribbling. Emphasize that each player stay with the opposition player he/she is guarding. *Variation:* Allow a maximum of 3 dribbles before passing.

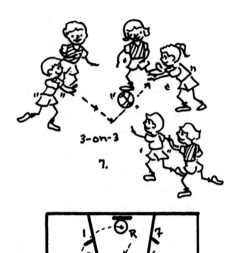

Cooling-down Activities/Games:

1. **Hot Shots.** Play in groups of 3 with one shooter, one passer, and one retriever. Each, in turn, takes 7 shots from designated spots on the keyway boundary lines as shown. Keep score. Who will be the hot shot for the first round?

   ● Mingle groups to form 3 new groups and play again.

2. **Legends of the Day!**

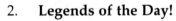

Fit Think Idea:

Discuss the term "one-on-one guarding" a player and the different sports in which this defense is used.

Lesson 32:
Baseball Pass/Passing Plays

Skill Builders: baseball pass technique, 2- and 3-player passing plays, cutting movement, shooting under pressure, hand–eye coordination, tracking, teamwork

Expected Student Performance:

Demonstrates competency in performing a baseball pass.

Demonstrates proficiency in performing 2- and 3-player passing plays.

Willingly cooperates and integrates with other class and team members.

Performs proficiently in heads-up dribbling and ball-handling warm-up.

Facility/Equipment Needed:

Gymnasium, undercover area, or outdoor basketball court

Cassette or CD player; popular music

1 basketball ("hands-on") per player or large playground ball

Several sets of colored bibs

Cones or dome markers

Teaching Points:

Baseball Pass. Used to make a long pass; that is, for throwing a long lead pass to a teammate cutting toward the basket, making an outlet pass to start a fast break, or inbounding the ball.

Start in a balanced position. See target without looking.

Pivot on back foot, turning body to passing-arm side.

Bring ball up to ear with elbow in, passing hand behind ball, and balance hand in front of ball.

As ball is passed, shift weight from back to front foot.

Step in direction of pass, extending legs, back, and passing arm forward toward the target.

Flex wrist forward, releasing ball off fingertips.

Follow-through by pointing fingers at target, with palm of passing hand down.

Catching the Ball in Position to Shoot

◆ Target with hands high between ear and shoulder and in shooting position.

◆ As pass is thrown, jump behind the ball squaring to the basket in position to shoot, feet shoulder-width apart, knees flexed, shoulders relaxed, elbows in.

◆ Let the ball come into your hands; do not reach for the ball.

◆ Catch ball with relaxed fingers, shooting hand behind ball and nonshooting hand under the ball. Do not catch ball with hands on the sides, then try to rotate ball into position.

Focus Word:

● *Cutting*

Warming-up Activity/Game:

Follow-the-ball. This is a follow-the-leader warm-up activity that gives dribblers further practice at heads-up dribbling. Each team starts in a designated spot—one behind the other, leader in front—everyone with a ball.

◆ On signal (whistle or music), activity starts. On one whistle blow, leader goes to the end of the file, and the next player takes over as the new leader. Encourage leaders to use all the basketball handling skills, dribbling skills, footwork, and bodywork skills they have learned.

◆ On two whistle blows (or music stops), activity finishes. Each group dribbles back to its starting spot and follows a leader through a series of stretches and more ball handling. Observe and offer feedback; better still, join in!

Skill Practice

1. **Baseball Passing.** Demonstrate baseball pass technique, emphasizing the key teaching points. Have players partner off with each partner standing opposite each other, about 10 yards away. Practice using a baseball pass to send the ball to partner. *Variation:* Try a baseball bounce pass to your partner!

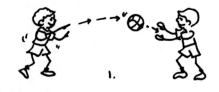

2. **Truck and Trailer Drill.** Partners line up alongside each other at each end of the basketball court, near free-throw line as shown. Player #1 on the inside holds the ball. On signal "Go!" both players move forward. Player #1 dribbles the ball to the center then baseball passes to player #2 who **cuts** at a 45-degree angle to the basket and attempts a layup. See diagram. Player #1 follows and rebounds the ball. Partners switch positions and join the opposite file. *Variation:* Run drill from both sides of the court.

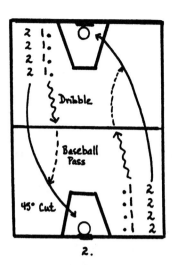

3. **Three-person Passing Weave.** Form groups of 3 players who position in wave formation at one end line of basketball court. Players in each group should be about 3 meters (10 feet) apart in a shallow V formation, with center player #1 holding the ball. Have players walk through the drill first, then jog, and finally at game speed. Remind all players to say to themselves, "Pass and go behind the player just passed to, then *cut* to center." Group changes positions each time weave is completed.

- **Pass and Weave Pattern:** Player #1 (middle player) passes to either side player; for example, player #2, as they move up the court. #1 then runs behind #2 and cuts back to center looking to receive the pass from #3; #2 player receives the ball and immediately passes across to #3. Player #2 then runs behind player #3 and cuts to center to receive a pass from #1 and so on.

4. **Five Passes.** Play game as for Lesson 31. Mark off several mini courts and play as a 3-on-3 game. Use a mini-ball or size 5 basketball. Have players partner up with an opposition player about the same size, and acknowledge each other with a "high 10." Object is to make 5 uninterrupted passes to score a point. Only the pivot step is allowed. Chest or bounce pass can be used. Now add the rules that at the most 3 dribble steps may be taken. Overhead, sidearm, and baseball can be used as well. *Variation:* Set up a "Five Passes" Tournament: A vs. B; C vs. D; A vs. C, B vs. D; A vs. D, B vs. C.

Cooling-down Activities/Games:

1. **"Bump."** Form groups of 6–8 at each hoop. Players position in a file behind the free-throw line. The first two players have a basketball. Object is for the player behind to try to "bump out" the player in front, by sinking the ball through the hoop before the front player does. First player shoots, then the second immediately after. Players must continue to shoot until they sink the ball or are bumped out. After scoring or being bumped each player retrieves his/her ball and hands it to the next player in line. Continue in this way. Once bumped out, players can watch while ball handling and cheer on the remaining players. *Variation:* Allow players to have two "lives." If possible, ability group the shooters, so that the better shooters are challenging each other; likewise for the weaker shooters.

"Bump!"

2. **Legends of the Day!**

Fit Think Idea:

Discuss how scoring in basketball is made up of 2- and 3-player plays such as the Truck 'n Trailer Drill. Create another 2- or 3-player play (such as Pass and Cut Drill, Two-on-One Drill).

Lesson 33:
Defense/Offense

Skill Builders: offensive and defensive skills, footwork, one-on-one guarding, ball dribbling and driving to basket to perform a layup in game-like situations

Expected Student Performance:

Performs proficiently in defensive and offensive footwork and handwork maneuvers.

Demonstrates competency in ball-dribbling skills and driving to the hoop while being guarded.

Willingly cooperates and integrates with other players.

Performs proficiently in aerobic, agility, and guarding demands.

Facility/Equipment Needed:

Gymnasium, undercover area, or outdoor basketball court

Cassette or CD player; popular music

1 basketball ("hands-on") per player or large playground ball

1 hoop per Dog 'n a Bone game

Cones or dome markers to set out corridors

Teaching Points:

"Balance" and "Quickness" are the most important physical skills a player requires to execute each fundamental movement skill in basketball. Balance and quickness are closely related to footwork which is basic to all fundamental movement skills. Developing good footwork is important to both offense and defense. Offensively, a well-balanced stance allows the player to move quickly, change direction, stop under control, and jump. Defensively, a player must be able to quickly move in any direction and change direction while maintaining balance.

Offense

Keep head over waist and back straight.

See the rim and the ball.

Position hands above the waist, elbows flexed, arms close to body.

Place feet at least shoulder-width apart, weight evenly distributed on balls of feet.

Flex knees to get low, so that you are ready to move.

Defense

- Keep head over waist to center gravity and back straight.
- Keep wide base with feet wider apart than shoulder-width and staggered, one foot in front of the other.
- Distribute weight evenly on balls of feet.
- Flex knees so body is low, ready to move in any direction.
- Position hands up above shoulders, elbows flexed.
- See opposition's midsection which will give movement direction.
- To guard a player on the ball side of the basket (called the **strong side**), take up a "denial stance"—one hand and one foot up in the passing lane.
- To guard a player on the opposite side of the basket (called the **weak or help side**), take a defensive stance several steps away so that you can see the ball and the player you are guarding.

Defensive Hand Positions

- One hand up on side of lead foot to pressure shooter; other hand at side to protect against passes.
- Both hands at waist level, palms up, to pressure dribbler (allows you to flick at ball with hand nearer the direction in which opponent is dribbling).
- Both hands above shoulders to force lob or bounce passes, to block shots, to rebound with two hands, to help prevent reaching fouls.

Focus Words:

- *Offense and Defense*

Warming-up Activities/Games:

Players start in a Home space inside the basketball court. Check for good spacing. On signal:

- **Change of Pace.** Change from fast running speed to slower, then quickly back to fast without changing basic running form.
- **Change of Direction.** Cut sharply from one direction to another without crossing your feet or losing balance!
- **Whistle.** Jump-stop with both feet landing simultaneously.
- **Rebound.** Jump up in the air to grab an imaginary ball, bring down into triple-threat position.
- **Forward Pivot.** Let chest lead the way as you turn, keeping weight on ball of pivot foot and stepping forward with non-pivot foot.

CHANGE OF DIRECTION   'REBOUND'

- **Reverse Turn (Drop Step).** Let your back lead the way to make a reverse turn, keeping weight on ball of pivot foot and dropping non-pivot foot back.

- **Defense.** Move backward, carefully changing hand positions.

- **Pitter-Patter.** Move feet quickly in place.

- **Hit the Deck.** Get onto all fours and do bent knee push-ups.

- **Periscope.** Stretch hamstrings from back lying position.

- **Arm Stretch.** Interlock fingers and stretch arms up, to each side, behind the back.

DROP STEP   DEFENSE   PITTER-PATTER

Skill Practice & Progressions:

1. **Hands in Defense Drill.** Players partner up with someone their own size and find a Home space. Partner A is the offensive player and holds a basketball in triple-threat position to start. Partner B is the defensive player who tries to take the ball off of A. Player A may use pivot steps only, taking the ball from high to low positions. Player B must not make any contact with Player A other than using hands to try to knock the ball away or steal the ball from Player A. Switch roles on signal. Emphasize safety.

2. **Corridor Drill Without Basketball.** (Use cone to mark off "corridors" that reach from sideline to the opposite sideline. Players pair off—one player is the defensive player; the other, the offensive player. Each pair is given a corridor to work in as shown.) Starting at one sideline, offensive player moves in a zigzag fashion (1-2-3 count, change direction) toward opposite sideline. Defensive player moves backwards, using shuffle steps, drop-stepping lead foot, and keeping always just in front of offense. Players switch roles once they reach the opposite sideline. Remind defense to focus on midsection of offensive player and keep hands up. Observe defensive movement and offer feedback.

2.

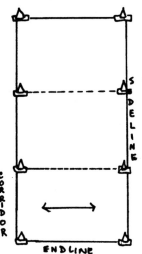

CORRIDOR

SIDELINE

ENDLINE

3.   **Corridor Drill with Basketball.** Offensive player dribbles ball down corridor to opposite sideline. Dribble with a 1-2-3 count, crossover dribble to other side, protecting ball. Remind dribbler not to turn back into defensive player while dribbling ball, but keep movement forward! Defensive player positions one hand up; one hand down, adjusting hands to ball side, as offensive player changes dribble hand. Defensive player offers "passive defense," not trying to take the ball away. Remind defensive player to keep moving backwards, keeping arm's reach away. *Variation:* On signal "Mingle" find new partners and continue. *Friendly Competition:* Offensive players try to get to opposite sideline, while defensive player is allowed to try to take ball "legally" off offensive player (that is, no body contact allowed!)

3.

4.   **One-on-one Layup Drill.** (Set up one offensive file of players and one defensive file of players on the right-hand side of basketball key, starting at center line, as shown. Use this setup in the other half of the court to have two drills going on simultaneously.) Both players must have a foot "tagged up" at center line. Defensive player gives the "Go!" signal for offensive player to drive to the basket (dribble basketball to hoop to execute a layup). Defensive player runs to get in front of offensive player to get good defensive position to prevent offensive player from scoring a layup. Both players try to get the rebound, but no more shots are taken. Players then switch files and the next two continue the drill.

Cooling-down Activities/Games:

1.   **Dog 'n a Bone Game.** (For each game have two teams of no more than 6 players number off and face each other on opposite lines as shown. Place a basketball in a hoop in the middle between the two groups. Each game is played in one half of the basketball court.) On signal "2's!" number 2's run to the hoop. Player to get possession of the ball is on the offense and tries to score a basket. Other player is the defensive player and tries to get into good defensive position to prevent scoring. Player succeeding earns a point for his/her team. Leaders keep track of score. Continue in this way until everyone has had a turn or after a set time. *Variation:* Set up a new game with different teams

challenging each other; for example, Round One: Team A vs. Team B, and Team C vs. Team D; Round Two: Team A vs. Team C, and Team B vs. Team D; and Round Three: Team A vs. Team D, and Team B vs. Team C.

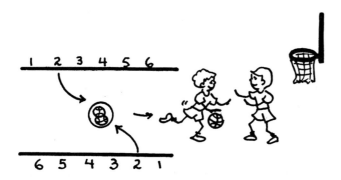

2. **Legends of the Day!**

Homework Ideas:

◆ Write a two-page report about a **basketball player** of your choice. Remember to include a bibliography of your research resources.

◆ Photocopy the Basketball Court Diagram (see the Appendix) and have players mark key lines and player positions for a jump ball.

Lesson 34:
Rebounding/Blocking Out

Skill Builders: introduce rebounding and blocking out, extend offensive and defensive positioning around keyway, hand–eye coordination, tracking, footwork and bodywork, leg strength, partner play, keyway play

Expected Student Performance:

◆ Demonstrates competency in rebounding and blocking out offensively and defensively.

◆ Demonstrates proficiency in strength, footwork, and bodywork demands.

◆ Willingly cooperates and integrates with other players.

Facility/Equipment Needed:

◆ Gymnasium, undercover area, or outdoor basketball court

◆ 1 basketball ("hands-on") per player or large playground ball

Teaching Points:

Successful team play depends on both offensive and defensive rebounding. The team that controls the backboards usually controls the game! Quickness and balance, jumping height and explosiveness, muscular endurance and strength, timing and positioning ("wanting the ball") are important factors to being an effective rebounder.

Defensive Rebounding

Two strategies for defensive rebounding:

◆ Blocking out or boxing out opponent's path to ball by pivoting your back to opponent's chest, then going for the ball, **or**

◆ Stepping in opponent's path and going for the ball.

Front Turn Defensive Rebounding Method: (best for blocking out the shooter)

◆ See ball and opponent.

◆ Take a defensive stance.

◆ Keep hand up in passing land.

◆ Front pivot on back foot.

◆ Step into shooter.

◆ Feel your back near opponent's chest.

◆ Keep a wide base and hands up.

◆ Go for the ball and catch with two hands.

◆ Spread eagle and protect ball in front of forehead.

◆ Land in a balanced stance.

Reverse Turn Defensive Rebounding

◆   See ball and opponent.

◆   Take a defensive stance.

◆   Keep hand up in passing land.

◆   Watch opponent's cut.

◆   Reverse pivot on foot closer to direction opponent is cutting in.

◆   Drop other foot back.

◆   Feel your back near opponent's chest.

◆   Keep a wide base and hands up.

◆   Go for the ball and catch with two hands.

◆   Spread eagle and protect ball in front of forehead.

◆   Land in a balanced stance.

Reverse Turn Defensive Rebounding Method (use when defending a player without the ball or off the ball)

◆   See ball and opponent.

◆   After the shot, first observe opponent's cut.

◆   Reverse pivot on foot closer to opponent's cut.

◆   Drop other foot back and away from opponent's cut.

◆   Go for the rebound.

Offensive Rebounding

◆   See ball and opponent.

◆   Take an offensive stance.

◆   When opponent front turns, cut straight by.

◆   Keep hands up and go for the ball.

◆   Catch ball with two hands.

◆   Spread eagle and protect ball in front of forehead.

◆   Land in a balanced stance.

Focus Word:

●   *Keyway* (See Basketball Court diagram in the Appendix.)

Warming-up Activities and Games:

1. **Rope Jumping Warm-up.** (Excellent activity for developing leg strength and power.) Single-rope jump to a steady beat for 1–3 minutes. Stretch during the breaks. Check for good spacing. Do Pepper Jumps for 30 seconds.

2. **Hoop Jumping.** One partner holds the hoop while the other partner jumps into it from a two-foot takeoff. Switch roles.

Skill Practice & Progressions:

1. Demonstrate key points for *offensive rebounding*. Stand in your Home space. Toss the ball upwards. Try to grab it in both hands at the height of your jump. Land in good rebounding position. Repeat. Can you catch the ball before your feet touch the ground?

2. **Wall Rebounding.** Stand facing a wall about 2 giant steps away. Practice shooting technique. Practice rebounding the ball off the wall.

3. **Hoop Rebounding.** Shoot the ball from marked positions around the keyway. Follow your shot to get the rebound and make a second shot.

4. **Blocking Out (Front and Reverse Turns).** (Demonstrate front turn to block out a shooter using the key teaching points.) Players partner up, with one player pantomiming the shooting action; the other player being the defensive player and blocking out the shooter. Shooter stands facing the hoop just outside the keyway; defensive player is about arm's length away just inside the keyway. Take turns practicing footwork and bodywork.

5. Shooter shoots a basketball and tries to follow shot to hoop to get the rebound; blocker tries to block out shooter's path to the basket and get the rebound. After 3 attempts, shooter and blocker change roles.

6. Demonstrate the key points for *reverse turn blocking out* when defending a player without the ball or off the ball. Partner practice the footwork and bodywork.

7. **Keyway Rebounding.** Divide the class into teams of 5. One team is offense; other team is the defense. Each team consists of 2 guards, 2 forwards, and 1 center. Use one keyway to demonstrate how the teams position around the keyway for a free throw to be taken as shown. A shooter from the offensive team takes a free throw. Keyway players react with offensive or defensive rebounding. If an offensive player gets the rebound, he/she tries to score. If a defensive player gets the rebound, he/she tries to dribble out to the side, then pass the ball to his/her teammate who moves out to the side from the 3-point semi-circle. This is called the outlet pass!

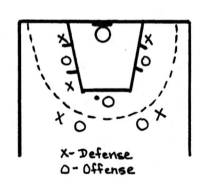

X– Defense
O– Offense

Cooling-down Activities/Games:

1. "Bump" as for Lesson 32, only allow one "life" before being out of the game.
2. **Legends of the Day!**

Fit Think Idea:

◆ Watch a basketball game in action—either live or on TV. Observe players rebounding for the ball and blocking out both offensively and defensively. Observe the outlet pass being executed.

◆ Check the local newspapers for the local as well as college and national Basketball League results. Check the website of your favorite basketball team.

Lesson 35:
Skill Builder Stations

Skill Builders: basketball fundamental skills of passing, speed dribbling, shooting, rebounding, modified team play, arm and leg strength, rhythm sense, fair play and cooperation

Expected Student Performance:

◆ Demonstrates competency in performing fundamental basketball skills.

◆ Demonstrates proficiency in strength tasks and sense of rhythm.

◆ Willingly cooperates and integrates with other class and team members.

◆ Demonstrates fair play and good sportsmanship.

Facility/Equipment Needed:

◆ Gymnasium, undercover area, or outdoor basketball court

◆ Cassette or CD player; station signs

◆ Station #1: 1–2 small or medium sized medicine ball(s)

◆ Station #2: several cone markers and other obstacles to create course

◆ Station #3: basketball keyway, 3 basketballs

◆ Station #4: 3–6 basketballs, free-throw line, basketball hoop

◆ Station #5: backboard and 1 #5 or mini basketball

◆ Station #6: 6 scooter boards, 2 large garbage bins, 1 #5 or mini basketball

◆ Station #7: 3 Fling-it™ Nets

◆ Station #8: 2 sets of Jump Bands or 4 double ropes

Skill Builder Basketball Station Ideas:

Station #1: Medicine Ball Pass. A medicine ball is a heavy leather ball about the size of a basketball and is used to develop finger, wrist, and arm strength in passing. Players stand in a circle and pass the ball carefully across the circle to another player. If two medicine balls are available, have players stand in triangle formation.

Station #2: Speed Dribble. Players, in turn, dribble through the course as quickly as possible, but in control. Record times.

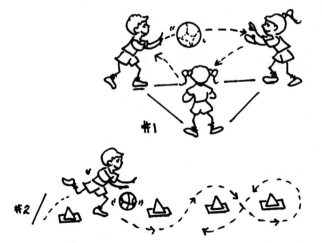

Station #3: Free-throw. (Refer to Lesson 30.) Players take free throws, one after the other, keeping track of total baskets scored.

Station #4: Layup/Rebound. (Refer to Lesson 30.) Players split into 2 lines, layup line and rebound line, as shown. Rebounders try to time the layup to grab the ball and then dribble on the outside to the layup line. After performing the layup, player runs on the outside to join the rebound line.

Station #5: Rebound Backboard Drill. Players stand in a long file facing one side of the backboard. First player has a ball and uses two hands to send the ball to the backboard. Next player in line tries to time the rebound and send the ball back up to the backboard, before landing. After doing so, the player joins the end of the file.

Station #6: 3-on-3 Scooter Basketball. Set up a small rectangular court. Use a large garbage bin as the goal or lowered basketball hoop. Play a 3-on-3 game with players sitting on scooter boards. Allow, at the most, 5 traveling steps before passing or shooting.

Station #7: Cooperative Fling-it™ Play. (Refer to Lesson 25, Station #5.) One pair sends an object into another pair's Fling-it™ Net; or all pairs send an object at the same time. Watch the fun!

Station #8: Jump Band Play (or Double Dutch Rope Play). (Refer to Lesson 7.)

JUMP BANDS

Lesson 36:
Lead-up and Modified Games

Skill Builders: applying fundamental basketball skills in game situations, court awareness, positional play, learning rules of the game, team play, fair play

Expected Student Performance:

◆ Performs proficiently in the basic fundamental skills of basketball in a game-like situation.

◆ Demonstrates proficiency in guarding, positional play, understanding and performing rules.

◆ Willingly cooperates and integrates with other team members in fair play.

◆ Meets fitness demands of aerobic endurance, arm/leg strength, speed, agility, alertness.

Facility/Equipment Needed:

◆ Gymnasium, undercover area, or outdoor basketball court

◆ For "Basketball Golf"—7 poly spots or dome markers, basketball keyway and hoop, size 5–6 basketball, basketball golf score card

◆ For each "Bucket Ball" game, 1 mini basketball, 2 buckets (small bin, box, or large cone), 4–6 sets of bibs, cone markers

◆ For "21," half-court and sideline basketball games use size 5 or 6 balls

Teaching Points:

The Player Positions. In class time, explain and illustrate the basketball playing positions:

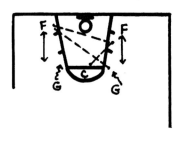

◆ **Center:** Usually the tallest player who positions around the keyway moving from low to mid to high post.

◆ **2 Forwards:** Right forward and left forward who travel down right or left side respectively of the court, and play to the sides of the basket near the key area and out toward the sideline along the baseline.

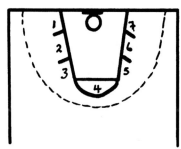

◆ **2 Guards:** Usually are quick and the best ball controllers who play primarily at the perimeter or away from the basket.

Focus Words:

● *Tip-Off (Jump Ball) and Team Play*

Lead-up Games:

1. **Basketball Golf.** Each partner must make the shot at each of 7 designated spots ("holes") on the basketball key lines ("golf course") before moving to the next spot. Which partner can complete the course in the fewer number of shots? Keep track of shots on a basketball golf score card.

2. **"21."** Divide class into groups of 3–5 with one basketball per group. Ideally position two groups at a keyway and demonstrate how players will line up. First player from each group shoots, follows his/her shot to try to grab the rebound. If the shot goes through the hoop and shooter is able to grab the ball before it touches the ground, shooter scores 2 points and gets to take a second "bank" (off the glass) shot for 1 point, for a possible total of 3 points. If the shot does goes through the hoop but shooter is unable to get the rebound before the ball hits the floor, then shooter is not allowed to take a second shot, and must collect the ball and pass it to the next team player. If shooter misses first shot, and gets rebound, a second shot for 1 point can be attempted. First team to reach 21 points wins.

   ◆ Observe teams. Try to balance them out so that one team does not dominate.

Modified Games:

1. **Bucket Ball.** For each game, depending upon the number of indoor or outdoor basketball courts that are available per game, create two teams of 5–6 with one opposing team wearing bibs. The team's goalie stands behind the opposition's end line and holds a "bucket" (small bin, box, or upturned large cone) in which a mini basketball must be caught in order to score a goal. Each game (and after a goal has been scored) begins with a *jump ball.* Players on opposing teams find someone their own size to guard, give high-10's to the opposition player, then position around a center jump ball circle as shown, with two opposing players standing in the jump circle and facing their respective goalies. This is called "the clock" positioning. Another player (from either team) tosses a mini basketball up between the two opposing players. Each player jumps up and tries to tip the ball to a teammate. Emphasize that the two center players must jump straight up—not breaking the vertical line between them. The ball is then "in play" and the rule of 3 goes into effect:

   - A player is allowed to bounce the ball, at the most, 3 times before passing or attempting to score.
   - A team must complete 3 consecutive passes before attempting to score in the opposition's half.
   - A player is allowed 3 seconds to hold the ball before passing or attempting to score or before the guarding player (and only this player) can try to take the ball away from this opposition player. Emphasize that no body contact is allowed. For each jump ball that takes place, have two different opposing players perform the tip-off. *Variations:*
   - As team play improves, increase the passing to 4 consecutive passes.

- Goalie positions in the opposition's keyway, and only the goalie is allowed in this area.

- Increase the size of the ball to a size 5 basketball.

- Designate court positions: 1 center, 2 forwards, and 2 guards. Allow players to switch positions on your signal.

JUMP-BALL / 'THE CLOCK'

2. **Half-court 3-on-3 Basketball.** Divide the class into teams of 3–4 and give each team a name, number, or letter. Assign two teams to a half court and have each team if possible wear a different set of colored bibs. Each game is played similar to regulation basketball rules (see the Appendix), but in a half court and only one hoop is used. Thus, two games can be going on at the same time in one basketball court. Substitute players (or extra, nonparticipating players) can be junior "referees" who reinforce the rules when not playing. Before each game starts, players must find an opposition player about their own size to guard. Establish a protocol to start each game; for example, center defensive player hands the ball to his/her offensive player who must pass the ball to another teammate to put it into play. If the offensive team scores, they keep possession of the ball and start again as just described. If the defensive team gets possession of the ball, they must pass or dribble the ball out to the 3-point circle, then they become the offensive team.

- Play 3-on-3 or 4-on-4 five-minute games, then set up a new game.

- Set up a half-court tournament. (Refer to the Appendix for a sample tournament draw.)

- If possible, adjust the height of the basketball hoop from the ground: suggest 8 feet for grade 4; 9 feet for grade 5; 10 feet for grade 6.

- Adjust the size of the ball: suggest size 5 for grade 4; size 6 for grades 5–6.

- Adjust the free-throw line distance (using floor tape): suggest 17 feet for grade 4; 18 feet for grades 5–6.

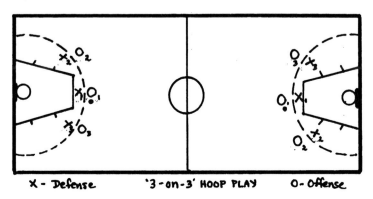

X - Defense   '3-on-3' HOOP PLAY   O - Offense

3. **Sideline Basketball.** Ideally for each sideline basketball game, create two even court teams of 5 players per team, and two sideline teams of 5 players per team: Team A1 vs. Team B1 start in "clock" position for the jump-off on the court; Team A2 players alternate with Team B2 players and stand in hoops on the sidelines as shown. Each court team and corresponding sideline team wears bibs. Court players find an opposing player who is about their size to guard. Game begins with a jump-ball at center by two opposing players. Play regulation rules (see the Appendix) except court players are allowed to dribble the ball, at the most, 5 times, then must pass to a sideline player on their team. An opposing sideline player can try to intercept a poorly thrown pass but is not allowed to step outside of his/her hoop. Encourage players to move to open spaces to get a good position for a pass. After a certain time (for example, every 5 minutes), sideline and court players change roles and a new game is started once again with a jump-ball at center.

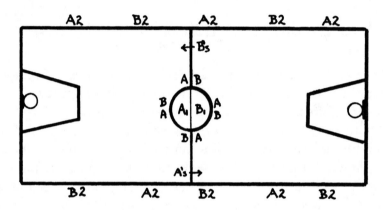

4. **Full-Court Game.** See the Appendix for the rules of the game, court diagram, and tournament draws. Several suggestions for modifying the game are included in the introduction and have also been included in this lesson.

Cooling-down Activity:

Legends of the Day!

Lesson 37:
Stick-handling Skills

Skill Builders: grip and dribbling technique, stick-handling, hand–eye coordination, footwork, cooperation

Expected Student Performance:

◆ Demonstrates competency in stick-handling and dribbling techniques.

◆ Willingly cooperates and integrates with other class and team members.

◆ Demonstrates proficiency in aerobic, strength and flexibility, ability/alertness demands.

Facility/Equipment Required:

◆ Gymnasium or smooth-surfaced outdoor playing area

◆ 1 plastic hockey stick and puck per player

◆ Obstacles such as cones, hoops, chairs

Teaching Points:

The Grip

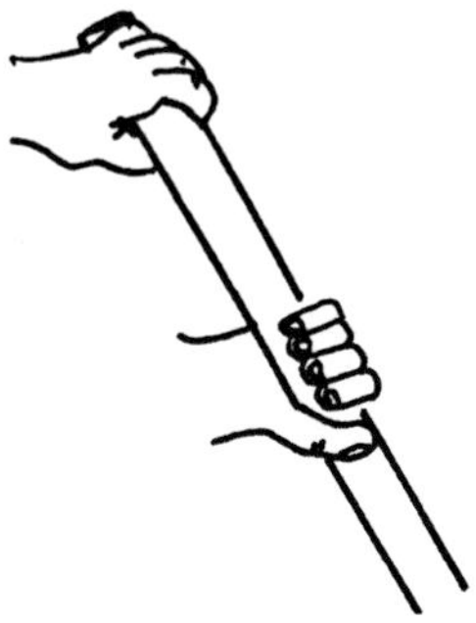

◆ Place one hand (usually left hand for right-hander) on top of stick as if shaking hands with it.

◆ Place other hand 10–12 inches (25–30 cm) below the first hand.

◆ Point thumbs toward the blade of the stick.

Dribbling

◆ Dribble by moving puck forward with short quick, controlled taps.

◆ Keep the puck 18–24 inches (48–60 cm) out in front.

Stick-handling

◆ Move the puck from side to side to make quick changes of direction.

◆ Try to "feel" the puck on the blade, keeping it in the middle of the blade.

Carrying the Puck

◆ Move the puck along the floor, keeping it in contact with only one side of the blade.

Focus Word:

● *Stick-handling*

Warming-up Activity/Game:

Aerobic Feet. Use popular music with a steady 4/4 beat. Everyone finds a Home space and walks in place to start, then changes motion on signal:

- *Jogging/Sprinting/Slide-stepping*
- *Side Kicks/Front Kicks/Back Kicks*
- *Prancing in place*
- *Side Jumps/Scissors Jumps/Cross-jumps*
- *Marching in place*
- *Grapevine Step/Pitter-patter*
- *Repeat above sequence.*

Skill Practice & Progressions:

1. Review and demonstrate grip technique. Reverse hands on stick and see which way feels more comfortable. Demonstrate dribbling and stick-handling techniques. Emphasize safety at all times!

2. Dribble puck along the lines of the floor or in a straight line. On whistle signal, change direction. Heads up! Move into open spaces.

3. Dribble puck, stick-handling puck as players move in and out of each other. Stick-handle in place (dribbling puck from side to other side of blade) on whistle signal.

4. **Obstacle Dribble.** Scatter several obstacles, such as cones, hoops, chairs, around the play area. Stick-handle puck in and around the obstacles, around the chairs or benches; in and out of cone markers or hoops, through the chair legs.

5. **Zigzag Relay.** Form teams of 3–4 and have each team stand in file formation behind a start line facing a column of 5 cones spaced 2 yards apart. On signal "Stick-Handle," each player in turn dribbles puck in and around the cone markers, then dribbles directly back to file to give the puck to the next player in line. Relay ends when everyone has had 3 turns. *Variation:* Form groups of 4 in shuttle formations and repeat zigzag relay.

6. **Hockey Pirates.** Select one-third of the class to be the Hockey Pirates who each have a stick and stand in the center of the play area to start. The remaining free players each have a stick and puck, and scatter throughout the play area. On signal "Hockey Pirates," the Pirates try to stick-handle the puck away from free players who then become Pirates, while the successful Pirate becomes a free player. Emphasize heads-up at all times, no body contact allowed, and fair play—cannot step on puck or pin it against a wall.

Cooling-down Activities/Games:

1. **Hockey Stick Stretches.** Check for good spacing.
   - *Overhead Stretch*
   - *Side Stretch*
   - *Behind-the-back Stretch*
   - *Hamstring Stretch*
   - *Sprinter Stretch*

2. **Legends of the Day!**

Fit Think Idea:

Discuss the importance of "safety" in hockey play and "fair play." What makes hockey such a good aerobic activity? Why is it sometimes called a "glide" sport?

Lesson 38:
Shooting and Goalkeeping

Skill Builders: wrist and sweep shot technique, goalkeeping, hand–eye coordination, tracking, alertness, cooperation

Expected Student Performance:

◆ Demonstrates competency in executing a wrist shot and sweep shot.

◆ Demonstrate proficiency in goalkeeping skills, tracking the puck, and alertness.

◆ Willingly cooperates and integrates with other class and team members.

◆ Meets fitness demands of aerobic warm-up activity, strength, and alertness/reaction.

Facility/Equipment Needed:

◆ Gymnasium or smooth-surfaced outdoor playing area

◆ 1 plastic hockey stick and puck per player

◆ 2 cones per goalie area

Teaching Points:

Shooting—Wrist Shot

◆ Use the wrist shot for short distances and quick execution.

◆ Check the puck, then concentrate on the target.

◆ Snap the wrists to propel the puck forward to the target.

◆ Keep both the backswing and follow-through short and low.

Sweep Shot

◆ Push the puck toward the goal. Do not flex the wrist.

◆ Ensure the puck is touching the blade before shooting.

◆ Follow-through low.

↑ GOALIE CREASE

Goalkeeping

◆ Keep in ready position, lightly crouched holding stick in front of body with one hand.

◆ Use other hand to catch or knock puck away.

◆ Watch the puck at all times.

◆ Place stick squarely in front of puck; use feet, legs, and body to stop puck.

◆ Clear puck by sweeping it or kicking it to the side.

Focus Word:

◆ High-sticking

Warming-up Activity/Game:

Fortune Cookie. (See the Appendix for sample reproducible cards.) Scatter a set of Fortune Cookie cards in the center of the hockey play area. Have players jog around the perimeter of the play area. On signal "Fortune Cookie," everyone jogs in place. Choose a player to run into the middle and select a "fortune cookie" that he/she reads out to the class. Teacher repeats this to ensure everyone has heard. Players perform the activity, then continue to jog (clockwise or counterclockwise) around the play area. Activity continues in this way until a warm-up effect is well observed.

Skill Practice & Progressions:

1. Demonstrate the wrist shot. Have players practice shooting at a wall. Discuss the danger of high-sticking or bringing the stick up too high when shooting and following through.

2. Demonstrate the sweep shot. Practice at the wall. Emphasize a low follow-through.

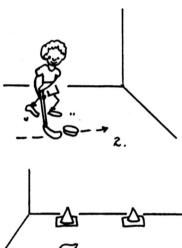

3. Partners set up mini-goals around the perimeter of the gym using 2 cone makers per pair as shown. Each partner, in turn, takes 2 shots to send the puck between the 2 cone markers and score a goal. Use the wrist shot for first shot, then the sweep shot for the second attempt. Experiment with cones 2 giant steps apart and 15 feet away, then gradually increase the shooting distance and narrow the goal "mouth" to 1 giant step apart. Partner must retrieve both pucks and send them to waiting partner.

4. Demonstrate goalie ready position and action. Players pantomime the action.

5. **Goalkeeping Drill.** Use the same set-up as for activity 3. One partner is the shooter; the other partner is the goalkeeper. Shooter takes 5 shots, then the two partners switch roles. Keep score.

6. **Team Shoot-Out.** Divide the class into 4 teams: A, B, C, D. Teams A and D are the goalie teams and position in front of each end line of a basketball court or marked-out play area. Teams B and C are the shooting teams and position in each half of the play area, facing a goalie team as shown. Each shooting team has 3 pucks. Goalie team tries to prevent the shooting team from scoring goals. The captain of each shooting team keeps track of the goals scored in a certain time limit; then the

goalie and shooting team exchange places. *Variations:*

- Increase the number of pucks used.
- Adjust the shooting distance to the ability level of the class or ability group of the teams, so that the weaker shooters have a shorter shooting distance to try to score.

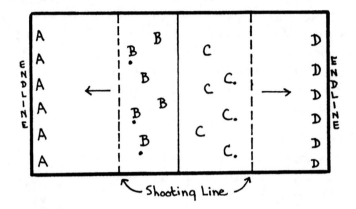

Shooting Line

Cooling-down Activities/Games:

1. Play "Team Gotcha." (See Lesson 7 for description.) Which team can score the most number of "Gotchas" each round?

2. **Legends of the Day!**

In Class Idea:

With a partner, create 5 Fortune Cookie activities that can be added to "Fortune Cookie" warm-up. Include two strength activities for upper body; two strength activities for lower body; one aerobic activity; and diagrams as needed. Put your activities on the card provided.

Lesson 39: Passing

Skill Builders: passing and receiving skills, tracking, stick-handling with control in game situations, shooting, alertness, cooperation

Expected Student Performance:

◆ Demonstrates competence and confidence in passing and receiving the puck.

◆ Willingly cooperates and integrates with other class and team members.

◆ Demonstrates proficiency in aerobic, strength, and agility/alertness demands.

Facility/Equipment Needed:

◆ Gymnasium or smooth-surfaced outdoor playing area

◆ 1 plastic hockey stick and puck per player

◆ 2 cones for goals, wall targets

Teaching Points:

Passing the Puck

◆ Keep your stick blade upright and use a smooth sweeping motion.

◆ Keep the backswing and follow-through low.

◆ Pass slightly ahead of the receiver (lead pass).

Receiving the Puck

◆ Track the puck as it comes toward you.

◆ Tilt the blade of the stick over the puck to gently trap it.

◆ Cushion the pass by giving with your stick blade at the moment of impact.

Receiving the Puck

Focus Word:

● *Cross-Checking/Slashing (See rules in the Appendix.)*

Warming-up Activity/Game:

Hockey Team Pirates. Divide the class into 2 teams, identified by the color of the stick each team player has. Players of one team, the "Stick-Handlers," each have a puck. Players of the other team, the "Pirates," try to capture as many pucks as they can before the whistle blows to stop the play. The number of pucks captured are counted and a score recorded. The two teams switch roles and the game continues. Emphasize heads-up and no body contact allowed. A player whose puck was captured can try to recapture a puck from a Pirate. *Variation:* Form 4 teams and let each team in turn be the Pirate Team who is given a certain time limit to try to capture as many pucks as possible.

Skill Practice & Progressions:

1. Partners, in stationary position, spaced 5 giant steps apart, practice passing the puck back and forth to each other. Emphasize getting the puck under control before passing it back to partner.

2. **Pepper Passes.** How many passes can be made in a certain time limit?

3. One partner stays stationary and sends a lead pass to the moving partner.

4. Partners move the length of the play area passing the puck to each other as shown.

5. **Hot Dog Passing.** Pass two pucks to each other at the same time.

6. **Pass and Shoot.** One partner passes the ball to the other partner who shoots the ball at a wall target or through a goal formed by 2 cones. Switch roles after 5 passes.

7. **Box and One.** Form groups of 5 with each group of 5 arranging in a square formation and one player in the center of the square. Four square players try to pass the puck to each other so that the center player cannot intercept it. If the center player does intercept the pass, then that player making the pass must take the place of the center player. If 5 unintercepted passes are made, then a new player comes into the center. Everyone should have a turn at being in the center. *Variation:* Repeat the above activities using a deck ring instead of a puck.

8. **Battle Puck.** Divide the class into teams of 8 and have each team number off from 1 to 8. Everyone has a hockey stick. For each game, have 2 teams position on a sideline, facing each other as shown. A puck is placed in the middle between the two teams. Teacher calls out a number. Players with that number run to the middle to try to gain possession of the puck, and score a goal by shooting the puck at the opposition's sideline players (who act as goalies). After a goal has been scored or the puck is fielded by one of the sideline players, the puck is returned to the middle and a new number is

called. Continue until all the numbers have been called. Have teams challenge a different team and play again. *Variations:*

- Call two numbers at a time. One pass must be made before a team can attempt to score.
- Use a deck ring instead of a puck.

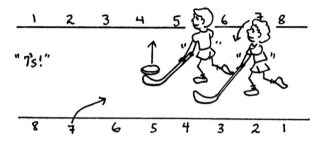

Cooling-down Activities/Games:

1. **Orbit Ball.** Use large beach balls or balloon balls for this activity. Divide the class into two teams. Players of one team lie on backs in "Dead Bug" position with feet and hands in the air. Second team players form a large circle around these players, spacing themselves arm's length apart. Circle team sends the ball into orbit. Middle players must keep it from touching the ground by using feet and hands to gently tap it upwards. Circle players help by keeping the ball from going out-of-bounds. After a certain time, switch roles. *Variation:* Divide the class into 4 teams and have two games going at the same time.

2. **Legends of the Day!**

Homework Idea:

If in season, watch an ice hockey game on TV or a live game in action. Observe the players' positioning, the goalies in action, and the conduct of the game. What penalties occurred and what was the consequence?

Lesson 40:
Facing-off/Offense & Defense

Skill Builders: facing-off, defensive and offensive play, player positions, stick-handling, dribbling, passing, shooting, goal-keeping in a game situation, teamwork, concentration

Expected Student Performance:

◆ Demonstrates proficiency in performing a face-off, and applying floor hockey skills in a game situation.

◆ Willingly cooperates and integrates with other class and team members.

◆ Demonstrates good understanding of player positions, and defensive and offensive play.

◆ Meets aerobic fitness and strength, and concentration demands.

Facility/Equipment Needed:

◆ Gymnasium or smooth-surfaced outdoor playing area

◆ 1 plastic hockey stick per player

◆ 1 hockey puck per group of 3

◆ 2 hockey goalie nets or large cone markers per game

◆ 1 hockey puck or ball per game

Teaching Points:

Playing Offense

◆ Be a team player and team maker, not a "solo" player.

◆ Play heads-up, following the path of the puck at all times.

◆ Move to open spaces when dribbling the puck and pass to the open teammate who is in a better position to score.

◆ Use short, quick passes to move the puck down the floor to avoid interception by the opposition.

◆ Use a lead pass, passing the puck ahead of the receiver, so that he/she can continue to run forward.

◆ Keep the backswing and follow-through low when shooting the puck.

Playing Defense

◆ Always face the puck, never turning your back toward the action or facing your own goal.

◆ Keep the stick below the waist when cross-checking.

◆ Avoid body contact with an opponent when trying to get possession of the puck.

◆ Stay on your assigned player when he/she is not in possession of the puck instead of trying to go after the puck.

Player Positions

◆ 1 Center—moves the entire length of the floor or field playing both offense and defense.

◆ 2 Forwards—play offense from the centerline forward.

◆ 2 Guards—play defense from the centerline back and try to pass to the center to get the puck back into offensive play.

◆ 1 Goalie—defends the goal area, moving around a goalie crease or goal box, and clearing the puck to the side away from the front of the net so that the guards can get the puck back into offensive play.

Focus Words:

● *Face-off, Defense, Offense*

Warming-up Activity/Game:

Fortune Cookie. Warm-up, using ideas generated from the "In Class Idea" in Lesson 38. Observe the players in action until a warm-up effect is achieved. Suggest 5–8 minutes.

Skill Practice & Progressions:

1. **Practice the Face-off.** Form groups of 3, and number off 1, 2, 3. Collect a puck for each group, and find a free space to practice. Players 1 and 2 stand facing each other about stick-length apart with stick blades resting on the floor and almost touching. Player 3 drops the puck between the two players. Each player immediately tries to gain control of the puck. After 3 face-offs, change roles until everyone has had a turn dropping the puck. *Variation:* Puck is positioned on the floor between the two sticks. Third player signals "Play" to start the action or a whistle is blown.

2. Review player positions and the role of each position.

3. Review and demonstrate defensive and offensive play. (Refer to teaching points.)

4. **Minky (3-on-3 Floor Hockey Game).** Form groups of 4. Mark out enough mini-rinks to accommodate everyone involved in a 3-on-3 game. For example, for a class of 32 players, mark out 4 mini-rinks, with 2 groups of 4 assigned to each rink. Benches turned on their sides can be used to create the side boundaries for the inside rinks. Use the walls of the gym to create the outside boundaries. If possible, clear everything away from the walls so that they can be used in the game. Game begins with a face-off at center. Players are allowed, at the most, 5 traveling steps before passing the puck. Strongly emphasize safe play—no high sticking, slashing, or cross-checking allowed. Encourage all players to take a turn at goal-keeping or have players change positions after each goal is scored. *Variation:* Set up a Minky tournament. (Refer to the Appendix for tournament draws.)

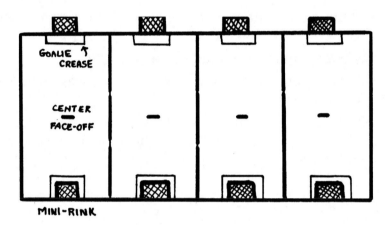

MINI-RINK

Cooling-down Activities/Games:

1. **Pink Panther.** (See Lesson 8.) Divide the class into 2 teams and select 3 players to be the "Pink Panthers" for each group. Which group can end up with more players lasting the length of the Pink Panther theme song without "waking up"?

2. **Legends of the Day!**

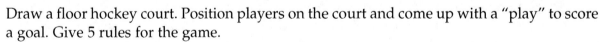

Homework Idea:

Draw a floor hockey court. Position players on the court and come up with a "play" to score a goal. Give 5 rules for the game.

Lesson 41:
Skill Builder Stations

Skill Builders: fundamental stick-handling, dribbling, shooting skills, goal-keeping, hand–eye coordination, 3-on-3 team play, cooperation

Expected Student Performance:

Demonstrates competency in performing fundamental floor hockey skills and applying in 3-on-3 games.

Willingly cooperates and integrates with other class and team members.

Demonstrates proficiency in offensive and defensive positional play and good sportsmanship.

Facility/Equipment Needed:

Gymnasium or smooth-surfaced outdoor playing area

Cassette or CD player; station signs

Station #1: 6 deck rings; 12 skittles, cones, or plastic jugs; 6 dome cone markers

Station #2: several large cone markers and other obstacles to create speed course

Station #3: 2 hockey nets, 6 hockey sticks, 6 pucks, 6 dome markers

Station #4: 2 large cones, floor tape, 6 scooter boards, 6 hockey sticks, 1 soft hockey puck

Station #5: 1 long rope, 2 floor posts (such as badminton posts), floor tape, large balloon ball

Station #6: 1 deck ring, 1 dowel stick per player, 2 sets of bibs, floor tape, 4 large cones

Skill Builder Station Ideas:

Station #1: Hockey Bowling. Each player, in turn, uses a 3-foot (1-meter) dowel stick (1-inch diameter) to propel 3 deck rings at a set of 6 skittles (plastic jugs, small cones) positioned as shown. Score according to the number of skittles knocked over. Vary the shooting distance to accommodate for different ability levels. Set up two mini-stations if possible.

Station #2: Speed Stick Dribble. Each player, in turn, dribbles through the course as quickly as possible. Record score each time.

Station #3: Goal-Keeping and Scoring. Set up two mini-stations using hockey nets and dome markers for scoring distances. Each player takes 3 shots from indicated spots to score. Goal-keeper tries to prevent a score.

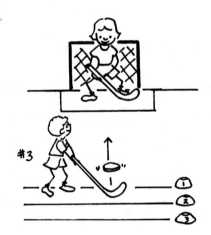

Station #4: Scooter Hockey Play. Set up a mini-hockey game in a small rectangular area, with cone markers and floor tape to mark off the goal box and goal net. Play a 3-on-3 game. Players sit on scooter boards and use mini-hockey sticks and soft hockey puck to score a goal. No goalies in this game!

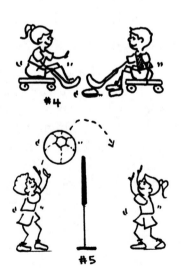

Station #5: 3-on-3 Balloon Ball. Use a rope positioned about head height and fastened between two poles to create the net. Three players are on each side and are allowed, at the most, 3 hits to send the ball over to the opposition's side. A player cannot hit the ball twice in a row. Take turns serving the ball into play from a taped mark on the floor.

Station #6: 3-on-3 Deck Ring Hockey. Use a deck ring propelled with a dowel stick to score goals. One goalie and two field players for each team can interchange positions. Only 3–5 traveling steps are allowed before the deck ring must be passed off or an attempt to score occurs. Emphasize absolutely no body contact or high-sticking. Keep the stick low along the floor to pass! A player guards only his/her player determined at the start of the game. Goal area and goal box need to be marked out.

Cooling-down Activity:

Legends of the Day!

Lesson 42:
Lead-up and Modified Games

Skill Builders: floor hockey fundamentals, court awareness and player positioning, offensive and defensive play, team play, fair play

Expected Student Performance:

◆ Demonstrates competency in performing fundamental floor hockey skills and applying in lead-up and modified games.

◆ Willingly cooperates and integrates with other class and team members.

◆ Demonstrates proficiency in offensive and defensive positional play and good sportsmanship.

Facility/Equipment Needed:

◆ Gymnasium or smooth-surfaced outdoor playing area

◆ 1 plastic hockey stick per player; 1 3-foot dowel stick (taped at one end) per player

◆ 1 puck per game; 1 deck ring per game

◆ 4 hockey nets and floor tape to mark out goalie box

◆ 4 sets of bibs

◆ 1 balancing feather or stick (3-foot, ½-inch dowel) per player

Teaching Points:

Refer to the Appendix for rules of the game and player positions.

Lead-up Games:

1. **Position Hockey.** For each game, mark off a large rectangular court or use the boundaries of a basketball court or outdoor tennis court. Within the court mark off a centerline and a face-off circle. Each game requires two opposing teams of 8 players: 1 Goalie, 1 Center, 2 Forwards, 2 Guards, and 3 Substitutes or players who stand in hoops on the designated sidelines as shown. Each player has a hockey stick and takes up position accordingly. Each team has a set of colored hockey sticks or wears bibs. Game begins with a face-off at center by the opposing centers, and occurs after each goal is scored. Centers are allowed to travel into front- or back-court; forwards must stay in the front-court (offensive court); guards must stay in their back-court (defensive court). Teams can use sideline players to pass to. A substitution can occur during stoppage of play in which a sideline player can trade position with any other team player. Encourage players to play at all positions. Emphasize no high-sticking, body contact, tripping, or any unsportsman-like conduct!

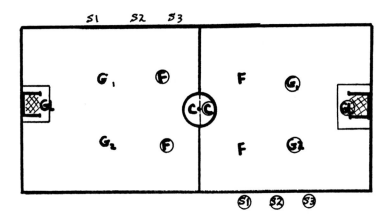

2. **End Zone Hockey.** Divide the class into two teams and give each player a number. The first 5 players from each team are the active players who play a regulation game in the court positions: goalie, 2 forwards, and 2 guards. The other players from the team play as goalies and position in front of their respective goal end line as shown in the diagram. After a certain time or after a goal has been scored, 5 goalie players become active players and everyone rotates accordingly. Emphasize safety at all times and playing fairly the rules of the game!

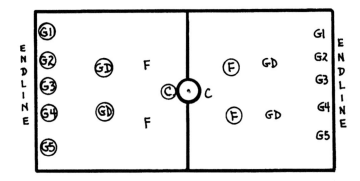

Modified Games:

1. **Ringette.** Popular lead-up game to ice hockey and particularly enjoyed by girls. In this game a deck ring is used as the puck and 3-foot dowel sticks taped at one end instead of the traditional hockey stick. The rink can be a large rectangular area such as a basketball court or an outdoor tennis court. Mark off a centerline and a face-off circle. Each game has two opposing teams of 6–8 players, with 6 players on the court at a time (1 goalie, 1 center, 2 forwards, and 2 guards), and the other players substituting in during stoppage of play. A player can only travel, at the most, 5 steps before passing or shooting the deck ring. Emphasize that only the player guarding the player with the deck ring may try to gain possession of the deck ring. Allow the ring to be played off the walls if indoors. Emphasize safety at all times! *Variation:* Set up several 4-on-4 Mini-Ringette games.

MINI-RINGETTE GAME

2. **Sideline Hockey.** For each game, mark off a large rectangular court or use the boundaries of a basketball court or outdoor tennis court. Within the court mark off a centerline and a face-off circle. Each game requires two opposing teams of 6–8 court players: 1 goalie, 1 center, 2 forwards, 2 guards, and 2 teams of 6–8 supporting sideline players for each team, who stand in hoops on the designated sidelines as shown. Each player has a hockey stick and takes up position accordingly. Each team has a set of colored hockey sticks or wears bibs. Game begins with a face-off at center by the opposing centers, and occurs after each goal is scored. Sideline players keep the puck "in play" and may advance the puck down the sideline or down the floor, but cannot score. Sideline and court players switch roles after every 3 minutes or after a goal has been scored. Regulation rules apply. If indoors, allow the puck to be played off the walls. This becomes another strategy for offensive (or defensive) play! Refer to the Appendix.

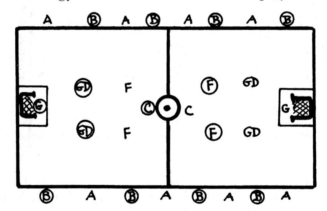

3. **Mad Ball Hockey.** Position hockey nets in the middle of both ends and at each side of a large play area. Mark off a goal box for each goal area using floor tape. Divide the class into two equal teams and distribute one set of bibs to each team. Assign each team an end net and one side net to defend and a goalie for each goal area. To start the game, have two face-offs in the designated spots shown in the diagram. Goalies keep track of the number of goals scored. After a certain time, play is stopped and goals are counted to give each team a score. A new game begins with new goalies in place. Strongly emphasize safety at all times: no high-sticking, keep backswing and follow-through low when attempting to score or pass, no body contact, no rough play of any sort, and poor sportsmanship behavior is not allowed.

Variation: As skill improves, add another puck and yet another until four pucks are in use.

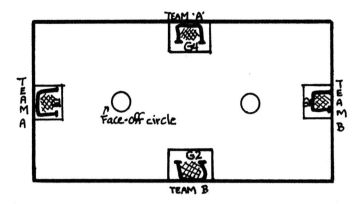

4. **Full-court Game.** See the Appendix for the rules of the game, court diagram, and tournament draws. Several suggestions for modifying the game are included in the introduction and have also been included in this lesson.

Cooling-down Activities/Games:

1. **Balance Feathers/Balance Sticks "Hotdog" Time.** Explore using balancing sticks or feathers on different parts of the body.

2. **Legends of the Day!**

Fit Think Idea:

Discuss the benefits of playing these games. Provide feedback on fair play and good sportsmanship observed while class is at play.

Lesson 43:
Underhand Serving

Skill Builders: underhand serving technique, accuracy serving, hand–eye coordination, partner play, finger/arm strengtheners, aerobic fitness

Expected Student Performance:

◆ Demonstrates proficiency in performing an underhand serve and serving with accuracy.

◆ Willingly cooperates and integrates with other class and team members.

◆ Demonstrates proficiency in aerobic fitness, strength, and flexibility demands.

Facility/Equipment Needed:

◆ 2 volleyball indoor or outdoor courts

◆ 2 volleyball nets and posts

◆ 1 volleyball per server

◆ 1 small balloon ball (about size of a volleyball) per server

◆ floor tape

◆ Cassette or CD player; popular music

Teaching Points:

Underhand Serve

◆ Stand with feet in a comfortable stride position, facing the net, with weight evenly distributed, knees bent.

◆ Keep shoulders square to net.

◆ Hold ball in nondominant hand across and in front of body, about waist level.

◆ Keep eyes on the ball.

◆ Swing arm back, transfer weight to rear foot.

◆ Swing arm forward, transfer weight to front foot.

◆ Contact the ball with the heel of the hand.

◆ Drop holding hand away from ball on contact.

◆ Follow-through in line of direction.

Focus Word:

● *Weight Transfer*

Warming-up Activities/Games:

1. **Volleyball Warm-up Circuit.** (Use the volleyball court boundary lines and net for this warm-up. Half the class positions on one end line of the court, the other half positions on the opposite end line. See diagram. Use popular music with a steady 4/4 beat.) Jog forward along one sideline. Shuffle-step along the net, hands held high. Jog backwards along the other sideline. Hop along the baseline or end line. Movement pattern should last for 2–3 minutes.

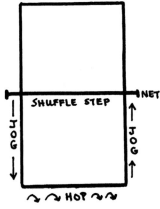

2. **Finger Push-ups.** Stand near a wall, facing it. Lean into the wall, taking weight on fingertips. Slowly push away from the wall. Repeat 10 times.

3. **Volleyball Sit-ups.** Start in hook lying position, holding a volleyball in both hands. Gently curl upwards to touch volleyball just past knees, and curl slowly down to starting position. Repeat 20 times.

4. **Volleyball Stretches.** Stretch volleyball high over head; stretch with volleyball to one side, other side. Do full body circles with volleyball tracing a large circle. Periscope touch volleyball to raised leg, then reverse legs. Hold stretches for 10–15 seconds.

Skill Practice & Progressions:

1. Demonstrate the teaching points of the underhand serve. Players pantomime the action. Use balloon or balloon balls to initially learn the technique.

2. **Wall Serve.** Have players collect a volleyball and find a free space facing a wall about 5 giant steps away. Position in serving stance. Practice the underhand serve. Serve the ball so that it hits above a line on the wall that is 10 feet (3 meters) from the floor. Gradually step farther away from the wall, until about 8–10 giant steps away.

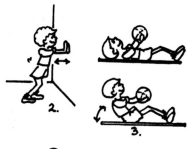

3. **Net Serve.** Set up 3 files just behind the "Attack Line" as shown. Each server has a volleyball. First 3 players underhand serve the ball, then go retrieve it, and join the end of their file. On signal, when safe, next 3 servers go.

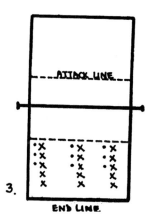

4. **Partner Serve.** Partners stand on opposite sides of a net and serve the volleyball to each other, so that the partner can catch it. Start 3 giant steps away from the net, and gradually increase the distance. On signal, have partners change positions so they are serving to a new area. Object is to improve the accuracy of the serve.

5. **End-line Serve.** Partners stand on opposite end lines and serve the volleyball to each other.

6. **Serving Grid.** Use floor tape to mark out a numbered Serving Grid on one side of the volleyball court as shown. Players partner up and collect 2 volleyballs. One partner stands on one of the serving lines as shown. Each partner in turn has two serves and tries to score points by landing the ball in one of the grid squares. The nonserving partner positions in the grid to retrieve each serve and note which square the ball lands in each time, keeping score. Ideally this could be set up as a skill builder station activity.

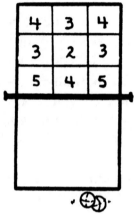

Cooling-down Activities/Games:

1. **Hand/Arm Yoga**

   ◆ Fingers stretch—opening and closing
   ◆ Fists—slow-motion boxing
   ◆ Wrist and fingers—flexing
   ◆ Interlock fingers and arms—stretching overhead
   ◆ Interlock fingers and arms—stretching behind
   ◆ Gentle arm waving
   ◆ Breathing—slowly, gently inhaling, exhaling with cross-arm circling

2. **Legends of the Day!**

Homework Idea:

Complete the Aerobic Activity Grid. (See the Appendix.)

Fit Think Idea:

Discuss why the serve may not go in the intended line of direction: hitting the ball with a closed fist, hitting off the side of the hand, not following through in the line of direction, not keeping eyes in contact with the ball.

Lesson 44:
Setting (Overhead Pass)

Skill Builders: overhead pass technique, hand–eye coordination, partner and team play, aerobic and strength fitness

Expected Student Performance:

> Demonstrates competency in performing a set pass.
>
> Willingly cooperates and integrates with other class and team members.
>
> Demonstrates proficiency in aerobic fitness, strength, and flexibility demands.

Facility/Equipment Needed:

> 2 volleyball indoor or outdoor courts
>
> 2 volleyball nets and posts
>
> 1 volleyball or volleyball trainer per player
>
> 1 balloon ball or large soft ball per pair

Teaching Points:

Ready Position

> Place feet in a slight stride, shoulder width apart, knees bent.
>
> Raise hands in front of forehead about 6–8 inches away, elbows flexed.
>
> Point thumbs toward the eyes.
>
> Form a "window" with the thumbs and pointer fingers.
>
> Watch the ball through this window.
>
> Square shoulders to the target.

Execution

> As contact is made, form hands to the shape of the ball, with only upper two joints of fingers and hands touching the ball.
>
> Fully extend body upward on contact, transferring weight toward target.
>
> Follow through with hands, arms, and legs extending toward target.
>
> Set the ball just above forehead level.

Focus Words:

- *Ready Position*
- *F-O-C-U-S*

Warming-up Activities/Games:

Indoor or Outdoor Exercise Hunt. (See the Appendix for Exercise Hunt ideas.) Have each team design an Exercise Hunt that can then be used as the warming-up activity for a lesson! Captains and co-captains would introduce the Hunt and briefly outline the activities involved. Each team would also create a Exercise Hunt card to give to the other teams to follow. Check activities for safety and good balance of aerobic, strength, agility, cooperative, stretching activities.

Skill Practice & Progressions:

Discuss focus word: "FOCUS"

F—Feel the ball on the hands.

O—Open the "window."

C—Concentrate, with eyes tracking the ball all the way.

U—Hands are a "Unit" working together; fingers relaxed.

S—Have a successful setting.

1. Demonstrate the "Ready Position" for *setting* the ball. Players pantomime the action. Demonstrate the movement involved to set the ball. Players pantomime the action.

2. **Volleyball Window.** Collect a volleyball and place it on the floor. Spread fingers to make a window on the ball and pick it up, positioning ball just in front of forehead. Toss ball in air and catch it in the window position. Pause to check correct hand positioning. Repeat several times. Gradually reduce the pause time.

3. **Toss and Set.** Toss the ball to yourself, set it once, and catch; toss again, set it twice and catch; toss again, set it three times and catch. Continue toss–set–catch pattern.

4. **Wall Set.** Stand about 2 giant steps away. Set the ball to the wall, let it rebound off the wall, and set it back. Set the ball just above forehead level each time. Pause slightly after catching ball, then gradually eliminate.

5. **Sit & Set.** Partners in wide-sit position set the volleyball back and forth to each other.

6. **Partner Set.** Partners, spaced 3 giant steps apart, set the ball back and forth to each other. Pause after catching the ball before setting back to partner, then gradually eliminate the pause.

7. **Balloon Ball Set.** Partners repeat activity 6 using a balloon ball, large soft ball, or Nerf™ ball.

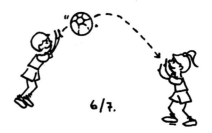

6/7.

Setting Games

1. **Keep It Up.** Teams of 5–6 players keep the ball from touching the floor by setting it back up. The same player cannot hit the ball twice in a row. Vary the type of ball used: balloon ball, Nerf™ ball, volleyball. Count the number of continuous sets made in a certain time limit.

2. **Mine!** Same formation as for game 1, but players set ball across the circle. Receiving player must call "Mine!" before setting the ball to another player. *Variations:*

   ● Establish a setting pattern, as shown.

   ● Create a new setting pattern.

Cooling-down Activities/Games:

1. **Five-Star Set.** Players in groups of 5 position in a star pattern as shown and set the ball around in a certain passing order. Passers are not allowed to set the ball to a player on either side. Use a small balloon ball, large soft Nerf™ ball, or large volleyball trainer ball. Change the order and establish a new star pass pattern.

2. **Legends of the Day!**

Homework Idea:

Use the Aerobic Activity Grid. (See the Appendix.)

Fit Think Idea:

Discuss different ways of strengthening fingers, wrists, and arms. How will this help to become a better setter?

Lesson 45:
Bumping (Forearm Pass)

Skill Builders: bumping technique, hand–eye coordination, partner and team play, aerobic and strength fitness, concentration, manual dexterity in juggling with scarves

Expected Student Performance:

◆   Demonstrates competency in performing a forearm pass.

◆   Willingly cooperates and integrates with other class and team members.

◆   Demonstrates proficiency in aerobic and strength demands, concentration, and manual dexterity.

Facility/Equipment Needed:

◆   2 volleyball indoor or outdoor courts

◆   2 volleyball nets and posts

◆   1 volleyball or volleyball trainer per player

◆   1 balloon ball per pair

◆   3 juggling scarves per player

◆   1 24-foot parachute

Teaching Points:

◆   Move to the ball and set your position.

◆   Position feet in an easy stride position, shoulder's width apart.

◆   Bend your knees, keeping body low, back straight.

◆   Interlock or cup fingers, thumbs parallel to each other, elbows locked and rotated inward so that the soft-flat part of forearms faces upward.

◆   Keep this platform with arms, holding them parallel to thighs and away from the body.

◆   Track ball with eyes and position the body directly behind the ball.

◆   Transfer weight forward.

◆   Slant platform toward target and watch ball contact arms.

◆   Absorb the force of the ball on forearms and direct ball toward target.

◆   Follow-through extending legs and arms toward the target.

◆   Contact ball with little or no arm swing, keeping arms below shoulder level.

◆   Watch ball's path to target.

◆   Keep motion smooth and continuous.

Focus Word:

- *Manual Dexterity*

Warming-up Activity/Game:

Parachute Play. See Lesson 4 for description of activities. Play Parachute Volleyball: Divide the circle players into two even teams, A and B. Place a volleyball in the middle of the chute. Object of the game is to send the volleyball off the chute on the opposition's side to score a point.

Skill Practice & Progressions:

1. Demonstrate the bumping technique, then have players pantomime the action of bumping, getting into ready position, execution, and following through. Repeat action several times. Observe and give feedback. *Variation:* Use balloon balls to practice bumping action.

2. **Partner Toss & Bump.** (Do the following tasks using a balloon ball, then a Nerf™ ball, and then a volleyball.) One partner gets into knee-sit position 3 giant steps from other partner. Standing partner tosses volleyball to kneeling partner who tries to bump it back. Catch the bumped ball and repeat the task 5 times, then change roles.

3. Partners now stand 4–5 giant steps apart. One partner tosses ball to other partner who tries to bump it back. Catch the ball and toss it again. Switch roles after 5 tosses.

4. **Free-Style Bumping.** Each player collects a volleyball and finds a free space. Toss the volleyball up in the air, move into position under the ball, arms in bumping position. Let ball contact forearms and simply let it bounce off. Repeat. Toss volleyball into the air, again position under it, and bump it to yourself. Catch it. Repeat several times. Now try to bump it twice, three times: "Throw–bump–catch;   throw–bump–bump–catch" pattern.

5. **Wall Bump.** Repeat activity 3 but bump the ball to a wall and catch it. Toss the ball at the wall and try to bump it back. Set the ball to the wall, and bump it back. Catch it.

6. **Partner Bump.** Gradually, as skill improves, partners bump the ball back and forth to each other. *Variation:* One partner bumps the ball to partner who sets it back.

Bumping Games

1. **Bump It Up.** Divide the class into circles of 6–8 players. Use a balloon ball, then a Nerf™ ball, then a volleyball. On signal "Bump!" the team tries to keep the ball in the air without it touching the ground or floor. Count the number of bumps made in a certain time. *Variations:*

    *   Repeat activity using a Nerf™ ball; a volleyball.
    *   Allow both setting and bumping the ball.

2. **Bump Volleyball Relay.** Divide the class into teams of 4 or 6 and position in shuttle formation, with each half file facing and standing about 3 giant steps away. Player #1 on signal "Bump!" bumps a balloon ball to the front player (#2) of the opposite file, then quickly runs to the end of his/her file. Player #2 bumps ball across to player #3, and so forth. Count the number of bumps made in a certain time. Repeat relay using a Nerf™ ball; a volleyball.

Cooling-down Activities/Games:

1. **Juggling Scarves.** (See the Appendix.)
2. **Legends of the Day!**

Homework Idea:

Use the Aerobic Activity Grid. (See the Appendix.)

Fit Think Idea:

Discuss when the bump is used in a volleyball game: receiving a serve, to send a low ball over the net when it cannot be set or attacked.

Lesson 46:
Overhand Serving

Skill Builders: overhand serve technique, hand–eye coordination, aerobic and strength fitness, partner and team play, court awareness

Expected Student Performance:

◆ Demonstrates proficiency in performing an overhand serve.

◆ Willingly cooperates and integrates with other class and team members.

◆ Demonstrates proficiency in meeting aerobic, strength, and flexibility demands.

Facility/Equipment Needed:

◆ 2 volleyball indoor or outdoor courts

◆ 2 volleyball nets and posts

◆ 1 volleyball or volleyball trainer per player

Teaching Points for Overhand Serve:

◆ Stand with feet in a slight stride position, facing the net, with weight evenly distributed.

◆ Keep shoulders square to net and noncontact side foot forward.

◆ Toss ball with nonhitting hand about 3 feet in front and above hitting shoulder, and close to body.

◆ As ball is tossed, bring hitting arm back with elbow high and hand close to ear.

◆ Keep eyes on the ball.

◆ Contact ball with heel of the open hand above the head.

◆ Transfer weight from rear foot to front foot as contact is made and arm swings through.

◆ Follow-through in line of direction, dropping hitting arm slightly.

Warming-up Activity/Game:

"Just Beat It" Challenges. See Lesson 2 "Games." Use the volleyball court markings to create different challenges. Emphasize safety at all times and fair play. Praise good effort.

END LINES- TOUCH TWO HANDS, TWO KNEES

Skill Practice & Progressions:

1. Demonstrate the teaching points of the overhand serve. Players pantomime the action. Use balloon or balloon balls to initially learn the technique.

2. **Wall Serve.** Have players collect a volleyball and find a free space facing a wall about 6–7 giant steps away. Position in serving stance. Practice the overhand serve. Serve the ball so that it hits above a line on the wall that is 10 feet (3 meters) from the floor. Gradually step farther away from the wall, until about 8–10 giant steps away.

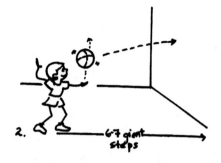

3. **Partner One-step Serve.** One partner overhand serves the ball to the other partner who must try to catch it and serve back. For each successful serve and catch set, partners are then allowed to take a step back from each other. Start at 6 giant steps apart.

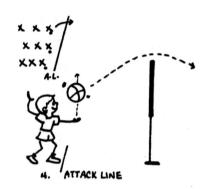

4. **Net Serve.** Set up 3 files just behind the Attack Line as shown. Each server has a volleyball. First 3 players overhand serve the ball, then go retrieve it, and join the end of their file. On signal, when safe, next 3 servers go.

5. **Partner Net Serve.** Partners stand on opposite sides of a net and overhand serve the volleyball to each other, so that the partner can catch it. Start 3 giant steps away from the net and gradually increase the distance. On signal, have partners change positions so they are serving to a new area.

Serving Games:

1. **Serving Attack.** Divide the class into two teams and have each team stand on a baseline of the volleyball court. Each team is given 5 volleyballs. Object of the game is to serve as many balls over into the opposition's court before a whistle blows to stop the game, and end up with a fewer number of volleyballs in your court! Players may serve from a marked service line which is about halfway between the attack line and the baseline. Emphasize safety when retrieving balls. Heads up! *Variation:* Allow overhand or underhand serves.

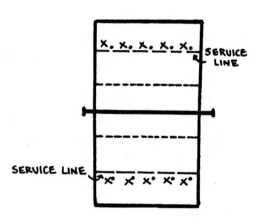

2. **Alley Serve.** Divide the court on both sides of the net into 3 alleys as shown. For each game assign 12 players who number off from 1 through 12: Players 1, 2, and 3 each position in an alley on one side; players 4, 5, and 6 on the other side of the net. These players are retrievers who catch or field the balls and return them by rolling the ball under the net to their teammates. Players 7, 8, and 9 position on one end line; players 10, 11, and 12 are on the other end line and serve into the corresponding alley on the opposite side of the court. On signal "Rotate," retrievers rotate one alley; servers rotate one alley. On signal "Switch," servers and retrievers exchange roles.

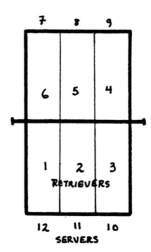

Cooling-down Activities/Games:

1. **Volleyball Wheel.** Teams of 6 players are in circle formation, spaced 2 giant steps apart, with one player in the center. Center player sets the ball to each "spoke" player who returns the set. Continue until everyone has had a turn in the center. Call "Mine!" Vary the type of ball used.

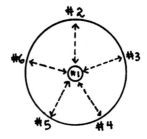

2. **Legends of the Day!**

Homework Idea:

Use the Aerobic Activity Grid. (See the Appendix.)

Fit Think Idea:

Discuss how performing an overhand serve is the same action as performing an overhand throw. Think of other sports that also involve an overhand throwing action (badminton smash, tennis smash and serve, and javelin throw).

Lesson 47:
Digging and Serve Reception

Skill Builders: dig technique, serve reception, serve–bump–set sequence, hand–eye coordination, aerobic fitness, partner and team play, court awareness

Expected Student Performance:

◆   Demonstrates competency in performing a dig and receiving a serve.

◆   Willingly cooperates and integrates with partner and team members.

◆   Demonstrates proficiency in meeting fitness demands.

Facility/Equipment Needed:

◆   1 Nerf™ ball, volleyball trainer, or volleyball per player

◆   2 volleyball indoor or outdoor courts

◆   2 volleyball nets and posts

◆   Cassette or CD player; popular music

Teaching Points:

A "dig" differs from a forearm pass (or "bump") in that the player must react quickly and play the ball with little time to position strategically. It is often combined with a roll or sprawl to prevent injury and recover quickly.

Digging

◆   Keep weight forward, one foot slightly ahead of the other.

◆   Bend at the knees, keeping hips low to get under the ball.

◆   Hold hands in bump position and arms out in front of body at waist height.

◆   Watch ball contact the arms.

◆   Contact ball with both arms parallel to floor.

◆   Extend body toward target.

◆   Flick wrist(s) to gain height.

◆   Follow eyes toward the target.

Receiving the Serve

◆   Set in ready "bump" position to receive the ball on the forearms.

◆   Track the ball as it comes toward you.

◆   Move quickly into position and execute the bump.

Focus Words:

- *Digging*
- *Serve Reception*

Warming-up Activities/Games:

Volleyball Court Aerobics. Divide class into 4 teams who position in a circle on each side of two volleyball courts. Play popular music with a steady 4/4 beat. Players respond to the different signals that are called out: Marchers (in place); Joggers (clockwise around the circle); Twisters (jump, twisting to the right, to the left); Bouncers (jump slightly in place); "Ready Position—Bump" (pantomime action); "Ready Position—Set"; Blockers (jump straight up into the air, arms extended upwards); Wall Push-ups; Wall Calf Stretch.

Skill Practice & Progressions:

1. **Bump and Set.** Partners collect a volleyball and space themselves about 3 giant steps apart in a free space. Partner A sets the ball to Partner B who bumps it back to partner A. Partner A catches the ball, then sets it back to Partner B who bumps. Reverse roles. Repeat activity #1 but have Partner A do a "pause" catch, then set the ball to Partner B. Gradually take the pause away.

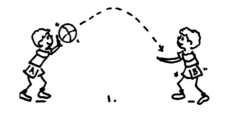

2. **Toss & Dig.** Demonstrate the dig and have players pantomime the action. Practice. One partner uses an overhead toss to send the ball quickly toward the other partner to the right, to the left, or short of the partner. Partner must quickly react to oncoming ball to make the dig.

3. **Serve and Bump (Dig).** Partners stand facing each other without a net. Partner A, with the ball, serves to Partner B, who bumps the ball back to Partner A. Reverse roles after 5 serves. Partner A then serves ball over the net to Partner B who bumps the ball so that it lands in a nearby hoop.

4. **Serve–Bump (Dig)–Set.** Three partners, A, B, and C, stand in a wide triangle formation as shown. Partner A serves to Partner B who bumps the ball to Partner C, who sets the ball to himself/herself. Change roles after every 5 serves.

5. **Serve–Net–Bump (Dig)–Set.** Partner A positions on one side of the net; Partners B and C position on the opposite side. Partner A serves the ball over the net to Partner B who makes the bump or dig and sends the ball to Partner C who sets it into a hoop.

Cooling-down Activities/Games:

1. **Bolleyball.** Divide the class into two equal teams and position each team on one side of the net. Ideally if two courts are available, have 4 teams of 6–8 players. Lower the net to 7 feet. One team has 3 volleyballs; the other team has 4. On signal "Bolleyball," players set or bump the balls over the net. The opposition players catch or quickly retrieve the ball and set or bump it back. Object of the game is to end up with fewer volleyballs in your court when a whistle is blown to stop the play. A count is taken. Teams rotate to a different court and a new game begins. Players may send ball directly over the net or pass to a teammate who then sends the ball over the net. *Variation:* As skill level improves, players bump (dig) or set the ball back over the net without catching it first.

2. **Legends of the Day!**

In Class Idea:

Indoor or Outdoor Exercise Hunt. (See the Appendix for Exercise Hunt ideas.) Have each team design an Exercise Hunt that can then be used as the warming-up activity for a lesson! Captains and co-captains would introduce the Hunt and briefly outline the activities involved. Each team would also create a Exercise Hunt card to give to the other teams to follow. Check activities for safety and good balance of aerobic, strength, agility, cooperative, and stretching activities.

Homework Idea:

Use the Aerobic Activity Grid. (See the Appendix.)

Lesson 48:
Introduction to Spiking and Tipping

Skill Builders: spiking technique, tipping technique, hand–eye coordination, aerobic fitness, leg and arm strength, partner and team play, net awareness

Expected Student Performance:

> Demonstrates proficiency in ability to tip or spike the volleyball.

> Willingly cooperates and integrates with other class and team members.

> Demonstrates proficiency in meeting fitness demands.

Facility/Equipment Needed:

> 1 balloon ball, Nerf™ ball, volleyball trainer, or volleyball per player

> 2 volleyball indoor or outdoor courts

> 2 volleyball nets and posts

Teaching Points:

Spiking is the action of forcefully hitting (smashing) the ball over the net to score a point or regain the serve. It is the third part of the serve–reception sequence: bump–set–spike. Adjust the height of the net to the jumping ability level of the class.

Spiking

> Approach net with as few steps as possible.

> Swing arms back to waist to prepare for jump.

> Take off on two feet by planting both heels first to change from forward to upward momentum.

> Swing arms forward and up.

> Jump straight up into the air, bring hitting arm back, elbow high and hand close to ear.

> Contact ball at full extensions in front of hitting shoulder.

Spiking

> Contact on top of the ball with heel of hand, snapping wrist as fingers roll over the top.

> Keep eyes on the ball through the contact.

> Do not let striking arm follow-through down, but drop hand to hip.

> Bend knees to cushion landing.

Tipping or Dinking

- Use the upper two finger joints to contact the ball for a tip or dink.
- Contact ball slightly below the center back.
- At contact, gently direct ball over or past the block so that it drops quickly to the floor.
- Return to floor with a 2-foot landing, bending at the knees.

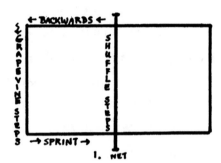

Tipping

Focus Words:

- *Spiking*
- *Tipping*

Warming-up Activities/Games:

1. **Volley Circuit.** Sprint forward along one sideline. Take 3 shuffle steps along the net, jump straight up with hands high in air to touch the top of the net, run backward along the other sideline, grapevine step along the baseline. Repeat movement pattern for 2–3 minutes.

2. **Partner Blocks.** Start back-to-back, take 3 giant steps away from each other, jump-turn, and face. Use a 3-step approach, jump and touch hands in air as high as possible. Repeat 5 times.

3. **Stretches:**

   - *Finger-Wrist Stretch*
   - *Sprinter Stretch*
   - *Hamstring Stretch*
   - *Calf Stretch*

Skill Practice & Progressions:

1. Demonstrate the action of spiking a ball. Players pantomime the action. Practice. Demonstrate the action of tipping the ball. Players pantomime the action.

2. Players use a balloon ball or Nerf™ ball for the following tasks and stand near a wall.
   - Hold the ball in the nonhitting hand at shoulder level. Hit the ball out of your hand, with the heel of the striking hand, to the floor.
   - Snap wrist through the ball to add force. Emphasize that arm does not follow-through downward, but drops to hip.
   - Toss ball upward in front of hitting shoulder. Watch it carefully to time jump, then hit ball downward toward floor between you and the wall. Repeat several times.

3. **Three-step Approach.** Players practice a 3-step approach, taking off on 2 feet, and pantomime spiking or tipping the ball. Teaching cues: Step left–right–left, two-foot takeoff–tip (spike).

4. **Jump and Spike/Tip.** In teams of 5–6, position at the net as shown in diagram. Lower the height of the net to suit the jumping ability level of the class. Class has two retrievers (Players 1 and 2), one ball holder (Player 3), and 2–3 Spikers/Tippers (Players 4, 5, 6). Player 3 stands on a chair holding the balloon ball, Nerf™ ball, or volleyball just above the net. After spikers/tippers have had two turns at tipping the ball and two turns at spiking the ball each, they become the retrievers and the ball holder.

5. **Toss & Spike or Tip.** Use the same formation as for activity 4. Net players toss the ball or set it up along the net. Hitter uses a 3-step approach to spike or tip the ball over the net. Rotate one position after every 4 tosses.

Cooling-down Activities/Games:

1. **Human Knots.** Teams of 5–6 players in circle formation, facing the center, find a free space in play area. Players join hands across the circle with any two players except a player who is on either side of them. Each hand-hold must be to a different player. Without letting hold of hands, each team untangles itself. *Variations:*

    ● Two teams join together for a giant human tangle.

    ● Which team can untangle itself and cross-leg sit first?

2. **Legends of the Day!**

In Class Idea:

Teams continue to develop Exercise Hunts as described in Lesson 47.

Homework Idea:

Use the Aerobic Activity Grid. (See the Appendix.)

Lesson 49:
Introduction to Blocking

Skill Builders: blocking technique, hand–eye coordination, aerobic fitness, leg strength, partner play, net awareness, applying bump–set–spike sequence in a lead-up game

Expected Student Performance:

◆ Demonstrates proficiency in performing a block and using volleyball skills in a game-like situation.

◆ Willingly cooperates and integrates with other class and team members.

◆ Demonstrates proficiency in meeting fitness demands.

Facility/Equipment Needed:

◆ 1 volleyball per pair

◆ 2 volleyball indoor or outdoor courts

◆ 1 long rope and posts

◆ 2 volleyball nets and posts

◆ 1 balloon ball, 1 volleyball trainer per game

Teaching Points:

Blocking is the action of intercepting the ball coming over the net with the hands and arms to deflect the ball into the opponent's court.

Blocking

◆ Stand facing and close to the net, hands at shoulder level.

◆ Time jump to that of the spiker's jump.

◆ Jump high enough so that the wrists will be slightly above the net.

◆ Jump straight up to meet the oncoming ball.

◆ Do not touch the net when blocking.

◆ Tense fingers together and tense as contact with ball is made.

◆ Deflect the ball downward off the hands and arms.

◆ Do not let the arms swing forward as you land, since a net foul could result.

◆ Land on two feet, bending knees to cushion landing.

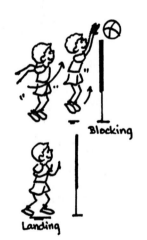

Blocking

Landing

Focus Word:

● *Blocking*

Warming-up Activity/Game:

Team Exercise Hunt. Each team is handed a card of activities/exercises to perform in the Hunt as explained by the team's captain and co-captain. The warm-up should last about 5 minutes.

Skill Practice & Progressions:

1. Demonstrate the action of blocking. Players pantomime the action. Remind players that a block does not count as a hit. After a player blocks the ball, he/she is allowed to hit it again. But a blocker is not allowed to block the opponent's serve.

2. **Partner Net Jump.** Partners are positioned one on each side of the net. They jump at the same time and touch fingertips over the net, without touching the net. Adjust the height of the net to the jumping ability of the class.

3. **Partner Toss and Block.** As for activity #2, but Partner A tosses ball just above the top of the net, while Partner B tries to block the ball from the other side. Change roles after 5 tosses.

4. **Partner Spike and Block.** Same set-up as for activity #2, but now Partner B is the spiker and pantomimes spiking action on one side of the net. Partner A is the blocker who tries to "read" the spiker's action and time the jump.

5. **4-on-4 Beach Ball or Balloon Ball Volleyball.** Stretch a long rope across the length of the gym or outdoor play area. Adjust height of net to suit the ability level of the class. Divide this area into 4 courts as shown. Divide the class into 8 teams, ability grouping if possible. Assign each team to one side of a court: Team A vs. Team B; Team C vs. Team D; Team E vs. Team F; Team G vs. Team H. Each team serves from a designated mark on the floor. Players take turns serving. A team is allowed, at the most, 3 hits per side. Encourage teams to use the bump–set–spike sequence. Blocking is allowed! No one is allowed to hit the ball twice in a row. Remind players to call "Mine!" if going to play the ball. After a certain time, rotate teams and begin new games. *Variation:* Vary the type of ball used. For the groups whose skills are developing well, use a Nerf™ or soft volleyball trainer.

Spiker   4.   Blocker

5. 4-on-4 V'BALL

Cooling-down Activities/Games:

1. Lightly stretch while discussing with the class player positions and playing your position rather than "cluttering" to the ball. Be a team player, not a ball hogger!

2. **Legends of the Day!**

Homework Ideas:

1. Use the Aerobic Activity Grid. (See the Appendix.)

2. Watch a volleyball game in action! Observe player positioning, bump–set–attack play, serving, and teamwork.

Lesson 50:
Skill Builder Stations

Skill Builders: fundamental volleyball skills of serving, bumping, setting, hand–eye coordination, double rope jumping, team play, cooperation

Expected Student Performance:

◆   Demonstrates competency in performing fundamental volleyball skills and other station tasks.

◆   Willingly cooperates and integrates with other class and team members.

◆   Meets fitness demands and demonstrates fair play and good sportsmanship.

Facility/Equipment Needed:

◆   Gymnasium or outdoor area with a hit-up wall

◆   Cassette or CD player; station signs

◆   Station #1: 1 hoop and volleyball per pair, volleyball net and posts

◆   Station #2: floor tape, 3 wall targets, 3 setting lines, 1 volleyball per player

◆   Station #3: 1 wall target line, 1 volleyball per pair

◆   Station #4: 1 balloon ball, 1 long rope, badminton posts

◆   Station #5: 2 sets of long ropes

◆   Station #6: 1 loop 'n catch™ per player, 1 Squellet™ or beanbag per pair

◆   Station #7: 1 Woosh Ring™ per 3 players, 1 low net and posts

Skill Builder Station Ideas:

Station #1: Hoop Serve. Place a hoop about 10 feet (3 meters) from a net on one side. Serve the volleyball using the underhand serve into the hoop from the opposite side.

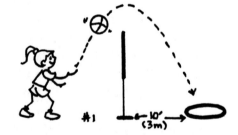

Station #2: Target Setting. Use floor tape to mark out 3 different sized wall targets, positioned at different heights on the wall. Mark off 3 different setting lines. Partners, at a target, take turns setting the volleyball into a wall target from a setting line. Try to get 3 or more sets in a row!

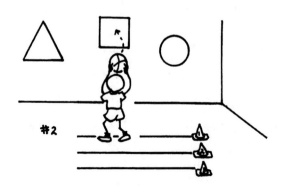

Station #3: Partner Wall Bumps. Partners, taking turns, try to bump the volleyball above a wall target line. Then partners try to bump the volleyball back and forth off the wall continuously to each other.

Station #4: 3-on-3 Balloonball Volleyball. Set up a 3-on-3 game using a long rope stretched between two badminton poles, as the net height. Mark off a serving box. One player serves the ball from the serving box; other two players are net players. One help on the serve is allowed. Players can have up to 3 hits per side before volleying ball into opposition's court.

Station #5: Double Dutch Rope Jumping. Experiment with jumping in two turning ropes. Turners may need to practice the technique of turning two ropes at once. Jumper needs to jump in when one rope is at the top of its turn.

Station #6: Loop 'n Catch™/Squellet™ Ball or Beanbag Ball. Partners use a loop to toss and catch a small object such as a Squellet™ ball or beanbag ball. Start about 2 giant steps apart and gradually increase the distance.

Station #7: 3-on-3 Woosh Ring™ Volleyball. Three players position on either side of a low net. Each group has a Woosh Ring™. Throw the rings over the net to the other side. Score a point if the ring touches the floor on the opposition's side.

Cooling-down Activity:

◆ **Legends of the Day!**

Homework Idea:

Photocopy a volleyball court diagram and have players mark out court with respect to key lines and player positions. (See the Appendix.)

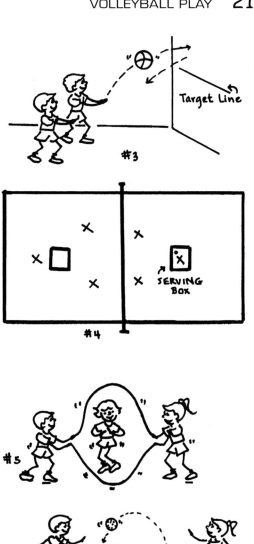

Lesson 51:
Lead-up and Modified Games

Skill Builders: fundamental volleyball skills of serving, bumping, setting, spiking, blocking, digging and tipping, hand–eye coordination, team play, court awareness and positional play

Expected Student Performance:

◆ Demonstrates competency in performing fundamental volleyball skills in game situations.

◆ Willingly cooperates and integrates with other class and team members.

◆ Demonstrates proficiency in positional play and team strategies.

Facility/Equipment Needed:

◆ Volleyball courts, nets, and posts

◆ 2 long ropes and volleyball posts

◆ Several volleyballs or volleyball trainers

◆ Several Foxtails™, Catchballs™, beanbags, spider balls, tennis balls, small Nerf™ balls

Teaching Points:

Discuss Rules of the Volleyball game.

See the Appendix.

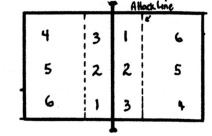

Court Positions (6 players)

Right forward (1), Center Forward (2), Left Forward (3), Left Back (4), Center Back (5), Right Back (6)

Court Position (9 to 12 players)

Players are positioned in 3 waves (net, middle, and back) and numbered off as shown. On signal "Waves," rotate one wave position: net wave goes to back, middle wave to net, back wave to middle, etc.

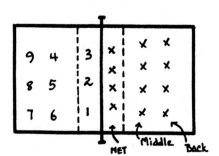

Lead-up Games:

1. **Newcomball.** Ideally two volleyball courts are required so that the class can be divided into 4 groups with 2 games going on simultaneously. Each team positions on one side of the net as shown. To start the game, a team player from each team serves the volleyball over the net from either of two designated court markings. The object of the game is to serve the volleyball over the net quickly to try to keep the opposition from catching the ball. A caught ball should be immediately served back but from the designated spot. If the ball is not caught, the serving team receives a point. Any player

who is unable to participate could be the scorekeeper. Rotate teams one court-side position and play again until all teams have challenged each other. Remind players to call "Mine!" if going to play the ball. *Variations:*

- Allow each team to have 2 volleyballs or volleyball trainers.
- Allow ball to be served from exactly where it was caught or hit the floor.
- Allow ball to be only served from anywhere behind the end line.
- Use Foxtails™ instead of volleyballs and watch the "flying" action.
- Lower the height of the net.

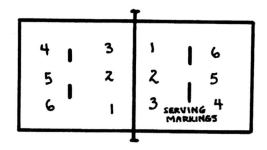

2. **UFO Volleyball.** Stretch a long rope across the length of the gym or outdoor play area, or use two volleyball courts across the length of the gym. Adjust height of net to suit the ability level of the class. Divide this area into 4 courts as shown. Divide the class into 8 teams, ability grouping if possible. Assign each team to one side of a court: Team A vs. Team B; Team C vs. Team D; Team E vs. Team F; Team G vs. Team H . Use a whistle to start and stop the play. Each team is given 2–3 objects (UFOs) to throw over the net. The opposition must prevent these objects from touching the floor or surface; otherwise, the opposition team is awarded a point. The idea is to throw the object immediately back over the net from where it was caught. To score a point, players look for "holes" or free spaces to throw the objects into. Any player who is unable to participate could be the scorekeeper. After a certain time, play is stopped, score accounted for, and teams rotate one court position in a counterclockwise direction. After all the teams have challenged each other, each team score is totaled and a grand winner declared. Remind players to call "Mine!" if going to play the ball. Use objects such as Foxtails™, Catchballs™, small Nerf™ balls, beanbags, spider balls, tennis balls.

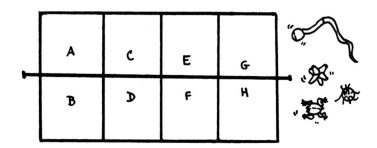

Modified Games:

Note: The first two games are ideal for large classes when only one court is available for play.

1. **Modified Volleyball.** For each game, form teams of 6–9 players per team. Each team positions on a side of the volleyball court. Adjust the height of the net to the ability level of the class. Teach the court positions and rotational order (refer to Teaching Points), then play regulation volleyball with any or all of the following modifications:

   ◆ Vary the type of ball used: balloon ball, Nerf™ ball, volleyball trainer, soft volleyball.
   ◆ Server serves from a designated floor marking in the center of the court.
   ◆ Server is allowed 2 attempts to serve the ball over the net.
   ◆ One "help" is allowed on the serve.
   ◆ A team may take more than 3 hits to send the ball over to the other side.
   ◆ The volleyball may be played after one bounce or in the air.
   ◆ Server calls out the score before serving.
   ◆ A point is scored to the opposition team when a foul occurs.
   ◆ The game is played to a set number of points or a certain time limit.
   ◆ Remind players to call "Mine!" if going to play the ball.
   ◆ Emphasize that the ball is rolled under the net to the opposition team when a loss of serve occurs ("Side out").

2. **Sideline Volleyball.** For each game, form 2 teams of 12–15 players and arrange each team on a side of a volleyball court as shown: 6–9 players are inside the court, while 6–9 players are along the sidelines. Remind players to call "Mine!" if going to play the ball, and to roll the ball under the net to the opposition team when a "side out" occurs. The game is played as in regulation volleyball with the following modifications:

   ◆ Sideline players must stay outside the volleyball court in their designated area.
   ◆ Sideline players may bump or set a loose ball back into their team's court as long as the ball has not touched the floor or surface.
   ◆ A hit by a sideline player does not count as one of the team hits.
   ◆ Sideline players may not pass the ball to each other.
   ◆ After a certain time, or a certain number of points have been scored, sideline and court players change positions.
   ◆ A balloon ball or volleyball trainer is used.

3. **Four-court Volleyball.** Using two long ropes and volleyball poles, set up a rope at right angles to the second rope to divide the play area into 4 volleyball courts as shown. Divide the class into four equal teams and assign each team, A, B, C, and D, to a court. Each team begins with 12 points. The object of the game is to finish with the best score after a certain time or to remain the only team with points left! A team becomes a sideline team if it has no points left! One team starts the game by serving the ball from a designated serving area into any of the other three courts. From then on, regulation volleyball rules go into effect. Each team tries to force one of the other teams to make an error. When a team makes an error, a point is deducted from its score. The ball is given to the next team in order upon loss of serve. Sideline players keep the ball into play unless the ball has touched the floor. Insist that ball is rolled under the net to the serving team when a "side out" occurs.

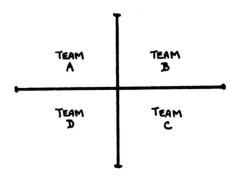

4. **Blindman's Volleyball.** For each game, form teams of 6–9 players a side with each team on one side of the net or long rope. Hang sheets over the rope using clothespins to secure the sheets and let the sheets hang down so that only the opposition's feet can be seen! Play regulation volleyball rules. Have players roll the ball under the sheets to the serving team. Emphasize fair play; no peeking allowed under or around the sheets! Have players call out the score before serving. Remind players to call "Mine!" if going to play the ball. Emphasize that players be in the "ready position" to move to the ball. Encourage team play. A ball in the back-court should be passed to the front line instead of trying to hit it directly over the net. *Variations:*

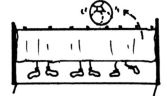

    -   Use a balloon volleyball to slow down the action.
    -   Use a volleyball trainer as ability level improves.
    -   Allow more than 3 hits per side.
    -   Allow a help on the serve and mark a serve spot in the center of the court. Once a player has a turn to serve, he/she serves from this area.
    -   Set up a tournament.

Cooling-down Activities/Games:

1.   **Juggling.** Continue from Lesson 45. (See the Appendix.)

2.   **Legends of the Day!**

Lesson 52:
Dribbling

Skill Builders: dribbling technique, foot–eye coordination, aerobic fitness, leg and arm strength, partner play

Expected Student Performance:

Demonstrates proficiency in technique.

Willingly cooperates and integrates with other class and team members.

Demonstrates proficiency in meeting fitness demands.

Facility/Equipment Needed:

Large grass oval or field or gymnasium

1 soccer-type ball or large playground ball

6 sets of rainbow-colored flags

cone markers, hoops

Teaching Points:

Use either foot to dribble.

Use the inside of the foot, outside of the foot, or toe to tap the ball lightly below center.

Keep the ball 1–2 feet in front of your feet, while maintaining control.

Focus eyes on the ball, but at the same time, dribble "heads up."

Focus Word:

● *Foot-Eye Coordination*

Warming-up Activities/Games:

1. **Team Tail Snatch.** Divide the class into 6 teams. Each team captain is given a set of colored tags: Red, Orange, Yellow, Green, Blue, Purple. Players tuck the flags into the back of their shorts or track pants and scatter in the play area. One team is designated the IT team. On signal ("Red"), the Red team gives chase trying to capture as many of the other flags as possible in a certain time (20 seconds). A player whose flag has been pulled must jog in place. On signal "Iceberg!," IT team comes to center circle. A quick count is taken, and the next team becomes IT. Continue until each team has been an IT team. Declare a Tail Snatch Champ!

Variations:

- Two teams are IT at the same time: Red–Orange; Yellow–Green; Blue–Purple. Change combinations.
- Vary the movement of the players whose flags have been pulled.

2. **Partner "Hoppo Bumpo."** Find a partner about the same size and stand facing in a free space. Each player stands on the right leg and holds left ankle with right hand behind the back. Grasp right arm behind the back with left hand. Gently try to bump partner so that he/she loses balance. Reverse leg/hand positions and challenge each other again. "Mingle!" New partner, new Hoppo Bumpo challenge.

3. **Partner Tug-o-war.** Stand facing, wrist hold. Try to pull your partner over a line. "Mingle," new partner and new tug-o-war game.

4. **Partner Tick-tocks.** Facing, interlocking fingers. Stretch to touch fingers to one side ("tick"), then to the other side ("tock"); 3 touches each side.

Skill Practice & Progressions:

1. Demonstrate moving the ball with the inside and outside of the feet. Players practice footwork on signals "Inside," "Outside," keeping the ball under control. On signal "Trap," players stop the ball by resting a foot on top of it.

2. **Obstacle Dribble.** Scatter several cones and hoops around the play area. Players dribble a ball in and out of the obstacles, trying not to let the ball touch any of the obstacles, using:

   - only the inside of either foot
   - only the outside of either foot
   - the toe of the foot
   - the inside or the outside of either foot

3. **Zigzag Dribble.** Groups of 5 zigzag dribble through sets of 5 cone markers as shown. As soon as the player in front has reached the third cone, the next player goes.

4. **Knock-out Dribble.** Everyone scatters with their ball to a free space, except for 3 IT players who stand in the middle without a ball. On signal "Knock-out!," the IT players give chase, trying to kick away another player's ball. This player then joins the IT team after placing his/her ball in a designated corner. Activity continues until all have become chasers!

5. **Circle Dribble Race.** Form circles of 6–8 players who number off 1, 2, 3, . . . 8. Call out a number. The players with that number must dribble a ball clockwise around their circle and back to place. Teams score points accordingly: first back—4 points; second—3 points; third—2 points; and fourth—1 point. Keep a record of the scores each time, until everyone's number has been called. Declare an overall Champ!

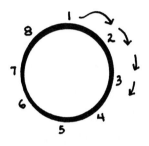

Cooling-down Activities/Games:

1. **Partner Stretching:**
   - **Bungee:** Hook sit, facing each other with soles of feet touching. Gently stretch arms through back area. Hold for 10–20 seconds.

Bungee Stretch

   - **Snake Roll:** In front lying position, facing and holding each other's arms with a wrist hold, gently roll to one side, then to the other side.

SNAKE ROLL

   - **Periscope:** One partner in periscope position; other partner gently pushes raised leg toward partner's head; 10 seconds each leg. Switch roles.

Periscope

2. **Legends of the Day!**

Fit Think Idea:

Many sports that are played today involve hand–eye coordination. Soccer involves foot–eye coordination and is the most universal played sport in the world. Think of ways to develop good footwork.

Lesson 53:
Passing and Receiving the Pass

Skill Builders: inside-of-the-foot pass and reception, outside-of-the-foot pass and reception, foot–eye coordination, aerobic fitness, leg and arm strength, partner play, team work

Expected Student Performance:

◆ Demonstrates competency in executing the different push passes and receiving a pass.

◆ Willingly cooperates and integrates with other class and team members.

◆ Demonstrates proficiency in meeting aerobic fitness demands.

Facility/Equipment Needed:

◆ Large grass oval or field or gymnasium

◆ CD or cassette player; popular music

◆ 1 soccer-type ball or large playground ball

◆ 1 cone or skittle or pin per pair

◆ Several dome markers

Teaching Points:

Push Pass (3 types)

   Inside-of-the-foot Pass:

◆ Use to pass the ball over short distances of 5–15 yards/meters.

◆ Face target and square shoulders as you approach ball.

◆ Focus on the ball.

◆ Plant nonkicking foot beside the ball and point toes toward the target.

◆ Position kicking foot sideways, ankle locked, toes pointed up, and contact ball with inside surface of kicking foot.

◆ Follow-through with kicking motion.

   Outside-of-the-foot Pass:

◆ Use this pass to make a diagonal pass to the right or left.

◆ Use for short and middle-distance passes.

◆ Place nonhitting leg slightly behind and to the side of the ball.

◆ Bring kicking foot downward and rotate inward.

◆ Keep arms out to sides for balance.

◆ Contact the ball with outside surface of the instep.

Use a short snap-like kicking motion of lower leg.

For longer passes, follow-through to generate more distance and speed on the ball.

Instep Pass (Instep is the part of the foot covered by the shoelaces.)

Use to send the ball over a long distance (25+ yards).

Approach the ball from a slight angle, eyes focused on the ball.

Place nonkicking foot beside the ball, leg slightly flexed, knee of kicking leg over the ball.

Contact the center of the ball with the instep of foot, toes pointed downward.

Drive the instep through the point of contact with ball with a powerful snap-like motion of the kicking leg.

Keep arms out to sides for balance, head steady.

Follow-through to chest level with kicking leg.

Inside-of-foot Reception

Keep eyes on ball and head steady.

Move toward ball and extend receiving leg to meet ball.

Position feet sideways.

Give with the leg and receiving foot to cushion its impact.

INSIDE-OF-FOOT

OUTSIDE-OF-FOOT

Outside-of-foot Reception

As for inside-of-foot reception above.

Position sideways to oncoming ball.

Receive ball on outside surface of instep.

Focus Word:

- *Instep*

Warming-up Activities/Games:

1. **Geronimo!** Use dome markers to mark off a large square track (or use the boundaries of a basketball court), and position four large cone markers at equal distances apart from each other on the perimeter of the track. Divide the class into 4 equal teams. Assign each team to a starting cone 1, 2, 3, or 4. On whistle signal or when the music starts, players jog in a clockwise direction around the outside of the track. On signal "Geronimo," the end

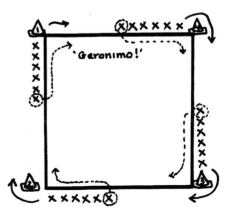

jogger of each team runs on the inside of track to take over the lead and calls out "1 Geronimo." This is the signal for the next end player to run the inside, take the lead, and call out "2 Geronimo!" One team cannot pass another team. Continue jogging pattern in this way until the music stops or whistle blows. Record each team's scores. Praise their efforts. *Variation:* Power walk instead of jogging.

2.   Finish warm-up with:

- **Hands Circle Walk:** Front support position, keep feet in one place, walk hands in a clockwise or counterclockwise circle.

- **Swimmer Dips:** In back support position, bend elbows to lower and raise body (dips).

- **Body Circles:** Clockwise, then counterclockwise.

Skill Practice & Progressions:

1.   **Inside-of-the-foot Pass.** Demonstrate the inside-of-the-foot pass and reception. Players practice at a wall. Players practice passing ball to a partner, spaced 5 giant steps away. Gradually increase the distance. Emphasize getting the ball under control, then passing.

2.   **Outside-of-the-foot Pass.** Demonstrate the outside-of-the-foot pass and reception. Players practice at a wall. Players practice passing ball to a partner, spaced 5 giant steps away.

3.   **Instep Pass.** Demonstrate the instep pass and reception. Players practice at a wall. Players practice passing ball to a partner, spaced 5 giant steps away.

4.   **"Gotcha" Soccer.** Partners position near a wall and pin or small cone as shown. Object is to knock the pin over using one of the push passes. One partner starts the activity and, if successful in knocking the pin over, the other partner must try to make the same type of pass using the same foot. If unsuccessful, the partner gets a letter "G." Continue in this way until one partner gets a "Gotcha!"

5.   **Zigzag Lead Pass.** Partners position side-by-side, spaced 3 giant steps apart as shown. Partner A starts with the ball. Partner B runs ahead to receive the ball passed by Partner A. Partner B makes the reception, gets the ball under control, then passes to Partner A who now runs ahead. *Variation:* Set up a passing file on each side of the play field as shown. Vary the type of pass used.

Cooling-down Activities/Games:

1. **Soccer Circle Passing.** Teams of 6 in circle formation pass the soccer ball in a certain pattern as shown.

2. **Legends of the Day!**

Fit Think Idea:

Four teams meet in class-time to create ideas for a Joker's Wild Warm-up. (See the Appendix for a sample "Joker's Wild.") Each team is given a suit (Hearts, Diamonds, Spades, or Clubs) and together players create 12 exercises/activities for each. (This activity will be used for Lesson 55.)

5.

Lesson 54:
Goal-kicking

Skill Builders: instep drive kick, introducing volley and half-volley kicks, foot–eye coordination and overall balance, aerobic fitness, partner and group play

Expected Student Performance:

◆   Demonstrates proficiency in performing an instep drive kick and volley and half-volley kicks.

◆   Willingly cooperates and integrates with other class and team members.

◆   Demonstrates proficiency in meeting aerobic fitness and coordination/balance demands.

Facility/Equipment Needed:

◆   Large grass oval, field, or gymnasium

◆   CD or cassette player; popular music

◆   1 soccer-type ball per player

◆   30 cones

◆   1 small balloon or balloon ball per player

◆   1 beanbag or hockey sac per player

Teaching Points:

Instep Drive Kick

◆   Approach ball from behind and at a slight angle.

◆   Square shoulders and hips to target.

◆   Plant nonkicking foot beside the ball, slightly flexing knee.

◆   Keep head steady and eyes focused on the ball.

◆   Keep arms out to sides for balance.

◆   Draw kicking leg back and extend kicking foot, keeping knee directly over the ball.

◆   Snap leg straight through.

◆   Contact center of ball with full instep of foot.

◆   Keep foot firm and toes pointed down as foot strikes the ball.

◆   Follow-through fully with kicking leg to maximize power on the shot.

Volley Kick (Ball is hit straight out of the air.)

◆ Move to the spot where the ball will drop.

◆ Face the ball square-on.

◆ Flex knee of nonkicking foot for balance and body control.

◆ Keep arms out to sides for balance.

◆ Draw kicking leg back and extend kicking foot.

◆ Keep head steady and eyes focused on ball.

◆ Snap kicking leg forward from knee.

◆ Contact center of ball with the instep, keeping kicking foot firm.

◆ Use a short powerful kicking motion as leg snaps straight.

Half Volley Kick

◆ Hit ball the instant it contacts the ground rather than directly out of the air.

Focus Word:

● *Volley*

Warming-up Activities/Games:

1. **Geronimo!** Set up the warm-up as for Lesson 53, but split the class into 2 teams only.

2. **Hotdog Soccer Juggling.** Using small balloon balls, players explore different ways to keep the ball up in the air using feet, knees, and head; anything but hands!

Skill Practice & Progressions:

1. **Instep Kick.** Demonstrate the kicking action. Players pantomime the action, then practice at a wall. Gradually increase the distance.

2. **Roll and Kick.** Partner A is the roller; Partner B is the kicker, spaced 10 giant steps apart. Partner A rolls the ball to Partner B who uses the instep kick to try to send the ball directly back to Partner A. Change roles after 5 kicks. Gradually increase kicking distance.

3. **Volley Kick.** Same as for activity #2, but partner A tosses the ball to Partner B who either volley kicks or half-volley kicks the ball to Partner A. Change roles after 5 tosses.

4. **Pass and Kick.** Get in groups of 3: 1 passer (A), 1 kicker (B), 1 retriever (C). Player A uses inside of foot to pass to Player B who tries to kick the ball between the two cone markers. Player C retrieves the ball and passes it to Player A. Rotate one posi-

tion after every 5 kicks. Start with a kicking distance of 6 yards and cones 2 yards apart, then gradually increase the kicking distance.

5. **Shoot-out.** (Ideally played indoors or in an enclosed area.) Divide the class into two teams and have each team position at a kicking line near the center line of each half-court as shown. Each player has a ball. Space 10 large cones or pins across each end line of a basketball court. On signal "Kick!," players from each team try to kick over their cone markers. Play is stopped after everyone has kicked. Knocked-over cones are counted for each team and recorded, cones are reset, then a new game begins.

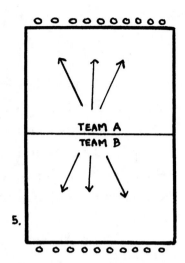

Cooling-down Activities/Games

1. **Hotdog Soccer Juggling.** Using feet and knees, players try to keep a beanbag or hockey sac in the air. Provide opportunity for players to "show off" their talents!

2. **Legends of the Day!**

Lesson 55:
Trapping

Skill Builders: trapping ball with sole of the foot, inside of either foot or lower legs, front of legs, thigh and/or chest, foot–eye coordination, aerobic fitness, partner and group play, communication and trust

Expected Student Performance:

Demonstrates competency in performing the different trapping techniques.

Willingly cooperates and integrates with other class and team members.

Demonstrates good communication and listening skills.

Demonstrates proficiency in meeting fitness demands.

Facility/Equipment Needed:

Large grass oval, field, or gymnasium

1 soft foam ball or soccer-type ball per player

Joker's Wild cards

CD or cassette player; popular music

Blindfolds, enough for half of the class

Several obstacles: benches, hoops, mats, chairs, cones

CD or cassette player; popular music

Teaching Points for Trapping:

Focus eyes on ball.

Position in line with the oncoming ball.

Cushion the impact of the ball to get control.

Use the inside of the foot or lower leg of either foot, the front of both legs to trap a ball traveling low to the ground.

Trap a ground ball by forming a wedge with the heel and sole of the foot and the ground as shown.

Trap an air ball by letting the ball hit the chest or thigh and letting the body absorb the force of the ball so that it drops straight downward to the ground after impact. (Girls are allowed to cross their arms over the chest when doing a chest trap.)

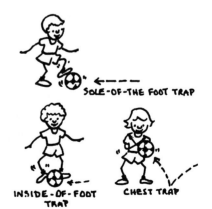

Focus Word:

- *Trapping*

Warming-up Activity/Game:

Joker's Wild—Jumbo Cards. See the Appendix for a sample Joker's Wild warm-up activity, or use each team's Joker's Wild warm-up created as a Fit Think Idea from Lesson 53.

Skill Practice & Progressions:

1. Demonstrate the sole-of-the-foot trap in which the rolling ball is trapped by the player, forming a wedge with the heel and sole of the foot and the ground. Emphasize keeping eyes on the ball and positioning in line with the oncoming ball.

2. **Toss and Trap Grounders.** Partners A and B space 6 giant steps apart. Partner A rolls the ball toward Partner B who traps it with a sole-of-the-foot trap. Change roles after 5 traps have been made.

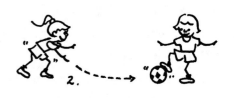

3. Demonstrate trapping the ball with the inside-of-the-foot trap using the inside of either leg, or the lower leg of either foot or front of both legs to trap a ball traveling low to the ground. Emphasize cushioning the impact of the ball to get control. Repeat activity #2 with partner tossing the ball low to the ground.

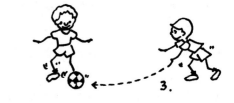

4. Repeat activity #2 with the partner calling out which foot to trap with. Roll the ball or toss it low to the ground so that it goes to the right or to the left of the other partner. Trapping partner moves to position in front of the ball using a sole-of-the-foot trap or inside of leg or front of legs to trap the ball.

5. Demonstrate trapping an air ball by letting the ball hit the chest or thigh (chest or thigh trap). Emphasize that the player let the body absorb the force of the ball so that it drops straight downward to the ground after impact.

6. **Toss and Trap Air Ball.** Partner A tosses the ball up in the air toward Partner B who uses a chest or thigh trap to stop and control the ball. Switch roles after 5 tosses.

7. **Toss, Trap, and Pass.** Groups of 3 position in a triangle formation. Partner A tosses the ball to Partner B who makes the trap, gets the ball under control, then passes the ball to Partner C. Partner C picks up the ball, tosses it to Partner A who makes the trap, then passes the ball to Partner B.

Partner B picks up the ball and passes it to Partner C who makes the trap; Partner C passes the ball to Partner A and the pattern begins again. Send the ball by rolling it or tossing it low to the ground, or tossing it about chest level. Partner making the trap must adjust.

Cooling-down Activities/Games:

1. **Trust Walk.** Players pair up and find a free space. One partner collects a blindfold and puts it on. Other partner carefully leads the "blind" partner through an "obstacle field" of moving over, under, through, across, on and off of, into and out of. If indoors, use soft background music. "Seeing" partner is not allowed to touch "blind" partner; can only give verbal directions. Change roles on signals. Observe interactions taking place and offer feedback when activity has ended.

2. **Legends of the Day!**

Fit Think Idea:

Discuss the art of communicating and the art of listening as equally important skills. Refer to the Trust Walk cooling-down activity.

Lesson 56:
Tackling

Skill Builders: block tackle, poke or side tackle, foot–eye coordination, aerobic fitness, partner and group play

Expected Student Performance:

◆　Demonstrates proficiency in a block tackle and a side or poke tackle.

◆　Willingly cooperates and integrates with other class and team members.

◆　Demonstrates proficiency in meeting fitness demands.

Facility/Equipment Needed:

◆　Large grass oval, field, or gymnasium

◆　1 soft foam ball or soccer-type ball per player

◆　Joker's Wild cards

◆　CD or cassette player; popular music

Teaching Points:

Tackling is the method used to take the ball away from an opponent. Two basic tackling techniques are presented: the "block" and the "poke." To be an effective tackler requires good judgment, confidence, and exact timing.

Block Tackle

◆　Use when opponent is dribbling directly at you.

◆　Play the ball, not the opponent, when tackling.

◆　Focus on the ball.

◆　Position feet in a staggered stance with one foot slightly ahead of the other.

◆　Get into a slightly crouched stance with knees flexed, arms out to sides for balance, to react quickly to dribbler's movements.

◆　Tackle the ball by blocking it with inside surface of foot.

◆　Position foot sideways, keep it firm, and drive it into the ball.

◆　Push ball forward, pass the opponent, and gain possession.

BLOCK TACKLE

Poke or Side Tackle

◆　Use when approaching an opponent from the side or from slightly behind.

◆　Close in on dribbler.

◆　Focus on the ball.

◆　Stay in a slightly crouched stance with knees flexed.

◆　Keep balance and body control.

" POKE/SIDE TACKLE

◆   Reach in with leg, extend foot, and poke ball away with toes.

◆   Play the ball, not the opponent.

Focus Word:

●   *Tackle*

Warming-up Activity/Game:

Joker's Wild. See the Appendix for a sample Joker's Wild warm-up activity, or use each team's Joker's Wild warm-up created as a Fit Think Idea from Lessons 53 and 55.

Skill Practice and Progressions:

1.   Demonstrate the *block* tackle. Demonstrate the *poke* tackle. Emphasize that the block tackle is made from the front of the opponent using the inside of the foot to take the ball away; the poke tackle is made from the side of the opponent using the toes of the foot to tap the ball away.

2.   Players partner up and find a free space. One partner is the dribbler; the other, the tackler. At first, dribbler plays passively and lets tackler take away the ball to practice the techniques. Change roles and repeat.

3.   **Soccer Tag.** Partners play soccer tag, trying to tackle the ball away from each other and gain possession. Emphasize safety at all times: A player must play the ball, not the opponent, and only go after his/her partner's ball!

4.   **Soccer Pirates.** Dribblers with the ball scatter throughout the play area. Pirates who do not have a ball start in the center of the play area. On signal "Pirates!," the Pirates try to tackle the ball away from dribblers. Once a dribbler loses possession of the ball, he/she becomes a Pirate. Game continues in this way.

Cooling-down Activities/Games:

1.   **Dog and a Bone (Soccer Ball).** For each game, two teams of 6–8 number off and stand facing each other on opposite sides of a sideline, 30 feet (10 meters) apart. A gap is left in the middle between each side of players as shown. A soccer ball is placed in the center between the two teams. When a number is called ("3"), players with that number run toward the ball and try to take possession of it by using a tackle, then dribble it over the gap line on their team sideline to score a point. Play until every number has been called. Mingle the teams and begin a new game. *Variation:* Call two numbers out at a time.

2.   **Legends of the Day!**

Lesson 57:
Goalkeeping

Skill Builders: goalkeeping skills, tracking the ball, alertness, reaction, aerobic fitness, partner and group play

Expected Student Performance:

◆ Demonstrates proficiency in tracking the ball and goalkeeping.

◆ Willingly cooperates and integrates with other class and team members.

◆ Demonstrates proficiency in meeting fitness demands.

Facility/Equipment Needed:

◆ Large grass oval, field, or gymnasium

◆ 1 soft foam ball or soccer-type ball per pair

◆ 2 cones per pair

◆ 1 large cone per group of 4

◆ Die

Teaching Points:

Ready Position

◆ Stand with knees bent, weight forward on balls of feet, ready to move quickly in any direction.

◆ Hold hands at waist to chest level, palms forward and fingers pointing upward.

◆ Keep head steady and focus on the ball.

◆ Move body in line with the oncoming ball.

◆ React quickly, using the shuffle step for any sideways movement.

Ready Position

Collecting the Ball

◆ For a ground ball, scoop it up into the arms.

◆ For an air ball, hold hands in an upward position for a ball taken above the waist; hands downward for a ball below the waist.

◆ For each catch, clutch ball against chest with the forearms.

◆ Roll or bowl ball to an offensive player over a short distance.

◆ Overhand throw the ball (baseball throw) or punt upfield over longer distances.

◆ Deflect shots using a punch shot with the fists or a push shot with open hand.

Deflect Shot

Kicking the Ball

◆ Punt kick (full volley) the ball by holding it with both hands in front of the waist.

◆ Bend knee and point toes of kicking leg downward.

◆ Straighten knee, contacting ball with the instep of the foot, and rise up on the toes of the nonkicking foot.

◆ Punt the ball out of the hands, fully extending leg on follow-through.

◆ Drop kick (half volley) by releasing the ball, then stepping forward to strike it just as the ball contacts the ground. Lean back and completely follow-through with the kicking leg fully extended.

Punt Kick

Focus Words:

● *Goalkeeping*

● *Drop Kicking*

● *Punting*

Warming-up Activity/Game:

Dice-ercise. Players run clockwise around the perimeter of the playing area (or one half of the large playing field). Teacher (or nonparticipating player) rolls the die out into the center of the play area. Players do the activity until the die is rolled again and a new number appears. This is a "dicy" game so if the same number appears again, have players do a modification of the same exercise (knee push-ups, wall push-ups)!

● "1"—Power walk clockwise around the play area.

● "2"—Jump rope for two minutes.

● "3"—Slide-step from one side to the opposite of playing field.

● "4"—Hit the deck and do knee push-ups.

● "5"—Drop into hook-sit position and do sit-ups on the spot.

● "6"—Grapevine step counterclockwise along the boundary lines of the play area.

Skill Practice & Progressions:

1. Demonstrate goalkeeping skills of ready position, catching a ground or air ball, deflecting a shot, and throwing the ball to a teammate. Emphasize teaching cues. Players pantomime the action.

2. Partners stand near a wall. One partner is the goalkeeper who positions in the goal area (2 cone markers, spaced 3 giant steps apart) as shown. The other partner is the thrower who throws the ball high, low, along the ground, trying to score a goal. Goalkeeper retrieves the ball and overhand throws or bowls it back to the thrower. Switch roles after every 5 throws.

2.

3. Now demonstrate goalkeeper making the catch and then punting the ball out of the hands, fully extending leg on follow-through. Demonstrate the drop kick or half volley by releasing the ball, then stepping forward to strike it just as the ball contacts the ground. Emphasize following through with the kicking leg fully extended.

4. Repeat activity #2, but have goalkeeper retrieve the ball and punt it back to the thrower. Switch roles after every 5 kicks.

5. Again use the same set-up as for activity #2. Partner now kicks the ball to try to score a goal from a kicking distance of 10 yards (meters). Other partner defends the goal, reacting to the flight of the oncoming ball. Goalkeeper deflects the shot by punching with a fist or pushing with the open hand. If goalkeeper catches the ball, he/she punts it back to the kicker. Change roles after every 5 kicks. *Variation:* Kicker can dribble in and attempt to score.

6. **3-on-1 Attack.** Set up in groups of 4 with 3 players in triangle formation, spaced 6–8 giant steps away from each other, and a goalkeeper in the center who tries to protect a large traffic cone. Triangle players take turns throwing the ball to try to hit the cone. The goalkeeper protects the cone, deflecting or catching the ball, and throws it back to a thrower. Thrower may pass quickly to each other to try to catch the goalkeeper off guard. A new goalkeeper takes over after every 6 throws.

Cooling-down Activities/Games:

1. **Dog and a Bone (Soccer Ball).** Play the game as for Lesson 56, but tackler now tries to get control of the ball and score on the opposition line who act as goalkeepers. *Variation:* Call out two numbers at the same time.

2. **Legends of the Day!**

Homework Idea:

Observe a soccer game in action either "live" or on a sports channel. Note how the players keep the ball under control, passing plays, player positioning, goalkeeping, and penalties that occur.

Lesson 58:
Heading the Ball/Throw-in

Skill Builders: heading the ball, tracking, timing and coordination, the throw-in, aerobic fitness, partner and group play

Expected Student Performance:

◆ Demonstrates proficiency in heading the ball and performing a throw-in.

◆ Willingly cooperates and integrates with other class and team members.

◆ Demonstrates proficiency in meeting fitness demands.

Facility/Equipment Needed:

◆ Large grass oval, field, or gymnasium

◆ 1 soft foam ball or soccer-type ball per pair

◆ 1 pair of color-n-dots dice

Teaching Points:

Heading the Ball

◆ Focus eyes on the ball.

◆ Move to position under the descending ball.

◆ Use a two-foot takeoff to jump.

◆ Use legs to propel trunk, neck, and head forward to meet the ball.

◆ Contact ball on forehead at the highest point of the jump.

◆ Time the jump so that the head hits the ball rather than the ball hitting the head.

◆ Send ball upward by heading it under the middle of the ball.

◆ Send ball downward by heading above the middle of the ball.

◆ Follow-through with the forehead.

◆ Land on both feet, bending at the knees to cushion impact.

Throw-in

Occurs whenever the ball goes out of play over the sidelines. Team to last touch the ball takes the throw. Another player must touch the ball before the thrower can touch the ball again. Cannot score a goal from the throw-in.

- ◆ Plant both feet behind the sideline and in contact with the ground.
- ◆ Throw ball from behind the head with both hands.

Focus Words:
- ● *Heading the Ball*
- ● *Throw-in*

Warming-up Activity/Game:

Double Dice Warm-up. Players pair up and find a free space. Use color-n-dots dice. Each face of the die is one of the rainbow colors: red, orange, yellow, green, blue, and purple.

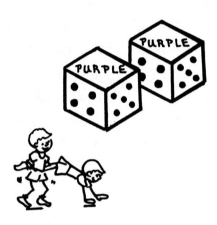

- ● Doubles (same number)—Sprint from one end line to the opposite end line.
- ● Odd Number (total of two dice)—Leapfrog with a partner from sideline to opposite sideline.
- ● Even Number (total of two dice)—"Thread the needle."
- ● Both "Red"—Ski jump back and forth along a sideline.
- ● Both "Blue"—Bicycling feet.
- ● Both "Yellow"—Inchworms.
- ● Both "Green"—Bucking broncos.
- ● Both "Blue"—Churn-the-butter.
- ● Both "Purple"—Wheelbarrow walk.
- ● Both different colors: Backward get-up.

Skill Practice & Progressions:

1. Demonstrate the throw-in and discuss the throw-in rule. Partners take turns to practice throw-in at a sideline of the court.

2. Demonstrate the technique of heading the ball. Use a balloon ball or softer, foam ball for this. Heading the ball can be used to pass the ball to a teammate, score a goal, or clear the ball away from the goal area.

3. **Toss and Head.** In a Home space, toss the ball in the air above your head and try to head the ball. Emphasize that contact is on the forehead. Jump to meet the ball, rather than the ball meeting the forehead!

4. **Wall Toss and Head.** Toss the ball high up against a wall and try to head the rebound back up against the wall. Then practice heading the ball downward.

5. **Partner Toss and Head.** Players pair up and collect a balloon ball and a foam or light soccer-type ball. Use the balloon ball first to practice heading the ball to each other, then the foam ball. Partner A underhand tosses ball so that it arches and drops toward Partner B's head. Partner B tries to head the ball forward and back to Partner A. *Challenge:* Try to head the ball back and forth to each other.

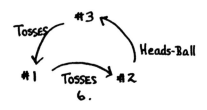

6. **Triangle Heading.** Players stand in a triangle formation about 2 yards part. Player #1 tosses ball to Player #2 who heads it to Player #3. Player #3 catches the ball and tosses it to Player #1 who heads the ball to Player #2; Player #2 catches the ball and tosses it to Player #3. Continue this pattern of tossing, heading, and catching. Reverse the direction. Emphasize that players move to get directly under the descending ball and then head it.

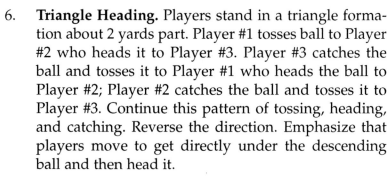

Cooling-down Activities/Games:

1. **Socceroo.** This game is an ideal indoor soccer lead-up game. Mark out the play area as shown. Ensure that the safe zones are 10 feet (3 meters) from the wall. Divide the class into 2 equal teams: kicking team and the batting team. Establish a girl–boy–girl–boy kicking order. Kicker stands at the center spot on one safety line, facing the fielding team. Remaining kicking team players stand or sit safely to one side. Bowler rolls the ball from a marked spot towards the kicker. Kicker must kick the ball over a kicking line, then try to run safely to the opposite safe zone, and tag up at the wall. Runner has the choice of staying here or trying to run back to the Home safe zone. But at most only 3 runners are allowed in the safe zone before the first runner to get there must return back. A runner scores one point for each way. Fielding team tries to retrieve the ball and hit the runner below the knees before he/she can reach the safe zone. If successful, that runner is out. A fly ball caught in the air or off a wall puts the kicker out, and no runner can go out of the safety zone. Fielders are not allowed to run with the ball, but may pass to another teammate who is in a better position to tag or hit the runner. Scores are recorded on a whiteboard as the game progresses. Teams change roles after everyone has had a turn at bat. *Variation:* Allow only two runners in the opposite safe zone.

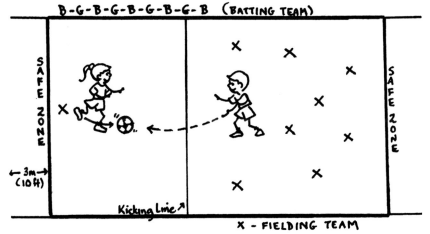

2.   **Legends of the Day!**

Homework Idea:

Make photocopies of soccer field and have players pencil in the field markings, plus player positions. (See the Appendix.) Discuss the "free kicks" situations that occur in a soccer game and the difference between a direct kick and an indirect kick. (Refer to Soccer rules in the Appendix.)

Lesson 59:
Skill Builder Stations

Skill Builders: fundamental soccer skills of dribbling, passing, shooting, trapping, tackling, heading, goalkeeping, throw-in, foot–eye coordination, balance and overall coordination, cooperation

Expected Student Performance:

◆ Demonstrates competence and confidence in performing fundamental soccer skills and applying to 3-on-3 mini-games.

◆ Willingly cooperates and integrates with other class and team members.

◆ Demonstrates competence and confidence in performing balancing tasks.

◆ Demonstrates fair play and good sportsmanship and meets fitness demands.

Facility/Equipment Needed:

◆ Large grass oval, field, or gymnasium

◆ Cassette or CD player; station signs

◆ Station #1: 2 large nets or wall targets, 1 soccer ball per player, floor tape or dome markers

◆ Station #2: 1 large balloon ball or soft trainer ball

◆ Station #3: obstacle course using cones, chairs, hoops, directional arrows, etc.

◆ Station #4: 2 hockey nets or 4 large cones, 1 soft soccer ball, 2 sets of bibs

◆ Station #5: balance boards or Duck Walkers™, tilt walkers, stilts, lo-lo bouncers, pogo bouncers

◆ Station #6: mini-hockey nets, mini-soccer ball, 6 scooters, 2 sets of bibs

Skill Builder Station Ideas:

Station #1: Kick & Score. If possible, use two large nets or wall targets, and mark out 4–5 different kicking spots as shown. Players take turns kicking ball from the spot to try to score a goal.

Station #2: Ball in Space. For groups of 3 in triangle formation. Using a small balloon ball, players keep the ball up in the air using only feet, knees, or head.

Station #3: Obstacle Dribble. Each player tries to dribble soccer ball through the obstacle course as quickly as possible. Record times. As soon as one player has reached halfway point, the next player can go. Partners can time each other.

Station #4: 3-on-3 Mini-soccer. For each team, one player is a goalie; second player is a defensive player; the third player is an offensive player. Each team wears a different set of colored bibs. Hockey nets or cones are used as goals. Players are allowed to change positions through the game. Soccer rules are enforced.

Station #5: Soccer Balancing: Use a variety of balancing equipment and let players explore balancing in different ways on the equipment, such as: balance boards or Duck Walkers™, tilt walkers, stilts, lo-lo bouncers, pogo bouncers.

Station #6: Scooter Board Soccer Ball. This is a 3-on-3 game played in a confined space, using a mini-soccer ball which can be hand or foot dribbled, passed by hand or foot. A goal is scored by throwing or kicking the ball into a net. No goalie is allowed, but each team can have a defending player. See diagram.

Cooling-down Activity:

Legends of the Day!

Lesson 60:
Lead-up and Modified Games

Skill Builders: fundamental soccer skills of dribbling, passing, shooting, trapping, tackling, heading, goalkeeping, throw-in, foot–eye coordination, team play, court awareness and positional play

Expected Student Performance:

Demonstrates competency in performing fundamental soccer skills in game situations.

Willingly cooperates and integrates with other class and team members.

Demonstrates proficiency in positional play and team strategies.

Facility/Equipment Needed:

Large grass oval, field, or gymnasium

1 soccer-type ball per circle game

Several cones or dome markers for mini-playing fields

6–8 sets of bibs

4 large cone markers per goal

Floor tape for goal box area and marking off zones

Hockey nets for goal area

Teaching Points:

Teach the rules of soccer. (See the Appendix.)

Demonstrate how fouls can occur and what action is taken.

Discuss the player positions and the roles of each.

Lead-up Game:

Circle Soccer. Divide the class into two teams and have each team position outside of a large marked-out circle, on one half of the circle. One team is given the ball. A player starts the game by kicking the ball toward the other team, trying to send the ball outside the circle to score a point. The opposing team players try to trap the soccer ball, preventing a goal from being scored, then kick it towards the opponent's half circle to attempt to score. The ball must stay below the opponent's waist (shoulders). Team players may pass the ball to each other before attempting to score. Try not to telecast where the kick is going!

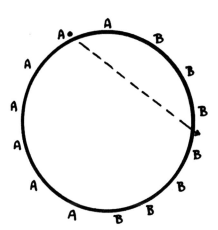

Modified Games:

1. **Sideline Soccer.** Each game requires 4 teams of 6–8 players: 2 teams are the active court players and 2 teams are the sideline players and assist their court team respectively. For each team there are 2–3 forwards, 2–3 mid-fielders, 2 defenders, and no goalkeepers. Each team wears a set of colored bibs for easy identification and change-over. Set up a hockey net goal on each end line as shown. Regulation rules are in play. Active players try to score a goal by kicking the ball over the end line. Sideline players keep the ball in play by passing it to a teammate on the court, but they cannot score. After a goal has been scored, sideline and court players change roles. Emphasize positional play. Have players switch to a different position after every change-over. (See the Appendix for soccer rules.)

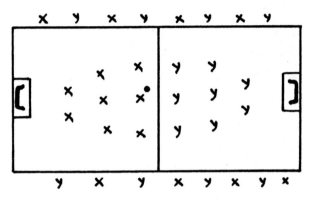

2. **Zone Soccer.** Divide each half of the playing field into 3 zones. Each team consists of 6–9 players who position as shown in the diagram: 3 forwards, 3 guards, 3 goalies. Only forwards may advance into each other's half-fields to try to kick a goal. Guards try to tackle the ball away; goalies are the last line of defense. Play regulation rules. (See the Appendix for soccer rules.) After a goal has been scored, players in their playing field rotate positions: goalkeepers to defense; defense to forwards; forwards to goalkeepers. *Variation:* Put two soccer balls into play!

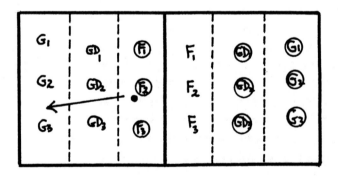

3. **Many-goal Soccer.** Use a soccer field or basketball court boundaries for this game, with goal nets positioned in the middle of each end line and middle of each sideline as shown. Each game requires two teams of 8–12 players; each team wears a set of colored bibs. Each team has a goalie for one end-line goal and for one sideline goal. See diagram. To start the game, each team has a soft foam soccer-type ball and kicks it into play per regulation rules which then go into effect. (See the Appendix for soccer rules.)

Teams try to score on either of the two opposition goals. For an indoor game, the ball may be played off the walls. Emphasize fair play and safe play at all times! Observe game in motion and offer feedback if necessary. Better still, get involved and play the game as well! Nonparticipating players can be umpires for the game.

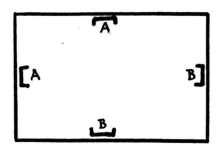

4. **4-a-side Soccer.** Mark out 4 mini-fields (60 feet by 40 feet) and divide the class into 8 teams of 4 players. Each team wears a set of bibs. Set up the games in the following order: Team A vs. Team B; Team C vs. Team D; Team E vs. Team F; Team G vs. Team H. Each team consists of a goalkeeper, 2 forwards, and 1 defensive player. Players are encouraged to switch positions and experience playing in each. *Variations:*

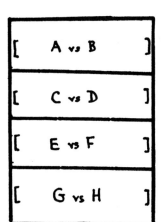

    ● Play 6-a-side soccer: 3 forwards, 2 defensive players, 1 goalie.
    ● Set up a tournament. Try to "balance" teams so that one team does not dominate the play.
    ● Have a girls tournament separate from the boys.

Cooling-down Activity:

Legends of the Day!

Lesson 61:
Throwing and Catching

Skill Builders: grip, overhand throwing and catching revision, tracking the ball, hand–eye coordination, aerobic fitness, partner and group play

Expected Student Performance:

◆   Demonstrates competency and confidence in overhand throwing and catching.

◆   Willingly cooperates and integrates with partners and team members.

◆   Demonstrates proficiency in meeting fitness demands.

Facility/Equipment Needed:

◆   Large open outdoor area or gymnasium

◆   1 fielding glove per player

◆   1 large softball-type per pair

◆   8 deck rings and 4 tall cone markers

◆   4 softball bases or carpet squares; 6 poly spots

◆   Wall targets

Teaching Points:

Grip

◆   Hold ball by the fingers and off the palm of the hand.

◆   Grip the ball tightly with the fingers across the seams.

◆   Use a 2-finger grip with the index finger and middle finger across the seams and the little finger resting on the side of the ball.

◆   For smaller hands use a 3-finger grip by placing the index, middle, and ring fingers across the seams.

◆   Place the thumb under the ball on the opposite side to the little finger.

WRIST SNAP

Throwing (See Lesson 15—Overhand Throwing)

◆   Stand side-on to target or receiver, one foot in front of the other, and the dominant leg back.

◆   Keep eyes on target.

◆   Grip ball in your fingers, wrist cocked.

◆   Pointer finger of nonthrowing hand points at target.

Throwing hand swings in a downward and backward arc, weight transfers onto back foot.

Elbow bends as throwing hand moves behind head, wrist cocked.

Front foot steps forward as weight transfers from back foot.

Hips, then shoulders, rotate forward.

Lead the arm motion with the elbow.

Release the ball with a wrist snap.

Follow-through in the intended direction of flight.

Catching

Position body squarely with the oncoming ball, and maintain a balanced stance.

Keep eyes focused on the ball, tracking it into the hands.

Reach for the ball, giving with the arms and hands to absorb its force.

For a high ball, position glove so that fingers are up.

For a low ball, position glove so that fingers point down.

Let ball come into glove, then use the other hand to trap the ball into the glove.

the glove.

Focus Words:

- *Tracking the ball*
- *"Giving" with impact*

Warming-up Activity/Game:

Base Tag. Mark out a large diamond-shaped play area and place bases or "floor squares" at each of the corners along with 6 floor spots, the safety spots, scattered throughout the play area as shown. Select one team to be the IT team. Each IT uses a whiffle ball as the tagging object. The IT team on signal gives chase. Any free player who is tagged must go to a corner square and jog in place. A player is safe if touching a safety spot with one foot, but is allowed only a 5-second count to stay there. A player who has been tagged can be freed by another free player if they run once around the outside of the diamond and do so while holding a deck ring between them. Two deck rings are located near each square on a tall cone marker and must be returned to the cone. After a certain time another team takes over as the IT team and the game continues. For each new game, change the movement of the tagged player. *Variations:* Finger Stretches, Arm Stretches.

SAFETY SPOT

BASE

IT

Skill Practice & Progressions:

1. Each student holds a softball-type ball. Demonstrate the 2- and 3-finger grips on the ball. Players "feel" the ball in their fingers. Demonstrate catching the ball in the glove. Emphasize using the other hand to trap the ball into the glove.

2. Players toss the ball upward and practice catching it in the glove. Catch the ball high; catch the ball low. Check for correct positioning of the glove.

3. Send the ball to a wall target with an overhand throw and practice catching the rebound off the wall using the glove.

4. Partners, spaced about 5 giant steps apart, throw the ball back and forth to each other. Partner A sets a target with his/her glove, reaching for the oncoming ball. Partner B overhand throws to the target. Emphasize overhand throw technique. Then reverse roles. Vary the target by shifting the glove's position every 2 throws. Emphasize that the catcher "give" with the ball and focus on correct glove placement. Gradually increase the throwing distance. As the distance demands a much greater throwing effort, emphasize that the thrower take a couple of steps before throwing the ball.

5. **Catch Me If You Can!** In a certain time limit see which pairs can make the most consecutive number of passes from a certain distance. If the ball is not caught, the count must begin again.

Cooling-down Activities/Games:

1. **Pattern Throw and Catch.** In large circles of 6–8 players, throw the ball to someone who is not on either side of you. Establish a throwing pattern. Practice the pattern. Which team can complete the pattern through 6 times the quickest?

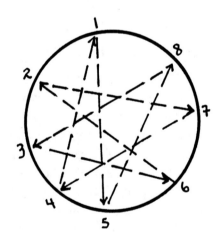

2. **Legends of the Day!**

Fit Think Idea:

Run Around Australia Project. (See the Appendix.) Each class member keeps track of the miles (km) he/she runs using the "Run Around Australia" Form. Two class captains monitor and record each team's total distance at the end of each week on a team barometer and use pins to indicate progress on the map of Australia.

Lesson 62:
Fielding Grounders/Sidearm Throw

Skill Builders: fielding a ground ball, tracking the ball, sidearm throwing, dodging and agility, partner and group play

Expected Student Performance:

◆ Demonstrates proficiency in fielding a ground ball and performing a sidearm throw.

◆ Willingly cooperates and integrates with other class and team members.

◆ Demonstrates proficiency in meeting fitness demands.

Facility/Equipment Needed:

◆ Large open outdoor area or gymnasium

◆ 1 fielding glove per player

◆ 1 large softball-type per pair

     1 whiffle ball or tennis ball per thrower

     8–12 cone markers for shuttle relay

Teaching Points:

Fielding Grounders—Ready Position

Get into a direct line with the path of the ball using the shuffle step.

Bend knees and lean forward with upper body so that glove and other hand touch the ground.

Position so that one leg is forward, the other slightly back (leg on throwing side).

Keep weight on the balls of the feet; seat low to the ground.

Keep glove and other hand in an open position to receive the ball and use the non-glove hand to trap the ball into the glove.

Fielding and Throwing

Keep arms and hands "soft" and relaxed.

Keep eyes tracking the ball all the way into the glove.

Give with the ball as you field it.

Bring it to the hip of the throwing side.

Keep the transition from fielding and throwing the ball one smooth and quick motion.

◆   Know where to throw the ball before you field it.

◆   Find the target, releasing the ball.

Sidearm Throwing

(Used for shorter and quicker throws than the overhand throw. An effective throw for infielders: shortstop to second baseman, pitcher to first base, etc.)

◆   Turn sideways, extending upper throwing arm out diagonally and down from shoulder.

◆   Forearm should be straight up from the elbow.

◆   Swing arm forward with the forearm parallel to the ground.

◆   Release ball and follow through with arm across the body.

Focus Words:

●   *T.E.A.M. (Together Everyone Achieves More)*

Warming-up Activity/Game:

Partner Throws & Tag. Partners start back-to-back with one partner holding a whiffle or tennis ball; both partners wear gloves. On signal or when the music starts, partners split away from each other and throw the ball using the overhand or sidearm throw. When music stops or whistle blows, partner with the ball is IT and gives chase to the free partner, trying to tag him/her before the music or start signal is given. If successful, IT scores a point; otherwise, the point is given to the free player who remains untagged. Which partner will have the best score at the finish of the game? Partners then mingle (find new partners), and a new game continues. Play until a good warm-up effect has been achieved.

Skill Practice & Progressions:

1.   **Demonstrate fielding a low or ground ball.** Remind players to use a staggered stance (or kneel on one knee.) Move to position directly in front of the oncoming ball. Bring the glove and hand into an open position. Track the ball all the way into the glove and then trap it there with the other hand. Give with the arms and hands to cushion the force of the rolling ball.

2.   Throw a large whiffle ball (tennis ball) low to a wall and practice fielding the rebound ball. Start only 5 giant steps

away, then gradually move farther away until about 10–15 yards away from the wall. Throw the ball at different angles so that you have to react left or right to field the ball.

3. **Demonstrate the sidearm throw.** Players practice at the wall sidearm throwing and fielding the ball. Emphasize and demonstrate the transition from fielding to throwing, making the motion smooth and quick. Players practice.

4. Partners stand about 20 feet apart and take turns fielding thrown ground balls. Fielding partner quickly scoops up the ball and throws it back to other partner using a sidearm throw or low overhand throw to target (receiving partner). Now throw ball so that it travels to the left or right of fielder, who must move to align body to the ball.

5. **Triangle Pick-off.** Players stand in a triangle formation, spaced about 10–12 yards apart. Player A sidearm throws ball to Player B, who tries to quickly field the grounder and overhand throw the ball to Player C—all in one smooth motion. Player C makes the catch, then sidearm throws to Player A, who fields the grounder and overhand throws to B; Player B makes the catch, and sidearm throws to Player C. Player C fields the grounder, then overhand throws to Player A, and the pattern of "sidearm throw—field—overhand throw—catch" repeats.

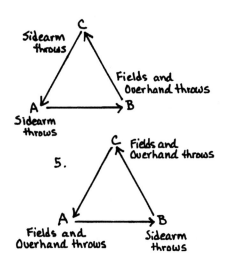

Cooling-down Activities/Games:

1. **Grounders Relay.** Teams of 6 players position in shuttle formation with each half spaced 8 yards apart. Use cone markers or lines on the floor to position each side. Player A sidearm throws to Player B who fields the grounder and sidearm throws to Player C, and so on. Player than goes to the end of his/her file. *Variation:* Overhand throw to opposite player. After the throw, run to position behind the file of the opposite side.

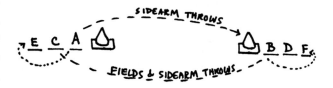

2. **Legends of the Day!**

Fit Think Idea:

Run Around Australia Project. (See the Appendix.) Collect running sheets and have captain record results.

Lesson 63:
Fielding Fly Balls

Skill Builders: fielding a fly ball, tracking the ball, transition from fielding to throwing, aerobic fitness, stretching and breathing, partner and group play

Expected Student Performance:

◆ Demonstrates proficiency in fielding a fly ball and making a smooth transition from fielding to throwing.

◆ Willingly cooperates and integrates with other class and team members.

◆ Demonstrates proficiency in meeting fitness demands.

Facility/Equipment Needed:

◆ Large open grassed field or oval, or gymnasium

◆ 1 fielding glove per player

◆ 1 large softball-type per pair

◆ 1 whiffle ball or tennis ball per thrower

◆ 8–12 cone markers for shuttle relay

Teaching Points:

Fielding a Fly Ball—Ready Position

◆ Track the oncoming ball, moving in toward the ball if necessary.

◆ Move quickly to position body in front of it.

◆ Keep glove pocket open and in front of throwing shoulder.

Transition from Fielding to Throwing

◆ Catch the ball on the throwing side of the body above eye level.

◆ Hold the glove fingers upward, and place other hand over the ball to trap it in the glove.

◆ If the ball falls short, extend the glove toward the oncoming ball, keeping it open and glove fingers pointed downward.

◆ Bend elbows to absorb the force of the ball.

◆ Hold throwing hand up near glove, ready to grab the ball and throw it.

◆ Know where to throw the ball before fielding it.

◆ Take a crossover step to plant the rear foot and produce more throwing force.

◆ Make the transition between catching the fly ball and throwing it in one smooth and quick action.

Focus Words:

● *Health and Fitness allows better and longer life! (H - F - A - B - L - L)*

Warming-up Activities/Games:

Six-Minute H - F - A - B - L - L Workout. (Head, Forward Trunk, Arms and Shoulder, Back, Lateral Trunk, and Leg with an aerobic movement)

● Jog for 30 seconds

● Head Nods

● Belly Button Swirls

● Prance for 30 seconds

● Arm Propellers and Shoulder Rotators

● Back Lifts

● Leg Kick for 30 seconds

● Side Benders

● Pantomime jumping a rope for 30 seconds

● Leg–Toes Flexors

Skill Practice & Progressions:

1. Demonstrate the ready position. Players pantomime the action of catching a fly ball. Demonstrate the transition from making the catch to making the throw. Practice the crossover footwork. Use the teaching cues.

2. At a wall, each player overhand throws ball high up onto the wall, then tracks it to pick off the rebound.

3. **Fly Ball Gotcha.** Partners stand at a wall. Partner A throws the ball high up onto the wall; Partner B catches the rebound, and quickly throws the ball back up along the wall. If a player misses making the catch, he/she gets a letter. Who will get to "gotcha" first?

4. **Pop-ups.** Partners, spaced 12 yards apart, throw high pop-ups to each other using a tennis ball or large whiffle ball or large soft ball. Vary flight and distance thrown. Emphasize receiving partner tracking the ball all the way and getting the body in front of the ball.

5. **Sky Ball.** For each team, circle players space themselves 5 giant steps away from a center player, Sky Thrower, who throws high pop-ups towards circle players and calls out a number. The player with that number must make the catch, then throw the ball back to the circle player. Change the Sky Thrower after each number has been called. Sky Thrower takes the place and the number of the circle player coming to the center. *Variation:* Earn points for making a catch. Subtract points if ball touches floor.

Cooling-down Activities/Games:

(Use soothing relaxing music.)

1. **H - F - A - B - L - L Cool-down.**

   - Head Stretch
   - Forward Trunk Stretch
   - Arms/Shoulder Stretch
   - Back Stretch
   - Lateral Trunk Stretch
   - Leg Stretch
   - Breathing: slowly inhaling; slowly exhaling

2. **Legends of the Day!**

Fit Think Idea:

Run Around Australia Project. (See the Appendix.) Collect running sheets and have captain record results.

Lesson 64:
Pitching and Back-catching

Skill Builders: pitching skills and back-catching skills, accuracy throwing, tracking the ball, hand–eye coordination, aerobic fitness, partner and group play

Expected Student Performance:

◆   Demonstrates competent and confident pitching and back-catching skills.

◆   Willingly cooperates and integrates with other class and team members.

◆   Demonstrates proficiency in meeting fitness demands.

Facility/Equipment Needed:

◆   Large open outdoor area or gymnasium

◆   1 softball-type ball per pair

◆   1 glove per player

◆   Wall targets, floor tape

◆   Cone markers

Teaching Points:

The Strike Zone for the batter is the area from the bottom of the armpits to the top of the knees, and over home plate.

Underhand Pitching

◆   Stand square-on to target, balanced, feet comfortably spread.

◆   Hold ball and pitching hand in the glove at waist level.

◆   Bend trunk slightly forward at waist level.

◆   Keep both feet in contact with pitching rubber or marker.

◆   Grip the ball with the fingers across the seams.

◆   Keep eyes focused on target or strike zone.

◆   Aim the ball at the catcher's glove.

◆   Extend throwing arm down and back, taking weight on back foot.

◆   Cock the wrists at the top of the backswing.

◆   Step forward with foot opposite to throwing arm when beginning the downward motion of the pitch.

◆   Transfer weight from back foot to front foot as throwing arm swings through.

◆   Snap the wrist releasing the ball between the waist and knee level.

◆ Follow through "up" and "out" in the intended direction of flight and step forward on back leg ready to react.

Back-catching

◆ Position just beyond the range of the swinging bat.

◆ Squat with feet shoulder-width apart, one foot slightly ahead of the other.

◆ Hold glove up as the target for the pitcher.

◆ Keep eyes focused on the ball, tracking it all the way into glove.

◆ Use the non-glove hand to trap the ball into the glove.

Focus Word:

● *Strike Zone*

Warming-up Activities/Games:

Splash Routine. See Lesson 10. Use popular music with a steady 4/4 beat. Add some sea creature actions such as:

● Crab Walk greeting

● Seahorse Bobs

● Octopus Crawl

Skill Practice & Progressions:

1. Demonstrate the stance and pitching motion. Emphasize teaching points/cues. Discuss the strike zone and demonstrate with a player in batter position at home plate. Talk about the pitching area (mound and rubber).

2. **Wall Target Pitch.** Use floor tape to mark off several pitching zones or strike zones as shown. Mark off a pitching line ("rubber") 8–10 yards from the wall. Players practice pitching from this distance into the target area. *Variation:* Mark off 3 different pitching lines that vary in distance from the wall (8, 10, 12 yards) to suit the different ability levels of the class.

3. Demonstrate the stance and back-catching skills. Players pantomime the action.

4. **Strike!** Partners collect a softball and base or carpet square. One partner is the back catcher who positions just behind the base near a wall as shown. Other partner is the pitcher who stands at a pitching line located 8–10 yards from the base.

Pitcher takes 10 pitches, back-catcher calls a "ball" or a "strike" on the pitch. Emphasize that back-catcher set a target with his/her glove for the pitcher.

Cooling-down Activities/Games:

1. **Three Deep.** Pairs scatter around the play area and stand one behind the other (file) just in front of a carpet square as shown, except for one pair (A and B) who start in the middle, standing back-to-back. On signal (music), game begins. Partner B counts to 5, while Partner A takes off. The object is for Partner B to try to tag A. Partner A moves in and out of the stationary pairs to avoid being caught. At any time A can choose to stand on a carpet square (3 deep). This is the signal for the end player to take over A's role. Partner B must now pursue this player. If Partner B does make the tag, the two players quickly change roles. *Variation:* Have 2 pairs that start in the middle—A vs. B; C vs. D—and play the game as above.

2. **Legends of the Day!**

Fit Think Idea:

Run Around Australia Project. (See the Appendix.) Collect running sheets and have captain record results.

Homework Idea:

If in season, ask children to watch a softball game. Note the player positions, playing field, and general rules of the game.

Lesson 65:
Batting

Skill Builders: grip, stance and swing, hand–eye coordination, tracking the ball, aerobic fitness, partner and group play

Expected Student Performance:

◆ Demonstrates proficiency in batting a ball off a tee, batting a pitched ball, and batting a ball thrown to self ("fungo batting").

◆ Willingly cooperates and integrates with partner and team members.

◆ Demonstrates proficiency in meeting fitness demands.

Facility/Equipment Needed:

◆ Large open grassed field or oval, or gymnasium

◆ 1 softball-type ball and 1 whiffle ball per pair

◆ 1 bat per pair, different lengths

◆ 1 softball glove per player

◆ 1 poly square or base per pair

◆ 1 batting tee per pair

◆ Cone markers

Teaching Points:

Grip (Right-hander)

◆ Hold bat firmly with hands together near the "butt" of the bat, with the dominant hand on top of the other. (Moving hands up the bat is called "choking up" on the bat.) Do not cross hands when gripping the bat.

◆ Check the bat length—should reach completely across the plate and not feel too heavy.

Stance

◆ Lift the rear elbow away from the body and hold bat off the shoulder with the trademark facing up.

◆ Stand in the batter's box with body facing home plate, feet parallel and shoulder-width apart, knees slightly bent.

Swing

◆ Focus eyes on the ball.

◆ Step forward with the front foot (about 12") as the swing is started with hands and arms.

◆ Keep the rear foot planted as the weight shifts forward.

Contact the ball in front of the plate, not over it.

Swing the bat as fast as you can.

Roll the top hand over the bottom during contact.

Swing the ball all the way around to the front shoulder during the follow-through.

Keep both hands on the bat at all times.

Swing with a smooth, continuous motion.

Do not throw the bat after hitting the ball!

Focus Word:

● *Batter's Box*

Warming-up Activity/Game:

Outdoor Exercise Hunt. (See the Appendix.) Teams finish at the Stretch Tree.

Skill Practice & Progressions:

1. **Demonstrate the grip, stance, and swing.** Emphasize players select the correct bat length. Players pantomime the action, taking up the batting stance near a poly square.

2. Partners practice the grip, stance, and swing. One partner swings the bat; other partner observes and offers feedback. Switch roles.

3. Partner A, the batter, hits a whiffle ball off a batting tee. Partner B retrieves the ball and replaces it on the batting tee. Players switch roles after every 5 hits.

4. **Pitch, Bat, & Field.** In groups of 5, each group—consisting of a batter, catcher, pitcher, and 2 fielders—find a free space. Check for good spacing between groups. Pitcher stands 5 yards away from the plate (poly square). Batter gets into batting stance, eyes focused on the ball. Pitcher pitches a whiffle ball or sponge softball; batter hits the ball and fielders retrieve it. Players switch positions after every 5 hits. *Variation:* Use a softer, larger softball-type ball and switch positions after every 5 hits.

Cooling-down Activities/Games:

1. **Fungo Batting.** (This skill of fungo batting may take some time to master and could be incorporated into a skill builder station before being used as a cooling-down activity. The stronger batters should be able to perform the required skill.) Teams of 6–8 players

scatter in an area of the playing field, spaced safely apart from each other. One player is the "fungo batter" who tosses the ball to himself/herself and hits it toward the fielders. A fielder attempting to retrieve the ball must call it "Mine!" After every 7 hits, a new fungo batter takes over.

2.   **Legends of the Day!**

Fit Think Idea:

Run Around Australia Project. (See the Appendix.) Collect running sheets and have captain record results.

Lesson 66:
Base Running

Skill Builders: base-running skills, agility, aerobic fitness, partner and group play

Expected Student Performance:

◆ Demonstrates proficiency in base running and understands how to run the different bases.

◆ Willingly cooperates and integrates with other class and team members.

Demonstrates proficiency in meeting fitness demands.

Facility/Equipment Needed:

◆ 4 bases or carpet squares per group

1 bat per group

1 softball per group

Teaching Points:

Base Running

Run from home plate to first base by stepping out of the batter's box with the rear foot.

Run in a straight pathway on the right side of the foul line (runners basically have the "right of way" to the right half of the base).

Run as quickly as possible, but also as safely as possible!

Keep eyes on the base, not on the ball, as you run.

Always turn to the right when overrunning first base.

Stop on second or third base; do not overrun either base.

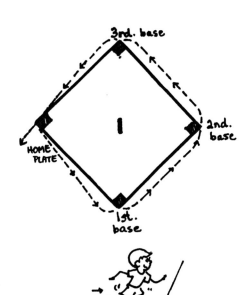

When trying to cover two or more bases, run in a slightly outward curved pathway, tagging base with the left foot on the outside corner of the bag.

In running to home plate, focus on the plate and run over and through the plate as you step on it.

Do not attempt to steal or lead off a base in softball. (Not permitted to leave the base until the batter swings at the ball.)

Focus Words:

- *Diamond*
- *Infield*
- *Outfield*

Warming-up Activities/Games:

1. **Base-Running Warm-up.** (Outdoor Circuit). Divide the class into 4 base-running teams, and set up 4 diamond circuits using bases or poly squares as shown. Each team starts in file formation behind home plate. Runner #1 starts with foot on home base. On "Go" signal, runner sprints to first base, jogs to second base, sprints to third, then jogs home. As soon as a runner tags second base, the next runner may go. Emphasize that runners touch the inside of each base with their foot. Also they should swing out slightly in their running path and avoid turning at right angles. Each team counts the number of "home runs" (one complete circuit) scored in a certain time limit. *Variation:* For an indoor circuit, set up one diamond circuit. Runners start in a snake formation on a sideline. Music starts the base-running action, and a leader takes the class through the circuit. The end runner sprints the inside of the bases to take over as the new leader. This earns the class "one home run." Challenge is to get as many "home runs" as possible in a certain time.

2. Do the following:
   - Calf Stretch
   - Sprinter Stretch
   - Periscope Stretch

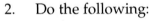

SPRINTER   PERISCOPE

CALF

Skill Practice & Progressions:

1. Observe how runners tag the bases in the base-running warm-up and provide feedback. Then demonstrate base-running skills, emphasize the pathway to different bases, foot tagging, which bases may or may not be overrun, and the rules involved.

2. **Home to First.** Players pair up and find a free space to place two bases, home plate and first base, 15 yards apart from each other. Partners practice base running to first. Swing an imaginary ball in the batter's box, then sprint in a straight pathway to tag up the base with the left foot on the outside corner of the base. Runner then jogs back to the start. Emphasize the strong push-off with the rear foot. Repeat, but this time, overrun the base turning to the right.

HOME   2.   FIRST

3. **Home to Second.** Set up as for activity #2, but add another base—second base placed 15 yards from first base and about 20 yards from home place as shown. Runners sprint from home in a slightly outward curved path stopping at second, then jog back to home base.

4. **Home Run.** Teams of 5–6 set up 4 bases in a diamond and space the bases 15 yards apart as shown. Runners practice running the bases to home plate. Emphasize that runners tag first, second, and third base on the inside corner with the left foot, then sprint to home, running over and through the plate as they step on it.

5. **Beat the Ball.** Set up in groups of 5 players: a runner; a catcher; first, second, and third base players. Group collects 4 gloves, 4 bases, and a soft softball. Arrange bases as shown in the diagram. Runner gets a head start and sprints to first base. As soon as runner has tagged the base, catcher throws the ball to first base player, who throws to the second base player, who throws back to catcher, trying to beat the runner back to home plate. Emphasize that each base player has one foot touching the outside of the base so that the runner's path is not obstructed and runner can tag each base on the inside corner of the bag. *Variation:* Group of 4 and only 3 bases.

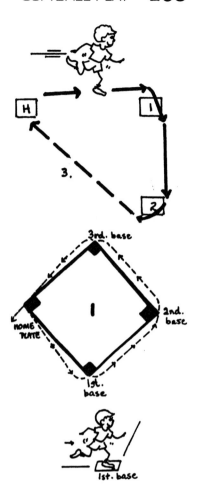

Cooling-down Activities/Games:

1. **Round-the-bases Relay.** Use the same set-up as for activity #4. Each team starts behind home plate. On signal "Home Run!" each player in turn runs to tag all four bases, then returns to home plate to tag the next runner. First team to complete the relay and cross-leg sit wins. One runner may have to run a second time if team numbers are not equal. *Variation:* Reverse the order: home–third–second–first–home.

2. **Legends of the Day!**

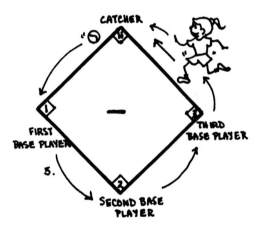

Homework Idea:

Using the distances in activity #3, have class use the Pythagorean theorem ($c^2 = a^2 + b^2$) to calculate the more accurate distance between home plate and second! Determine the distance from home plate to second using a distance of 16 yards (from home plate to first, and from first to second base); 18 yards; 20 yards. Draw the triangle to scale.

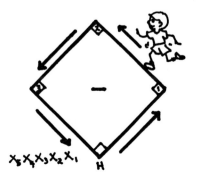

Lesson 67:
Skill Builder Stations

Skill Builders: fundamental softball skills of throwing, catching, pitching, introducing bunting, introducing batting with a cricket bat, agility base running, cooperation

Expected Student Performance:

◆   Demonstrates competency in performing fundamental softball skills.

◆   Demonstrates proficiency in bunting the ball and hitting the ball with a cricket bat.

◆   Willingly cooperates and integrates with other class and team members.

Facility/Equipment Needed:

◆   Large open grass field or oval, or gymnasium

◆   Cassette or CD player; station signs

◆   Station #1: 2 sets of 4 bases, 2 stopwatches

◆   Station #2: 1–2 Foxtails™, 1 glove per player

◆   Station #3: wall targets, 3 skittles or cones, bench, suspended hoop, floor tape or throwing cone markers, 6 soft softballs

◆   Station #4: 3 baseball bats, 3 soft softballs, 3 softball gloves

◆   Station #5: 1 cricket bat and stumps, 5 cone markers, 1 large whiffle ball, large field area

◆   Station #6: 3 vortex footballs, open field

Skill Builder Station Ideas:

Station #1: Base-running Clock. Each player in turn runs the bases in order: Home, First, Second, Third, Home. Players take turns being the timer, trying to beat their own time on the next go. Set up a station with bases only 15 yards apart; a second station with bases 20 yards apart. *Variation:* Two players start at the same time, in reverse order. Emphasize safety when their paths cross! Which base runner will get back to home first?

Station #2: Foxtail™ Fly Balls. Using 1–2 Foxtails™, one player throws fly balls to the other players who call for the ball and try to catch it in the glove. Change throwers every 5 throws.

Station #3: Target Pitching. Set up different targets, such as wall targets, skittles or cones on a bench, suspended hoop target. Vary the throwing distance. Players pitch the softball into wall targets and suspended hoop, and overhand throw at the skittles or cones on the bench.

Station #4: Bunting. Pairs take turns practicing bunting the ball from an underhand pitch. Batter squares to the oncoming ball, slides upper hand about halfway up the bat. Bat is positioned parallel to the ground just behind the hitting place. Give with the bat to soften the hit as ball contact is made. Angle the bat to send the ball into fair territory. Change roles after every 5 pitches.

Station #5: Cricket Batting. Introduce the cricket bat and wicket stumps. One player "bowls" (overhand throwing so that the ball bounces on the ground about two-thirds of the way between the batter and the bowler). Batter tries to hit it in any 360-degree direction; fielders retrieve the ball. Rotate positions after every 3 bowls.

Station #6: Vortex Throw & Catch. Players pair off and throw a vortex football back and forth to each other. Gradually increase the throwing distance. Emphasize tracking the football all the way into the hands.

Cooling-down Activity:

◆ **Legends of the Day!**

Fit Think Idea:

Discuss the player positions. Have each class member place the infield and outfield positions onto a photocopied field diagram. (See the Appendix.) Ask class to think about which position they would like to play. Discuss fitness involved to play softball.

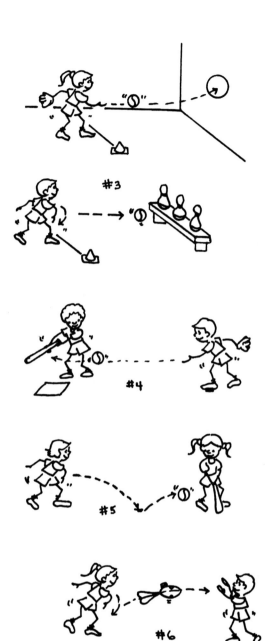

Lesson 68:
Lead-up and Modified Games

Skill Builders: fundamental softball skills of throwing and catching, fielding grounders and fly balls, batting, pitching, back catching, base running, hand–eye coordination, team play, field awareness, and positional play

Expected Student Performance:

◆   Demonstrates competency in performing fundamental softball skills.

◆   Willingly cooperates and integrates with other class and team members.

◆   Demonstrates proficiency in positional play and team strategies.

Facility/Equipment Needed:

◆   Large open field free of obstructions

◆   20 dome markers, 2–3 bats

◆   Small playground ball, 4 bases

◆   1 slo-ball per game

◆   1 softball glove per player

Focus Word:

◆   Inning (An inning is completed when both teams have had a turn at bat.)

Teaching Points—Player Positions: (Use a whiteboard to illustrate softball field and player positions.)

First Base Player

◆   Must have good catching and throwing skills, and be able to handle different thrown balls.

◆   Play the inside of the base on throws from the infield.

◆   Play about 6 feet to the right and behind the base with no runner on base.

◆   Cover the base, but do not interfere with oncoming runner.

Second Base Player

◆   Must be quick to move left or right to field grounders.

◆   Must have good hands to relay the ball to first or third base.

◆   Play about 10–12 feet left of behind the base.

Third Base Player

◆   Must have quick reactions and good agility.

◆   Must have a strong throwing arm.

◆   Must be able to field hard-hit grounders to this area.

◆   Play 6–10 feet left of the base and slightly behind it.

Shortstop

Must be the most agile of the infielders, quick to move in both directions.

Must be the best infielder of ground balls and have a strong throwing arm.

Initiate double play by getting the ball quickly to second base player who in turn throws it to first to put out both runners, or from second to third.

Play between second and third base, about 10–12 feet behind the base line.

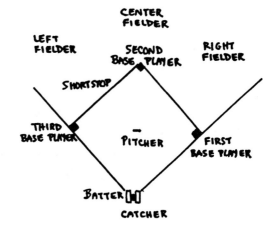

Catcher

Must have good hand–eye coordination to make catches.

Set "targets" for the pitcher to try to strike out the batter.

Must have a good throwing arm to make the throw to any of the base players.

Must be able to field thrown balls to home plate.

Batter

Keep eye focused on the pitched ball.

Hold the bat firmly, but do not tense the entire body.

Be ready to hit every pitched ball.

Judge ball carefully—don't swing at pitches outside strike zone.

Drop bat without throwing it after the hit.

Run out each batted ball because fielder could make an error.

Learn to place hit the ball into open field.

Base Runner

Be ready to run with each pitched ball.

Lead off slightly on every pitch only when it passes over home plate.

Know how many outs there are.

Try to get to the next base so that the base behind is free for the next runner.

Do not run on a fly ball with less than two outs: On short fly ball only go halfway.

On a long fly ball, tag up to move on to the next base.

Outfielders

Must have good "eyes" to field grounders and judge fly balls.

Must have good running speed to get to the ball.

Must have strong throwing arms and very accurate throws.

Lead-up Games:

1. **Semi-circle Softball.** For each game, form teams of 6–8 players. One team bats, while the other team fields. Mark out a semi-circle of 8–10 dome markers about 15 yards from home plate. Batting team lines up behind the home as shown. Fielding team consists of a pitcher, back catcher, and fielders who stand at the cone markers, facing the batter. Batters try to score points by hitting the ball past or over the semi-circle of dome markers. Change the pitcher after every 3 throws. Teams change roles after everyone on the batting team has had a turn. Team captain records score after team has batted. Bat in a girl–boy–girl–boy order. Play for 3 innings.

G–B–G–B–G–B–G
BATTING TEAM

2. **Soccer Softball.** Divide the class into 2 teams: a kicking team and a fielding team. Set up a softball diamond, with bases 15 yards apart. Establish a girl–boy–girl–boy batting order and have the batting team stand safely off to one sideline. Use floor tape to mark out where bowler stands. Bowler rolls the ball to kicker who stands just in front of the home base. Kicker must try to kick the ball past a kicking line into the field. He/she then runs to tag up at first base, or further. Play softball rules except for the following: A fly ball that bounces off a wall and is caught by a fielder puts the kicker out. Teams change roles after everyone on the kicking team has had a turn. Use a small rubber playground ball. *Variations:* Kicker kicks the ball and runs the bases. Fielding team retrieves the ball, lines up one behind the other, and passes it through their legs to the end player who calls out "Freeze!" Runner must stop at the base he/she just touched.

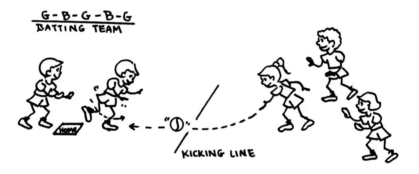

3. **Knock-pin Softball.** Set up four bowling pins or skittles or plastic bottles on the outside corner of first, second, third, and home bases. Mark out a pitcher's plate about 8 yards from home base. Form two equal teams of batters and fielders. Number the players in each team consecutively to establish batting order and fielding positions. Batters stand safely to one side in a boy–girl–boy–girl order. Fielders take up position as shown in the diagram. Pitcher underhand pitches ball to the batter who hits the ball and then runs around all the bases back to home base before the fielding team can retrieve the ball and pass it to each of the base players and back to home. Base players must knock down the bowling pin at their base before throwing the ball to the next base. Runner scores a point if successful; otherwise, fielding team is awarded a point for their efforts. Batter is out if a fielder catches a fly ball, all the pins are knocked over before the batter tags home base, or the batter knocks over any of the pins. Teams

change roles after everyone in the batting team has had a turn. Scores are recorded and continuously updated as the game progresses.

Modified Games:

1. **Double Scrub.** Each game requires 9 to 11 players. Each position is numbered. A player draws a number to see which of the 11 positions he/she will play to determine the starting positions. *Play Softball rules except for the following:* Two batters start the game. These batters work together as a pair. The first batter after hitting the ball has two choices: run to first base or run all the bases for a home run. If batter reaches first base safely, he/she may "walk" to third base. Second batter tries to get on base and to hit the first batter home. If a fielder catches a fly ball, then that player and the batter immediately exchange places. When a batter is out, all players rotate one position: batter to right field, right field to center field, center field to left field, left field to shortstop, shortstop to second base, second base to first base, first base to pitcher, pitcher to catcher, catcher to batter. If one batter dominates the batting, then after 5 successful hits, have this batter step down and everyone rotate one position.

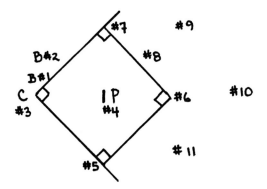

2. **Slo-pitch.** Each game consists of a batting team and a fielding team of 10 players each. The fielding team takes up the 9 softball positions. The extra player is a "rover" who plays in the outfield or between first and second base. Slo-Pitch is played with regulation Softball rules, except a large slo-pitch ball is pitched in a 3-meter (10-foot) arch from the ground and must travel across the plate in the strike zone. Batter is not allowed to bunt the ball. Base runners are not allowed to lead-off or steal a base. If the batter hits a foul ball on the third strike, he/she is also out. After 3 outs the batting

team and fielding team change roles. *Variations:* Allow 5 outs before the batting team retires to field. Have everyone on the batting team take a turn, then exchange places with fielding team.

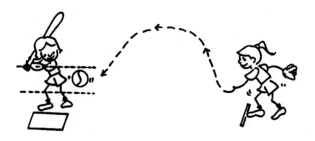

Cooling-down Activity:
Legends of the Day!

Lesson 69:
Bowling

Skill Builders: bowling skills, footwork, hand–eye coordination, accuracy throwing, aerobic fitness, partner and group play

Expected Student Performance:

◆ Demonstrates proficiency in bowling the ball.

◆ Willingly cooperates and integrates with other class and team members.

◆ Demonstrates proficiency in meeting fitness demands.

Facility/Equipment Needed:

◆ Small playground ball or tennis ball per player

◆ Dome markers for bowling lines and popping crease

Teaching Points:

Use a whiteboard or overhead transparency to show a cricket playing field and the location of these areas on the field. (See the Appendix.)

Basic Grip

◆ Hold ball by the fingers and off the palm of the hand.

Grip the ball tightly with the fingers across the seams.

Use a 2-finger grip with the index finger and middle finger across the seams and the little finger resting on the side of the ball.

For smaller hands use a 3-finger grip by placing the index, middle, and ring fingers across the seams.

Place the thumb under the ball on the opposite side to the little finger.

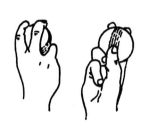

Footwork and Bowling Action (Right-hander)

Stand side-on to target or receiver, one foot in front of the other, and the dominant leg back.

Grip ball in your fingers and hold ball near chin (coil position).

Concentrate—focus on the line to bowl.

Keep head steady and eyes level.

Lean back, extending front arm up.

Eyes look behind front arm towards target.

Place back foot at right angles to intended bowling direction.

◆   Transfer weight from back foot to front foot and anchor it.

◆   Move bowling arm high over the head.

◆   Pull the front arm strongly down the target line, keeping elbow close to the body.

◆   Bowling arm should brush the ear, then follow-through across the body.

◆   Eyes now look over bowling shoulder.

Focus Words:

●   *Popping Crease*

●   *Bowling Crease*

Warming-up Activity/Game:

Conspiracy: One player is IT and holds a small Nerf™ ball; all the others scatter inside the oval area. IT gives chase until he/she tags someone or hits them below the knees with the ball. Tagged player must wear a bib, then joins the IT team. Now IT player can no longer run with the ball, but can only pivot and pass. Other IT players try to close in on a free player and use quick passes to try to tag the player or hit him/her below the knees. Eventually as the game progresses, there will be more IT players than free players. Challenge is to last the length of the game without getting tagged!

Skill Practice & Progressions:

1.   Demonstrate the grip, stance, and bowling action. Point out that the bowler does not use a throwing action, but a straight arm action to release the ball. Ball should bounce just in front of the batter. Players pantomime the footwork, arm action, and follow-through.

2.   Bowler collects a small playground or tennis ball and stands about 10 yards (10 giant steps) from a wall. Practice bowling action at the wall. Ball should hit the floor first, then the wall.

3.   Partners collect a small playground or tennis ball and space 12–15 yards apart from each other. Practice bowling the ball to each other. Observe partner's arm action—not allowed to throw the ball. Ball should hit the floor or ground just in front of the receiving partner.

4.   **Hoop Bowl.** Mark out two parallel bowling lines, 20 yards in length, and 3 yards apart from each other. Place a hoop at the 5-yard mark at each end as shown. One pair of bowlers stands behind one popping crease; the other pair stands behind the opposite popping crease. Bowlers take turns trying to bowl the ball so that it lands in the hoop,

one pair versus the other pair. Each pair keeps its own score. Challenge other pairs. *Variation:* Use a small playground ball, then a tennis ball, then a soft cricket ball.

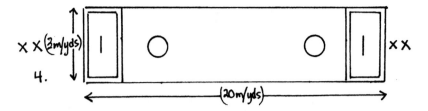

Cooling-down Activities/Games:

1. **Heads, Tails, or Pockets.** Divide the class into three equal groups: "Heads" who have favorite hand on head, other hand free; "Tails" who have favorite hand on backside, other hand free; and "Pockets" who have favorite hand in pocket, other hand free. Players mingle and scatter waiting for the start signal in a home space. On whistle or when music starts, players give chase to other players. If a Pocket tags a Head, then that Head is transformed immediately into a Pocket, and so on. Whistle signal stops play and a count is taken to see how many of each group remain. Players are only allowed to walk! Play fairly!

2. **Legends of the Day!**

In Class Idea:

Photocopy a diagram of the playing field and have class mark the key areas and player positions. (See the Appendix.)

Lesson 70:
Batting/Fielding

Skill Builders: batting grip, stance, striking motion, wicket-keeping ready position and fielding, overhand throwing, hand–eye coordination, aerobic fitness, partner and group play

Expected Student Performance:

◆ Demonstrates proficiency in striking the ball with a cricket bat.

◆ Willingly cooperates and integrates with other class and team members.

◆ Demonstrates proficiency in meeting fitness demands.

Facility/Equipment Needed:

◆ 1 cricket bat per pair; 1 small playground ball or tennis ball per pair

◆ 1 cone marker or low batting tee per pair, 2 large cone markers

◆ Long ropes and dome markers to mark out large oval

◆ Wicket-keeper protective gloves, shin pads, and helmet

◆ Several sets of wicket stumps and bails

Teaching Points:

Set up a wicket and explain the different parts. Show in a diagram where the wicket is positioned and where the wicket-keeper stands.

Basic Grip and Stance (Right-hander)

CRICKET BAT

◆ Lay bat face down on ground with handle pointing toward batter.

◆ Pick up bat with both hands together in the middle of the handle.

◆ Position hands so that the first finger and thumb form a V.

◆ Point the V formed by the hands down the bat.

◆ Hold bat firmly with hands close together on handle.

◆ Place dominant hand just below the other hand.

◆ Stand side-on to oncoming ball in the popping crease.

◆ Place feet shoulder-width apart, with knees relaxed and slightly bent.

◆ Keep balanced, weight forward on balls of feet.

◆ Keep the eyes level, chin just above the toes from front on and midway between the toes from side on.

◆ Rest the bottom of the bat lightly against the little toe of the back foot (or place the bat in front of the back foot).

◆ Rest the knuckles of the top hand against the front thigh.

Striking the Ball

Keep head up and still, eyes focused on oncoming ball.

Lift bat high as bowler is about to release the ball.

Coordinate the backlift with the bowler's delivery stride.

Keep the hands in close to the body.

Point the toe of the bat between off stump and second slip.

In backlift position the arms form a number 6.

Square body to the ball and keep head in line with it.

Swing bat down and across to hit the ball well in front of the body.

Transfer nearly all body weight to front foot, lifting rear heel.

Let body weight follow the stroke.

Wicket-keeping

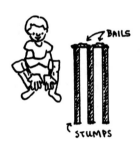

Position directly behind the wickets, knees bent and feet shoulder-width apart.

Keep weight forward on the balls of the feet, ready to react in any direction.

Wear protective gloves which are touching the ground with little fingers together and palms open to the ball, facing the bowler.

Watch the ball right into the gloves, and position hands ready to react to the ball.

Keep totally involved in the game, the major focus being the ball!

Focus Words:

- *Wicket, Stumps, and Bails*
- *Wicket-Keeper*

Warming-up Activities/Games:

1. Review overhand throwing and fielding skills, Lessons 15 and 18.

2. **Grand Prix Circuit Warm-up.** Use the cricket oval to create the track. Refer to Lesson 9 for complete description of the warm-up activity.

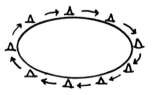

Skill Practice & Progressions:

1. Point out to class the difference between a cricket bat and a softball bat, noting that the cricket bat is flat on one side and humped on the other for strength. Ball is hit only on the flat side of the bat. Bat is not dropped after the batter strikes the ball, but carried with the runner.

2. Demonstrate the grip, batting stance, and position of the bat. Players practice the ready position. Demonstrate striking motion with the cricket bat. Players pair off and practice the action, striking a tennis ball sitting on top of a low batting tee or small cone. Batter tries to hit towards the fielder who positions in different spots around the cone as shown. Emphasize that the ball can be hit through 360 degrees into the cricket oval.

3. Set up a wicket that consists of 3 stumps and 2 bails which sit in the grooves of the stumps as shown. Position the wicket behind the batter and mark out the batter's box. Show how the wicket-keeper positions behind the wicket. Players practice the set-up position. Discuss the protective shin pads, gloves, and helmet worn by the batter and wicket-keep-er. Players stand square to a wall in semi-crouch position and throw a tennis ball (or golf ball) to rebound first off the concrete, then off the wall (and vice versa) before catching it.

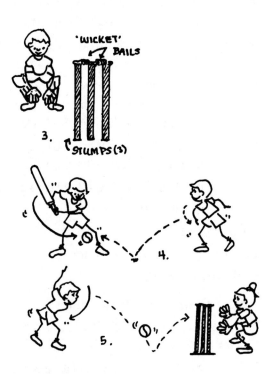

4. **Bat & Wicket-keep.** Players still in pairs: One partner is the batter; the other partner, the wicket-keeper. Wicket-keeper throws a tennis ball to the batter who hits it on one bounce towards the wicket-keeper now in a semi-crouch position. Partners change roles after every 5 throws.

5. **Bowl Wicket-keep.** Same set-up as for activity #4 except one partner is the bowler; the other partner is the wicket-keeper in ready position just back of the wicket stumps or large cone marker. Bowler practices trying to hit the stumps and knock the ball over; wicket-keeper practices fielding the ball.

Cooling-down Activities/Games:

1. **Imagery.** Using soothing music, have everyone quietly and comfortably sitting or lying, eyes closed, body relaxed, breathing slowly and peacefully. Ask class to imagine that they are now floating in warm water—feel the water, feel its warmth, feel the sunshine, body totally relaxed. Now feel heavy, very heavy. Slowly lift yourself to standing position, with the head being last. Stand stretch, open eyes, breathe slowly in, breathe slowly out.

2. **Legends of the Day!**

Homework Idea:

Observe a cricket game on one of the sport channels or a live game in action. Note the pitch, position of the wickets, position of the players in the playing field, bowler's bowling action.

Lesson 71:
Lead-up and Modified Games

Skill Builders: fundamental cricket skills of batting, bowling, fielding, overhand throwing, hand–eye coordination, aerobic fitness, positional play and team play

Expected Student Performance:

◆   Demonstrates proficiency in fundamental cricket skills and team play.

◆   Willingly cooperates and integrates with other class and team members.

◆   Demonstrates proficiency in meeting fitness demands.

Facility/Equipment Needed:

◆   Dome markers to mark out large oval area

◆   Set of wicket stumps per game, large cone marker or bin

◆   3 small playground balls, tennis balls, or soft cricket balls per game

◆   2 kanga cricket bats and balls per game

◆   2 low tees

Teaching Points:

The game consists of two teams of 11 players; one team bats first, while the other team fields. The fielding team is made up of a wicket-keeper; bowler; mid on, mid off, and mid wicket players; covers; point; slips; gully; third man; long on; and fine leg. The busiest players are the bowlers and the wicket-keepers. Players close to the bat (mid off, mid on, point, and short leg) are attacking positions and are positioned to take catches that pop up from defensive batting strokes. Such positions are generally disallowed or discouraged in junior cricket. Fielders are placed in positions as shown in the diagram with those players near the boundary referred to as outfielders. Two batters from the batting team take up a position at each end of the cricket pitch, standing behind each popping crease and in front of a wicket that consists of 3 stumps and 2 bails which sit in grooves atop the adjacent pairs of stumps. A wicket-keeper positions just behind the wicket stumps. A bowler has a cricket ball and may bowl from either side of the wicket with a run-up.

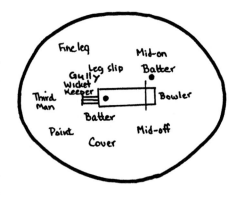

◆   Put strongest throwers in the outfield.

◆   Use players who are good at reflex catches in the slips and gully positions.

◆   Use quick and agile players in the cover and mid-wicket positions.

◆   Some players will naturally take to wicket-keeping, but also encourage them to develop other skills such as bowling.

Lead-up Games:

1. **Wicket Cricket.** For each game, a circle team of 6–8 players tries to bowl out a batter defending a wicket in the center of a large circle, 20-yard diameter. Batter can only use cricket bat to deflect oncoming balls. If a bowler is successful, then the bowler and batter change places; otherwise, batter stays in the middle for 10 bowls. Bowlers take turns bowling the ball and are allowed to make quick passes to another circle bowler to try to catch the batter off guard. *Variations:*

    - Vary the type of ball used: small playground ball, tennis ball, soft cricket ball.

    - Use a large cone or bin if not enough wickets to go around.

    - For added challenge use two tennis balls!

2. **Bowl & Strike.** In teams of 6: batter (1), wicket-keeper (2), bowler (3), and three field-ers (4, 5, and 6). Bowler bowls a small playground ball so that the ball bounces up towards the batter. Batter tries to strike the ball in different directions. Each batter takes 6 bowls (this is called an "over"), then players rotate one position as shown. Check for good spacing between the groups so that no interference occurs. *Variation:* Batter runs to touch bat to a circle and returns to touch his batting box before balls can be knocked off the stumps. Each batter keeps track of the number of runs he/she scores in 6 bowls.

Modified Games:

1. **Continuous Cricket.** For each game form two equal teams of 10–12 players. Number the players of each team from 1 to 12. If possible, bat in a boy–girl–boy–girl order. Place a wicket in a hoop and a marker in a hoop about 6 meters (20 feet) apart. Batting team positions in a file near batter's wicket, but at a safe distance away. Fielding team players space themselves around the batter's wicket at least 10 yards away. Batter stands just in front and to one side of the wicket holding a kanga bat to the ground, inside a wicket circle, to protect the wicket.

◆ Bowler bowls the ball toward the wicket so that it bounces just in front of the batter and then will hit the wicket. After every 6 bowls a new bowler takes over.

◆ Batter protects the wicket by hitting the ball in any direction. Batter scores runs by carrying bat to touch the marker circle and back to touch the wicket circle. Score one point for each round trip.

◆ Fielding team tries to put the batter out by catching a fly ball or hitting the wicket before the batter can return to the wicket circle.

◆ If batter is bowled or put out, another batter quickly takes his/her place to guard the wicket before the bowler bowls again.

◆ After all the batting players have had a turn, the fielding team comes to bat.

◆ Scores are recorded on a whiteboard (indoor) or clipboard (outside).

◆ After each team has batted, a winner is determined.

◆ Set up a new game and have different teams challenge each other.

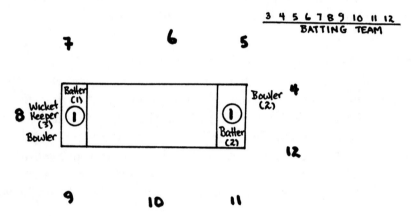

2. **Kanga Cricket.** (See the Appendix for Cricket rules.) Play this game the same as for Continuous Cricket except use two wickets in a wicket circle, spaced 15 yards apart. A batter protects each wicket and a bowler positions near the side of each wicket. Each bowler, in turn, has 6 bowls to try to put out the batter. Batters score runs by exchanging places and must run every hit.

3. **Pairs Cricket.** Each game requires 5–6 pairs which number off as follows: Pair #1—batters; Pair #2—bowler/wicket-keeper; Pairs #3, #4, #5, and #6 take up field positions as shown. Pairs will rotate through these positions so that every player will have the opportunity to bat, bowl, run, and field. The playing area ideally should be a low-cut grassy playing field or oval. Length of the pitch should be appropriate to the ability level of the players. Suggest 12–14 yards for grades 4–5; 14–16 yards for grade 6. A set of wickets is placed at each end of the pitch in a wicket circle. Two kanga bats and two kanga balls are used. No gloves, pads, or helmets are required. The boundary should be at least 20 m/yards from the pitch. For safety, fielders should stand at least 10 yards away from the batters.

◆ Bowler takes 6 bowls, bowling the ball towards the batter so that it bounces just in front of the batter; then the wicket-keeper takes over as bowler.

◆ Batter attempts to strike the ball in any direction and then batters score a run for each time they cross safely to the other end and touch the ground inside the wicket circle.

◆ Each pair keeps track of the number of runs scored.

◆ Fielding team tries to put the batter out by catching a fly ball (*caught*), or hitting the batter's wicket before he/she can return to the wicket circle (*run out*), or by the bowled ball hitting the wickets and knocking over the bails (*bowled*). If the batters go out, they simply swap ends. They do not stop batting until they retire.

◆ Pairs rotate one position after every 12 bowls (2 overs or 6 bowls per over).

Variation: When batting, the batters can hit the ball off the tee if they miss the bowled ball as long as the bowled ball does not hit the stumps, and on the condition that the batter has tried to hit the bowled ball. The ball on the tee must be hit in front of the wicket, not behind or backward, for safety reasons. The batter only gets one swing at the tee ball!

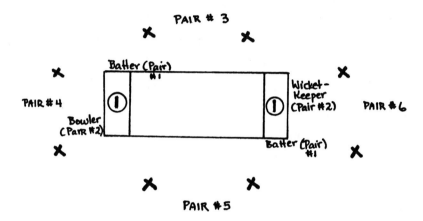

Cooling-down Activity:

Legends of the Day!

Lesson 72:
Passing and Catching/Footwork

Skill Builders: passing and catching skills and the rules involved, tracking the ball, dodging skills, footwork, one-to-one checking or guarding, 2-on-2 and 4-on-4 play

Expected Student Performance:

◆ Demonstrates competency and confidence in performing a variety of passes and in catching ability, and in performing correct footwork.

◆ Demonstrates proficiency in one-on-one guarding in a game-like situation.

◆ Willingly cooperates and integrates with other class and team members.

◆ Demonstrates proficiency in meeting fitness demands.

Facility/Equipment Needed:

◆ Netball court, basketball court, or tennis court

◆ 1 small playground ball per pair

◆ 5–6 sets of bibs

Teaching Points:

Passing

◆ Allowed to throw the ball in any manner and in any direction to another player.

◆ Allowed to bounce the ball with one or both hands in any direction to another player.

◆ After contacting a ball by using one bounce or bat, or by tipping it in an uncontrolled manner, a player may pass (or direct) it to another player by batting or bouncing it as before.

◆ A ball may not be thrown over a whole third of the court, crossing two transverse lines. (A free pass or throw-in is given to the opposition team at the point where the ball entered the incorrect third.)

◆ Aim pass at a point in space where the receiver will arrive by the time the ball has traveled through the air (lead pass).

◆ For a long pass, draw arm well back to provide for a long pull forwards and gather speed to produce power.

◆ Release ball with a flick of the wrist, as if fingers are trying to push through the ball.

◆ Exaggerate follow-through to ensure intended direction of flight.

Catching

◆ Keep eyes tracking ball all the way to your hands.

◆ Keep hands in ready position to receive the ball.

◆ Reach and absorb impact of pass by bending elbows.

◆ Look immediately to make the next pass.

◆ Time the catch, making the catch with one or both hands.

◆ Allowed prior to catching the ball to bat or bounce the ball once, or tip the ball in an uncontrolled manner.

◆ Having caught or held the ball, a player may not drop the ball and replay it. "Replay" means the player may neither catch the ball again nor bat/bounce it for another teammate to catch or retrieve.

Footwork

◆ A player making the catch must land on one foot (usually the right foot is chosen for a right-handed player).

◆ A right-foot landing followed by a left-foot landing provides a good base for efficient throwing.

◆ If the landing in on two feet, a player may choose which foot to move.

◆ After completing a catch with just one foot on the ground, a player may step with the other foot in any direction, lift the landing foot and throw or shoot before this foot is regrounded.

◆ While in possession of the ball, the player may not jump from one foot and land on the same foot (hop); nor may he/she jump from two feet and land back on two, although he/she may land on one.

Warming-up Activities/Games:

1. **Artful Dodger.** (See Lesson 19.) Emphasize that a player stay close to the player she/he is following, but no body contact is allowed.

2. **Up and Over (Down and Through) Pass.** Partners stand back to back, half a step away from each other, and pass ball with two hands through legs, overhead.

3. **Side-to-side Pass.** Partners, back-to-back, now pass the ball from side to side to other partner.

4. **Side Twists and Pass.** Partners in back-to-back position, turn right shoulders to pass ball, then left shoulders to pass ball.

Skill Practice & Progressions:

1. Demonstrate the different passes that can be used: overhand pass, underhand pass, one-handed and two-handed bounce, overhead pass. Emphasize keeping eyes on ball. Discuss the passing rules in the Teaching Points, including batting or tipping the ball.

2. **Pepper Passes.** Partners make quick passes to each other in 30 seconds. Vary the type of pass used.

3. **One in the Middle.** Each group of 3 finds a free space, with one player in the middle. Check for good spacing. Middle player tries to intercept the pass. Encourage passers to use all kinds of passes and make the passes "snappy!" Once a player has caught the ball, allow only 2 steps to be taken before passing. Passer whose ball gets intercepted becomes the middle player, or after 7 uninterrupted passes, switch the middle player.

4. **Footwork.** Demonstrate the footwork involved in making a catch. Have players practice landing on the right, followed by a left-foot landing; then pivoting on the landing foot in any direction any number of times. Players pass the ball back and forth to each other, and practice catching the ball with correct foot-work.

5. **Two-on-two Passing.** Confine the space that this game is played in for each group of 4. Players pair off with each player of the pair guarding an opposition player. Observe players' ability to guard their opposition players. Demonstrate movements to get open to receive a pass when their partner has the ball. Emphasize correct footwork when making the catch.

6. **Five Passes.** Divide the play area into 3 zones or use the thirds of a netball court. A 4-on-4 game is played in each zone. Each team wears a different set of bibs. Each player has an opposition player to guard. A team earns a point for every 5 completed unintercepted passes. One team starts the game with a throw-in from the side. Allow at the most 2 traveling steps before passing. A player can then only hold onto the ball for 3 seconds.

7. Play the game **Beanbag Conspiracy** from Lesson 16 using a small playground ball instead of beanbags.

Cooling-down Activities/Games:

1. **Star Pass & Follow.** Set up in groups of 5 in a star pattern as shown. Players pass across the star in a certain order. Challenge the teams to see which team can complete a certain number of star patterns or can complete the most number of star patterns in a certain time limit.

2. **Legends of the Day!**

Fit Think Idea:

Discuss the fitness that is involved in playing the game of netball. Discuss the footwork involved: Is a jump stop a better way to land than a stride stop?

In Class Idea:

Photocopy a diagram of a netball court and have the class mark the key lines and player positions. (See the Appendix.)

Lesson 73:
Goal-scoring

Skill Builders: goal-shooting skills, passing skills, hand–eye coordination, aerobic fitness, partner and group play

Expected Student Performance:

- Demonstrates proficiency in goal shooting.
- Willingly cooperates and integrates with other class and team members.
- Demonstrates proficiency in meeting fitness demands.

Facility/Equipment Needed:

- Netball court, basketball court, or tennis court
- 1 small playground ball or size-5 netball
- 6 netball posts and rings
- 5–6 sets of colored bibs
- 40–50 beanbags and/or deck rings
- Floor tape or dome markers

Teaching Points:

Goals can only be scored from within the goal circle and only a goal shooter or goal attack can attempt to shoot goals. A goal is scored by throwing the ball through the team's ring located in the opposition's end zone. A shooter must be completely within the circle to shoot and may make no contact with the ground outside the circle either during the catching of the ball or while holding it. Shooters may retrieve their own missed shot and shoot again, as long as the ball touches any part of the goal post including the net. Defending player (goalkeeper) is allowed to lean forward and extend a hand towards the ball.

Goal Shooting

- Hold ball in both hands and position ball behind the head.
- Keep eyes focused just above and to the back of the ring, not on the defender's hand.
- Keep balance, with one foot slightly ahead of the other, weight evenly distributed on both feet.
- Keep in a vertical body position with arms high in line.
- Release the ball off the fingers in a high arc towards the goal ring.
- Follow-through with both hands in the intended direction of flight.

Warming-up Activities/Games:

1. **Mission Possible.** See Lesson 15.

2. **Shuttle Pass.** Teams in shuttle formation pass the ball back and forth to each other from a distance of 7 yards. (Adjust distance according to ability level.) After passing, each player follows the pass to join the opposite file. Emphasize quick passes and that each pass is made before the feet move! Encourage players to use a variety of passes.

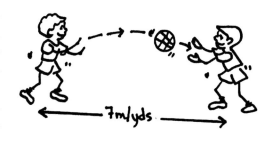

Skill Practice & Progressions:

1. **Lead Pass.** Partners, spaced about 5 giant steps apart, move up the court passing the ball back and forth to each other with lead passes. Emphasize keeping hands in the ready position to receive the pass and correct footwork.

2. Demonstrate the *goal-shooting motion.* Players pantomime the action. Discuss the rules involved in goal-shooting.

3. **Wall Shoot.** Mark off high wall targets about the same height as the goal net from ground, 10 feet. Partners, in turn, practice shooting the ball into the wall target.

4. **Net Shoot.** At each goal net, groups of 4 players position as shown in the diagram. Each player has a ball. (If not enough balls for every player, give each shooting side 2 balls.) Each shooter shoots at the goal, then retrieves the ball and joins the opposite side's file. *Variations:*

    -   Each shooter joins his/her own file. Each file keeps track of the number of goals scored in a certain time, or which team can score a certain number of goals the quickest.

    -   Set up 3 shooting files 1, 2, 3 with a player from each file shooting at the same time. Retrieve ball and join end of the file. On signal, files then rotate one position. Each file keeps track of the number of goals scored.

Cooling-down Activities/Games:

1. **Pass and Shoot Relay.** For each netball court, teams of 5 set up as shown in the diagram. Mark off 4 passing positions and 1 shooting position. Object is to pass the ball from Player 1 to Player 2, from Player 2 to Player 3, and so on until Player 5 has the ball in the goal circle and shoots.

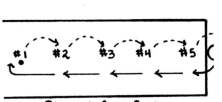

PASS AND SHOOT RELAY

The shooter retrieves the ball and runs to the start of the line to begin the passing sequence again. Meanwhile, the other players advance one position. Continue until everyone has had two turns at shooting. Team captains keep score.

2. **Legends of the Day!**

Homework Idea:

Observe a netball game on one of the sport channels or a live game in action. Note the netball court, positions of the players in each third of the court, passing and goal scoring action, and team play.

Lesson 74:
Lead-up and Modified Games

Skill Builders: fundamental skills of netball—passing and catching skills, goal-scoring, guarding, hand–eye coordination, footwork, court awareness and positional play, partner and team play

Expected Student Performance:

Demonstrates competency in fundamental passing and catching and shooting skills.

Understands court positions and can play the different player positions.

Willingly cooperates and integrates with other class and team members.

Demonstrates proficiency in meeting fitness demands.

Facility/Equipment Needed:

Netball courts, or basketball court, or tennis courts

1 size-5 netball or small playground ball per game

4–6 netball goals or posts

6 sets of bibs (or netball bibs)

Teaching Points:

Before class participates in the lead-up and modified games, teach the player positions and responsibilities for each position. On whiteboard, put a diagram of a netball court. (See the Appendix.)

Netball is played by two teams of 7 players each. Players' movements are restricted on the court according to the position played:

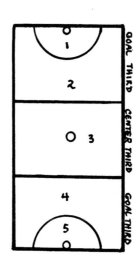

Goal Shooter (GS) is allowed in areas 1 and 2. The GS has the main responsibility of shooting goals; has height and good hands for catching the ball; accurate shooting skills.

Goal Attack (GA) is allowed in areas 1, 2, and 3. The GA can also shoot goals and leads the attack.

Wing Attack (WA) is allowed in areas 2 and 3. The WA has the responsibility of passing the ball to the shooters.

Center (C) is allowed in areas 2, 3, and 4. The C plays the whole court except for the goal circles and joins the defensive and attacking sides of his/her team together.

Wing Defense (WD) is allowed in areas 3 and 4. The WD defends the wing attacker, playing in the defense and center thirds.

Goal Defense (GD) is allowed in areas 3, 4, and 5. The GD defends the goal attacker and plays in the defense and center thirds, including the goal circle.

Goalkeeper (GK) is allowed in areas 4 and 5. The GK is the defense third that includes the goal circle.

Lead-up Game:

Zone Bucketball. For each game, mark out 3 zones in a rectangular play area and mark a goal area (semi-circle area) in each end zone as shown. Divide the class into teams of 6–8, and have players take up a position, 2 players per zone from each team. Each team wears a colored set of bibs to identify the team. A goalie for each team stands in the opposite goal area. No one else is allowed in the goal area except for the goalkeeper. Players must stay in their assigned zone. Object of the game is to pass the ball up court to the attacking players who attempt to score a goal. A goal is scored by a goalie catching the ball in a small bucket. To start the game, a center player passes the ball to a teammate who is just behind him/her. A player with the ball is allowed 2 traveling steps. A team must complete 3 consecutive passes before attempting to score. After a certain time, have players rotate to the next zone so that they experience playing in each zone. *Variations:* Players can only pivot, no traveling steps are allowed. A player can only hold the ball for 3 seconds.

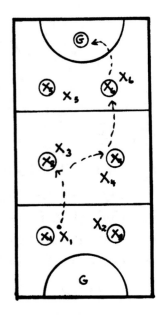

Modified Game:

Netta Netball. (See the Appendix.) This is a modification of the regulation game of netball. A size-4 ball or small playground ball is used. Ring is positioned at 8 feet (2.4 meters) instead of 10 feet. Teams consist of 7 players with 3 substitutes. Length of the game is four 10-minute quarters. Players are allowed up to 6 seconds to throw the ball. Enforce one-to-one defense and allow defender to defend from 1.2 meters/yards (about 1 giant step). A player with the ball is allowed 2 traveling steps and may pivot on landing foot.

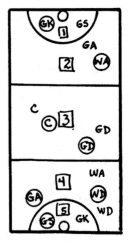

Cooling-down Activity:

Legends of the Day!

Lesson 75:
Handball Play/Forehand Stroking/Footwork

Skill Builders: ready position, footwork, forehand stroking skill, bounce-serve, hand–eye coordination, aerobic fitness, partner and group play

Expected Student Performance:

Demonstrates proficiency in executing a forehand stroke using the hand.

Willingly cooperates and integrates with other class and team members.

Demonstrates proficiency in meeting fitness demands.

Facility/Equipment Needed:

1 small balloon per player or small balloon ball per pair

1 large whiffle ball per pair

1 small playground ball per game

Teaching Points:

Ready Position

Face the net with feet shoulder-width apart, knees bent, and weight slightly forward on the balls of the feet.

Hold the hands out from your body, waist high, so that the striking hand is ready to hit the ball.

Footwork and Forehand Stroking

Watch the oncoming ball and quickly move into position.

Start drawing the paddle head back before turning and planting the back foot.

Step to a side-on position with the foot on the non-striking side.

Draw the hand back and plant weight on back foot.

Swing the hand forward by stepping into the ball, shifting weight onto the front foot.

◆   Keep wrist locked.

Keep eyes on the ball right through the contact.

◆   Contact the ball just ahead of your trunk.

◆   Stroke through the ball, finishing with the hand pointing up and over the opposite shoulder.

Warming-up Activities/Games:

1. **Partner Ring Tag.** Use a basketball court if inside, or the boundaries of a tennis court if outside. Players pair off and each hold a deck ring between them. Designate two pairs to be the IT pairs. They must also each hold a small playground ball as the tagging objects. On signal "Ring Tag!" ITS give chase to the free pairs trying to tag them. A pair that is tagged becomes the IT team and now has the tagging objects. Continue in this way. *Variations:*

   ◆ A tagged pair must get a tagging object each and join the IT team.

   ◆ Stop the game, signal "Mingle!" and have players find new partners. Then play another game.

2. **Partner Ring Tugs.** Partners stand on opposite sides of a line, holding a deck ring between them in their right hands. On signal, try to pull each other across the line. Repeat using a left-hand hold.

   ◆ Wring-the-Dishrag using deck ring.

   ◆ Leg Lifts with deck ring on end of foot.

   ◆ Leg Stretches with deck ring on end of foot; other foot.

Skill Practice & Progressions:

1. Discuss the type of games that are played with a racquet: tennis, badminton, squash, racquetball, table tennis, pickle-ball, as well as handball in which the hand is like a racquet. First demonstrate ready position and footwork that is important to hit the ball successfully. Use teaching cues.

2. **Ready Position.** Class faces a wall or one side of the play area. Demonstrate the square-on ready position. (Point out that this ready position is almost the same as for the volleyball ready position.) Players pantomime the action.

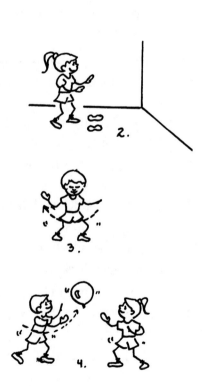

3. Demonstrate the footwork and forehand stroke. Players pantomime the action: Start to draw racquet hand back as you turn side-on, swing hand forward by stepping into (imaginary) ball. Keep eyes on the ball right through contact. Follow-through with hand up and over opposite shoulder. Practice. Do this with your eyes closed.

4. **Balloon Handball.** Partners get a balloon ball and find an open space to hit the balloon ball back and forth to each other using either open hand. Emphasize stepping side-on to partner with the opposite foot.

5. **Partner Handball.** Each pair collects one small playground or whiffle ball, and stands facing each other about 5 giant steps apart. Partner A tosses the ball so that it bounces in front of Partner B's hitting side. Partner B, from ready position, pivots and makes a forehand stroke to hit the ball back to Partner A. Switch roles after 5 tosses. Players try to hit the ball back and forth off one bounce. This is called "rallying."

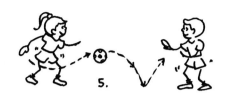

5.

6. **Bounce-serving.** Players face a wall about 3 giant steps away. Practice bounce-serving a whiffle or small playground ball to the wall. Turn side-on to the wall. Drop the ball from the nonstriking hand and hit it on the first bounce with the open hand. Ball should hit the wall first, then the floor. Practice. Then try to hit the ball back to the wall using a forehand stroking action, catch the ball, and bounce-serve again. Practice. Now bounce-serve, and try to hit the ball back to the wall continuously, until you miss. Bounce-serve again.

6. BOUNCE-SERVE

Cooling-down Activities/Games:

1. **Two-square.** Use floor tape or paint to mark out several 1 meter by 2 meter (4 feet by 8 feet) courts, including a center line to divide the court into two half courts as shown. Have players pair off and each pair collect a whiffle ball or small playground ball or tennis ball. Partners position in each half of the two-square court. One partner starts the game by bounce-serving the ball into the other partner's square. Continue hitting the ball with either hand until one player misses. Play to 10 points, then challenge another player. Ball landing on the line is considered in. Ball must clear the center line and bounce in the other player's side. Play heads up and fairly!

2. **Legends of the Day!**

Lesson 76:
Paddle Ball Play/Forehand Stroking/Footwork

Skill Builders: ready position, footwork, forehand stroking skill, bounce-serving, hand–eye coordination, aerobic fitness, partner and group play

Expected Student Performance:

◆ Demonstrates proficiency in forehand stroking and bounce-serving using a paddle bat.

◆ Willingly cooperates and integrates with other class and team members.

◆ Demonstrates proficiency in meeting fitness demands.

Facility/Equipment Needed:

◆ 1 small balloon per player or small balloon ball per pair

◆ 1 lightweight paddle ball racquet (wooden or plastic) per player

◆ 1 hand racquet per player

◆ 1 large whiffle ball per pair

◆ 1 small Koosh™ or yarn ball per pair

◆ 1 small playground ball per game or tennis ball

◆ Floor or wall tape

Teaching Points:

Handshake Grip

◆ Shake hands with paddle so that the V formed by thumb and index finger is centered on top of grip.

◆ Slightly separate the index finger from the other fingers.

Ready Position

◆ Face the net with feet shoulder-width apart, knees bent, and weight slightly forward on the balls of the feet.

◆ Hold the paddle throat lightly with the non-paddle hand.

◆ Hold paddle out from your body, waist high, so that the head of the paddle is vertical to the ground, and the handle is pointing to your belly button.

"V"

Shake Hands Grip

Footwork and Forehand Stroking

♦   Watch the oncoming ball and quickly move into position.

♦   Start drawing the paddle head back before turning and planting the back foot.

♦   Step to a side-on position with the foot on the non-paddle side.

♦   Draw the paddle back behind the shoulder and plant weight on back foot.

♦   Swing the paddle forward by stepping into the ball, shifting weight onto the front foot.

♦   Keep wrist locked and grip firmly.

♦   Keep eyes on the ball right through the contact.

♦   Contact the ball just ahead of your trunk.

♦   Stroke through the ball, finishing with the paddle head pointing up over the opposite shoulder.

Bounce-Serve

♦   Stand side-on to the wall or net.

♦   Step forward with the foot opposite your serving hand.

♦   Hold the ball in the other hand.

♦   Drop the ball and allow the ball to bounce once.

♦   Swing paddle forward to strike the ball against the wall using the forehand stroke.

Warming-up Activity/Game:

Parachute Play Warm-up. See Lesson 4 for warm-up ideas. Excellent activity for developing arm strength, and strong wrists and fingers in such a fun way!

Skill Practice & Progressions:

1.   Introduce the paddle: head, throat, handle. Demonstrate the ready position with the paddle. Players pantomime the action. Emphasize holding the paddle throat lightly with the non-paddle hand.

2.   Demonstrate the footwork and forehand stroke using the paddle racquet. Use teaching cues. Players pantomime the action.

3.   **Balloon Ball Paddle.** Partners hit a balloon ball back

and forth to each other using their paddle racquet.

4. **Paddle Ball Tasks.** Find a home space with your paddle racquet and whiffle ball (or small playground ball or tennis ball).

- Bounce the ball with the paddle racquet to the floor.
- Start low, then gradually bounce the ball higher. Emphasize staying in control!
- Place the ball on the paddle. Try to continuously bounce the ball up in the air each time. How many hits can you make before the ball touches the floor? Try this with a Koosh™ ball.
- Now try to bounce the ball twice against the floor, then twice into the air off your paddle.
- Walk around the play area while bouncing the ball on the floor with your paddle; while bouncing the ball in the air off your paddle; alternating floor and in the air.

5. Demonstrate the bounce-serve using the paddle racquet. Players practice bounce-serving the ball to a wall using the paddle. Then try to hit the ball back to the wall using a forehand stroking action off the bounce-serve. Practice. Bounce-serve, and try to hit the ball back to the wall continuously until you miss. Bounce-serve again.

Cooling-down Activities/Games:

1. **Wall Ball.** Mark off a serving line on the floor and a ball line on the wall as shown. Players partner up and collect a whiffle ball (small playground ball or tennis ball). Partner A starts the game with a bounce-serve to the wall. The ball must hit the wall above the ball line. Partner B must hit the rebound ball on the first bounce, and send it back to the wall using a forehand stroke. Practice. Then play a game, scoring a point each time the other partner fails to return the ball. If you win the point, you get to serve. Play to 5 points, then challenge another player.

2. **Legends of the Day!**

Homework Idea:

Watch a tennis game, badminton game, or some other racquet sport on the sports TV channel, or watch a live game in action. Observe player positions, hitting the ball with the forehand, backhand, and serving.

Lesson 77:
Backhand Stroke/Footwork

Skill Builders: footwork and backhand stroking skills, hand–eye coordination, aerobic fitness, partner and group play

Expected Student Performance:

◆   Demonstrates proficiency in footwork and performing a backhand stroke.

◆   Willingly cooperates and integrates with other class and team members.

Demonstrates proficiency in meeting fitness demands.

Facility/Equipment Needed:

◆   1 small balloon per player or small balloon ball per pair

◆   1 lightweight paddle ball racquet (wooden or plastic) per player

◆   1 large whiffle ball per pair

◆   1 small playground ball or tennis ball per game

1 deck ring per player

1 short rope per court, 4 dome markers per court

Floor tape to mark off Ping-Pong courts

Teaching Points:

Backhand Grip

Shake hands with the racquet, then rotate hand inward slightly so that the V is on the left top of the racquet handle.

Spread thumb across the back of the grip.

Footwork and Backhand Stroking

Keep eyes on the oncoming ball and quickly get into position.

Rotate shoulders so that the racquet side of your back is facing the net and weight is on your back foot.

Shift weight forward and swing parallel to the ground.

Backswing straight, taking racquet across the body.

Keep wrist locked and hold with a firm grip.

Contact the ball ahead of the forward foot.

Swing through toward the net across the front of the body, letting the racquet rise slightly.

Keep eyes on the ball right through the contact.

Follow-through toward the target.

Warming-up Activity/Game:

Blob-o-link Attack! Select 3 players to be Baby Blobs to start the game. They stand in the center of the play area; everyone else scatters. Everyone holds a deck ring (or "blob-o-link"). On signal "Blob Attack!" Baby Blobs give chase to free players. A player caught must link up with the Baby Blob and together they give chase. As more players are caught, the blob will grow into a mini-blob, maxi-blob, and then a mega-blob! Emphasize that the Blob must stay linked together and keep heads up throughout the game. *Variation:* Once a Blob grows to 6 players, it can break off into mini-blobs of 3 players and continue to grow.

Skill Practice & Progressions:

1. Revise the ready position and footwork. Stand in ready position facing a wall. *For forehand stroke,* pivot on the right foot, step left forward in front of right so that left shoulder is at right angles to the target. Then perform a forehand stroke. *For backhand stroke,* pivot on left foot and step right foot in front of left so that the back of the right shoulder faces the target.

   1. Forehand   Backhand Stroke

   - *Use the cue words: "Ready Position, Forehand, Backhand!"*
   - *Now have players do footwork with eyes closed.*

2. Demonstrate the backhand stroke action. Players pantomime the action. Cue words: "Ready Position, Backhand Stroke!"

3. Partners hit a balloon ball back and forth to each other with paddle racquets using backhand strokes.

4. Partners collect one small playground or whiffle ball, and stand facing each other about 5 giant steps apart. Partner A tosses the ball so that it bounces in front of Partner B's backhand side. Partner B, from ready position, pivots and makes a backhand stroke to hit the ball back to Partner A. Switch roles after 5 tosses.

5. Repeat activity #4 above, but have partners mix up the tosses. Toss to forehand; toss to backhand. Exchange roles.

6. **Rally the Ball.** Use dome markers to create a court. Use a rope to divide the court into two equal halves as shown. Partners try to rally the ball back and forth off of one bounce, using forehand and backhand strokes.

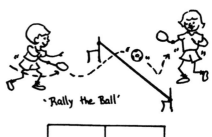

'Rally the Ball'

Cooling-down Activities/Games:

1. **Play Four Square or Floor Ping-pong.** (See Lesson 81 for Lead-up Games.)

2. **Legends of the Day!**

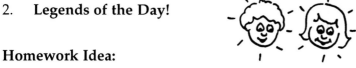

Homework Idea:

Activity Pyramid and Nutrition Pyramid. (See the Appendix.)

A	B
D	C

Lesson 78:
Ground Strokes and Volleys

Skill Builders: footwork and ready position revision, body positioning and preparation, forehand and backhand ground strokes, introduction to volleying the ball, hand–eye coordination, aerobic fitness, partner and group play

Expected Student Performance:

◆   Demonstrates competency in footwork and performing forehand and backhand strokes.

◆   Demonstrates proficiency in volleying the ball.

◆   Willingly cooperates and integrates with other class and team members.

◆   Demonstrates proficiency in meeting fitness demands.

Facility/Equipment Needed:

◆   1 junior tennis racquet per player

◆   1 large and small whiffle ball per pair

◆   1 small playground ball or tennis ball per game

◆   1 short rope per court, 4 dome markers per court

◆   Tennis courts or badminton courts, nets, and posts

Teaching Points:

Ground Stroking

◆   Start in ready position: Face the net with feet shoulder-width apart, knees bent, and weight slightly forward on the balls of the feet.

◆   Hold throat of racquet lightly with the non-racquet hand; relax racquet hand grip.

◆   Keep eyes focused on the approaching ball; move into position.

◆   Draw the racquet back early, pivot side-on to the net, and step into the ball shifting weight forward.

◆   Keep wrist grip firm and try to contact ball in the center of racquet.

◆   Let eyes follow the ball onto the racquet in the contact.

◆   Swing through the ball as if you were trying to knock several glasses off a table or trying to hit three balls coming in a row.

◆   Follow-through with the racquet face perpendicular to the court surface, and racquet arm coming upwards and rotating slightly over at the completion of the swing.

◆   Don't crowd the ball; position to take it arm's length away.

◆   After following through, quickly return to ready position.

Volley

- ◆ Keep eyes focused on the ball and knees flexed throughout the volley.

- ◆ Keep racquet in front of you and arms extended.

- ◆ Keep wrist and grip firm; use a short backswing.

- ◆ Step into the volley, and "punch" the ball, contacting it early.

- ◆ Use very little follow-through; stop racquet head just after it strikes the ball.

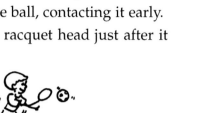

Warming-up Activities/Games:

1. **Aerobic Snake.** Class in snake formation lines up on one sideline of the tennis court. Leader takes the class through different movement patterns as the snake winds its way around the court. Start by power walking, then use a variety of locomotor movements.

2. H - F - A - B - L - L (Refer to Lesson 63.)

Skill Practice & Progressions:

1. Introduce the junior tennis racquet. Players shake hands with the racquet and get into ready position. Revise the footwork and stroking action **using** key teaching cues:

   - Ready Position—Forehand Pivot—Stroke
   - Ready Position—Backhand Pivot—Stroke

2. Demonstrate the key teaching points in positioning to hit a ground stroke, racquet preparation, eye focus, making contact, and following through. Players pantomime the action. Observe and give feedback.

3. Discuss the term "volley" and demonstrate how to volley the ball. Emphasize keeping eyes on ball at all times! Players pair up with one partner tossing the ball to the other partner who volleys the ball. After 5 volleys, change roles.

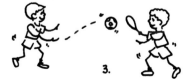

4. Divide the class into two groups: Ground Strokers and Volleyers. In each group have players partner up. Lower the net or use a long rope stretched between two posts at waist height.

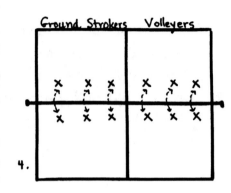

- Ground Strokers: Position so that a partner is on one side of a net. Check for good spacing. Start at the service line to hit the ball back and forth to each other on one bounce, then gradually move further back.

- Volleyers: Partners stand about 5 giant steps apart and volley a large whiffle ball back and forth to each other. Emphasize adjusting racquet to forehand or backhand grip.

- After sufficient practice has taken place (about 8–10 minutes), have the two groups switch roles.

Cooling-down Activities/Games:

1. **Control the Ball.** Form 2 groups, Ground Strokers and Volleyers, and set up as for activity #4 in the Skill Practice & Progressions session. *Ground Strokers pairs*, hitting back and forth to each other, try to get to 10 consecutive hits before losing control of the ball. Start at the service line. After every successful 10 hits, the pair steps back to the next rally line (see diagram). Continue in this way. *Volleyers* start 5 giant steps away and try to volley ball 5 times in a row or more before losing control. If successful, pairs take one step away and continue challenge. On signal, ground strokers and volleyers change roles.

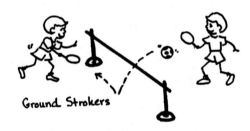

2. **Legends of the Day!**

Homework Idea:

Activity Pyramid and Nutrition Pyramid. (See the Appendix.)

Lesson 79: Serving

Skill Builders: introduction to serving technique, hand–eye coordination, aerobic fitness, partner and group play

Expected Student Performance:

◆ Demonstrates proficiency in performing an overhand serve.

◆ Willingly cooperates and integrates with other class and team members.

◆ Demonstrates proficiency in meeting fitness demands.

Facility/Equipment Needed:

◆ 1 junior tennis racquet per player

  1 large and small whiffle ball per pair

◆ 1 small soft playground ball per game or tennis ball

◆ 1 short rope per court, 4 dome markers per court

  Tennis courts or badminton courts, nets, and posts

Teaching Points:

Overhand Serve (Right-handers)

  Stand with left hip and shoulder side-on to the net and left foot pointing to opposition's serving court or diagonally forward.

  Hold racquet in a relaxed forehand grip.

  Hold ball lightly in the fingers of the left hand.

  Gently rest this hand against the throat of the racquet.

  Hold the racquet head up, pointing it towards the opposition's service court.

  Start the ball hand and racquet downward together.

  Swing the racquet hand away and behind the body.

  Toss the ball in front and above the hitting shoulder.

  Follow ball toss with the eyes, right through to contact.

  Time the ball toss and racquet moving upwards from behind the back.

  Lead with the elbow as racquet swings upward and forward.

- ◆ Shift weight forward, rising up on the toes.
- ◆ Contact the ball with full arm extension, slightly closing racquet face over the descending ball.
- ◆ Follow-through swinging out, across, and down while stepping forward with the back foot.

Warming-up Activity/Game:

Star Wars. (See Lesson 16.)

Skill Practice & Progressions:

1. Players spread out along the service lines of a tennis court(s) or wall (if indoors). If possible, use "footprints" or chalk out footprints for feet and body positioning side-on to net.

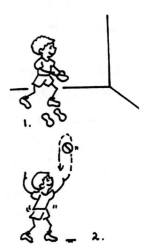

2. Demonstrate the ball toss. Players practice. Emphasize that the tossing hand follows the ball upwards in the intended direction of flight. Observe that the ball is tossed in front and above the hitting shoulder and released at top of extended arm. Check landing spot which should be 12–15 inches (30–38 cm) in front of forward foot. Practice several times.

3. Demonstrate serving action without the ball in small-step progressions. Point out that the overhand serve is similar to the overhand throw. Have players overhand-throw ball at a wall.

4. Players pantomime the serving action:
   - Position side-on to net (wall), check feet positioning.
   - Hold ball in non-racquet hand against racquet throat.
   - Start ball and racquet downward together.
   - Swing racquet head away and behind—backscratch position.

   - Toss ball upwards and move racquet up and forward.
   - Keep eyes on ball throughout toss and contact.
   - Contact with full arm extension; shift weight up and down into the ball.
   - Follow-through out, across, and down while stepping forward with back foot.

   Allow for ample practice so that players have a good mental "feel" for the total serving action.

5. **Wall Serve.** Players practice the complete serving action at the wall. For younger grades, let players start the serve in the back-scratching position instead of the full swing. Observe and offer one-to-one feedback.

6. **Net Serve.** Players practice serving across a net (or stretched rope) from about mid-court. For each tennis court, set up so that 3 players serve from the right-hand court; 3 serve from the left-hand court. Each player takes 5 serves from each court. After serving from one side, the player serves from the other side. On the opposite side of the net, have 3–4 ball retrievers whose job is to field the ball and roll it back under the net to the serving group. Use badminton courts for practicing inside.

   - If only two tennis courts are available, set-up serving groups on each side. Emphasize safety.

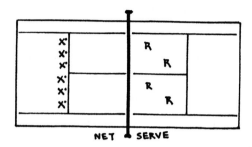

NET SERVE

Cooling-down Activities/Games:

1. **Tennis Balls and Cans Tricks.** Each player has a tennis ball and tennis can and finds a home space.

   - Hold tennis can upside down and rest the tennis ball on the bottom of the can. Balance the ball in this way while walking, jogging, skipping, side-shuffling.

   - Try to send the ball upward, quickly flip the can over and catch the ball in the can on the first bounce. Try without a bounce.

   - Toss the ball up, kneel down, and catch the ball in the can on the first bounce.

   - Toss the ball up, turn around, catch it on one bounce in the can. Then no bounce.

   - Invent another trick of your own.

   - Toss ball back and forth to a partner and catch it in the tennis can on one bounce.

   - Invent a partner trick.

2. **Legends of the Day!**

Homework Idea:

Activity Pyramid and Nutrition Pyramid. (See the Appendix.)

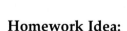

Lesson 80:
Skill Builder Stations

Skill Builders: racquet fundamentals such as ready position, footwork, forehand stroking, backhand stroking, serving, hand–eye coordination, partner and group play

Expected Student Performance:

◆ Demonstrates proficiency in executing racquet fundamentals using the hand or racquet.

◆ Willingly cooperates and integrates with other class and team members.

◆ Demonstrates proficiency in meeting fitness demands.

Facility/Equipment Needed:

◆ Cassette or CD player; station signs

◆ Station #1: 3 square and/or circular wall targets, floor tape, dome markers

◆ Station #2: 3 benches, 12 cone markers, 6 paddle racquets, 3 large whiffle balls

◆ Station #3: 1 tennis ball and empty tennis can per player; wall area

◆ Station #4: 1 Loop'n Catch (paddle racquet) and Squellet™ ball per player; 3 beanbag balls or tennis balls

◆ Station #5: a batting tee, 3 bases, 2 tennis or paddle ball racquets, 1 large whiffle ball

◆ Station #6: 1 Odd-Bounder per pair or group of 3; 6 paddle racquets; wall area

Skill Builder Station Ideas:

Station #1: Wall Targets. Two players per target take turns bounce-serving the ball into a wall target off the racquet. Use wall tape to mark out 3 large square or circular targets. Mark 3 different distances from the wall. *Variation:* Use the overhand serve.

Station #2: Bench Ball. Use cones to mark out 3 mini-paddle racquet courts and place a bench in the center of each one. (If not enough benches, use a rope stretched at waist height between two posts as shown.) Mark a serving spot in each court. Players pair off, with a player of each pair standing on one side of the bench. Start the game with a bounce-serve from the serving mark. Each server gets two serves. A point is scored to the side not faulting. Use forehand and backhand strokes to send the ball back to the opponent player. Play to 5 points, then challenge another player.

Station #3: Tennis Balls & Cans. Each player has a tennis ball and an empty tennis can. Players are given the following tasks to do:

◆ Toss ball up, bounce, catch it on one bounce in the can held by other hand. Try to do this 3 times in a row.

◆ Switch hands and repeat.

◆ Toss ball up and catch it on the full in the can held by other hand. Try to do this 3 times in a row.

◆ Switch hands and repeat.

◆ Toss ball to a wall, catch rebound in the tennis can off one bounce; off no bounce.

◆ One partner tosses ball to a wall; other partner catches it in the tennis can off one bounce.

Station #4: Loop'n Catch™. Loop'n Catch™ is a wide body aluminum tennis-type racquet. A Squellet™ ball is a transparent vinyl ball filled with red, yellow, and blue plastic beads. Both innovative items are available from major sports catalog companies. Each player holds a Loop'n Catch™ racquet and uses it to send the Squellet™ ball back and forth to each other. Start in close and gradually move farther apart. Experiment with tossing and catching using the nondominant hand. If enough equipment is available for each player, toss and catch to self. *Variations:*

● Use a beanbag ball or tennis ball.

● Use a paddleball racquet with beanbags.

Station #5: Paddleball T-ball. Set-up consists of a batting tee, 3 bases, 1 back catcher, 2 batters, 4 fielders, 1 whiffle ball, and 2 junior tennis racquets or paddleball racquets. Play game as for Double Scrub (see Lesson 68). *Variations:*

● No batting tee; instead add a pitcher who tosses the ball towards batter who hits it off one bounce.

● Fungo Batting using a junior tennis racquet (see Lesson 65).

Station #6: Odd-bounder. This is a small plastic ball with 6 bumps on it that send it off in odd directions and make it a challenge to track and catch. This manipulative equipment is available from major sports catalog companies. Partners space about 8 giant steps apart and overhand throw the Odd-Bounder to each other. *Variations:*

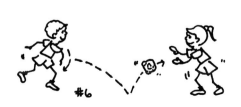

● Use the smaller Z-Ball which is more challenging!

● Partners toss and catch the Odd-Bounder off a wall.

Cooling-down Activity:

Legends of the Day!

Lesson 81:
Lead-up and Modified Games

Skill Builders: racquet fundamentals such as ready position, footwork, forehand stroking skill, backhand, serving, hand–eye coordination aerobic fitness, partner and team play, court awareness, player positioning, rules

Expected Student Performance:

◆   Demonstrates proficiency in executing racquet fundamentals.

◆   Willingly cooperates and integrates with other class and team members.

◆   Demonstrates proficiency in meeting fitness demands.

Facility/Equipment Needed:

◆   1 large whiffle ball per pair or game

◆   1 small playground ball per game

◆   1 paddle ball or tennis racquet per player

◆   3 bases and 1 batting tee per game

◆   Floor tape or paint

Lead-up Games:

1. **Four Square.** Use floor tape (or painted lines) to mark out as many 2.5-meter (8-foot) square courts as there are groups of 4 players. Divide the court into 4 smaller squares. Call each square by a letter: A, B, C, and D. Player in court A begins the game with a bounce-serve with one hand to a player in any of the other 3 squares. Receiver must allow the ball to bounce once, then can hit it with the open hand to a player in any other square. A player is allowed to step out of the square to play the ball, but not into anyone else's square. The server receives a point if the receiver misses the ball or does not return it properly to another square. A receiver gets a point whenever the previous player sends the ball out-of-bounds, or not over the line properly. Mingle groups and play with new players.

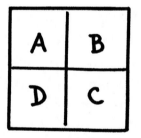

2. **Paddleball T-ball.** Set-up consists of a batting tee, 3 bases, 1 back catcher, 2 batters, 4 fielders, 1 whiffle ball, and 2 junior tennis racquets or paddle ball racquets. Play game as for Double Scrub (see Lesson 68). *Variations:*

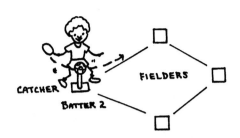

- No batting tee; instead add a pitcher who tosses the ball towards batter who hits it off one bounce.

- Fungo Batting using a junior tennis racquet (see Lesson 65).

Modified Games:

1. **Paddle Ping-Pong.** Use floor tape to mark off 10-feet by 5-feet (3 m by 1.5 m) courts. Players pair up and each pair takes up a position in one half of the Ping-Pong court which is divided into two half courts by a low net. On each side, a line through the vertical center creates a right-hand service area and a left-hand service area. One partner stands in service area. Toss a coin to see which pair will serve first. Begin the game with a bounce-serve from right-hand area which must travel over the net and land in the opposition's right-hand service area. The opposition player is then allowed to return the ball on one bounce anywhere on the other side. One partner serves for five points at a time, then the other partner serves. When each pair on a side has served, then the opposition pair serves, starting with the player in the right-hand service area. A pair earns points for their side when the opposition pair commits a fault: hitting the ball out-of-bounds, under the net, hitting the ball on the full, or on two or more bounces; failing to return the ball over to the opposition's side. "On the line" is considered in. Play to 11, 15, or 21 points.

2. **Paddle Ball Tennis.** (See the Appendix.) Play this game in a badminton court, or if outside, tennis courts. Lower the net to 3 feet (1 m) height. Use a large whiffle ball to start. As skills improve, use a small whiffle ball or tennis ball. Use paddle ball racquets or junior tennis racquets.

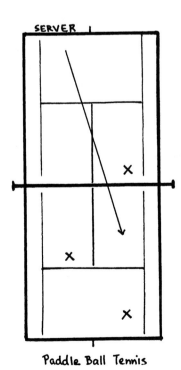

Paddle Ball Tennis

- Doubles Play: Server stands behind the base line on the right-hand side of the court and bounce-serves the ball across the net into the receiver's right-hand side. Receiver must let the ball bounce once before hitting it back over the net. From then on, the ball may be played by either player on one bounce or on the full.

- Scoring: Server serves out a game which is played to 4 points, then the opposition team serves. Keep score: 0 points = love; 1 point = 15; 2 points = 30; and 3 points = 40. If score is tied at 40–40 (deuce), server serves to see which side will win the game. A score of 30–15 means the server has won 2 points, the opposition has won 1 point.

3. **Paddle Ball Volleyball (3-on-3 paddle ball).** For each game position 3 players on each side of a badminton net. Use a small or large whiffle ball. Mark on each court a service spot. Each side has at the most 3 hits to send the ball over to the other side. "Help" is allowed on the serve; that is, another player can help the ball get over the net on the serve. No player can hit the ball twice in a row. If a team commits a fault, then their team is given a point. Play to 21, then challenge another team for a new 3-on-3 game.

Paddle Ball Volleyball

Cooling-down Activity:

Legends of the Day!

Lesson 82:
Passing and Catching

Skill Builders: grip, throwing a football, receiving a football, tracking the ball, hand–eye coordination, aerobic fitness, partner and group play

Expected Student Performance:

◆ Demonstrates proficiency in throwing a spiral pass.

◆ Demonstrates competency in receiving the ball.

◆ Willingly cooperates and integrates with other class and team members.

◆ Demonstrates proficiency in meeting fitness demands.

Facility/Equipment Needed:

1 large playing field or gymnasium

◆ 1 football per pair

◆ Grass Drills cards

Volleyball courts, net, and posts

Teaching Points:

Grip

Place the thumb underneath the ball.

Spread the other fingers across the seam (laces) of the football.

Use the nonthrowing hand to support the ball on the front inside part.

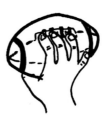

Stance and Throwing Action

Stand with the foot of the nonthrowing side forward.

Start the throwing action with the throwing arm and hand cocked back slightly behind the head. Nonthrowing hand provides support to the ball almost to this point, then drops away.

Keep eyes focused on the target.

Release ball by throwing flexed elbow forward and snapping wrist downward so that ball spins in a spiral motion to receiver or target.

Follow-through in the intended direction of flight.

Receiving

◆ Make a target with your hands.

◆ Spread fingers wide and point thumbs in toward the body for an above-the-waist catch. Keep little fingers together for a below-the-waist catch.

◆ Relax the hands.

◆ Track the ball with your eyes right into the hands.

◆ Always try to catch the ball with both hands.

◆ Reach for the ball, letting it fall into the cradle of your hands.

◆ As the ball meets the hands, bring the ball, hands, and arms into the body to absorb the force of the throw.

◆ Get ball under control and tuck it into the forearm, covering the tip of the ball with the hand to protect it as you run with the ball.

Warming-up Activities/Games:

Grass Drills. (Commonly used in football training, this requires players to respond to signals that alternate aerobic or running-type movements with ground exercises. Emphasis is on alertness and agility. Suggest aerobic signal start at 20 seconds and gradually increase in duration; ground exercise starts at 10 seconds.) Players stand in wave formation, spaced arm's length apart. Signals:

Knee Push-ups

BACK

Seal Walk

Inchworm

Periscope

● "Jog!"—Jog in place with knees high and clap hands to knees.

● "Front"—Hit the dirt, do bent knee push-ups.

● "Jog"—"Front!"—"Jog"—"Front" . . .

● "Rope Jump"—Pantomime rope jumping in place.

● "Back"—Quickly and safely get into back lying position and grab ankles.

● "Rope Jump"—"Back"—"Rope Jump"—"Back" . . .

● "Jumping Jacks"—Gently and lightly jump feet apart, then feet together.

● "Inchworm"

● "Side-Kicks"—Hop and kick leg out to side; other leg.

● "Seal Walk"—Front support position, drag feet, and move on forearms.

- "Twist Jumps"—Jump, twisting from side to side.
- "Jump Turns"—Quarter-jump turns.
- "Hit the Dirt"—"Pencil Stretch"—"Periscope!"

Skill Practice & Progressions:

1. Each player has a football and finds a free space. For younger children, use smaller and softer junior footballs. Demonstrate the grip on the football. Players check for proper grip.

2. Demonstrate the throwing action. Emphasize trying to achieve a spiraling motion on the ball. No wobbling. Need to release the ball with a firm snap of the wrist. Demonstrate the key points for receiving a pass. Emphasize tracking the ball right into the hands; hands relaxed; and bringing the ball, hands, and arms into the body to absorb the force of the throw.

3. Partners practice the throwing and receiving action. Emphasize receiver setting a target with the hands. Passer concentrates on sending the ball in a spiraling motion. Start 5 giant steps apart, and gradually get farther apart.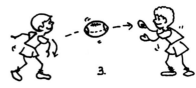

4. Thrower now practices sending the ball to the receiver with a lead pass. Emphasize passing the ball far enough in front of the receiver, so that the receiver doesn't have to stop to catch the ball. Receiver moves to the right, to the left, and forward.

Cooling-down Activities/Games:

1. **Star Football.** Pass ball to a partner, counting the passes each makes. Five caught passes in a row earn a letter "S," five more consecutive caught passes earn letter "T," and so on until the letters spell the word "STAR." *Variation:* Set up in groups of 3, 4, or star pattern. Group must make 5 successful catches to earn a letter.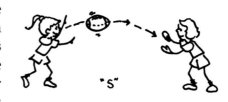

2. **Net Football.** See Lead-up Games, Lesson 89.

3. **Legends of the Day!**

Fit Think Idea:

Discuss why an oval-shaped (elliptical-shaped) ball would travel farther than a round-shaped ball on an overhand throw.

Lesson 83:
Ball Snap and Lateral Pass

Skill Builders: ball-snapping technique, laterally passing the ball, catching, hand–eye coordination, aerobic fitness, partner and group play

Expected Student Performance:

◆ Demonstrates proficiency in executing a ball snap and lateral pass.

◆ Willingly cooperates and integrates with other class and team members.

◆ Demonstrates proficiency in meeting fitness demands.

Facility/Equipment Needed:

◆ Large outdoor playing field or gymnasium

◆ 1 football per pair

◆ Soft or Nerf™ ball per player

◆ 5–6 folding mats

◆ 12–15 dome markers

Teaching Points:

Center Snap

◆ Grip the ball the same way as for passing.

◆ Spread feet wide apart, bending at the knees.

◆ Look back through the legs to see the quarterback before snapping the ball, but look heads up to face the opposition when actually snapping the ball.

◆ Release the ball with one hand, snapping the wrist.

◆ Extend snapping hand and arm back through the legs into the hands of the quarterback who positions about 5 yards behind the snapper. Non-snapping hand rests on the knee.

◆ Ball should spiral into the quarterback's hands at about chest height.

Lateral Pass (One-Hand Underpass)

◆ Grip the ball with the favorite (dominant) hand.

◆ Place the palm of the passing hand under the ball, fingers spread.

◆ Snap the wrist back to make the underhand toss and impart spin.

◆ Ball should spiral as it travels to the receiver.

◆ Pass to the side (laterally) or backwards to a player.

◆ Note that a forward lateral pass beyond the line of scrimmage is illegal.

Warming-up Activity/Game:

The Wall. Position an equal number of players at both ends of a large playing area or half a playing field. At center, mark off a "wall" using dome markers or 5–6 long folding mats stretched across the area and taped to each other so they stay in position. On the wall are positioned 3–4 defenders who try to "capture" free players by tagging them with a soft Nerf™ ball as they try to cross over to the other side. A tagged player must also get a Nerf™ ball and become a wall defender. Gradually the wall will have more defenders than free players. Free players can run back and forth at will, but once they enter into the wall zone (as shown), they must continue to cross the wall. Emphasize safety at all times!

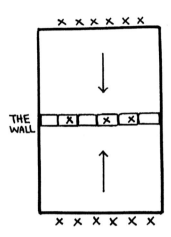

Skill Practice & Progressions:

1. Demonstrate the technique of snapping the ball and explain when this action occurs in the game: ball is snapped to the quarterback who then passes to a receiver or runs with the ball himself/herself.

2. Players partner up. Partner A is the snapper; Partner B is the quarterback who signals "1-2-3 HIKE!" Snapper hikes the ball to the quarterback. Switch roles after 5 snaps. Emphasize using a snap of the wrist to put a spiral spin on the ball.

3. Demonstrate the teaching cues for the lateral pass or underhand pass. Explain that this pass can only be made to the side or backwards to a player. A forward lateral pass is illegal.

4. Partners standing about 5 giant steps apart practice laterally passing the ball back and forth to each other from a stationary position. Emphasize that the passer uses one hand and tries to put a spiral spin on the ball. Practice passes to the left and to the right.

5. Partners moving together down the field and staying about 5 giant steps apart practice laterally passing the ball back and forth to each other. Switch sides and continue moving back up the field laterally passing.

6. **Snap, Pass, & Crackle.** Players form groups of 3 with one ball snapper, one quarterback, and one receiver who position 5 giant steps apart as shown. Snapper hikes the ball to the quarterback, who lateral passes the ball to the receiver moving forward. After 3 goes, players rotate positions until everyone has had a turn.

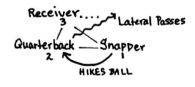

Cooling-down Activities/Games:

1. **Foxtail™ Throwing** (see Lesson 15) or **Woosh™ Ring Throwing** (see Lesson 19).

2. **Legends of the Day!**

Lesson 84:
Pattern Running and Defensive Guarding

Skill Builders: pattern running, dodging and faking, alertness and reaction, throwing and catching, tracking, hiking the ball, aerobic fitness, partner and group play

Expected Student Performance:

◆   Demonstrates proficiency in pattern running, dodging, and faking maneuvers.

◆   Willingly cooperates and integrates with other class and team members.

◆   Demonstrates proficiency in meeting fitness demands.

Facility/Equipment Needed:

◆   1 football per pair

◆   1 flag or flag belt and flags per player, 1 die

◆   Large cone markers

◆   1 bucket with 6 rainbow-colored beanbags

◆   1 corresponding rainbow card for each corner

◆   1 stretch chart

Teaching Points:

Pattern running consists of running and making at least one quick change of direction (or "cut") to get free from a defender and into an open space to receive a pass from the quarterback.

Pass Running Pattern

◆   "Cut" by pushing off the inside of the foot opposite to the intended direction of the cut: to cut to the right, push off from the inside of the left foot.

◆   Run at a certain pace, then bend at the knees and use small steps to make a quick movement to change direction.

◆   Add a head or body fake by a quick movement in one direction to go into the opposite or a different direction.

◆   After making the cut, keep trunk and lower body moving in the intended line of direction, but turn head back to see the quarterback releasing the ball and track the flight of the ball into your hands.

Defending the Receiver

◆   Watch the quarterback for clues to see where the pass will go.

◆   Keep within 3 giant steps of the player you are guarding, but never let the receiver get behind you.

- Be alert, ready to react to the receiver's cut.
- Try to knock the ball away or intercept the pass to the receiver.
- No body contact is allowed until the receiver touches the football, then you can try to pull the flag.

Warming-up Activity/Game:

Even and Odds Tag. Players pair off; each tucks a flag in the back of his/her shorts so that three-fourths of the flag is showing, and together start in a home space, standing side-by-side. Each pair decides who is "Even" and who is "Odd." A die is thrown. If the die rolls an even number, then that player is the IT player who must count to 3, then give chase to try to pull the "Odd" partner's flag before the die rolls again. Score a point for each flag successfully pulled. *Variation:* One partner is "Heads"; other partner, "Tails." Flip a coin to decide who is IT.

Skill Practice & Progressions:

1. Demonstrate "cutting" footwork. Players practice running in one direction, and on signal "cut" into another direction.

2. Demonstrate running a pattern to receive a pass, such as "down and out"—run forward on right-hand side, and cut at right angles to the right; or run forward on left side and cut at right angles to the left. Players practice running this pattern.

3. Display the patterns shown on the right on a whiteboard or large posterboard. Pair students and have them practice the different running patterns. Encourage pairs to create a pass running pattern of their own.

4. **Making the Play.** Partners now get into a "huddle" to decide on the pass-and-run pattern that is to happen. Ball snapper partner hikes the ball to the quarterback partner, then ball snapper runs a pass pattern, looking for the pass from quarterback partner.

5. **Hike, Pass, Pattern.** Form groups of 3 consisting of a ball snapper, quarterback, and receiver. Quarterback sets up the "play" or pass-running pattern for the receiver. Ball is hiked to quarterback, receiver runs the pattern, and quarterback makes the pass. Practice two different patterns, then rotate positions.

6. **Hike! Hike!** Use the teaching cues for defending or covering a receiver, and demonstrate the whole play sequence of activity #5. Add a defender who will guard the receiver, but only passively. Offensive team gets a 5-second huddle to decide on the pass-pattern play. The hike, snap, pass is executed and the defender must react.

Cooling-down Activities/Games:

1. **Football Corners.** Designate 6 colored corners on the playing field as shown: Red, Orange, Yellow, Green, Blue, and Purple. Players may run to any corner of their choice and stay there jogging lightly in place. From the bucket of corresponding colored beanbags, draw out a color. Players in the corresponding colored corner are "caught out" and must come to the center circle and stretch. (A stretch chart is positioned at the center circle for players to follow.) Once a certain color has been drawn, players cannot go to that corner. Players who forget and go to the corner already eliminated are "caught out." Emphasize fair play! Which player or players will remain after the fifth beanbag has been drawn? Start a new game. *Variations:*

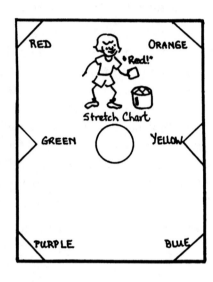

-   Replace the beanbags in the bucket after each draw. Make the rule that players must always move to a new corner each time a beanbag has been drawn.
-   Use a die and number the corners from 1 through 6.
-   Use different polygonal shapes for each corner. Draw the name of the shape.

2. Legends of the Day!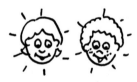

In Class Idea:

Pair players off and have each pair develop 4 running plays and 4 passing plays. One partner is the recorder; the other creates the diagrams.

Lesson 85:
Ball Carrying and Handing-off

Skill Builders: ball-carrying and handing-off skills, dodging and alertness, partner and group play

Expected Student Performance:

Demonstrates proficiency in ball-carrying and handing-off skills.

Willingly cooperates and integrates with other class and team members.

Demonstrates proficiency in meeting fitness demands.

Facility/Equipment Needed:

1 football per pair

1 flag or flag belt and flags per player

Large cone markers

Teaching Points:

Handing-off

Ball carrier holds ball in two hands to begin.

As receiver approaches, move ball across to that side with the hand under the ball and the elbow bent.

Hold ball now slightly out from the body.

Hand the ball to the receiver; do not throw.

Receiver approaches the ball carrier and raises the arm on the side of the quarterback.

Elbow is bent at right angle at shoulder level, forearm directly in front of body, and palm down.

Bend the other arm's elbow at right angle, position just below the waist, directly in front of the body, with the palm facing up.

Let quarterback hand-place the ball into your hands; don't reach for it.

As exchange takes place, clasp the ball from above with the top hand and from below with the other hand.

Do not stop but run through the ball as it is handed to you.

Shift ball to the carrying position.

Hand-Off   Carrying the Ball

Carrying the Ball

◆ Cradle the ball firmly into the crook of the elbow and your chest and cover the front tip of the ball with the hand.

◆ Carry the ball against the side away from the defender(s).

◆ Run with head up and into open space; keep alert.

Common Running Plays

◆ "Pitch-out"—Quarterback underhand tosses ball to a running back.

◆ "Sweep"—Quarterback gives a hand-off to a running back who follows teammate(s) usually down a sideline.

◆ "Reverse"—Quarterback runs in one direction and hands off a running back traveling in the opposite direction.

Warming-up Activity/Game:

Football Tag. Mark off a large rectangular playing area with an end zone at either end and a center circle. Players are in teams of 5–6; each team selects the name of a football team: Broncos, Roughriders, Lions, and so on. Each team is given a certain colored set of flags: red, orange, yellow, green, blue, and purple. Each player must tuck his/her flag into the back of the shorts so that three-fourths of the flag is showing. A corresponding set of beanbags is placed in a bucket. One beanbag is drawn out and the color determines which team is the IT team. IT team stands in a center circle. Other players scatter throughout the play area. On signal "Tackle," IT team gives chase to the other teams. A player whose flag has been pulled must go to either end zone area and jog in place. A whistle stops the play after a certain time limit (30 seconds). Caught players are quickly counted and a score recorded for the IT team. Another beanbag is drawn, and another IT team takes over. Game continues in this way. Which team will be the best tagging team?

Skill Practice & Progressions:

1. Demonstrate the hand-off. Emphasize the teaching cues. Players pair up and take turns practicing the action. One partner is the quarterback; the other, the receiver. Quarterback stands in place with the ball and hands it off to the receiver who walks past on the right side. Repeat action on the left side. Receiver then runs past the quarterback who hands off the ball. Practice each side. Switch roles and repeat.

   ● Now players practice walking towards each other and making the exchange.

   ● Players practice running towards each other for the hand-off.

   Emphasize cradling the ball into carrying position.

2. Demonstrate the skill of carrying the ball. Have players practice carrying the ball and zigzag running through a set of cones.

3. **Practice Hike/Hand-off/Carry Sequence.** Use the same set-up as for activity #5 from Lesson 84: Snapper hikes the ball to quarterback, receiver runs past to receive the hand-off, and carries the ball another 5 yards. Introduce and demonstrate the three common running plays: pitch-out, sweep, and reverse play. Practice faking the hand-off and passing the ball to the receiver who runs a pass pattern.

4. **One on Three.** For each team mark out several corridors using dome markers and 3 equal zones in each corridor. Each team positions as shown in the diagram: 3 ball carriers at one end, 1 defender in each zone. Each team has 2 footballs and 6 flags. Each ball carrier has 3 flags tucked into the back of the waistband. Ball carrier starts at one end and, carrying the football, tries to run and dodge his/her way past each defender without getting "tackled" (a flag pulled). Each defender must stay in his/her own zone and can pull only one flag. After each ball carrier has had a turn, the defenders and ball carriers switch roles. Emphasize heads up at all times!

Ball Carrier   Defender

Cooling-down Activities/Games:

1. **Shuttle Hand-off & Carry Relay.** Teams of 6 to 8 players set up in shuttle formation. Player 1 runs and carries football across to opposite side to hand-off to Player 2, who runs across to hand-off ball to Player 3, and so on. Which team can make the most number of crossings in a certain time limit? Which team can make *x* number of crossings the quickest?

#6   #4   #2   #1

2. **Legends of the Day!**

Lesson 86: Punting and Place-kicking

Skill Builders: place-kicking, punting, foot–eye coordination, passing and catching, tracking the ball, aerobic fitness, partner and team play

Expected Student Performance:

◆ Demonstrates proficiency in punting the ball and place-kicking.

◆ Willingly cooperates and integrates with other class and team members.

◆ Demonstrates proficiency in meeting fitness demands.

Facility/Equipment Needed:

◆ Large outdoor playing field

◆ 1 football and kicking tee per pair

◆ 1 mini-football per game

◆ 1 Nerf™ or vortex football per game

◆ 1 set of colored bibs per team

◆ Cones and dome markers

Teaching Points:

Place-kicking

◆ Slowly approach the ball from about 5–8 yards/meters away.

◆ Plant the non-kicking foot to the side of the ball and about a foot behind it.

◆ Keep eyes focused on the ball right through the kick.

◆ Bend the kicking leg at the knee and straighten as the foot contacts the ball.

◆ Lock angle at contact so that supporting foot and kicking foot are at right angles.

◆ Contact the ball just below the midline.

◆ Follow-through in the intended direction of flight with the kicking leg lifting the kicker off the ground.

Punting

◆ Grip the ball with the laces up and center the ball over the kicking leg.

◆ Place one hand on the back of the ball and the other hand on the front.

◆ Keep eyes focused on the ball through the kick.

◆ Take a 1-2-3 step-and-kick approach: step with non-kicking leg (1), then kicking leg (2), then non-kicking leg (3), and kick.

◆ Drop the ball onto the top of the kicking foot instep.

♦ Point kicking toes down as you kick the ball.

♦ Follow-through with kicking leg in intended direction of flight, keeping hands out for balance.

♦ If ball is punted correctly, it will spiral which will significantly add traveling distance to the ball.

Warming-up Activities/Games:

1. Play **Five Passes** in 4-on-4 mini games. Each team wears a set of colored bibs. The playing area for each game is marked out by dome markers. Object of the game is to score 5 uninterrupted passes to score a point. A mini football is used per game. Have players stand by the player they will guard and shake hands to start the game. Emphasize that each player stay with the player he/she is guarding instead of cluttering to the ball. Use head and body fakes to get away from the defending player. Allow 5 traveling steps before passing the ball. *Variations:*

   ● Use a junior Nerf™ football or a vortex football.

   ● Allow only 3 traveling steps.

2. Do the following **Leg Stretches:**
   ● Hamstring Stretch
   ● Calf Stretch
   ● Sprinter Stretch

Skill Practice & Progressions:

1. Demonstrate the placement of the ball in the kicking tee and the place-kicking action. Start with a one-step approach. Emphasize keeping eyes focused on the ball, planting foot at the right spot, and contacting the ball below center to get it airborne. Discuss when the place-kick in a regulation game occurs, that is, at the start of each half of the game and to kick a point after a touchdown.

2. Players pair off and practice place-kicking skill. One partner is the kicker; the other partner, the retriever. After 5 place-kicks, switch roles. Check for good spacing so that one pair does not interfere with another pair. Start with a one-step approach, then gradually take a full run at the ball.

3. Demonstrate the punting action, emphasizing the 3-step approach, and dropping ball onto the top of the kicking foot instep.

4. Partners practice the punt kick, punting the ball back and forth to each other. Ensure pairs are safely spaced apart.

5. **Snap, Punt, Retrieve.** Each group of 3 consists of a ball snapper, a punter, and a retriever. Group sets up in a free open space. Check for good spacing. Rotate one position after every 3 punts.

Cooling-down Activities/Games:

1. Play **The Punting Game.** See Flag Football Lead-up Games, Lesson 89.

2. **Legends of the Day!**

Lesson 87:
Blocking* and Tackling

Skill Builders: introduction to the screen and shoulder blocking skills and rules, reinforcement of tackling and rules, aerobic fitness, partner and group play

Expected Student Performance:

◆ Demonstrates proficiency in blocking and tackling techniques.

◆ Willingly cooperates and integrates with other class and team members.

◆ Demonstrates proficiency in meeting fitness demands.

Facility/Equipment Needed:

◆ Large outdoor playing field

◆ Dome or cone markers for corridors

◆ 12–16 colored bibs

2 flags per player

◆ 1 junior football per group

Teaching Points:

Tackling

(In flag football a defensive player can only make the "tackle" by pulling a flag off the offensive ball carrier.)

Keep eyes focused on the flags of the runner.

Keep alert to any head or body fakes and be ready to react.

Stay balanced with weight evenly distributed on the balls of the feet, ready to move in any direction.

Get in good body position to move in quickly and grab the flag. Remember, no body contact is allowed.

Tackling

Setting the Block

(Blocker sets into a three-point stance: one hand and both feet in contact with the ground.)

Position feet shoulder-width apart, side-straddled, and weight evenly distributed on the balls of the feet, knees slightly flexed.

Place other arm across the thigh once in set position.

Keep body weight forward on the fingers of the hand resting on the ground.

Keep seat down, head up, and look straight ahead.

Setting the Block

*Suggest that blocking be introduced at Grade 6 level only!

Screen Blocking

- Blocker simply places her/his body between the ball carrier and the tackler.
- Absolutely no body control can occur.
- Tackler cannot push blocker out of the way, but must try to go around her/him.

Screen Blocking

Shoulder Blocking

(This is the only body blocking allowed in flag football. A blocker is not allowed to block an opposition player below the knees or on the back, use the hands to grab an opponent, or leave his/her feet to block an opponent.)

- Place the shoulder against the opposition's shoulder, chest, or mid-section.
- Keep in a balanced, forward stride position, knees slightly flexed and body crouched, head up.
- Make contact, driving the opponent downfield.

Warming-up Activities/Games:

1. Demonstrate tackling skills before warm-up game is played. Emphasize heads up to avoid collisions.

2. **Team Tail Tackle.** Divide the class into two even teams: "A" Team and "B" team. One team must wear colored bibs. Each player tucks two flags in the back of his/her shorts. A player from Team A finds a player from Team B to guard. The two shake hands, then stand face-to-face. A signal is given, Team A quickly indicates that Team A is the defensive team. The objective is then to try to capture as many flags as possible in a certain time limit, but a player can only pull the flag of the player he/she is guarding and only pull one flag at a time. Once a player has had both flags pulled, he/she must go to either end zone of the play area and jog in place. The defensive player who has successfully captured both flags then goes to either sideline and jogs in place. A whistle stops the play and a count is taken to determine the defensive team's score. Score 1 point for every flag pulled. Flags are returned and a new game begins with Team B being the defensive team.

ENDZONE

TEAM TAIL TACKLE

Skill Practice & Progressions:

1. Discuss "blocking" and the rules that go with it. Demonstrate how to set a **three-point stance.** Emphasize getting into a balanced position, seat down, head up, ready to move. Players practice the technique.

1.

2. Demonstrate the **Shoulder Block.** Players pair up with a player who is the same size. One partner is the blocker who faces a defending partner about 1 giant step away. Each player sets in the three-point stance. On signal "Block," partners step toward each other. The blocker, using a shoulder block, tries to control the defender for a 5-second count. Switch roles. Repeat the action with partners starting 2 giant steps apart from each other. Emphasize that partners do not try to knock each other down; action is a firm pushing action.

3. Demonstrate the **Screen Block,** emphasizing the "screening" action in slow motion. Players then get into groups of 3: one blocker, one ball carrier, one defender. Everyone has a flag tucked into the back of the shorts. Each group starts on one sideline of the playing field in a marked-out corridor as shown. Ball carrier runs the ball over to the opposite sideline, staying inside the corridor boundaries. Blocker tries to stay between the tackler and the ball carrier. Do this passively at first, emphasizing that absolutely no body contact is allowed! No flags are pulled.

4. **The Blocking Game.** Set up as for activity #3 above. Tackler tries to pull the ball carrier's flag. Switch roles each time so that players get ample practice at each position.

5. **Hike, Run, Block Game.** Form groups of 6 with each group made up of a quarterback, ball snapper, receiver, defender, and 2 blockers. Check that each group is safely spaced apart. Game is played from one sideline to another in corridors as for activities #3 and 4. Ball is snapped to quarterback who tries to pass the ball to a receiver. One blocker tries to get past the ball snapper to pull the quarterback's flag before he/she can pass the ball; other blocker tries to set a screen block for the receiver so that the defender cannot tackle the ball carrier. Emphasize safety at all times! Players rotate one position after 2–3 tries. Each quarterback is allowed a 10-second huddle to set up a "play." Encourage quarterback to call at least 2 running plays and 2 passing plays.

Cooling-down Activities/Games:

1. **Changing Motions.** Use the "sticky popcorn" signal to get the class quickly into a large circle and hook sit. Count down from 5. Select one player to be the blocker who must stand outside the circle with back facing the circle players. Secretively select another player to be the quarterback who starts a certain motion. Everyone else follows the quarterback's actions. Blocker is asked to step inside the circle and has 3 tries to guess who the quarterback is. When blocker is not looking, the quarterback changes the motion.

2. **Legends of the Day!**

Homework Idea:

Watch a football game in action either on TV or live. Observe the player positions, the scoring system, and the rules being played.

Lesson 88:
Skill Builder Stations

Skill Builders: flag football fundamentals, accuracy passing and receiving, throwing for distance, punting and place-kicking, agility running, cooperation, 3-on-3 play

Expected Student Performance:

◆ Demonstrates proficiency in accuracy throwing and catching with a football.

◆ Willingly cooperates and integrates with other class and team members.

◆ Demonstrates competency in agility demands.

Facility Equipment Needed:

◆ Cassette or CD player; station signs

◆ Station #1: 3 vortex howlers (regular and junior sizes)

◆ Station #2: 1 suspended hoop, 2–3 fixed hoops, bench, 3 junior footballs, floor tape or dome markers

◆ Station #3: 6–8 tires or hoops, stopwatch or digital watch

◆ Station #4: 3 junior footballs, kicking tees, goal posts

◆ Station #5: mini-basketball, 2 sets of bibs, basketball or netball posts

◆ Station #6: 3 Fling-It™ nets, variety of tossing objects

Skill Builder Station Ideas:

Station #1: Vortex Football Throw. Partners throw back and forth to each other. With every successful catch made by each partner, take a step back. Emphasize good catching skills.

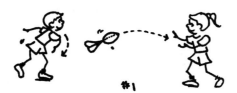

Station #2: Target Throw. Suspend a hoop from a basketball ring, or set up a hoop on a bench. Use a junior football. For suspended hoop, players stand on either side and try to throw the football through the hoop to the opposite player. For hoop targets on a bench, mark off three throwing distances.

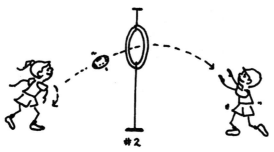

Station #3: Agility Tire Circuit. Place tires or hoops in a pattern as shown in the diagram. Players time each other to run through the tire/hoop pattern.

Station #4: Kicking. Players partner off and practice kicking the ball to each other. Practice place-kicks and punting through the goal posts if possible.

Station #5: Mini-netball or 3-on-3 Basketball Game. See Lessons 36 and 74.

Station #6: Fling-it™ Net Play. Partners explore using different objects to fling off the net and catch.

Cooling-down Activity:

Legends of the Day!

Lesson 89:
Lead-up and Modified Games

Skill Builders: football fundamentals such as footwork, running and dodging, passing and receiving, punting; hand–eye coordination; aerobic fitness; partner and team play; field awareness; player positioning; rules

Expected Student Performance:

Demonstrates proficiency in executing football fundamentals and team play.

Willingly cooperates and integrates with other class and team members.

Demonstrates proficiency in meeting fitness demands.

Facility/Equipment Needed:

Large playing field

Variety of footballs (Nerf™, junior, mid-size)

Cone and dome markers, safety spots

2 kicking tees per game

Teaching Points:

Offensive Positions

Offensive set consists of 8 players: a quarterback, a center (ball snapper), 2 tackles, 2 ends, and 2 running backs.

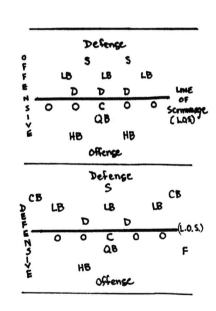

Quarterback calls the plays in the huddle, gives the hiking signal for the ball snapping, and passes or hands-off the ball to the receiver. Also has the option of running with the ball.

Center lines up in front of the ball at the line of scrimmage, and on quarterback's signal, hikes or snaps the ball to the quarterback, then sets a shoulder block.

Tackles help to protect the quarterback by setting shoulder blocks.

Two ends and the running backs are all eligible to catch a pass, and any player can run with the ball after it is snapped into play.

Defensive Positions

Defensive set consists of 5 defensive linemen and 3 defensive backs (or 3 defensive linemen and 5 backs).

KEY:
QB – Quarterback
C – Center
O – Offensive Lineman
HB – Half back
LB – Line backer
D – Defensive Lineman
CB – Corner back
S – Safety
F – Flanker

- Linemen are responsible for rushing the quarterback and tackling the ball carrier.

- Defensive backs are responsible for stopping the sweep, running, and preventing receivers from catching the ball. Usually the fastest defensive backs defend against the long pass.

- In one-to-one defense, a defensive back guards the receiver wherever he/she runs.

- In zone defense, the defensive backs guard receivers who come into the zone or area they are defending.

Lead-up Games:

1. **Net Football.** For each game play on a mini-volley-ball court with a 6-foot high net and a small junior-sized football. One team positions on each side of the net as shown. Player #6 from one team starts the game by throwing a mini-football over the net into the opposition's side. Player making the catch immediately throws the football, looking for "holes" in the court. Score one point if the opposition fails to catch the football or return it over the net fairly.

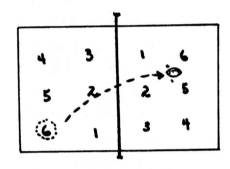

2. **The Punting Game.** For each game have one team of six to eight players against another team of six to eight players. Each team starts in its own half of a large playing field marked off with end zones at either end as shown. Flip a coin to see which team will start the game with a place kick, taken 5 yards/meters from center line. Players advance the ball by punting it into the opposition's court. The ball must be kicked from where it is caught. If the ball is dropped, the team is given a 3-yard penalty and the ball is positioned 3 yards back from where it was dropped. A team scores a goal by kicking the ball into the end zone on the full. After a score, the opposition team puts the ball into play again with a place kick. Emphasize that players take turns punting the ball. *Variations:*

   - Allow the team to advance 3 yards/meters forward if an opposition's punt is caught on the full.

   - Use a dome marker to indicate where the ball is to be punted from.

   - Vary the type of football used.

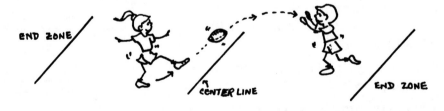

3. **Capture the Football.** Divide a large rectangular play area into two halves using dome markers. Place a football on a cone marker at the middle of each end line. Place a hoop at each diagonal corner ("The Prisons") of the playing area. Place two safety squares or spots in each half of the play area. To start, each team lines up in its own half at a scrimmage line as shown. Every player has a flag tucked in the back of his/her shorts.

The object of the game is for one team to "capture" the opposition's football and carry it into that team's own half before the other team can do the same. The football may be laterally passed to another teammate or handed-off, but the receiver must run with the football over the center line without being tackled (flag pulled). If in the opposition's half, a player can seek the safety of one of the two spots. But only one player can stand on a safety marker at a time. If a defender pulls an opponent's flag, then that player must go to "Prison" and remain there until a teammate is able to free that player. Both players can then return to their half by walking on the outside of the play area. A player can only free one prisoner at a time. Prisoners must have one foot inside the hoop. *Variation:* Allow prisoners to link up with the first prisoner to be taken at the front of the link.

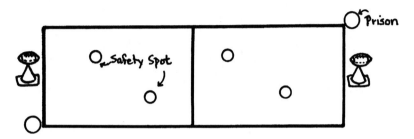

Modified Games:

1. **Three-pass Flag Football.** Mark out a large playing field with a goal crease (20-foot or 6-meter radius) at each end as shown. Each game requires two teams of 6–8 players: 1 goalie, 3 offensive players, and 3 defensive players. Each team wears a set of colored bibs and starts in its own half of the field. Every player has a flag tucked in the back of his/her shorts. Players line up at center and each shake hands with the player he/she will guard. Each team's goalie takes up position in the opposite goalie crease. The team winning the toss of a coin gets possession of the football.

   Play starts by a place-kick taken at the mid-point mark of each half. Once the football is received by a player in the opposition field, players may advance into each other's half.

   The football can only be advanced up the field by the overhand pass or hand-off.

   The defensive team will try to intercept the pass and get possession to attempt to score.

   A "touchdown" is scored when the team's goalie catches a pass from a teammate and after 3 uninterrupted passes have been made.

   After each goal a place-kick is taken by the team that made the goal.

   A player receiving the pass may take at the most five traveling steps before passing off the football or attempting to score.

   The football is awarded to the defensive player making the flag pull at the spot where this occurs. The football is put into play by a free pass from this point.

   The football is awarded to the opposition team where the violation occurs if the offensive player steps on or into the goalie crease; takes more than five steps with the ball; steps out-of-bounds with the football; or the pass goes out-of-bounds.

◆ Absolutely no body contact is allowed. A 3-minute penalty is given to a player who trips, pushes, holds, or deliberately knocks another player to the ground. That player must sit out for the 3-minute penalty on the sideline; the opposition team now has a player advantage.

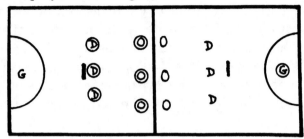

2. **Basketball Football.** Play the game as for "Three-Pass Flag Football" except now the goal becomes the basketball hoop. Score 1 point for hitting the backboard or ring; 2 points for sending the football through the ring.

3. **Netball Football.** Assign players to netball positions. Score a goal by passing or running the ball over the end line.

4. **Flag Football.** See the Appendix for description of the game and rules.

Cooling-down Activity:

Legends of the Day!

Lesson 90:
The Bird Dance/Balance Feathers

Skill Builders: skipping, elbow swinging, partner and group interaction, aerobic rhythm signals, hand–eye coordination, balance, development of rhythm sense

Expected Student Performance:

Demonstrates competency and confidence in performing dance steps.

Demonstrates proficiency in fine motor balancing.

Willingly cooperates and integrates with partner and group members.

Demonstrates proficiency in meeting fitness demands.

Facility/Equipment Needed:

CD player or cassette player

Popular music with a steady 4/4 beat

Quiet music with a steady 4/4 beat

1 balance feather per dancer

Teaching Points:

Teach each part of the dance first—small-step progressions.

Make sure everyone can clearly hear and see you.

Get dancers to listen to the music and clap the rhythm first.

Walk through steps first without music, then with the music.

Write out the teaching cues on whiteboard.

Use verbal teaching cues.

Use popular music that dancers can identify with. But also, if possible, use the traditional music of the dance.

Gradually expand dancers' movement vocabulary.

Provide opportunity to mingle the dancers so that they are interacting more with each other.

"STAMP-STAMP"

Warming-up Rhythms:

Aerobic Mingler. Use popular music with a steady 4/4 beat.

- **March and Clap:** March in place clapping on the fourth count.

- **Scrambled Eggs—March!** March in general space, changing directions every 8 counts; clap on the eighth count.

MARCH & CLAP

- **Step Kicks:** In place alternate stepping on one leg, kicking other out in front 8 counts; snap fingers every 4 counts.

- **Clockwise Jog & Stamp:** Jog clockwise around the play area for 12 counts, then stamp feet in place for 4 counts.

- **Counterclockwise Jog & Stamp:** Jog counterclockwise around the play area for 12 counts, stamp feet in place for 4 counts.

STEP-KICK

- **Right Elbow Swing:** Find a partner and hook right elbows while skipping in a clockwise circle for 8 counts.

- **Left Elbow Swing:** Find a partner and hook left elbows while skipping in a counterclockwise circle for 8 counts.

RIGHT ELBOW SWING

- **Scrambled Eggs—Hopping!** Hop in general space changing hopping foot every 4 counts.

- **Mingle Swing:** Find a new partner, join both hands, and swing once around in a circle clockwise (4 counts); counterclockwise (4 counts).

'MINGLE - SWING'

- **March and Clap:** March in place and clap hands.

Dance Progressions:

The Bird Dance. (This popular novelty dance involves the basic steps of skipping and elbow swinging and is danced throughout the whole world by young and old!) Have dancers pair off and form groups of four. Each group finds a free space. In each group, one pair of dancers faces the other pair, about 2 giant steps apart. Check for good spacing. Use the "Bird Dance" song available from major sports catalog companies.

Part A

- **Cheep, cheep, cheep, cheep:** Imitate a bird's beak opening and closing by opening and closing fingers and thumb (4 counts).

- **Flap, flap, flap, flap:** Imitate a bird flapping its wings by hooking thumbs under armpits, and moving elbows up and down (4 counts).

- **Wiggle, wiggle, wiggle, wiggle:** Imitate a bird ruffling its feathers by swaying hips from side to side (4 counts).

- **Clap, clap, clap, clap:** Clap hands together (4 counts).

'CHEEP - CHEEP!'   FLAP - FLAP!

' WIGGLE - WIGGLE'   'CLAP - CLAP!'

Part B

- **Swing-2-3-4-5-6-7-8:** Hook right elbows with partner and skip clockwise in a circle (8 counts).

- **Swing-2-3-4-5-6-7-8:** Hook left elbows with opposite partner and skip counterclockwise in a circle (8 counts). Repeat from the beginning. *Variation:* Repeat Part B, but on the last 4 counts of the left elbow swing, everyone quickly form new groups of four, partner up, ready to begin dance again.

SWING -2-3- ...: B

Cooling-down Rhythms:

Use relaxing background music for this activity.

1. **Balance Feathers.** Dancers explore balancing the feather on different body parts; then experiment with transferring the balance feather from one body part to another. Emphasize that focus will shift from the top of the feather to the bottom part and back to the top again as transference takes place. *Variation:* Now challenge dancers to transfer one balance feather from one partner to the other, using different body parts!

2. **Legends of the Day!**

Homework Idea:

Aerobic Grid. (See the Appendix.) Dancers fill in the grid squares each time they do different aerobic activity, including their P.E. dance class!

Lesson 91:
The Bunny Hop/The Stepping Routine

Skill Builders: rhythm footwork routine, side-close steps, Bunny Hop steps, partner and group interaction, development of rhythm sense

Expected Student Performance:

◆ Demonstrates competency and confidence in performing dance steps.

◆ Willingly cooperates and integrates with other class and team members.

◆ Demonstrates proficiency in meeting fitness demands.

Facility/Equipment Needed:

◆ CD player or cassette player

◆ Popular music with a steady 4/4 beat

◆ Quieter, new age music for cooling-down activity

◆ 1 large hoop or center circle in play area

Teaching Points:

Hallelujah Routine

◆ Teach each part of the dance first—small-step progressions.

◆ Make sure everyone can clearly hear and see you.

◆ Get dancers to listen to the music and clap the rhythm first.

◆ Walk through steps slowly at first without music, then with music; moderate tempo, then quicker tempo.

◆ Call out teaching "cues" as dancers perform the steps.

◆ Teach side-close and finger snapping.

◆ Have dancers practice in their own free space.

◆ Use popular music that dancers can identify with.

◆ Face the same direction as the dancers when teaching the steps.

SIDE - CLOSE

Bunny Hop Steps

◆ Demonstrate and teach the basic steps of the dance first: hop on one foot and kick the other foot out diagonally to the side.

◆ Have dancers practice in their own free space.

◆ Ensure that all can clearly hear and see you.

◆ Listen to the music and clap the beat, then Bunny Hop in rhythm.

◆ Put the teaching "cues" on the whiteboard or posterboard to help dancers remember the sequence.

◆ Call out teaching "cues" as dancers perform the steps.

◆ Face the same direction as the dancers when teaching the steps.

HOP - KICK

Warming-up Rhythms:

Hallelujah Routine. (This routine involves quick footwork, but should be introduced at a slow tempo first, then gradually increase the tempo. Dancers stand in wave formation with each "wave" spaced about 3 giant steps from the other. Make sure everyone can hear and see clearly.)

- **Side-close (1), side-close (2), side-close (3), side-close (4) . . . (8 counts).** Begin with right foot, and step right foot to side, close left foot to right; step left foot to left side, close right foot to left. Finger snap on each close.

- **Side, front, side, back (4 counts).** Touch right foot to right side, to front, to right side, to back.

- **Step right, crossover left, step right, and hop-turn (4 counts).** Step right foot to right side, cross left foot behind right, step right foot again, and on that same foot do a quarter hop-turn to the right.

- **Back (1-2)-back (3-4), stamp-stamp-stamp-pause (5-6-7-8 counts).** Step back on left foot, step back on right foot; then quickly stamp left, stamp right, stamp left, and pause.

- **"Shimmey down (1-2), shimmey up (3-4)" (8 count total).** Wiggle down, wiggle back up. Repeat pattern twice.

- **Start from the beginning: "side-close, side-close, . . ."**

Variation: Add other footwork to the routine; for example, kick right side, kick left side.

Dance Progressions:

The Bunny Hop. Dancers in free space practice the hop-kick-jump sequence:

- **Kick right, kick right (4 counts).** Hop on left foot and kick right foot diagonally out to side.

- **Kick left, kick left (4 counts).** Hop on right foot and kick left foot diagonally out to side.

- Jump forward (1-2), jump back (3-4).

- Jump–jump–jump–pause (4 counts).

Bunny Hop in teams, with dancers holding on at the hips of the dancer in front. Teams move in a certain pattern as shown.

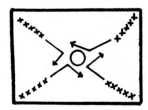

Cooling-down Activities/Games:

1. **"Flowing Pockets" in pairs.** Partner A moves into a certain shape and holds it; Partner B fills in the space ("pockets") created by Partner B's shape. Partner A then slowly changes her/his shape to fill in the pockets created by B's shape. Dancers continue in this way filling in the pockets created by each other's shape. Emphasize that movement transitions are smooth and in slow motion. *Variation:* Flowing Pockets in threes; in fours; teams. Establish a flowing order: Dancer A, then B, then C, etc.

2. **Legends of the Day!**

Homework Idea:

Aerobic Grid. (See the Appendix.) Dancers fill in the grid squares each time they do different aerobic activity, including their P.E. dance class!

Lesson 92:
The Twist/The Schottische

Skill Builders: twisting action, schottische pattern of step-hops, partner and group interaction, development of rhythm sense

Expected Student Performance:

Demonstrates competence and confidence in performing twisting action.

Demonstrates competence and confidence in performing schottische steps.

Willingly cooperates and integrates with partner and other group members.

Demonstrates proficiency in meeting fitness demands.

Facility/Equipment Needed:

CD player or cassette player

Popular music with a steady 4/4 beat

Chubby Checker's "Let's Twist Again"

Teaching Points:

Ensure that all can clearly see and hear you.

Walk through steps first without music, then with the music.

Introduce patterns slowly at first, then pick up the tempo.

Have dancers practice individually at first.

Call out teaching "cues" as dancers perform the steps.

The Twist Warm-up

Demonstrate the twisting action:

Keep knees bent and swivel body on the balls of the feet.

Move arms freely to help the twisting action.

Keep relaxed and loose.

Listen to the music and twist in time with it.

Schottische Step

Have dancers move to the drumbeats, then music.

Step-step-step-hop pattern: Beginning with right foot, step right, step left, step right, and hop on right; step left, step right, step left, and hop on left.

Step-hop pattern: Beginning on right foot, step, then hop on right foot; step, then hop on left foot.

Warming-up Rhythms:

The Twist Routine. The twisting action is similar to "toweling your backside and rubbing your feet into the ground!" Find a free space, listen to the music, and twist away!

- Twist from a high level to a low level. How low can you go?
- Twist from a low level to a high level.
- Twist with your feet together, then gradually twist them farther and farther apart; gradually twist feet together again.
- Twist and move sideways; twist around in a circle.
- Jump up in the air, land, and keep twisting again.
- Don't forget to smile!
- Twist with a partner. Copy each other's twisting actions.
- Twist away from each other; towards each other.
- One partner twists clockwise while the other partner twists counterclockwise.
- One partner twists high, the other low; vice versa.
- Invent another twisting action with your partner.
- Create your own twisting routine with your partner.

TWISTING PAIRS

Dance Progressions:

1. **Demonstrate the Schottische Step.** Beginning with right foot, step right, step left, step right, and hop on right; step left, step right, step left, and hop on left. Dancers keep in time to drumbeats as they do 8 Schottische steps clockwise, then 8 Schottische steps counterclockwise. Repeat pattern slowly at first, then pick up the tempo.

2. **Demonstrate the Step-hop Pattern.** Beginning on right foot, step, then hop on right foot; step on left foot, then hop on left foot; continue this pattern for 8 Step-Hops. Now in place do 4 Step-Hops circling clockwise, then 4 Step-Hops circling counterclockwise.

STEP   R – L – R

2.   'STEP – HOPS'

3. **Demonstrate the Schottische Pattern.** Dancers move in a large circle in a clockwise direction doing 4 Schottische steps, followed by 4 Step-Hops. Repeat, but Step-Hop in a clockwise circle. Repeat again, but Step-Hop in a counterclockwise circle.

4. **Partner Schottische pattern.** Dancers pair up, join inside hands, and stand side by side around a large circle. Check for good spacing. Starting with inside feet, dancers do 4 Schottische steps, followed by 4 Step-Hops in the line of direction. *Step-Hop Variations:*

- One partner step-hops in place, while the other partner step-hops, circling under the stationary partner's raised hand. Switch roles on the next step-hop sequence.

- Both partners circle away from each other while step-hopping.

- Partners "Wring-the-dishrag" while step-hopping in place.

5. **Horse and Buggy Schottische.** Dancers form sets of four, with one couple behind the other couple, facing counterclockwise. Each pair joins inside hands and joins their outside hands to the other couple as shown.

- **Step, step, step, hop (four times):** Starting with the outside foot, and moving forward, each group does 4 Schottische steps.

- **Step-hop, step-hop, step-hop, step-hop:** Front couple drops inside hands and step-hops around the outside of the back couple, who step-hop forward. Front couple then rejoins hands behind the other couple, so that the positions are now reversed; then Schottische pattern is repeated from beginning. *Variation:* On step-hop pattern, front couple continues to hold hands as they step-hop backward under the upraised hands of the back couple who step-hop while turning away from each other to untwist and become the front couple.

Cooling-down Activities:

1. **Rock, Paper, Scissors.** This is an ideal concentration activity to cool down the dancers after their high energy output in performing the Twist and Schottische! Rules are simple: "Paper covers rock; rock crushes scissors; and scissors cut paper." Hand actions are simple, too:

- "Rock" is made by placing one fist on top of the other.

- "Paper" is made by spreading one hand flat on top of bottom fist.

- "Scissors" is made by spreading pointer and middle finger apart on top of bottom fist.

Dancers pair up and sit facing each other. On signal "1,2,3,Show!" each dancer taps one hand fist on the other three times, then shows either "rock," "paper," or "scissors" action. A win is decided; for example, if partner A shows paper, while partner B shows rock, then A wins (since paper covers rock) and partner A gets 1 point. Play to 5 points, then challenge someone else.

2. **Legends of the Day!**

Fit Think Ideas:

- ◆ **Aerobic Grid.** (See the Appendix.) Dancers fill in the grid squares each time they do different aerobic activity, including their P.E. dance class!
- ◆ Discuss the word "D-A-N-C-E" as a feel-good experience and ask the class to create an action word for each letter; for example, "D"—determination, "A"—(positive) attitude, "N"—nutrition, "C"—cooperation, and "E"—enthusiasm!

Lesson 93:
The Hustle/Rhythmic Ribbons

Skill Builders: aerobic workout routine, foot pattern routine, rhythmic ribbons, listening and following instructions, development of rhythm sense, coordination

Expected Student Performance:

Demonstrates proficiency in performing the aerobic and footwork routines.

Demonstrates competence and rhythm sense in using rhythmic ribbons.

Willingly cooperates and integrates with other class members.

Demonstrates proficiency in meeting fitness demands.

Facility/Equipment Needed:

CD player or cassette player

Popular music with a steady 4/4 beat

1 rhythmic ribbon per dancer

Teaching Points:

Sweat-it-out Routine

This aerobic routine consists of a sequence of actions that is repeated for the duration of the music.

Select music that is popular and has a lively 4/4 beat.

Demonstrate each action and have dancers practice.

Put the teaching "cues" on the whiteboard or posterboard to help dancers remember the sequence.

Call out teaching "cues" as dancers perform the steps.

Ensure that all can clearly see and hear you.

Teach the steps facing in the same direction as the dancers.

Change the focus point by moving to another side of the wave formation to start another sequence of actions.

Rhythmic Ribbons

Purchase a set from sports catalog companies or make rhythmic ribbons by attaching a 4- to 5-yard/m length of satin or synthetic ribbon to a 20-foot long dowel rod. Use a fishing line swivel and trace, screw-eye, and about 12 inches of fishing line to connect the two parts as shown.

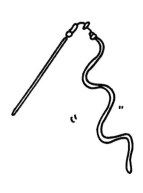

Keep the rod in line with the arm and hold the end in the palm with the pointer finger extended.

Keep ribbon moving continuously to create good flow.

Use the wrist movement for most ribbon patterns using the shoulder as the axis.

◆ Emphasize taking good care of the ribbon and how to wrap the ribbon for storage.

◆ Check for good spacing so that ribbons do not become entangled.

Warming-up Rhythms:

1. **Sweat-it-out Routine.** Teams set up in wave formation, spaced arm's length apart. Each wave is about 3 giant steps from the other.

   ● **Jog in Place:** Jog in place, clapping hands and keeping in time to the music. (16 counts)

   ● **Elbow-Knee:** Hop on the right foot while lifting the knee of the left leg to touch the right elbow. Hop on left foot and touch right knee to left elbow. (16 counts)

   ● **Jumping Crossovers:** Place hands on hips, jump feet apart, then jump and cross feet, jump apart, jump, and cross. Alternate the front foot each time when crossing feet. (8 counts)

   ● **Skipping Step:** 8 skips clockwise in a circle; 8 skips counterclockwise in a circle. Snap fingers every second count. (16 counts)

   ● **Twist Hops:** Extend arms sideways to shoulder level. Keep feet together and jump, twisting upper body to one side; lower body to other side. (8 counts)

   ● **Side Kicks:** Swing right leg out to right side while hopping twice on the left foot; then swing left leg out to left side while hopping twice onto right. (16 counts)

   ● **Quarter Jump—Turn to right–Stamp–Stamp–Stamp (4 counts).**

   HEART RATE
   CHECK

   Repeat sequence from the beginning until music stops. Do a 10-second count Heart Rate Check before and after the routine.

2. **2-minute Stretching Sequence.** Stretch through the full range of motion, rhythmically and smoothly: Full Body Circles, Side Stretchers, Leg Lunges. Do another 10-second count Heart Rate Check before and after the routine. Ask dancers to compare their active heart rate with recovery heart rate.

Dance Progressions:

The Hustle: This popular American line dance involves dancers learning a foot-pattern routine. Any popular music with a steady 4/4 beat can be used. Dancers form waves of about 6–10 dancers, all facing the same direction and spaced arm's length apart. When teaching the dance, face the same way as the dancers to avoid confusion.

1. **Back-2-3-4; Forward-2-3-4.** Beginning on right foot, dancers take three steps backwards, swing left foot out in front as they lean back and clap. Beginning on left foot, dancers take three steps forward, swing left foot out in front as they lean back and clap. Repeat twice.

2. **Side-front-side Kick; Side-front-side Kick.** Beginning with right foot, dancers take three steps to right side, crossing left foot in front of right. Place right foot down, and kick left foot to right and clap. Then reverse to the left, beginning with the left foot.

3. **Step-kick; Step-kick.** Step right foot in place, kick left leg to right side. Step left foot in place, kick right leg to left side. Repeat twice.

4. **Jump Forward-Pause; Jump Backward-Pause; Forward-Backward-Click-Click.** Jump forward with feet together, pause. Jump backward with feet together, pause. Jump forward; jump backward, then click heels together twice, pivoting on balls of feet.

5. **Touch Forward-Touch Backward; Forward-Backward-Sideways-Turn.** Touch right foot forward twice. Touch right foot backward twice. Touch right foot forward, backward, sideways, and pivot a quarter hop-turn to left on left foot, keeping right foot off the floor.

Repeat dance routine from beginning, facing the new direction. *Variation:* In step 2, dancers do step-turns as they step right, left, right, and kick left foot.

Cooling-down Rhythms:

1. **Rhythmic Ribbons.** Check for good spacing to avoid ribbons tangling. Have dancers use dominant hand at first, then try ribbon patterns holding the ribbon in the nondominant hand. Add footwork to complement ribbon movement. At the end, dancers wrap ribbons gently around the stick and put in storage.

   WINDSHIELD WIPERS   TRAFFIC COPS

   HELICOPTERS   BUTTERFLIES

   - **Windshield Wipers:** Swing ribbon from side to side.
   - **Traffic Cops:** Swing ribbon forward and back.
   - **Helicopters:** Circle ribbon overhead.
   - **Propellers:** Circle ribbon in front.
   - **Wheels:** Circle ribbon at either side.
   - **Butterflies:** Swing in a figure-8 pattern in front.

- **Bows:** Swing ribbon in figure-8 pattern at either side.
- **Ribbons:** Swing ribbon in figure-8 pattern overhead.
- **Coils:** Make bigger and bigger circles; then smaller and smaller circles.
- **Zingers:** Make spirals from left to right; right to left.
- **Air Snakes:** Raise and lower arms to a wiggle pattern in the air.
- **Floor Snakes:** Lower arm and flick wrist to make ribbon wiggle along the floor.

2. **Legends of the Day!**

Fit Think Ideas:

- Discuss dancing as a fitness activity. Does dancing make your heart beat faster? What makes it a dance and what makes it a fitness activity? What are the benefits of dancing?
- Remind dancers to fill in their **Aerobic Grid!**

Lesson 94:
Aerobic Ropes/La Raspa/The Limbo

Skill Builders: bleking steps, step-hop steps, elbow-swinging, rhythmical rope turning and jumping routine, enhancement of rhythm sense, partner and group interaction

Expected Student Performance:

Demonstrates competency in performing bleking and step-hop steps.

Demonstrates good rhythm sense in aerobic rope warm-up, flexibility, and overall body coordination in the cool-down activity.

Willingly cooperates and integrates with other class and team members.

Demonstrates proficiency in meeting fitness demands.

Facility/Equipment Needed:

CD player or cassette player

Popular music with a steady 4/4 beat

1 long pole or rope per group of 4

Teaching Points:

Bleking Step

Place hand on hips, and hop lightly on left foot, extending right heel forward to touch the floor.

Hop lightly on right foot, extending left heel forward.

Step-Hop-Step

With hands on hips, step on right foot, and hop on that foot; then step on left foot and hop on left foot.

Continue this step-hop-step pattern.

Warming-up Rhythms:

1. Aerobic Ropes Routine (See Lesson 7.)

    Helicopters while jogging in place (8 counts)

    Propellers while jumping feet apart, feet together (8 counts)

    Wheelers while doing pogo springs (8 counts)

    Figure-8 while doing Twisters (8 counts)

    Rocker Steps (8 counts)

    Joggers (8 counts)

    Boxer (8 counts)

    Side-jump, Side-jump (8 counts)

    Dancers add their own rhythm rope jump (8 counts)

HELICOPTERS   PROPELLERS

FIGURE-EIGHTS

2. Repeat the sequence above until the music stops, then do the following:
   - Rope Yanks
   - Periscope
   - Thread the Needle
   - Rope Stretchers

ROPE YANKS THREAD THE NEEDLE

Dance Progressions:

1. Demonstrate the bleking step and have dancers practice individually.

2. Demonstrate the step-hop pattern. Dancers practice at first without music and then to the music.

R L   L R

1.

STEP - HOP

2.

3. Dancers pair off and find a free space. Check for good spacing. Partners face each other, but turn slightly counterclockwise away so that they are standing right shoulder to right shoulder. Practice the sequence: 3 fast bleking steps, pause; and clap hands twice. On the pause, dancers quickly change to face diagonally left shoulder to left shoulder, and repeat sequence.

4. **La Raspa.** (This Mexican folk dance, meaning "the rasp" or "the file," involves the bleking and step-hop steps and elbow swinging.)

   - **Part 1: Fast-fast-fast: pause and clap-clap.** Facing diagonally, right shoulder to right shoulder, dancers do 3 fast bleking steps; pause on the fourth count, and clap hands twice. Change to face diagonally left shoulder to left shoulder and repeat 3 bleking steps and 2 hand claps. Repeat Part 1 a total of eight times, changing the diagonal direction each time the bleking step-clap sequence is repeated.

BLEKING STEPS

   - **Part 2: Swing-2-3- . . . -7. Clap; Swing-2-3- . . . -7, Clap:** Partners hook right elbows, bend left elbows, and point left hand upwards. Dancers do right-elbow swings with seven step-hops; release hands and clap on eighth count. Then dancers do left-elbow swings with seven step-hops; release hands and clap on the eighth count. Repeat Part 2 again. Dancers repeat entire dance from the beginning.

'ELBOW-SWINGS'

Variations:

Part 3: Left and Right Grand Around the circle.
Have couples form a single circle, partners facing. Shake right hands with partner, then walk past your partner to meet the next oncoming dancer, and shake left hands. Continue right and left handshakes until you meet your partner (or until you meet the seventh dancer for a mixer), then folk dance repeats from the beginning.

Cooling-down Rhythms:

1. **The Limbo.** (This activity involves coordination and balance, and good flexibility, particularly of the back area.) Use suitable music such as Chubby Checker's "Limbo Rock" available through the music stores. Each team has its own limbo corner. Check for good spacing. Two dancers hold long pole (PVC piping) or stretch a rope between them starting at waist height. Dancers take turns "limbo-ing" under the rope or pole: keep belly button upward, do not let hands touch the floor, and move with a two-foot shuffle under the rope. Feet will go first, head last! Gradually lower the pole. Who in your team will limbo the lowest? Challenge another group. *Variation:* Have a class challenge and declare a Limbo boy and girl champ.

2. **Legends of the Day!**

Fit Think Ideas:

- **Aerobic Grid.** (See the Appendix.) Dancers fill in a square on the grid for each aerobic activity session.

- Discuss the phrase "rhythm sense." What does it mean, and how does having good rhythm enhance our movement?

Lesson 95:
Barn Dance/Mayim/Rhythm Sticks

Skill Builders: grapevine step pattern (footwork), rhythm patterns using rhythm sticks, development of rhythm sense, partner and small group interaction

Expected Student Performance:

◆ Demonstrates proficiency in performing grapevine-step pattern.

◆ Demonstrates good rhythm sense in using rhythm sticks.

◆ Willingly cooperates and integrates with partner and group members.

◆ Demonstrates proficiency in meeting fitness demands.

Facility/Equipment Needed:

◆ CD player or cassette player

◆ Popular music with a steady 4/4 beat

◆ 2 rhythm sticks per dancer

Teaching Points:

1. **Grapevine Step.** (Basic step to many Mediterranean folk dances.) Have dancers practice individually, then in a line formation, then in a circle with hands joined. Use a tambourine to beat out the rhythm, and have dancers do grapevine steps to the music. Perform steps slowly at first, then gradually to dance tempo.

   • **Step right, step left in front pattern:** Step right foot right, cross left foot in front of right. Step right foot right, and cross left foot in front. Repeat this foot pattern.

   • **Step right, step left behind pattern:** Step right foot right, then cross left foot behind. Step right foot right, then cross left foot behind. Repeat this foot pattern.

2. **Grapevine-step.** (Combination of above.)

   • **Step right, cross left in front; step right, cross left behind pattern.** Step right foot right, cross left foot in front of right. Step right foot right, cross left foot behind. Repeat pattern. *Reverse pattern:* Step left, cross right in front; step left, cross right behind.

Warming-up Rhythms:

Movement is done to popular music with a strong 4/4 beat.

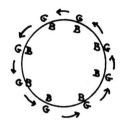

1. **A Barn Dance Warm-up.** Partners pair up and take the barn-dance (basic dance) hold: Boys on the inside and girls on the outside; pairs facing in a counterclockwise direction in a large circle formation. Boy partner starts with left foot; girl partner with right foot. Demonstrate the basic dance hold: Partners face each other with boy partner putting his arm around the girl's waist and the girl partner resting her left hand on his right shoulder.

   - **Forward, two, three, kick; back, two, three, together:** Pairs walk three steps forward and kick with inside leg, then walk four steps backward.

   - **Out, two, three, clap; in, two, three, clap:** Partners release hand-hold, and take four slide steps sideways away from each other. Clap on the fourth beat each time.

   - **Slide-step, slide-step sideways; slide-step, slide-step back:** Partners in basic dance hold take two slide steps sideways counterclockwise, then two slide steps back in a clockwise direction.

WALK AND KICK

2. **Waltz.** Partners in the waltz position circle twice in clockwise direction using a skipping step. Then girls jog in place while boy partners walk two steps counterclockwise towards a new partner. The new partners position for the forward walk and kick. Dance routine repeats from the beginning.

WALTZ POSITION

Dance Progressions:

1. Demonstrate the grapevine step progressions of the Teaching Points. Have dancers practice individually to your teaching cues at first, then to music. Gradually increase the tempo of the music. Encourage dancers to use a light, springy step, accenting the first step.

2. **Line Grapevine.** Dancers get in groups of 6–8. In each group dancers join hands and stand side by side to form a long line. Grapevine-step in one direction; grapevine in the opposite. Try to keep in time with the music.

2.

3. **Circle Grapevine.** Two groups combine to form a single circle, facing inward. Grapevine-step clockwise to the beat of the music, then grapevine-step counterclockwise.

4. **Mayim, Mayim.** (This is a simple Jewish folk dance that involves the grapevine step [tscherkessia] and running steps. Mayim means "water." The dance movements

express the joy of finding water in a very dry land and emulate the motion of the waves breaking on the shore.) Dancers form a simple circle, with hands joined and held down; everyone facing inward.

- **Step right, cross left in front; Step right, cross left behind:** Moving clockwise direction, perform 4 grapevine steps.

- **Center-2-3-4; Back-2-3-4:** With right foot dancers take 4 running steps into the center. On first step, they leap lightly, bending at the knees, gradually raising joined hands above heads. Dancers then return to place with four running steps, and gradually lower joined hands down to sides. Repeat sequence.

- **Run-Toe Touch-Clap; Run-Toe Touch-Clap; Run-Toe Touch-Clap; Run-Toe Touch-Clap:** Dancers move clockwise with three running steps, beginning with right foot. Turn to face center. Hop on right foot and touch left foot across front to right side; hop on right, touch left to side. Repeat hopping sequence three more times.

- **Hop-Toe Touch-Clap; Hop-Toe Touch-Swing Arms:** Hop on left foot, touch right foot in front to left side and clap hands directly in front. Hop on left, touch right to side, and swing arms out to sides, shoulder high. Repeat hop-clap-arm swing sequence three more times.

Repeat dance from beginning.

Cooling-down Activities:

1. **Rhythm Sticks.** Make rhythm sticks from dowels cut into 1-foot lengths with a 3/4-inch diameter. Have sticks painted as an art project, two sticks per child. Use music with a strong 4/4 beat. Each dancer finds a free space, knee-sits, and explores creating different tapping patterns:

alternate

- Tap sticks in front on floor, 2 counts.
- Tap sticks in air, 2 counts.
- Tap sticks in front on floor, 2 counts.
- Tap sticks in air, 2 counts.
- Alternate tapping sticks to each side, 2 counts.
- Alternate tapping sticks in front, 2 counts.
- Flip one stick, catch; flip the other stick, catch (4 counts).

in the air

flip & catch

Repeat pattern. Dancers pair up and partners face each other in knee-sit position. Create a tapping routine with your partner; for example:

- Tap sticks in front on floor, 2 counts.
- Tap partner's sticks, 2 counts.
- Tap sticks in front, 2 counts.
- Tap partner's sticks.

2. **Legends of the Day!**

Homework Idea:

Create a rhythm stick "dance" to your favorite music!

Fit Think Idea:

Dancers fill in the square(s) for the **Aerobic Grid.**

Lesson 96:
Parachute Dance/Virginia Reel

Skill Builders: grapevine steps, elbow swinging, do-si-do, sashays, casting off, reeling the set, rhythm patterns and rhythm sense, cooperation, partner and group interaction

Expected Student Performance:

◆ Demonstrates competency and confidence in performing parachute and dance routines.

◆ Willingly cooperates and integrates with partner and group members.

◆ Demonstrates proficiency in meeting fitness demands.

Facility/Equipment Needed:

◆ CD player or cassette player

◆ Popular music with a steady 4/4 beat

◆ 1 large parachute

Teaching Points:

◆ Teach each part of the dance through small-step progressions.

◆ Walk through steps first, then at tempo.

◆ Make sure everyone can clearly hear and see you.

◆ Get dancers to listen to the music and clap the rhythm first.

◆ Use popular music that dancers can identify with.

◆ Also, if possible, use the traditional music of the dance.

◆ Write out the teaching cues on whiteboard.

◆ Call out teaching "cues" as dancers perform the steps.

◆ Gradually expand dancer's movement vocabulary.

Warming-up Rhythms:

1. **Rhythmic Parachute Warm-up Routine.**
   - **Parachute shuffle and ruffle:** Using palms-down grip, facing chute, slide step counterclockwise for 8 counts, stamp-stamp-stamp-pause, then clockwise for 8 counts, stamp-stamp-stamp-pause. Gently shake the chute.
   - **Parachute salute:** Raise chute upwards and walk 4 steps into center, then 4 steps back out (8 counts). Repeat twice.
   - **Grapevine clockwise:** Step left, cross right foot in front of left; step left, cross right foot behind left; step (8 counts).
   - **Grapevine counterclockwise:** Step right; cross left in front of right; step right, cross right foot behind left (8 counts).
   - **2 Heel-toe's** (right foot); 2 Heel-Toe's (left foot). Repeat (8 total counts).

- **Skip clockwise** for 8 counts; jump-turn, jump-turn skip counterclockwise for 8 counts (one-hand hold); jump-turn, stamp-stamp.

Repeat routine from the beginning.

2. **Parachute Stretches.**

   - Gentle parachute wave, up-2-3; down-2-3.
   - Palms-up grip, facing chute, plant feet, and lean back.
   - Palms-down grip, back to chute, plant feet, and lean.

Dance Progressions:

The Virginia Reel. This popular American folk dance involves skipping, arm swinging, do-si-dos, sashay, slide-stepping, and casting off. The ideal formation for this lively dance are longways sets of six pairs per set. Partners face each other across the set, spaced about 3 yards apart from each other and arm's length apart from the dancer on either side. The head couple is closest to the music. Walk couples through the figures first, then have them listen to the music and perform at the music's tempo. Use popular music with a lively 4/4 beat, or traditional music of this folk dance.

- **Forward-2-3-4; Back-6-7-8:** Each line takes four skipping steps towards the other. Partners greet each other with a "high ten," then take four skipping steps back to place, clapping on the eighth count. Repeat this pattern twice.

- **Right Elbow Swing-3-4; Skip back-6-7-8; Left Elbow Swing-3-4; Skip back-6-7-8:** Skip to the middle, meet your partner, link right elbows and swing once around, then skip back to place (8 counts). Repeat, linking left elbows and swinging around once.

- **Two-Hand Swing-3-4; Back-6-7-8:** Skip to middle, meet partner, and join both hands. Swing clockwise once around, then skip back to place.

- **Do-Si-Do-3-4; Back-6-7-8:** Skip toward your partner, pass by right shoulder to right shoulder, back to back, and then return to place passing left shoulders.

- **Head couple, Sashay Down-3-4- . . . -8; Sashay Up-3-4 . . . -8:** Head couple joins hands in the middle and slide-steps for 8 counts down the set, then slide-steps back up to place. Other couples clap and foot-stomp in time to music. Yahoos and whistles are allowed too!

- **Cast Off-3-4-5-6-7-8:** Head couple casts off by turning outwards and leading the file as you skip down to the foot of the set. Dancers in your file follow in order. At the foot, Head Couple meets again, forms an arch by joining hands overhead. Each pair meets up, joins hands, and slide-steps through the arch and up the set back to place. Next pair in set becomes the new head couple and the dance starts again. Repeat the dance until each pair has had a turn as head couple.

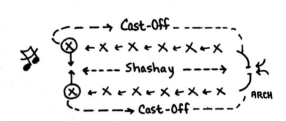

Variations:

Reel the Set. (Add this pattern to the dance between the Sashay and Cast Off figures.)

- Head couple skips toward each other, does a right elbow-swing one and a half times around. Then dancers separate and skip toward the opposite line. The head boy partner turns the second girl dancer around once with a left elbow-swing, while the head girl partner does a left elbow-swing with the second boy dancer.

- Head couple then meets in the middle of the set again for a right elbow-swing. Separate and skip to the opposite third dancer for a left elbow-swing.

- Continue down the set in this way, swinging partner with a right elbow-swing, then swinging the opposite dancer with a left elbow-swing.

- When head couple has "reeled" all five couples and is now at the foot of the set, they do a right elbow-swing halfway around so that they are on their starting sides, join hands, and sashay back to the head of the set. Skip back into place, ready for the cast-off.

" Reel The Set"

Cooling-down Activities:

1. **The Pow-wow.** Use Native American drumming music or aboriginal music. Dancers cross leg-sit in one large circle, each dancer with a pair of rhythm sticks. Establish a drumming sequence. Choose a "chief" to lead the group. *Variations:* Split drummers into 3–4 groups and select a chief for each group. Each group creates its own drumming patterns. Groups may decide to add dance footwork to their drumming.

2. **Legends of the Day!**

Fit Think Ideas:

◆ Dancers fill in the square(s) for the **Aerobic Grid.**

◆ Discuss why these dances are called folk dances.

Lesson 97:
Grand March/Cha-cha

Skill Builders: marching rhythm and marching patterns, cha-cha-cha steps, basic dance hold, even and uneven rhythms, rhythm sense, cooperation

Expected Student Performance:

◆   Demonstrates competency and confidence in performing marching patterns.

◆   Demonstrates proficiency in performing the cha-cha routine.

◆   Willingly cooperates and integrates with partner and class members.

◆   Demonstrates proficiency in meeting fitness demands.

Facility/Equipment Needed:

◆   CD player or cassette player

◆   Popular music with a steady 4/4 beat

◆   Variety of rhythm instruments and rhythm sticks

Teaching Points:

◆   Teach each part of the dance first through small-step progressions without music, then with music.

◆   Walk through basic steps first, then at tempo.

◆   Make sure everyone can clearly hear and see you.

◆   Get dancers to listen to the music and clap the rhythm first.

◆   Provide opportunity to mingle the dancers so that they are interacting more with each other.

◆   Use popular music that dancers can identify with.

◆   Also, if possible, use the traditional music of the dance.

◆   Write out the teaching cues on whiteboard.

◆   Use verbal teaching cues.

◆   Gradually expand dancers' movement vocabulary.

Basic Partner Dance Hold (Closed Position)

◆   Boy partner takes the girl partner's right hand in his left and holds it at a comfortable height, about level with boy's left shoulder.

◆   Boy's right hand is placed under girl's left arm and rests on girl partner's lower left shoulder blade.

◆   Girl's left hand is placed on boy's right shoulder.

Warming-up Rhythms:

Grand March. Use the boundaries of a basketball court or similar play area. Half of the class positions in a "snake" formation along one sideline; other half stands in a snake formation on the other side of the play area. Teacher stands on the middle end line at the head of the play area; dancers face the foot (opposite end line) as shown. Use music with a strong 4/4 marching tempo.

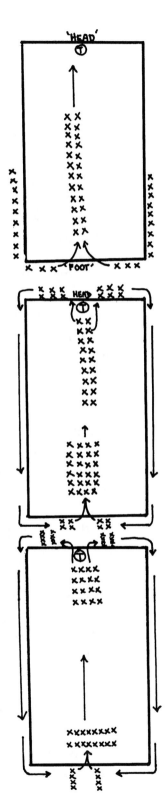

- **March down the middle in two's:** Each line marches forward to the foot of the play area, turns the corner, and continues toward the center of the foot. Meet another dancer there, and together turn and march up the middle toward the head end line.

- **Split two to left; two to right:** When dancers reach the teacher, the first pair turns to the left; second pair to the right; third pair to the left; fourth pair to the right, and so on. Dancers continue to march along the end line, turn the corner, and march down the sideline towards the foot.

- **March down the middle in four's:** As for the first pattern, but now one pair meets another pair, and together the group of four marches side-by-side up the middle.

- **Split four to left; four to right:** First group of four turns and marches left; second group of four turns and marches right, and so on. Each group marches down the sideline towards the foot.

- **March down the middle in eight's:** Groups of four meet at the center of the foot and form groups of eight who march side-by-side down the middle towards the head.

- **Four left and four right:** Now reverse the pattern: group of eight splits into groups of four; one group of four turns and marches to the left; while the other group of four turns and marches to the right. Each group of four marches down its respective sideline, turning the corner at the foot. At the middle of the foot, each group, alternating sides, turns down the middle. March up the middle in fours.

- **Two left, and two right:** When each group of four reaches the head, the group splits back into two groups; the first group of two turns to the left; the second group of two turns to the right. Each group marches along the head end line, down the respective sidelines, and turns the corner to march along the foot end line. At the middle, alternating sides, each pair marches up the middle.

- **Split one to the left; one to the right:** When each pair arrives at the center of the head end line, the pair splits, with one dancer turning to the left, and the other dancer turning to the right. Dancers march down the sidelines into original starting position.

Dance Progressions:

Cha-cha-cha. (This light bouncy popular Latin American social dance originated in Cuba in the 1950s.) Teach the basic "Cha-cha" pattern individually and slowly, without music. Have dancers count aloud the rhythm pattern: "1-2-Cha-cha-cha." Then have dancers pair up and practice the basic step pattern in Close and Open Positions.

1. Demonstrate and teach the forward basic pattern, and back basic pattern. Dancers in own space practice without music, then with music.

   - **Forward-Back-Step-Step-Step (Slow-Slow-Quick-Quick-Slow):** Step left forward, step back with right foot, accenting the step, then do the "'Cha-cha-cha" by stepping left in place, step right in place, step left in place.

   - **Back-Forward-Step-Step-Step (Slow-Slow-Quick-Quick-Slow):** Step right backward; step left forward in place, accenting step, and again "Cha-cha-cha" by stepping right in place, stepping left in place, and stepping right in place.

2. **Partner Cha-cha-cha.** Partners can face each other joining hands, or get into the basic dance hold position. Boy partner starts with the forward basic pattern; girl partner, with the back basic pattern.

   - **Forward-Back-Step-Step-Step (Slow-Slow-Quick-Quick-Slow):** Boy partner step forward L, back R; girl partner step back R, forward L "Cha-cha-cha," boy partner L R L; girl partner R L R.

   - **Back-Forward-Step-Step-Step (Slow-Slow-Quick-Quick-Slow):** Boy partner steps back R, forward L; girl partner steps forward L, back R "Cha-cha-cha," boy partner R L R; girl partner L R L.

3. **Opening Break Pattern.** Partners face with both hands joined.

   - **Forward-Back-Cha-cha-cha:** Both partners do a forward basic pattern.

   - **Right Crossover, Cha-cha-cha:** Partners then cross over right foot in front of left, step left, and Cha-cha-cha R L R. Drop left hand hold as you do this.

   - **Left Crossover Cha-cha-cha:** Then cross over left foot in front of right, step right, and L-R-L Cha-cha-cha. Change to left hand hold.

4. Partners practice these basic patterns. Then have each pair create a "Cha-cha-cha" routine of their own!

Cooling-down Activities:

1. **The Marching Band.** Dancers explore even and uneven rhythms and rhythm patterns in personal and general space, using a variety of rhythm instruments. Form 3 groups:

   - Shakers (tambourines, maracas)
   - Strikers (drums, rhythm sticks)
   - Ringers (cymbals, triangles, wrist bells)

   Dancers march in general space keeping in time to the music with their instruments and feet! On the loud drum beat, dancers change direction. On the whistle, dancers march in place and trade their instrument with someone else.

2. **The Orchestra.** Each group—Shakers, Strikers, and Ringers—collects in a certain area and creates a rhythm pattern that dancers will play. Teacher is the "Conductor" and uses a conductor's wand (rhythm stick) to point and signal each group to play this rhythm pattern with the rhythm instruments. On the "cut" signal with the wand, that group immediately stops. Explore bringing in different combinations: Groups 1 and 2; Groups 1 and 3; Groups 2 and 3; all 3 together; one at a time.

   CONDUCTOR   'SHAKERS'

3. **Legends of the Day!**

Fit Think Ideas:

◆ Dancers fill in the **Aerobic Grid.**

◆ Discuss what is meant by a "social dance" and why Latin American dancing is so popular today!

Lesson 98:
Square Dancing

Skill Builders: square dance formation: setting the square and positions, square dance figures, square dance jargon, cooperation, rhythm sense

Expected Student Performance:

◆   Demonstrates proficiency in performing square dance figures.

◆   Willingly cooperates and integrates with partner and group members.

◆   Demonstrates proficiency in meeting fitness demands.

Facility/Equipment Needed:

◆   CD player or cassette player

◆   Popular music with a steady 4/4 beat

◆   Traditional square dance music with calls

◆   1 pair of jump bands per group of 4

Teaching Points:

Setting the Square (See diagram.)

◆   Dancers pair off and form groups of four couples.

◆   Each couple of the group stands on one side of a square, facing inward about 3 yards from the other pairs.

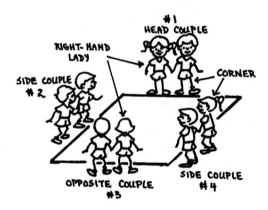

◆   The girl partner is always on the boy's right.

◆   Head couple, with backs to the music, is couple #1.

◆   Opposite couple is couple #3; side couples are #2 and #4.

◆   Couple #2 is to the right of the head couple.

Positions

◆   *Partner* is each dancer of the pair.

◆   *Corner, Corner Lady,* or *Left-Hand Lady* is the dancer on the boy's left.

◆   *Right-Hand Lady* is the dancer in the couple to the boy's right.

◆   *Opposite* or *Opposite Lady* is the dancer directly across the set.

◆   *Active* or *Leading Couple* is the couple designated by the caller to perform the action.

Basic Step: Shuffle Step

◆   Shuffle-step is a quick walk or half-glide step.

Warming-up Rhythms:

Square Dance Signals. Dancers move in general space using the shuffle-step in time with the music. Dancers are introduced to the basic square dance calls as signals and do the movements. Each time dancers hear a new square dance call, they find a new partner and together perform the movement.

- **Hit the Trail:** Shuffle-step in time to the music moving in different directions. Shuffle-step is a quick walk or half-glide step.

- **Stop, Clap 'n Stomp:** Dancers immediately stop and keep in time to the music by clapping hands and foot stomping.

- **Swing your partner (corner):** *Waist Swing:* Partners stand side by side, right hip to right hip. Each puts right arm around partner's opposite side at hip. Shuffle once around each other, leaning slightly away. *Right (left) Elbow-Swing:* Hook right (left) elbows with a dancer and turn once around in place. *Two-Hand Swing:* Dancers join both hands, lean away from each other and circle clockwise once around. *Do-Si-Do:* Cross arms in front at chest level. Pass dancer right shoulder to right shoulder, back to back, and shuffle step back to place.

Dance Progressions:

1. Illustrate and demonstrate "setting the square" and the positions in a square dance formation. Then have dancers pair up with 4 pairs setting up in square dance formation. Teach the following square dance figures as well as the square dance signals that were used in the warming-up activity.

- **Honor your partner:** Bow to your partner.
- **Honor your corner:** Bow to the corner who bows back to you.
- **Allemande left:** Boy partners face their corner, hook left elbows, and shuffle once around the corner, returning to partner.
- **Promenade:** Each couple joins right hands over left joined hands (skater's position) and walk side by side in a clockwise direction once around, then return to home position.
- **Do-si-do:** Cross arms in front at chest level. Pass dancer right shoulder to right shoulder, back to back, and shuffle step back to place.
- **Right-hand Star:** Hold right arms at the wrist at shoulder level of the dancer in front of you and shuffle-step clockwise once around.

- **Left-hand Star:** Hold left wrist of the dancer in front of you and shuffle step counterclockwise once around.

2.   Practice the following routine:
- Honor your partner; honor your corner.
- Circle left; Do-si-do partner; Swing your corner.
- Girls' star right; Boys' star left.
- Allemande left and Promenade home.
- Head couple bow; Side couples bow.

3.   Have dancers mingle and find new partners. Set the square again and practice the above routine.

4.   Each square set designs its own square dance routine.

Cooling-down Activities:

1.   **Jump Bands Play.** (See Lesson 7.) If possible, keep dancers in groups of 4: 2 jumpers and 2 steppers. Use popular music with a strong 4/4 beat. Dancers take turns being the jumpers and the steppers. Encourage steppers to experiment with creating different footwork actions. (See diagram.) Jumpers move in the following pattern: apart 1-2; together 1-2; apart 1-2; together 1-2. Check for good spacing.

2.   **Tinikling.** (See the Appendix.)

3.   **Legends of the Day!**

Fit Think Ideas:

- Dancers fill in the **Aerobic Grid.**
- Discuss tinikling and the history behind this name. See the Appendix for reference.

Lesson 99:
The Butterfly/The Troika

Skill Builders: step and hop sequence; elbow swings; running, stamping, and arching sequence; concentration; rhythm patterns; interaction in groups of 3

Expected Student Performance:

    Demonstrates proficiency in performing rhythm pattern sequences.

    Demonstrates competence and confidence in performing dance steps.

    Willingly cooperates and integrates with other class members.

    Demonstrates proficiency in meeting fitness demands.

Facility/Equipment Needed:

    CD player or cassette player

    Popular music with a steady 4/4 beat

Teaching Points:

    Teach each part of the dance first through small-step progressions.

    Walk through steps first, then at tempo.

    Make sure everyone can clearly hear and see you.

    Get dancers to listen to the music and clap the rhythm first.

    Provide opportunity to "mingle" the dancers so that they are interacting more with each other.

    Use popular music that dancers can identify with. Also, if possible, use the traditional music of the dance.

    Write out the teaching cues on whiteboard.

    Call out the cues as dancers perform the actions.

    Gradually expand dancers' movement vocabulary.

Warming-up Rhythms:

The Butterfly Warm-up. This is a popular social dance often performed by the participants at a wedding reception, and involves a slow part followed by a fast part. Dancers must listen carefully for changes of tempo in the music. The circle dance is performed in groups of 3 with each group equally spaced around a large circle. In each group dancers stand side-by-side, facing counterclockwise. The middle dancer holds each outside partner around the waist, while the outside dancers put their inside hands around the waist of the middle dancer. Encourage dancers to whistle and "yahoo!" on the fast part.

- **Part 1: Slow part (to music in 6/8 time):** *Step right, hop-hop and lift.* Start with right foot and step onto right foot (1 count). Hop twice on right foot (counts 2–3), while lifting left leg diagonally to right. *Step left, hop-hop and lift.* Step on left foot (count 4); hop twice on left foot (counts 2–3), while lifting right leg diagonally to left. Continue this step-hop pattern counterclockwise around the circle. Accent the first and fourth beats. Listen for temp to change.

- **Part 2: Fast part (to music in 2/2 time):** *Right elbow-swing; Clap and stomp.* Middle dancer right elbow-swings dancer on right, turning once around while third dancer claps hands and stomps feet in place. *Left elbow-swing; clap and stomp.* Middle dancer left elbow-swings dancer on the left, turning once around, while the other dancer claps hands and stomps feet in place. Continue this pattern until tempo changes. Quickly regroup so that a different dancer is in the middle.

Variations:

Have dancers hold deck rings instead of holding on at the waist of middle dancer. In Part 2, swing is done by each dancer holding a deck ring in each hand and using the skipping step.

Dance Progressions:

The Troika. (This traditional Russian folk dance means "three horses" and involves dancers in groups of three moving counterclockwise or clockwise around a large circle, using running steps and stamping.) Dancers form groups of 3 and stand side-by-side around a large circle (just like the spokes of a wheel), facing counterclockwise, holding inside hands shoulder high and placing outside hands on hips.

- **Run-2-3-4-5- . . . 16:** Together in each group take sixteen running steps forward.

- **Arch-2-3-4-5-6-7-8; Arch-2-3-4-5-6-7-8:** Dancer on the right-hand side of middle placer (outside dancer) takes eight small running steps under the arch formed by the middle and left (inside) dancers who run in place. Middle dancer follows the right dancer under the arch turning in place to face starting position.

- **Arch-2-3-4-5-6-7-8; Arch-2-3-4-5-6-7-8:** Dancer on the left-hand side takes eight small running steps under the arch formed by the middle and right dancers who run in place. Middle dancer follows the left dancer under the arch turning in place to face starting position.

- **Circle-2-3-4-5- . . . -12; Stamp-Stamp-Stamp; Circle-2-3-4-5- . . . -12; Stamp-into-side-by-side.** Each trio joins hands to make a circle and takes twelve small running steps clockwise, and three stamps in place; then trio takes twelve running steps counterclockwise, then stamps three more times at the same time getting back into side-by-side formation and switching positions.

Repeat from the beginning.

Variations:

- **Troika Mixer:** On last 3 stamps, middle dancers run forward to become the middle dancer for the next group.

- Instead of the circle-stamp sequence, use a right-hand star and a left-hand star.

- Inside dancer goes under the arch first; then the outside dancer.

Cooling-down Rhythms:

1. **Concentration, Concentration.** This is an alertness, listening, concentration, and cooperation activity. Dancers in groups of 8–10 sit cross-legged in a circle and number off 1, 2, 3, . . . 10. Number ones are the leaders who start the activity. Dancers practice the **slap-clap-snap** rhythm first: Slap knees twice, clap hands twice, then snap fingers. Keep rhythm steady and slow to moderate in tempo.

   `·SLAP — CLAP — SNAP·`

   - Leader starts the rhythm: "Slap-slap; clap-clap; snap-snap." Second time through, leader on the "snap-snap" calls out own number, then the number of another dancer in the group; for example, "slap-slap; clap-clap; "1"–"7.""

   - Now the dancer whose number has been called waits until the next "snap-snap" and says his/her own number and number of another dancer: "7"–"3." (May call the number of the dancer who just called your number!)

   Challenge: Form groups of 6. Get "two lives" to stay in the game, then if you say the wrong number sequence, you must sit out but can still do the slap-clap-snap rhythm sequence. Now the challenge becomes for those players still in the game to remember the numbers left!

2. **Legends of the Day!**

Fit Think Ideas:

- Dancers fill in the square(s) of the **Aerobic Grid.**

- Discuss how a dance can become a "mixer" or "ice breaker."

Lesson 100:
The Madison/Progressive Jiving

Skill Builders: footwork rhythm routine, hand rhythm routine, basic partner dance hold, side-together-side-tap jiving steps, partner interaction

Expected Student Performance:

◆ Demonstrates competence and confidence in performing jiving steps.

◆ Demonstrates proficiency in performing footwork and hand rhythm routines.

◆ Willingly cooperates and integrates with partner and other class members.

◆ Demonstrates proficiency in meeting fitness demands.

Facility/Equipment Needed:

◆ CD player or cassette player

◆ Popular music with a steady 4/4 beat

Teaching Points:

◆ Teach each part of the dance first through small-step progressions.

◆ Walk through steps first, then at tempo.

◆ Make sure everyone can clearly hear and see you.

◆ Get dancers to listen to the music and clap the rhythm first.

◆ Provide ample opportunity for dancers to practice the dance steps involved.

◆ Provide opportunity to mingle the dancers so that they are interacting more with each other.

◆ Use popular music that dancers can identify with.

◆ Also, if possible, use the traditional music of the dance.

◆ Write out the teaching cues on whiteboard.

◆ Use verbal teaching cues.

◆ Demonstrate dance steps facing the same direction as dancers.

◆ Gradually expand dancers' movement vocabulary.

Basic Partner Dance Hold (Closed Position)

◆ Boy partner takes the girl partner's right hand in his left and holds it at a comfortable height, about level with boy's left shoulder.

◆ Boy's right hand is placed under girl's left arm and rests on girl partner's left shoulder blade.

◆ Girl's right hand is placed on boy's right shoulder.

Warming-up Rhythms:

The "Madison" Warm-up. (Use popular music with a lively 4/4 beat.)

> **Touch side right, touch side right:** Touch right foot to the side; close right foot to left foot (twice).
>
> **Touch side left, touch side left:** Touch left foot to the side; close left foot to right foot (twice).
>
> **Touch right back, touch right back:** Touch right foot backwards; close right foot to left foot (twice).
>
> **Touch left back, touch left back:** Touch left foot backwards; close left foot to right foot (twice).
>
> **Right knee lift, right knee lift:** Lift right knee up and across body and lower (twice).
>
> **Left knee lift, left knee lift:** Lift left knee up and across body and lower (twice).
>
> **Kick right, Kick left:** Kick right foot across body. Kick left foot across body.
>
> **Jump turn apart, together:** Do a quarter jump turn, feet apart. Jump feet together and start again.

Repeat routine until the music stops.

Dance Progressions:

Have dancers form a circle that will move in a counter-clockwise direction. Boy partner positions on the inside of the circle facing out; girl partner stands on the outside of the circle facing in.

1. **Teach the Basic Jiving Step:** "Side-together-side-tap" steps. Boy partner starts with left foot; girl partner, with right foot. Use popular music with a 4/4 beat or classic rock 'n roll songs like Bill Haley and the Comets' "Rock Around the Clock."

2. **Boy Partner steps: Side-together-side-tap:** Step left foot to side; feet together. Step left foot to side, then right foot taps next to left foot. Step right foot to side; feet together. Step right foot to side; left foot taps next to right foot.

3. **Girl Partner steps: Side-together-side-tap:** Step right foot to side; feet together. Step right foot to side, then left foot taps next to right foot. Step left foot to side; feet together. Step left foot to side; right foot taps next to left foot.

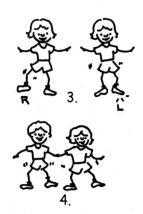

4. **Side-together-side-tap; returning to side-by-side. Side-together-side tap; returning to original position:** Partners turn counterclockwise to be side-by-side with each other. Hands may be joined or apart. Partners step away from each other. Boy partner to the center; girl partner to the outside.

5. **Side-together-side-tap:** Partners step away from each other again.

6. **Walking 1,2,3,4,5,6 (new partner):** In the next 6 walking steps, the girl turns under the raised joined hands (boy partner holding girl partner's left hand in his right hand). Boy partner moves clockwise; girl partner moves counterclockwise. Release hold towards the end so that the girl can move onwards one place around the circle (counterclockwise) to new partner, and repeat progression from beginning.

Once Progressive Jive is learned, have partners create a new step to add to the routine.

Cooling-down Activities:

1. **Hand Jiving.** This is a lively and enjoyable icebreaker clapping routine. Teach at a slow tempo at first, then pick up the tempo. Use a wave formation or a semi-circle formation and music with a steady 4/4 beat.

    - **Pat thighs twice, clap hands twice.**
    - **Cross right, cross left:** Palms down, cross right hand over left twice. Then cross left hand over right twice.
    - **Hit right fist on left; hit left fist on right:** Make two fists, hit right fist on top of left twice. Then hit left fist on top of right twice.
    - **Touch right elbow and shake right pointer; Touch left elbow and shake left pointer.**
    - **Lasso-2-3-4; Lasso-2-3-4:** Circle right arm over head (4 counts). Circle left arm overhead (4 counts).
    - **Hitchhike-3-4; Hitchhike-3-4:** Point right thumb over right shoulder (4 counts). Point left thumb over left shoulder (4 counts).
    - **Grab a fly, put it in your hand, squish it, flick it away, and stamp on it:** Reach up in the air and catch an imaginary bug, put it in the palm of your hand, squish it, flick it away, and stamp on it.

Repeat from beginning.

Variations:

- Add other movements between elbow touches and '"lassos," such as swimming strokes (breaststroke, front crawl, back crawl).
- Teams create 2–3 new movements to add to routine and teach to rest of dancers.

2. **Legends of the Day!**

In Class Ideas:

◆ Dancers fill in square(s) of **Aerobic Grid.**

◆ Dancers create other jive moves with a partner in the classroom.

APPENDIX

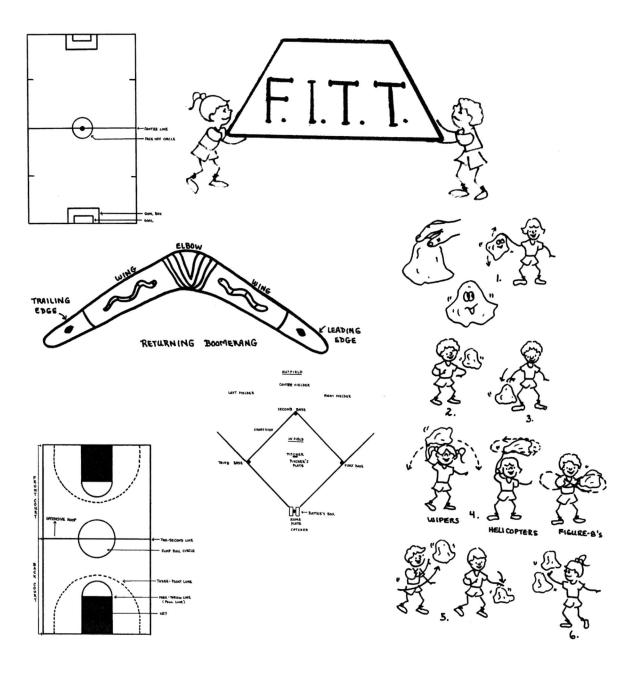

Pre-sport Skills Teaching
Pointers and Rules

BASKETBALL PLAY POINTERS
Dribbling

Control Dribbling

Use the control dribble when closely guarded and to keep the ball protected and under control. Maintain a well-balanced stance, basic to the control dribble, which will allow you to move quickly, change direction or pace, be a "triple threat" to shoot, pass, or drive, and stop under control.

Position in a diagonal stance, feet at least shoulder-width apart, weight evenly distributed on balls of feet, knees flexed, body low, foot opposite dribbling hand slightly forward.

Learn to dribble without looking at the ball.

Keep head over your waist and back straight.

Keep elbow of dribbling hand close to your body.

Relax dribbling hand, thumb relaxed and fingers comfortably spread.

Dribble off finger pads with fingertip control, not the palm of hand, flexing wrist and fingers to impart force to the ball.

Do not pump your arm. Don't pat or slap the ball!

Dribble ball at knee level or lower, keeping the ball close to your body and bouncing it in the "pocket" created by the diagonal stance.

Keep nondribbling hand in a protective position close to the ball.

Position body between your defender and the ball.

Crossover Dribbling

Use in the open court on a fast break, to get open on your drive to the basket, or to create an opening for a shot. The effectiveness of this dribble depends on how sharply dribble is changed from one direction to another.

◆ Cross the ball in front at a backward angle.

◆ Switch the dribble from one hand to the other.

◆ Dribble the ball close to you at knee level or lower with a control dribble (waist level for a speed dribble).

◆ When making change of direction, bring nondribbling hand up and change lead foot and body position for protection.

Speed Dribbling

Useful when not closely guarded to move ball quickly up court or to open spaces, or to drive to the basket.

- Push dribble forward at waist level.
- Keep head up and see the entire court and rim of the hoop.
- Ball must leave hand before lifting pivot foot.
- Dribble ball off finger pads, flexing wrist and fingers to put force on the ball.

Shooting

One-handed Set Shot (Right-Hander)

- Stand square to target, feet shoulder-width apart, with right foot slightly ahead of the other.
- Keep eyes on target, knees flexed, shoulder relaxed, head over the waist and feet.
- Hold basketball in finger pads, not the palm of the hand.
- Place shooting hand directly behind the ball, index finger directly at its midpoint.
- Place nonshooting hand to the side and slightly under the ball for balance. This is sometimes called the "T" position in which the thumbs form the letter "T" on its side.
- Hold ball comfortably in front of and above shooting-side shoulder, between ear and shoulder. Keep shooting elbow in and shooting arm bent at a right angle. Check alignment: right knee, right elbow, hand, eye, ball.
- Shoot ball with a smooth, rhythmical lifting motion.
- Start with knees slightly flexed, bend knees, and then fully extend legs in a down-and-up motion.
- As shot starts, tip ball back from balance hand to shooting hand, dropping wrist back only until there is wrinkle in the skin.
- Release ball off index finger with soft fingertip touch to impart backspin on ball and soften shot.
- Keep balance hand on ball until point of release.
- Follow-through keeping arm up and fully extended, index finger pointing straight to target.
- Palm of shooting hand should face down; palm of balance hand should face up.
- Hold arm up in this complete follow-through position until ball reaches the hoop.
- Keep in a balanced position throughout the shot.

Lay-up (Right-hander)

- Begin by holding ball in both hands, triple-threat position.
- Approach path is at a 45- to 60-degree angle to the basket.
- Step forward with the left foot and let ball bounce once near this foot.
- Protect ball by keeping it to right side of your body.
- Pick ball up in two hands with right hand on top, left hand on side for balance.
- Step right foot as you take ball in two hands, then left foot.
- Push upward off left foot, driving the right knee up to increase height of jump.
- Keep both hands on the ball until you reach the height of your jump, bringing ball into the shooting position.

Cock the right-hand wrist back and release ball off index finger with a soft touch.

Aim for the top right corner of the backboard square.

Keep balance hand on the ball until the release.

Keep eyes focusing on target.

Let fingers follow-through and balance hand come off the ball but stay in the air to protect the shot.

Passing & Catching

Chest Passing

Start in a balanced stance.

Hold ball with your fingers (not hand) in front of chest, one hand on each side of the ball. Spread fingers, thumbs up, elbows in. Hands should be slightly behind the ball in a relaxed position.

See your target without looking at it.

In one motion, step in the direction of pass and force your wrists and fingers "through" the ball.

Release the ball off the first and second fingers of both hands to impart backspin and give the ball direction.

Follow-through with arms fully extended and fingers pointing towards the target with palms facing down.

Aim for the receiver's hand target (chest level).

Bounce Passing

Start position is similar to the chest pass.

Start by holding ball at your waist with fingers spread on each side of ball; thumbs up, elbows in.

In one motion, step in direction of pass and force wrist and fingers "through" the ball.

Use fingertip release off first and second fingers to impart backspin and accuracy.

Aim for a spot on floor about two-thirds of the way or a few feet in front of target. Ball should bounce to receiver's waist.

Follow-through by pointing fingers at target with palms of hands facing downwards.

Overhead Pass

Use when a player is closely guarded and has to pass over the defender, as an outlet pass to start a fast break against pressing defenders, and as a lob pass to a player cutting "backdoor" [behind defender] to the basket.

See target without looking.

Start in a balanced stance, holding ball above forehead with elbows in and flexed about 90 degrees.

Do not bring ball behind your head from where it can be stolen or takes longer to execute a pass.

Step in direction of target, extending legs and back to get maximum power.

Pass ball quickly, extending arms and flexing wrists and fingers.

◆ Release ball off first and second fingers of both hands.

◆ Follow-through by pointing your fingers at the target, palms down.

Sidearm Pass

Similar to the overhead pass in execution, use when closely guarded to pass around a defender. A sidearm bounce pass can also be used to feed the ball to a low post player.

◆ See the target without looking.

◆ Using two hands as in the overhead pass, start by moving the ball to one side, between shoulder and hip, and step to that side.

◆ Do not bring ball behind the body where it can be stolen.

◆ Follow-through by pointing fingers toward the target, palms to the side.

◆ With one hand, place passing hand behind the ball.

◆ Keep nonpassing hand in front and on the ball until point of release.

Baseball Pass

Used to make a long pass; that is, for throwing a long lead pass to a teammate cutting toward the basket, making an outlet pass to start a fast break, or in-bounding the ball.

◆ Start in a balanced position. See target without looking.

◆ Pivot on back foot, turning body to passing-arm side.

◆ Bring ball up to ear with elbow in, passing hand behind ball, and balance hand in front of ball.

◆ As ball is passed, shift weight from back to front foot.

◆ Step in direction of pass, extending legs, back, and passing arm forward toward the target.

◆ Flex wrist forward, releasing ball off fingertips.

◆ Follow-through by pointing fingers at target, with palm of passing hand down.

Catching a Pass (away from the scoring area)

◆ See ball and go to meet the pass.

◆ Land with feet shoulder-width apart, knees flexed, balanced stance.

◆ Use hands to set a target, facing your partner, and "asking for the ball."

◆ Keep eyes on the ball, tracking it all the way into your hands.

◆ Catch the ball with both hands with thumbs and fingers relaxed.

◆ Give with the ball on catch, bringing arms and hands into position in front of chest.

◆ After receiving the pass, land with a one–two stop.

◆ Be ready to make the next pass or shoot.

Catching the Ball in Position to Shoot

◆ Target with hands high between ear and shoulder and in shooting position.

◆ As pass is thrown, jump behind the ball squaring to the basket in position to shoot, feet shoulder-width apart, knees flexed, shoulders relaxed, elbows in.

◆ Let the ball come into your hands; do not reach for the ball.

◆ Catch ball with relaxed fingers, shooting hand behind ball and nonshooting hand under the ball. Do not catch ball with hands on the sides, then try to rotate ball into position.

Offending & Defending

Offense

◆ Keep head over waist and back straight.

◆ See the rim and the ball.

Position hands above the waist, elbows flexed, arms close to body.

Place feet at least shoulder-width apart, weight evenly distributed on balls of feet.

Flex knees to get low, so that you are ready to move.

Defense

Keep head over waist to center gravity and back straight.

Keep wide base with feet wider apart than shoulder-width and staggered, one foot in front of the other.

Distribute weight evenly on balls of feet.

Flex knees so body is low, ready to move in any direction.

Position hands up above shoulders, elbows flexed.

See opposition's mid-section which will give movement direction.

To guard a player on the ball side of the basket (called the **strong side**), take up a "denial stance"—one hand and one foot up in the passing lane.

To guard a player on the opposite side of the basket (called the **weak or help side**), take a defensive stance several steps away so that you can see the ball and the player you are guarding.

Hand Position

Three basic defensive hand positions:

One hand up on side of lead foot to pressure shooter; other hand at side to protect against passes.

Both hands at waist level, palms up, to pressure dribbler (allows you to flick at ball with hand nearer the direction in which opponent is dribbling).

Both hands above shoulders to force lob or bounce passes, to block shots, to rebound with two hands, to help prevent reaching fouls.

Player Positions

Center: Usually the tallest player who positions around the keyway moving from low to mid to high post.

2 Forwards: Right forward and left forward who travel down right or left side respectively of the court, and play to the sides of the basket near the key area and out toward the sideline along the base line.

2 Guards: Usually are quick and the best ball controllers who play primarily at the perimeter or away from the basket.

Rebounding & Blocking Out

Successful team play depends on both offensive and defensive rebounding. The team that controls the backboards usually controls the game! Quickness and balance, jumping height and explosiveness, muscular endurance and strength, timing and positioning ("wanting the ball") are important factors to be an effective rebounder.

Defensive Rebounding

Two strategies for defensive rebounding:

◆ Blocking out or boxing out opponent's path to ball by pivoting your back to opponent's chest, then going for the ball, *or*

◆ Stepping in opponent's path and going for the ball.

Front Turn Defensive Rebounding Method (best for blocking out the shooter)

◆ See ball and opponent.

◆ Take a defensive stance.

◆ Keep hand up in passing land.

◆ Front pivot on back foot.

◆ Step into shooter.

◆ Feel your back near opponent's chest.

◆ Keep a wide base and hands up.

◆ Go for the ball and catch with two hands.

◆ Spread eagle and protect ball in front of forehead.

◆ Land in a balanced stance.

Reverse Turn Defensive Rebounding

◆ See ball and opponent.

◆ Take a defensive stance.

◆ Keep hand up in passing lane.

◆ Watch opponent's cut.

◆ Reverse pivot on foot closer to direction opponent is cutting in.

◆ Drop other foot back.

◆ Feel your back near opponent's chest.

◆ Keep a wide base and hands up.

◆ Go for the ball and catch with two hands.

◆ Spread eagle and protect ball in front of forehead.

◆ Land in a balanced stance.

Reverse Turn Defensive Rebounding Method (use when defending a player without the ball or off the ball)

◆ See ball and opponent.

◆ After the shot, first observe opponent's cut.

◆ Reverse pivot on foot closer to opponent's cut.

◆ Drop other foot back and away from opponent's cut.

◆ Go for the rebound.

Offensive Rebounding

◆   See ball and opponent.

◆   Take an offensive stance.

◆   When opponent front turns, cut straight by.

◆   Keep hands up and go for the ball.

◆   Catch ball with two hands.

◆   Spread eagle and protect ball in front of forehead.

◆   Land in a balanced stance.

BASKETBALL RULES

Teach these rules in the classroom so that players will develop a better understanding of the game and skills involved. These rules can be modified to the developmentally appropriate ability level of the children so that a positive, enjoyable, and successful experience will be guaranteed. The lesson plans in the basketball unit provide for specific suggestions to modify the equipment used—the size of the ball, the shooting distance from the free-throw line to the hoop, the distance of the hoop from the floor, the size of the court, as well as the number of players on the court, the length of playtime, the number of dribbles or passes allowed, and the type of goal that is used.

1. **Basketball Court and Team Positions (See Diagram A)**

   The basketball court is a rectangular surface 50 feet by 84 feet in dimensions. The boundary lines at each side are specifically called the sidelines; the end boundary lines of the court are called the end line or base line. A team's front-court refers to the half of the court where the basket to be scored upon is located; back-court refers to the other half of the court where a team defends the basket. A team has 10 seconds to advance the ball over the mid-court line. Once the ball is in the front-court, a violation occurs if the ball is returned to the back-court. Three circles are marked on the court: a free-throw circle at each end and a center circle. A *keyway* area (usually painted in a different color from the floor) connects the free-throw circle to the base line. Players position between the hash marks along each side of the keyway lines for a free-throw set-up. A 3-point arc is marked out from the base line to the top of the key. Basketball is played by two teams of 5 players consisting of: 1 center, 2 forwards, and 2 guards. All positions can be interchangeable in learning the game at the entry level. These court positions are introduced, but not overly emphasized, in the Pre-Sports Skills Resource.

2. **The Game Play**

   The game is started with a jump-ball at center. A basketball referee tosses the ball up between two opposing players who stand at mid-court in the basketball circle. These two center players face the hoop at which they will be trying to score, and try to tip the ball to a teammate. Players should position around the center circle in the 12 o'clock, 3 o'clock, 6 o'clock, and 9 o'clock positions. A jump-ball will also occur if two or more players lock up the ball by holding onto it at the same time. The game is monitored by two or three referees, a timer, and a scorekeeper. Each team attempts to score a goal by dribbling, passing, and shooting. The nonstop play continues until a team commits a violation or foul. A change of possession follows a violation and the opposition team takes the ball out-of-bounds. A foul results in an opposition player shooting two free throws or the opposition awarded the ball out-of-bounds. A team has 5 seconds to inbound the ball, and 10 seconds to bring the ball from back-court into front-court before loss of possession occurs. Once the ball has entered the front-court, the offensive team cannot take it back into the team's half of the court (cross-court or over and back rule).

3. **Playing Time**

   Regulation basketball consists of two 20-minute halves (college), with a 5-minute halftime break, or 8-minute quarters (high school), or 12-minute quarters (professional). Author suggests two 15-minute halves for upper elementary.

4. **Scoring**

   A field goal is scored when an offensive player shoots the ball from the field into the opposition's hoop. Two points are awarded for a basket scored within (including on) the 3-point arc; three points for outside of the 3-point line and one point for each free throw made. After a goal has been scored, the team not scoring the goal has 5 seconds to put the ball into play from out-of-bounds behind the base line near its own basket.

5. **Violations**

   A violation is a minor infraction of the rules and results in the ball being given to the opposition team outside the sideline and opposite the spot where the infraction occurred. Violations occur for:

   traveling or taking more than one step while in possession of the ball (sometimes called "carrying the ball")

   double-dribbling or dribbling the ball, stopping, then dribbling again or dribbling with two hands instead of one

   out-of-bounds caused by stepping on or over a boundary line while in possession of the ball, or passing or knocking the ball out of bounds

   kicking the ball intentionally

   three-second rule which allows an offensive player to stay in the opposition's keyway for only 3 seconds (5 seconds for upper elementary level) while his/her team has possession of the ball

6. **Fouls (Personal/Technical)**

   Personal fouls occur when a player holds, trips, blocks, pushes, kicks, or charges an opponent or engages in rough or unsportsmanlike play. If the referee feels the foul was intentional, the player being fouled is awarded 2 free throws from the foul line. If a foul occurs while a player is in the act of shooting, the shooter is awarded 2 (or 3 if shooting from outside the 3-point circle) free throws. If the ball touches the rim but does not go in on the second free throw, play continues; if the ball fails to touch the rim, the ball is given to the defending team on the sideline. Five personal fouls on any one player results in disqualification from the game. This may be extended to six personal fouls in junior basketball games.

   A *technical foul* occurs when a player or coach acts in an unsportsmanlike way, such as using unacceptable language and deliberate aggressive negative behavior, for delay of game, failing to report a substitution to the officials, and leaving the court. Two free throws are awarded and ball possession afterward.

The Basketball Court
Diagram A

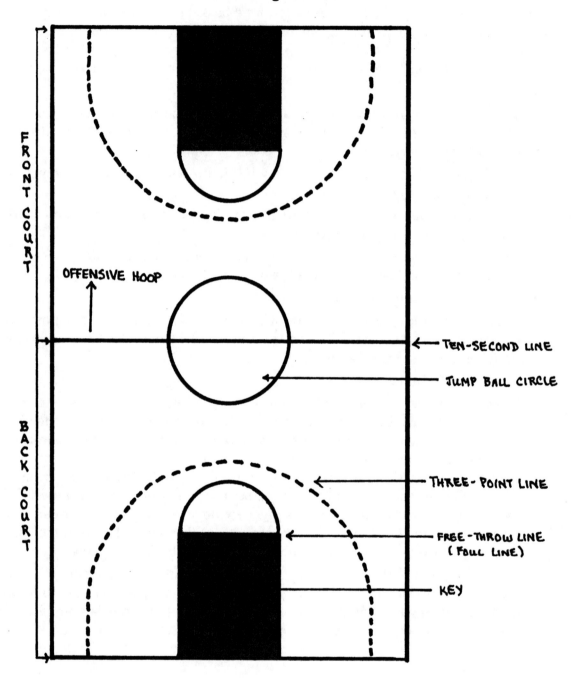

FLOOR HOCKEY PLAY POINTERS

Gripping the Stick

Place one hand (usually left hand for right-hander) on top of stick as if shaking hands with it.

Place other hand 10–12 inches (25–30 cm) below the first hand.

Point thumbs toward the blade of the stick.

Dribbling

Dribble by moving puck forward with short quick, controlled taps.

Keep the puck 18–24 inches (48–60 cm) out in front.

Stick-handling

Move the puck from side to side, to make quick changes of direction.

Try to "feel" the puck on the blade, keeping it in the middle of the blade.

Carrying the Puck

Move the puck along the floor, keeping it in contact with only one side of the blade.

Shooting

Wrist Shot

Use the wrist shot for short distances and quick execution.

Check the puck, then concentrate on the target.

Snap the wrists to propel the puck forward to the target.

Keep both the backswing and follow-through short and low.

Sweep Shot

Push the puck toward the goal. Do not flex the wrist.

Ensure that puck is touching the blade before shooting.

Follow-through low.

Goal Keeping

Keep in ready position, lightly crouched holding stick in front of body with one hand.

Use other hand to catch or knock puck away.

Watch the puck at all times.

Place stick squarely in front of puck, or feet, legs and body to stop puck.

Clear puck by sweeping it or kicking it to the side.

Passing & Receiving

Passing the Puck

Keep your stick blade upright and use a smooth sweeping motion.

Keep the backswing and follow-through low.

Pass slightly ahead of the receiver (lead pass).

Receiving the Puck

◆ Track the puck as it comes towards you.

◆ Tilt the blade of the stick over the puck to gently trap it.

◆ Cushion the pass by giving with your stick blade at the moment of impact.

Playing Offense

◆ Be a team-player and team-maker, not a "solo" player.

◆ Play heads-up following the path of the puck at all times.

◆ Move to open spaces when dribbling the puck and pass to the open teammate who is in a better position to score.

◆ Use short, quick passes to move the puck down the floor to avoid interception by the opposition.

◆ Use a lead pass, passing the puck ahead of the receiver, so that he/she can continue to run forward.

◆ Keep the backswing and follow-through low when shooting the puck.

Playing Defense

◆ Always face the puck, never turning your back toward the action or facing your own goal.

◆ Keep the stick below the waist when cross-checking.

◆ Avoid body contact with an opponent when trying to get possession of the puck.

◆ Stay on your assigned player when he/she is not in possession of the puck instead of trying to go after the puck.

Player Positions

◆ **1 Center:** Moves the entire length of the floor or field playing both offense and defense.

◆ **2 Forwards:** Play offense from the centerline forward.

◆ **2 Guards:** Play defense from the centerline back and try to pass to the center to get the puck back into offensive play.

◆ **1 Goalie:** Defends the goal area, moving around a goalie crease or goal box, and clearing the puck to the side away from the front of the net so that the guards can get the puck back into offensive play.

FLOOR HOCKEY RULES

The game of floor hockey, which evolved as an adaptation of ice hockey, can be easily learned because the rules are simple and the skills are not very specialized. Teach these rules in the classroom so that players will develop a better understanding of the game and skills involved. These rules can be modified to the developmentally appropriate ability level of the children so that a positive, enjoyable, and successful experience will be guaranteed. The lesson plans in the floor hockey unit provide specific suggestions to modify the equipment used, including the size of the net or goal, the type of stick (plastic or 3-foot dowel taped at one end), the type of ball or puck (can tape a puck to make it travel slower), the size of the play area, as well as the number of players on the court, the length of playtime, and the number of dribbles or passes allowed. Safety must be strongly emphasized and enforced at all times. Players need to be taught not to raise their sticks above their waist (high sticking) and that no body contact is allowed (which includes elbowing, tripping, and hooking, butt-ending, pushing, cross-checking and slashing, charging and interference).

1. **Floor Hockey Court and Team Positions (See Diagram B)**

   The floor hockey court is usually 50 feet by 84 feet (or 15m by 25.2m) in dimensions with a center or mid-line, but can be played on any flat area such as a basketball court (indoor or outdoor), tennis court, or large multipurpose tiled floor area. The equipment consists of plastic hockey sticks, plastic pucks or balls (in Unihoc® the ball used is a small whiffle ball), 2 hockey nets, and 2 goalie sticks (a goalie stick is wider and squarer than a regular hockey stick). The goal area should be 2 feet by 6 feet and a goal box around the goal should be 4 feet by 8 feet. A team consists of 6 players: 1 goalie, 1 center, 2 forwards, and 2 guards. The center player moves the entire length of the floor or field playing both offense and defense. Forwards play offense from the center or mid-line forward. Guards play defense from the centerline back, always facing the puck and never turning their back to the action. The goalie stays most of the time in the goalie crease or between the goal and the puck defending the goal and clearing the puck to the side away from the front of the net.

2. **The Game Play**

   The object of the game is to shoot the puck into the opposition's goal. The game begins with a face-off at center, and also occurs after a goal has been scored to restart the game. Play two 8-minute halves, with a 2-minute halftime change-over. To face-off, two opposition players face each other with their stick blades resting on the floor. An official drops a puck between them. Each player tries to gain control of the puck and either dribble away with it, pass it, or try to score. Players should be continually on the move so that play is almost continuous. Players need to be reminded to watch the puck or ball rather than their opponents. A regulation game consists of three 8-minute periods with a 5-minute break between each period.

3. **Fouls**

   ◆ When the puck goes out-of-bounds, the last team to touch it loses possession.

   ◆ Players can use their feet to advance the puck, but cannot use their feet to kick it into the goal; otherwise, they lose possession of it.

   ◆ The goalie is allowed to catch or throw the puck to the side, but not toward the other end of the playing area. Players can stop the puck with the hand, but cannot hold, pass, or throw the puck. Stepping on, holding, or lying on the puck results in the puck being given to the opposition at a place near where the foul occurred.

◆ The puck must be ahead of the offensive players across the centerline.

◆ If the puck gets trapped against the wall, then a face-off takes place at the nearby spot.

4. **Violations**

A 2-minute penalty results in removing the offender from the game for 2 minutes (for an unintentional violation) or 4 minutes (for an intentional violation):

◆ Elbowing, pushing or cross-checking, slashing, butt-ending, high sticking or raising the stick higher than knee level, tripping or hooking with a stick or foot, and any unsportsmanlike contact. Raising the puck higher than knee level results in a penalty shot on opposition's goal being awarded. The penalty shot may be taken anywhere outside the goalie's crease. Play then continues with a center face-off.

◆ Guards or forwards cannot go forward of the centerline. Center may go back and forward over the centerline.

The Floor Hockey Court
Diagram B

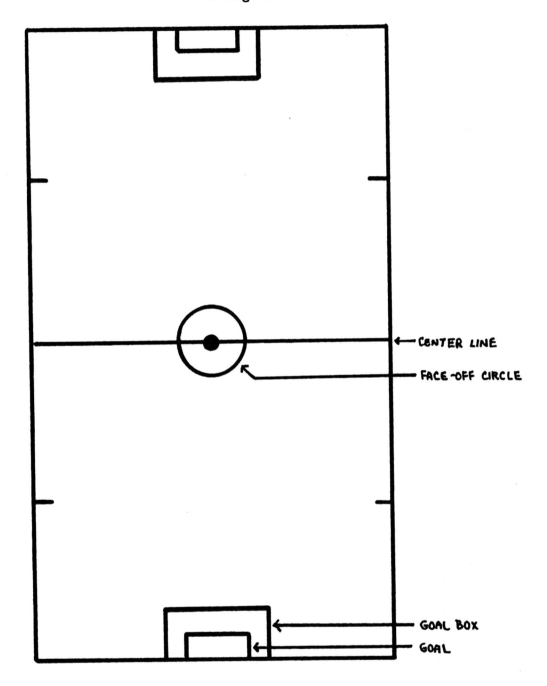

CENTER LINE

FACE-OFF CIRCLE

GOAL BOX

GOAL

VOLLEYBALL PLAY POINTERS

Serving

Underhand Serve

◆ Stand with feet in a comfortable stride position, facing the net, with weight evenly distributed, knees bent.

◆ Keep shoulders square to net.

◆ Hold ball in nondominant hand across and in front of body, about waist level.

◆ Keep eyes on the ball.

◆ Swing arm back, transfer weight to rear foot.

◆ Swing arm forward, transfer weight to front foot.

◆ Contact the ball with the heel of the hand.

◆ Drop holding hand away from ball on contact.

◆ Follow-through in line of direction.

Overhand Serve

◆ Stand with feet in a slight stride position, facing the net, with weight evenly distributed.

◆ Keep shoulders square to net and non-contact side foot forward.

◆ Toss ball with nonhitting hand about 3 feet in front and above hitting shoulder, and close to body.

◆ As ball is tossed, bring hitting arm back with elbow high and hand close to ear.

◆ Keep eyes on the ball.

◆ Contact ball with heel of the open hand above the head.

◆ Transfer weight from rear foot to front foot as contact is made and arm swings through.

◆ Follow-through in line of direction, dropping hitting arm slightly.

Receiving the Serve

◆ Set in ready "bump" position to receive the ball on the forearms.

◆ Track the ball as it comes towards you.

◆ Move quickly into position and execute the bump.

Digging

A "dig" differs from a forearm pass (or "bump") in that the player must react quickly and play the ball with little time to position strategically. It is often combined with a roll or sprawl to prevent injury and recover quickly.

◆ Keep weight forward, one foot slightly ahead of the other.

◆ Bend at the knees, keeping hips low to get under the ball.

◆ Hold hands in bump position and arms out in front of body at waist height.

◆ Watch ball contact the arms.

◆ Contact ball with both arms parallel to floor.

◆ Extend body toward target.

- Flick wrist(s) to gain height.
- Follow eyes towards the target.

Passing

Setting (Overhand Pass)
Ready Position

- Place feet in a slight stride, shoulder-width apart, knees bent.

Raise hands in front of forehead about 6–8 inches away, elbows flexed.

Point thumbs towards the eyes.

Form a "window" with the thumbs and pointer fingers.

Watch the ball through this window.

Square shoulders to the target.

Execution

As contact is made, hands form to the shape of the ball, with only upper two joints of fingers and hands touching the ball.

Fully extend body upward on contact, transferring weight towards target.

Follow-through with hands, arms, and legs extending towards target.

Set the ball just above forehead level.

Bumping (Forearm Pass)

Move to the ball and set your position.

Position feet in an easy stride position, shoulder-width apart.

Bend your knees, keeping body low, back straight.

Interlock or cup fingers, thumbs parallel to each other, elbows locked and rotated inward so that the soft-flat part of forearms face upwards.

Keep this platform with arms, holding them parallel to thighs and away from the body.

Track ball with eyes and position the body directly behind the ball.

Transfer weight forward.

Slant platform toward target and watch ball contact arms.

Absorb the force of the ball on forearms and direct ball towards target.

Follow-through extending legs and arms towards the target.

Contact ball with little or no arm swing, keeping arms below shoulder level.

Watch ball's path to target.

Keep motion smooth and continuous.

Attacking & Blocking

Spiking

Spiking is the action of forcefully hitting (smashing) the ball over the net to score a point or regain the serve. It is the third part of the serve-reception sequence: bump–set–spike. Adjust the height of the net to the jumping ability level of the class.

- Approach net with as few steps as possible.
- Swing arms back to waist to prepare for jump.
- Take off on two feet by planting both heels first to change from forward to upward momentum.
- Swing arms forward and up.
- Jump straight up into the air, bring hitting arm back, elbow high and hand close to ear.
- Contact ball at full extension in front of hitting shoulder.
- Contact on top of the ball with heel of hand, snapping wrist as fingers roll over the top.
- Keep eyes on the ball through the contact.
- Do not let striking arm follow-through down, but drop hand to hip.
- Bend knees to cushion landing.

Tipping or Dinking

- Use the upper two finger joints to contact the ball for a tip or dink.
- Contact ball slightly below the center back.
- At contact, gently direct ball over or past the block, so that it drops quickly to the floor.
- Return to floor with a 2-foot landing, bending at the knees.

Blocking

Blocking is the action of intercepting the ball coming over the net with the hands and arms to deflect the ball into the opponent's court.

- Stand facing and close to the net, hands at shoulder level.
- Time jump to that of the spiker's jump.
- Jump high enough so that the wrists will be slightly above the net.
- Jump straight up to meet the oncoming ball.
- Do not touch the net when blocking.
- Tense fingers together and tense as contact with ball is made.
- Deflect the ball downward off the hands and arms.
- Do not let the arms swing forward as you land, since a net foul could result.
- Land on two feet, bending knees to cushion landing.

Court Positions (6 players)

Right forward, Center Forward, Left Forward, Left Back, Center Back, Right Back

VOLLEYBALL RULES

The game of volleyball was invented in 1895 by William Morgan, a YMCA director in Holyoke, Massachusetts, as an alternative to basketball, and promoted by the YMCAs. In 1928 the Volleyball Association of the United States was formed and the game evolved into a power game of specialized skills and action. Rules of the game could be taught as each skill lesson is developed and then recapped in the classroom so that players will develop a better understanding of the game and skills involved. These rules can be modified to the developmentally appropriate ability level of the children so that a positive, enjoyable, and successful experience will be guaranteed. The lesson plans in the volleyball unit provide specific suggestions to modify the equipment used, including the type and size of ball used (balloon or beach ball, soft foam ball, volleyball trainer), the size of the play area, as well as the number of players on the court, the length of play time, the type of net used (volleyball net, badminton net, long rope), the height of the net from the floor (adjusted to the ability level of the class), and modifications of certain rules (e.g., more than 3 hits per side; "help" on the serve). Safety and court etiquette (e.g., rolling the ball under the net to the serving team; "calling" for the ball during play) are to be emphasized and enforced at all times.

1. **Volleyball Court and Team Positions (See Diagram C)**

   Volleyball is played by 2 teams each having 2–6 players on a 9-meter square (about a 30-foot square) court with the two courts separated by a net. Regulation volleyball has 6 players on a side: 3 are front row or forward players: left front (LF), center front (CF), and right front (RL); 3 are back row players: left back (LB), center back (CB), and right back (RB). Players rotate counterclockwise to establish the serving order with the right forward being the first player to serve.

2. **The Game Play**

   The objective of each team is to hit the ball over the net into the opponent's court so that the opponents are not able to return the ball. The game begins with a toss of a coin to determine which team will serve on court side. The right forward serves first from behind the end line in the right back corner. (Current rules allow for service to occur anywhere behind the end line of the court.) The server has 5 seconds to initiate the serve from the service area. Only the serving team may score points. The server will continue to serve until a fault occurs by the serving team. A service fault occurs when the ball served by the server touches the net on the way over or passes under the net or passes outside the legal portion of the net, the ball touches a serving team member before going over the net, the ball lands outside the court boundary lines, or the server steps on or over the end line before the ball leaves his/her hands. The ball remains in play if it touches the legal portion of the net in play.

   When the receiving team commits a fault, the serving team is awarded a point. If the serving team commits a fault, a *side-out* occurs and the opposition team is awarded service. Following a side-out, the server rotates one position after the team receives the ball. A ball landing on a court boundary line is considered in. Play continues until one teams gets to 15 points with at least a 2-point lead; otherwise, play continues until a 2-point advantage is obtained. At the end of each game, teams exchange sides. The losing team begins the new game.

3. **Faults**

The following team faults result in points for the opposition or loss of serve (side-out):

- The ball hits the floor.
- The ball is hit by a player more than once in a row.
- The ball is hit by a team more than three times in a row.
- The ball touches a player below the waist.
- The ball is carried or held.
- The ball hits the ceiling.
- The ball is hit out-of-bounds.
- The ball is touched by an opponent reaching under the net.
- The net or volleyball posts are touched by a player.
- A player completely crosses over the centerline to play the ball.
- A player tries to help the serve over the net.
- A team is out of position at service.
- Blocking the service.

4. **Special Notes**

- A blocked ball is not considered a hit.
- The ball may only be spiked within the spiking zone. (See Diagram C.)
- A back row player may spike only when the take-off is made from behind the attack line.
- A player may not spike the ball until part of the ball is on that player's side of the net.
- A player may go off the court to play a ball.
- Today's rules allow a player to head or kick the ball to a teammate or send it over the net.

The Volleyball Court
Diagram C

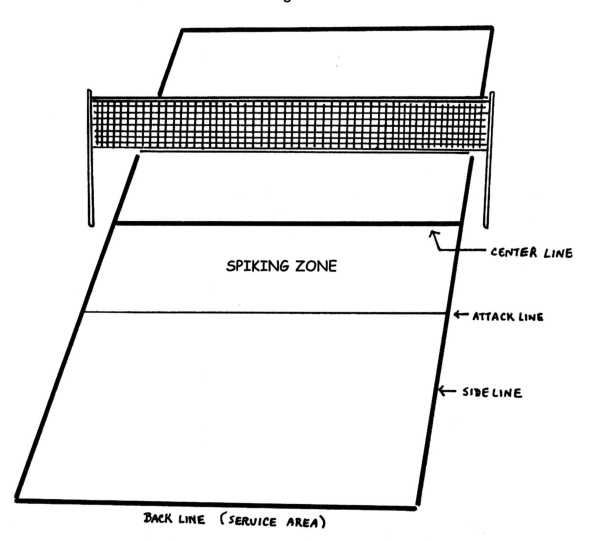

SPIKING ZONE

CENTER LINE

ATTACK LINE

SIDE LINE

BACK LINE (SERVICE AREA)

SOCCER PLAY POINTERS

Footwork

◆   Use either foot to dribble.

◆   Use the inside of the foot, outside of the foot, or toe to tap the ball lightly below center.

◆   Keep the ball 1–2 feet in front of your feet, while maintaining control.

◆   Focus eyes on the ball, but at the same time, dribble "heads up."

Passing & Receiving

Inside-of-the-foot Pass

◆   Use to pass the ball over short distances of 5–15 yards/meters.

◆   Face target and square shoulders as you approach ball.

◆   Focus on the ball.

◆   Plant nonkicking foot beside the ball and point toes toward the target.

◆   Position kicking foot sideways, ankle locked, toes pointed up, and contact ball with inside surface of kicking foot.

◆   Follow-through with kicking motion.

Outside-of-the-foot Pass

◆   Use this pass to make a diagonal pass to the right or left.

◆   Use for short and middle-distance passes.

◆   Place nonhitting leg slightly behind and to the side of the ball.

◆   Bring kicking foot downward and rotate inwards.

◆   Keep arms out to sides for balance.

◆   Contact the ball with outside surface of the instep.

◆   Use a short snap-like kicking motion of lower leg.

◆   For longer passes, follow-through to generate more distance and speed on the ball.

Instep Pass

(Instep is the part of the foot covered by the shoelaces.)

◆   Use to send the ball over a long distance (25+ yards).

◆   Approach the ball from a slight angle, eyes focused on the ball.

◆   Place nonkicking foot beside the ball, leg slightly flexed, knee of kicking leg over the ball.

◆   Contact the center of the ball with the instep of foot, toes pointed downward.

◆   Drive the instep through the point of contact with ball with a powerful snap-like motion of the kicking leg.

◆   Keep arms out to sides for balance, head steady.

◆   Follow-through to chest level with kicking leg.

Inside-of-foot Reception

◆   Keep eyes on ball and head steady.

◆   Move toward ball, extend receiving leg to meet ball.

◆   Position feet sideways.

◆   Give with the leg and receiving foot to cushion its impact.

Outside-of-foot Reception

◆   As for inside-of-foot reception above.

◆   Position sideways to oncoming ball.

◆   Receive ball on outside surface of instep.

Trapping

◆   Focus eyes on ball.

◆   Position in line with the oncoming ball.

◆   Cushion the impact of the ball to get control.

◆   Use the inside of the foot, lower leg of either foot, or the front of both legs to trap a ball traveling low to the ground.

◆   Trap a ground ball by forming a wedge with the heel and sole of the foot and the ground.

◆   Trap an air ball by letting the ball hit the chest or thigh and letting the body absorb the force of the ball so that it drops straight downward to the ground after impact. (Girls are allowed to cross their arms over the chest when doing a chest trap.)

Kicking

Instep Drive Kick

◆   Approach ball from behind and at a slight angle.

◆   Square shoulders and hips to target.

◆   Plant nonkicking foot beside the ball, slightly flexing knee.

◆   Keep head steady and eyes focused on the ball.

◆   Keep arms out to sides for balance.

◆   Draw kicking leg back and extend kicking foot, keeping knee directly over the ball.

◆   Snap leg straight through.

◆   Contact center of ball with full instep of foot.

◆   Keep foot firm and toes pointed down as foot strikes the ball.

◆   Follow-through fully with kicking leg to maximize power on the shot.

Volley Kick

(Ball is hit straight out of the air.)

◆   Move to the spot where the ball will drop.

◆   Face the ball square on.

◆   Flex knee of nonkicking foot for balance and body control.

- Keep arms out to sides for balance.
- Draw kicking leg back and extend kicking foot.
- Keep head steady and eyes focused on ball.
- Snap kicking leg forward from knee.
- Contact center of ball with the instep, keeping kicking foot firm.
- Use a short powerful kicking motion as leg snaps straight.

Half Volley Kick

- Hit ball the instant it contacts the ground rather than directly out of the air.

Tackling

Tackling is the method used to take the ball away from an opponent. Two basic tackling techniques are presented: the block and the poke. To be an effective tackler requires good judgment, confidence, and exact timing.

Block Tackle

- Use when opponent is dribbling directly at you.
- Play the ball, not the opponent, when tackling.
- Focus on the ball.
- Position feet in a staggered stance with one foot slightly ahead of the other.
- Get into a slightly crouched stance with knees flexed, arms out to sides for balance, to react quickly to dribbler's movements.
- Tackle the ball by blocking it with inside surface of foot.
- Position foot sideways, keep it firm, and drive it into the ball.
- Push ball forward, pass the opponent, and gain possession.

Poke or Side Tackle

- Use when approaching an opponent from the side or from slightly behind.
- Close in on dribbler.
- Focus on the ball.
- Stay in a slightly crouched stance with knees flexed.
- Keep balance and body control.
- Reach in with leg, extend foot, and poke ball away with toes.
- Play the ball, not the opponent.

Heading the Ball

- Focus eyes on the ball.
- Move to position under the descending ball.
- Use a 2-foot takeoff to jump.
- Use legs to propel trunk, neck, and head forward to meet the ball.
- Contact ball on forehead at the highest point of the jump.
- Time the jump so that the head hits the ball rather than the ball hitting the head.

Send ball upward by heading it under the middle of the ball.

Send ball downward by heading above the middle of the ball.

Follow-through with the forehead.

Land on both feet, bending at the knees to cushion impact.

Throw-in

Occurs whenever the ball goes out of play over the sidelines. Team to last touch the ball takes the throw. Another player must touch the ball before the thrower can touch the ball again. Cannot score a goal from the throw-in.

Plant both feet behind the sideline and in contact with the ground.

Throw ball from behind the head with both hands.

Goalkeeping

Ready Position

Stand with knees bent, weight forward on balls of feet ready to move quickly in any direction.

Hold hands at waist to chest level, palms forward and fingers pointing upward.

Keep head steady and focus on the ball.

Move body in line with the oncoming ball.

React quickly, using the shuffle step for any sideways movement.

Collecting the Ball

For a ground ball, scoop it up into the arms.

For an air ball, hold hands in an upward position for a ball taken above the waist; hands downward for a ball below the waist.

For each catch, clutch ball against chest with the forearms.

Roll or bowl ball to an offensive player over a short distance.

Overhand throw the ball (baseball throw) or punt up field over longer distances.

Deflect shots using a punch shot with the fists or a push shot with open hand.

Kicking the Ball

Punt kick (full volley) the ball by holding it with both hands in front of the waist.

Bend knee and point toes of kicking leg downward.

Straighten knee, contacting ball with the instep of the foot, and rise up on the toes of the nonkicking foot.

Punt the ball out of the hands, fully extending leg on follow-through.

Drop kick (half volley) by releasing the ball, then stepping forward to strike it just as the ball contacts the ground. Lean back and completely follow-through with the kicking leg fully extended.

Soccer Rules

Soccer is the most universal played sport in the world! Also known as "football" (except in the United States), soccer first evolved as an English game in the Middle Ages and now is the national sport of almost every country in South America, Europe, Asia, and Africa. Rules of the game could be taught as each skill lesson is developed and then recapped in the classroom so that players will develop a better understanding of the game and skills involved. These rules can be modified to the developmentally appropriate ability level of the children so that a positive, enjoyable, and successful experience will be guaranteed. The lesson plans in the soccer unit provide specific suggestions to modify the equipment used, including the type and size of ball used (a soft foam ball or Nerf™ ball, large playground ball, slightly deflated ball), the size of the play area, the number of players on the court, the length of play time, the size of the goal area, and modifications of the more technical rules. Safety and court etiquette need to be emphasized and enforced at all times. For example, girls are permitted to cross their arms over their chest when doing a chest block. The goalkeeper should wear gloves as well as pads for the elbows, hips, and knees.

1. **The Playing Field and Player Positions (See Diagram D)**

   The soccer field must be 100–130 yards/meters long and 50–100 yards/meters wide, the length always exceeding the width (modified to 80 by 60 yards/meters for elementary school). A halfway line divides the playing area into two equal halves and a center spot marks the center of the field. A center circle with a radius of 10 yards surrounds the center spot. A goal is positioned at each end of the field on the center of the goal line, with a goal box and penalty area box marked out along each goal line. Penalty kicks are taken from a penalty spot located in the penalty area. At each corner of the field is an arc area, with a l-yard radius from which corner kicks are taken.

   A regulation soccer team has 11 players, one of whom is the goalkeeper, but up to 15 players per teams can be allowed. Each team consists of 4–5 forwards, 3–4 mid-fielders, 4–5 defensive players, and 1 goalkeeper.

2. **The Game Play**

   The object of the game is to send the ball into a goal using the feet and head, but not the hands, to propel the ball. The game begins with a kick-off by one team. The player making the kick-off cannot touch the ball again until it has been touched by another player. All players position themselves outside the center circle in their own half of the field for the kick-off. A kick-off also occurs after a goal has been scored and after halftime. The ball is "in play" when it travels into the opposition's half of the field. A goal cannot be scored directly from the kick-off. A ball kicked over the sidelines is out of play. The team that touched the ball last before it went out of bounds loses possession and the other team gets a throw-in. A goal cannot be scored from a throw-in. The team scoring more goals by the end of the game is the winner. Regulation games consist of two 45-minute halves.

3. **Free Kicks**

   ◆ Two types of free kicks, *direct* and *indirect,* occur in the game. A goal can be scored directly by the kicker from a direct free kick. The ball must be played or touched by a player other than the kicker before a goal can be scored from an indirect free kick. *A direct free kick* is awarded when a major foul occurs: handling the ball; striking, kicking, tripping, holding, pushing an opponent; jumping at an opponent; charging from behind; and unsportsmanlike conduct. An *indirect free kick* is awarded when a minor foul occurs and includes obstruction and dangerous play; off-sides; the goalkeeper taking too many steps.

◆ A *goal kick* is awarded to the defending team if an offensive player causes the ball to go out of bounds over the end line, but not into the goal. The kick is taken from within the goal area usually by the goalie or a defensive player.

◆ A *corner kick* is awarded to the offensive team if a defensive player causes the ball to go out of bounds over the end line. Offensive players can stand near the kicker, but the opposition team must be 10 yards away.

◆ A throw-in occurs whenever the ball goes out of play over the sidelines. The team that did not touch the ball last takes the throw. The thrower must remain behind the sideline, both feet must be in contact with the ground, and the ball must be thrown from behind the head with both hands. Another player must touch the ball before the thrower can touch the ball again. A goal cannot be scored from a throw-in.

◆ *Offside rule* states that if in the opposition's half, an attacking player must have at least two opponents (including the goalie) in front of him/her at the time the ball was passed ahead. Violation of the rules results in an indirect free kick being awarded to the other team.

The Soccer Field
Diagram D

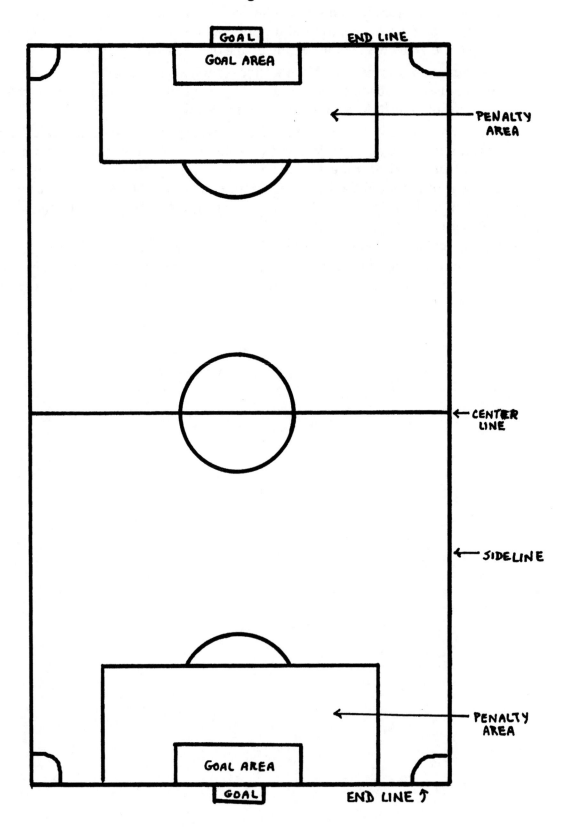

SOFTBALL PLAY POINTERS

Ball Grip

Hold ball by the fingers and off the palm of the hand.

Grip the ball tightly with the fingers across the seams.

Use a 2-finger grip with the index finger and middle finger across the seams and the little finger resting on the side of the ball.

For smaller hands, use a 3-finger grip by placing the index, middle, and ring fingers across the seams.

Place the thumb under the ball on the opposite side to the little finger.

Throwing & Catching

Throwing

(Also refer to Lesson 15—Overhand Throwing.)

Stand side-on to target or receiver, one foot in front of the other, and the dominant leg back.

Keep eyes on target.

Grip ball in your fingers, wrist cocked.

Pointer finger of nonthrowing hand points at target.

Throwing hand swings in a downward and backward arc. Weight transfers onto back foot.

Elbow bends as throwing hand moves behind head, wrist cocked.

Front foot steps forward as weight transfers from back foot.

Hips, then shoulders, rotate forward.

Lead the arm motion with the elbow.

Release the ball with a wrist snap.

Follow-through in the intended direction of flight.

Catching

Position body squarely with the oncoming ball, and maintain a balanced stance.

Keep eyes focused on the ball, tracking it into the hands.

Reach for the ball, giving with the arms and hands to absorb its force.

For a high ball, position glove so that fingers are up.

For a low ball, position glove so that fingers point down.

Let ball come into glove, then use the other hand to trap the ball into the glove.

Side Arm Throwing

Used for shorter and quicker throws than the overhand throw. An effective throw for infielders: shortstop to second base, pitcher to first base, etc.

Turn sideways, extending upper throwing arm out diagonally and down from shoulder.

♦   Forearm should be straight up from the elbow.

♦   Swing arm forward with the forearm parallel to the ground.

♦   Release ball and follow-through with arm across the body.

Fielding Grounders

Ready Position

♦   Get into a direct line with the path of the ball using the shuffle step.

♦   Bend knees and lean forward with upper body so that glove and other hand touch the ground.

♦   Position so that one leg is forward, the other slightly back (leg on throwing side).

♦   Keep weight on the balls of the feet; seat low to the ground.

♦   Keep glove and other hand in an open position to receive the ball and use the non-glove hand to trap the ball into the glove.

Fielding and Throwing

♦   Keep arms and hands "soft" and relaxed.

♦   Keep eyes tracking the ball all the way into the glove.

♦   Give with the ball as you field it.

♦   Bring it to the hip of the throwing side.

♦   Keep the transition from fielding and throwing the ball one smooth and quick motion.

♦   Know where to throw the ball before you field it.

♦   Find the target, releasing the ball.

Fielding a Fly Ball

Ready Position

♦   Track the oncoming ball, moving in toward the ball if necessary.

♦   Move quickly to position body in front of it.

♦   Keep glove pocket open and in front of throwing shoulder.

Transition from Fielding to Throwing

♦   Catch the ball on the throwing side of the body above eye level.

♦   Hold the glove fingers upwards, and place other hand over the ball to trap it in the glove.

♦   If the ball falls short, extend the glove towards the oncoming ball, keeping it open and glove fingers pointed downward.

♦   Bend elbows to absorb the force of the ball.

♦   Hold throwing hand up near glove, ready to grab the ball and throw it.

♦   Know where to throw the ball before fielding it.

♦   Take a crossover step to plant the rear foot and produce more throwing force.

♦   Make the transition between catching the fly ball and throwing it one smooth and quick action.

Underhand Pitching

The strike zone for the batter is the area from the bottom of the armpits to the top of the knees, and over home plate.

Stand square-on to target, balanced, feet comfortably spread.

Hold ball and pitching hand in the glove at waist level.

Bend trunk slightly forward at waist level.

Keep both feet in contact with pitching rubber or marker.

Grip the ball with the fingers across the seams.

Keep eyes focused on target or strike zone.

Aim the ball at the catcher's glove.

Extend throwing arm down and back, taking weight on back foot.

Cock the wrists at the top of the backswing.

Step forward with foot opposite to throwing arm when beginning the downward motion of the pitch.

Transfer weight from back foot to front foot as throwing arm swings through.

Snap the wrist, releasing the ball between the waist and knee level.

Follow-through up and out in the intended direction of flight and step forward on back leg ready to react.

Back-catching

Position just beyond the range of the swinging bat.

Squat with feet shoulder-width apart, one foot slightly ahead of the other.

Hold glove up as the target for the pitcher.

Keep eyes focused on the ball, tracking it all the way into glove.

Use the non-glove hand to trap the ball into the glove.

Batting

Gripping the Bat (Right-hander)

Hold bat firmly with hands together near the butt of the bat, with the dominant hand on top of the other. (Moving hands up the bat is called "choking up" on the bat.) Do not cross hands when gripping the bat.

Check the bat length—should reach completely across the plate and not feel too heavy.

Stance

Lift the rear elbow away from the body and hold bat off the shoulder with the trademark facing up.

Stand in the batter's box with body facing home plate, feet parallel and shoulder-width apart, knees slightly bent.

Swing

Focus eyes on the ball.

- Step forward with the front foot (about 12 inches) as the swing is started with hands and arms.
- Keep the rear foot planted as the weight shifts forward.
- Contact the ball in front of the plate, not over it.
- Swing the bat as fast as you can.
- Roll the top hand over the bottom during contact.
- Swing the bat all the way around to the front shoulder during the follow-through.
- Keep both hands on the bat at all times.
- Swing with a smooth, continuous motion.
- Do not throw the bat after hitting the ball!

Base-running

- Run from home plate to first base by stepping out of the batter's box with the rear foot.
- Run in a straight pathway on the right side of the foul line (runners basically have the "right of way" to the right half of the base).
- Run as quickly as possible, but also as safely as possible!
- Keep eyes on the base, not on the ball, as you run.
- Always turn to the right when overrunning first base.
- Stop on second or third base; do not overrun either base.
- When trying to cover two or more bases, run in a slightly outward curved pathway, tagging base with the left foot on the inside corner of the bag.
- In running to home plate, focus on the plate and run over and through the plate as you step on it.
- Do not attempt to steal or lead off a base in softball.

Player Positions

The Infielders:

First Base Player

- Must have good catching and throwing skills and be able to handle different thrown balls.
- Play the inside of the base on throws from the infield.
- Play about 6 feet to the right and behind the base with no runner on base.
- Cover the base, but do not interfere with oncoming runner.

Second Base Player

- Must be quick to move left or right to field grounders.
- Must have good hands to relay the ball to first or third base.
- Play about 10–12 feet left of behind the base.

Third Base Player

- Must have quick reactions and good agility.
- Must have a strong throwing arm.

◆ Must be able to field hard-hit grounders to this area.

◆ Play 6–10 feet left of the base and slightly behind it. (Not permitted to leave the base until the batter swings at the ball.)

Shortstop

Must be the most agile of the infielders, quick to move in both directions.

◆ Must be the best infielder of ground balls and have a strong throwing arm.

Initiate double play by getting the ball quickly to second base player who in turn throws it to first to put out both runners, or from second to third.

Play between second and third base, about 10–12 feet behind the base line.

Catcher

Must have good hand–eye coordination to make catches.

Set "targets" for the pitcher to try to strike out the batter.

Must have a good throwing arm to make the throw to any of the base players.

Must be able to field thrown balls to home plate.

Batter

Keep eyes focused on the pitched ball.

Hold the bat firmly, but do not tense the entire body.

Be ready to hit every pitched ball.

Judge ball carefully—not swinging at pitches outside strike zone.

Drop bat without throwing it after the hit.

Run out each batted ball because fielder could make an error.

Learn to place hit the ball into open field.

Base Runners

Be ready to run with each pitched ball.

Lead off slightly on every pitch only when it passes over home plate.

Know how many outs there are.

Try to get to the next base so that the base behind is free for the next runner.

Do not run on a fly ball with less than two outs: On short fly ball, only go halfway; on a long fly ball, tag up to move on to the next base.

Outfielders

Must have good "eyes" to field grounders and judge fly balls.

Must have good running speed to get to the ball.

Must have strong throwing arms and very accurate throws.

SOFTBALL RULES

Softball was first developed in 1887 by George Hancock and during the over 100 years of its existence, the game has evolved as one of the most popular outdoor or indoor games played today. Rules of the game could be taught as each skill lesson is developed and then recapped in the classroom so that players will develop a better understanding of the game and skills involved. These rules can be modified to the developmentally appropriate ability level of the children so that a positive, enjoyable, and successful experience will be guaranteed. The lesson plans in the softball unit provide specific suggestions to modify the equipment used, including the type and size of ball used (such as a softball-size whiffle ball, rubber softballs, tennis balls), size and type of bat, the size of the softball field or play area, the number of players, the length of playtime, the size of the infield (distances between the bases and between home plate and the pitching mound), and modifications of the rules. Safety and court etiquette need to be emphasized and enforced at all times. All field players should wear proper baseball gloves when fielding a thrown or batted ball. Catcher should wear a protective mask and chest protector. Hitting team should be positioned safely away from the play when waiting a turn at bat. Emphasize that the bat is put down, not thrown down, after a hit has been made!

1. **The Playing Field and Player Positions (See Diagram E)**

   The infield consists of four bases—first base, second base, third base, and home—spaced in a diamond shape 60 feet (18 meters) apart. Home plate is 46 feet (13.8 meters) from the pitching mound located in the center of the diamond. A regulation team consists of 10 players: pitcher, catcher, first baseman, second baseman, third baseman, shortstop, right fielder, left center fielder, right center fielder, and right fielder. (Could play only 9 positions with a left fielder, middle fielder, and a right fielder.) Shortstop plays between second and third bases.

2. **The Game Play**

   Toss a coin to decide which team will start batting. Players of that team take turns batting while the fielding team tries to put each batter out by: tagging the batter after a hit ball before he/she gets to first base, catching a batted fly ball, striking the batter out, touching a base ahead of the runner who must advance to that base, or tagging the runner on the way to the base. Suggest that batting order be organized according to the field positions: catcher (1), pitcher (2), first baseman (3), second baseman (4), third baseman (5), shortstop (6), left fielder (7), middle fielder (8), right fielder (9). Batting team is allowed only 3 outs, then the teams switch roles and the fielding team goes to bat. Each team is allowed 3 outs per inning; a regulation game consists of 7 innings. A player scores a run by advancing around all four bases. The team that scores more runs wins the game.

   The pitcher starts the game by underhand throwing (pitching) the ball to the batter who attempts to hit the ball. The ball must be hit inside the third and first base lines to be considered in play. A ball hit outside of the base lines is called a foul ball and is out of play; a ball hit between the two base lines is a fair ball and must be played by the defensive team. The batter hitting the ball must try to reach first base before the ball. If the ball is caught in the air (fly ball) or if the ball beats the batter to first base, the batter is out. If the batter reaches first base before the ball (assuming that the ball is not caught in the air), the batter is safe and the next team player comes to bat. The base runner at first now tries to run around all the bases to score a run without being put out.

3. **Pitching Rules**

The pitcher must face the batter and stand with both feet on the pitching mound. The ball must be held in front with both hands. The pitcher is allowed only one step forward and must deliver the ball while making the step. The ball must be thrown underhand. The pitcher is not allowed to fake or make any motion toward the batter without delivering the ball. The pitcher is not allowed to deliver the ball until the batter is ready.

A "strike" is a pitch thrown over home plate between the top of the knees and the bottom of the armpits of the batter, called the "strike zones." A "ball" is a pitch that does not go through the strike zone.

4. **Batting Rules**

The batter may swing at a pitched ball or let it go by. If the batter misses a pitched ball, it is a strike. A ball hit into "foul" territory is called a strike unless the batter already has two strikes. Three strikes put a batter out. If the batter hits a foul ball on the third strike that is caught by the catcher, he/she is out. A batter receiving 4 pitched balls or who is hit by a pitched ball, is "walked," that is, he/she gets to go to first base.

5. **Base-Running Rules**

There is no stealing or leading-off base in softball. The runner is not allowed to leave the base until the batter swings at the ball. When sprinting to first base after a hit, always turn to the right when overrunning the base. Do not overrun second or third base; stop at the base. Run in a straight pathway on the right side of the foul line. Runners are given the right half of the base to tag up.

The Softball Field
Diagram E

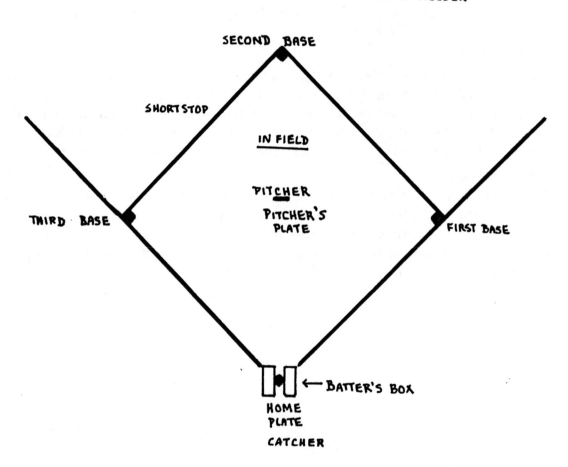

OUTFIELD

CENTER FIELDER

LEFT FIELDER

RIGHT FIELDER

SECOND BASE

SHORT STOP

IN FIELD

PITCHER

PITCHER'S PLATE

THIRD BASE

FIRST BASE

← BATTER'S BOX

HOME PLATE

CATCHER

RACQUET AND BALL PLAY AND TENNIS POINTERS

Ready Position

◆ Face the net with feet shoulder-width apart, knees bent, and weight slightly forward on the balls of the feet.

◆ Hold the hands out from your body, waist high, so that the striking hand is ready to hit the ball.

Footwork and Forehand Stroking

◆ Watch the oncoming ball and quickly move into position.

◆ Start drawing the paddle head back before turning and planting the back foot.

◆ Step to a side-on position with the foot on the nonstriking side.

◆ Draw the hand back and plant weight on back foot.

Swing the hand forward by stepping into the ball, shifting weight onto the front foot.

◆ Keep wrist locked.

Keep eyes on the ball right through the contact.

Contact the ball just ahead of your trunk.

Stroke through the ball, finishing with the hand pointing up and over the opposite shoulder.

Handshake Grip

Shake hands with paddle so that the "V" formed by thumb and index finger is centered on top of grip.

Slightly separate the index finger from the other fingers.

Ready Position

Face the net with feet shoulder-width apart, knees bent, and weight slightly forward on the balls of the feet.

Hold the paddle throat lightly with the non-paddle hand.

Hold paddle out from your body, waist high, so that the head of the paddle is vertical to the ground, and the handle is pointing to your belly button.

Footwork and Forehand Stroking

Watch the oncoming ball and quickly move into position.

Start drawing the paddle head back before turning and planting the back foot.

Step to a side-on position with the foot on the non-paddle side.

Draw the paddle back behind the shoulder and plant weight on back foot.

Swing the paddle forward by stepping into the ball, shifting weight onto the front foot.

Keep wrist locked and grip firmly.

Keep eyes on the ball right through the contact.

- Contact the ball just ahead of your trunk.
- Stroke through the ball, finishing with the paddle head pointing up over the opposite shoulder.

Bounce-serve

- Stand side-on to the wall or net.
- Step forward with the foot opposite your serving hand.
- Hold the ball in the other hand.
- Drop the ball and allow the ball to bounce once.
- Swing paddle forward to strike the ball against the wall using the forehand stroke.

Backhand Grip

- Shake hands with the racquet, then rotate hand inward slightly so that the "V" is on the left top of the racquet handle.
- Spread thumb across the back of the grip.

Footwork and Backhand Stroking

- Keep eyes on the oncoming ball and quickly get into position.
- Rotate shoulders so that the racquet side of your back is facing the net and weight is on your back foot.
- Shift weight forward and swing parallel to the ground.
- Backswing straight, taking racquet across the body.
- Keep wrist locked and hold with a firm grip.
- Contact the ball ahead of the forward foot.
- Swing through toward the net across the front of the body, letting the racquet rise slightly.
- Keep eyes on the ball right through the contact.
- Follow-through toward the target.

Ground Stroking

- Start in ready position: Face the net with feet shoulder-width apart, knees bent, and weight slightly forward on the balls of the feet.
- Hold throat of racquet lightly with the non-racquet hand; relax racquet hand grip.
- Keep eyes focused on the approaching ball; move into position.
- Draw the racquet back early, pivot side-on to the net, and step into the ball shifting weight forward.
- Keep wrist grip firm and try to contact ball in the center of racquet.
- Let eyes follow the ball onto the racquet in the contact.
- Swing through the ball as if you were trying to knock several glasses off a table or trying to hit three balls coming in a row.

Follow-through with the racquet face perpendicular to the court surface, and racquet arm coming upwards and rotating slightly over at the completion of the swing.

Don't crowd the ball; position to take it arm's length away.

After following-through, quickly return to ready position.

Volley

Keep eyes focused on the ball and knees flexed throughout the volley.

Keep racquet in front of you and arms extended.

Keep wrist and grip firm, and use a short backswing.

Step into the volley, and "punch" the ball, contacting it early.

Use very little follow-through; stop racquet head just after it strikes the ball.

Overhand Serve (Right-handers)

Stand with left hip and shoulder side-on to the net and left foot pointing to opposition's serving court or diagonally forward.

Hold racquet in a relaxed forehand grip.

Hold ball lightly in the fingers of the left hand.

Gently rest this hand against the throat of the racquet.

Hold the racquet head up, pointing it towards the opposition's service court.

Start the ball hand and racquet downward together.

Swing the racquet hand away and behind the body.

Toss the ball in front and above the hitting shoulder.

Follow ball toss with the eyes, right through to contact.

Time the ball toss and racquet moving upwards from behind the back.

Lead with the elbow as racquet swings upward and forward.

Shift weight forward, rising up on the toes.

Contact the ball with full arm extension, slightly closing racquet face over the descending ball.

Follow-through swinging out, across, and down while stepping forward with the back foot.

TENNIS RULES

Tennis, which was introduced into America in the mid-1870s by Mary Outerbridge, has become a popular high-profile sport worldwide. The game can be played all year around on lawn, clay, asphalt, concrete surfaces, requires only 2-4 players, is affordable for everyone, and is suitable for all age groups and both sexes. Rules of the game could be taught as each skill lesson is developed and then recapped in the classroom so that players will develop a better understanding of the game and skills involved. These rules can be modified to the developmentally appropriate ability level of the children so that a positive, enjoyable, and successful experience will be guaranteed. Suggestions to modify the equipment used include the type and size of ball (such as a whiffle ball, larger tennis balls), size and type of racquet, the size of the court, the number of players, the length of play time or number of sets, the height of the net, and modifications of the rules (allow the ball to bounce more than once after the serve). Tennis is a relatively safe game to play. Proper court shoes should be worn and any dangerous racket swinging dealt with immediately. Tennis is a game of court etiquette and protocol that need to be emphasized at all times.

1. **The Playing Area (See Diagram F)**

   The tennis court is a rectangular area, 78-foot (23.77-meter) sidelines, and 36-foot (10.97-meter) base line. The court is separated into two half courts by a net 3′6″ in height positioned across centerline. Each half court consists of a back-court area, a right and left service court and service line, and singles and doubles sidelines. Each base line has a center hash mark as shown. In a single match, the singles side boundaries are used; in doubles, the alleys are used.

2. **The Game Play**

   This racket-and-ball game can be played by two opposing players (singles) or two teams of two players (doubles). The object of the game is to win points by hitting the tennis ball over the net and into the opposition side of the court so that the opposition cannot return the ball before it bounces twice.

   Usually a spin of the racket occurs to determine who will serve first, in which "rough" or "smooth" is called (knots on the string) or "up" or "down" of the letter on the heel of the handle is called. The player winning the call has a choice of service or side.

   The game starts with a player serving from anywhere behind the base line to the right of the center mark and to the left of the doubles sidelines. The ball is usually served by being thrown up and hit on the full with an overarm throwing action of the racket. An underarm action is also allowed. The server has two tries to serve the ball into the diagonal service box. If the server fails to hit the ball into the proper court, or if the ball strikes the net but does not go over, or if the serve steps over the base line before completing the service action (foot fault), then the opposition gets a point. The server continues to serve, alternating serving courts, until the game is over; then the opposition player serves.

   The server may not serve until the receiver is ready and the receiver must let the ball bounce once before returning it. If the serve is good and returned, the play continues until the ball is hit out of court or into the net. The team not making the error scores a point. A ball landing on the line is considered "in" and is still in play. A served ball touching the net on the way over and falling into the proper court is called a "let." A "let" is also called when a distraction occurs during the play; for example, a ball from another court rolls onto the court during play. This results in the point being replayed, or during a serve, the serve being replayed.

3. **Scoring**

A set consists of six games, but must be won by two games. A match is the best two out of three sets or three out of five sets. A tie-breaker set is played if the games go to six each. In this case, the tie-breaker is played to 7 points, but must be won by at least 2 points. A game ends when one team scores 4 points or until one team is ahead by 2 points after 3 points have been played. Scoring system follows:

 ◆ The game begins at zero-all or love-all; 1 point equals "15"; 2 points equal "30"; 3 points equal "40" and 4 points equal the game. If the score is tied at 3 points, this is called "deuce" and each point scored thereafter is called "add-in" (server) or "add-out" (receiver). A team scoring 2 add-ins (or add-outs) in a row wins the game. For example, a score of 40–30 means the serving team leads 3 points to 2 points; a score of 15–40 indicates that the receiving team leads 3 points to 1 point; 40–40 is deuce. Players change ends each time the total games played is an odd number.

4. **Faults**

A team wins a point if the opposition double faults on serve; fails to return the ball in-bounds; lets the ball double bounce; touches the net or post with the racket, clothing or person; reaches across the net to return a ball (allowed to follow-through across the net); or plays the ball more than once on one side.

The Tennis Court
Diagram F

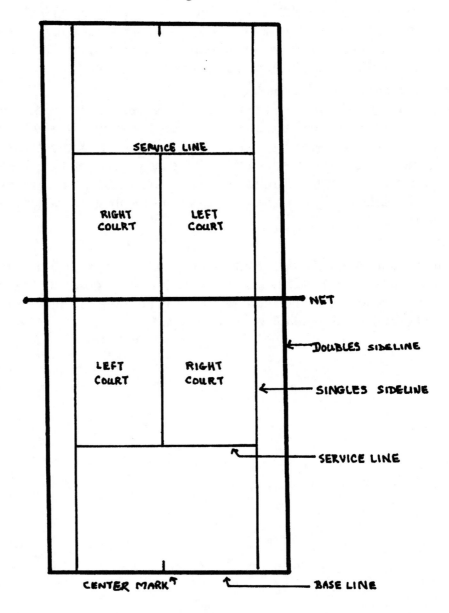

CRICKET PLAY POINTERS

Bowling

Basic Grip of Ball

Hold ball by the fingers and off the palm of the hand.

Grip the ball tightly with the fingers across the seams.

Use a 2-finger grip with the index finger and middle finger across the seams and the little finger resting on the side of the ball.

For smaller hands, use a 3-finger grip by placing the index, middle, and ring fingers across the seams.

Place the thumb under the ball on the opposite side to the little finger.

Footwork and Bowling Action (Right-hander)

Stand side-on to target or receiver, one foot in front of the other, and the dominant leg back.

Grip ball in your fingers and hold ball near chin (coil position).

Concentrate—focus on the line to bowl.

Keep head steady and eyes level.

Lean back, extending front arm up.

Eyes look behind front arm towards target.

Place back foot at right angles to intended bowling direction.

Transfer weight from back foot to front foot and anchor it.

Move bowling arm high over the head.

Pull the front arm strongly down the target line, keeping elbow close to the body.

Bowling arm should brush the ear, then follow-through across the body.

Eyes now look over bowling shoulder.

Batting

Basic Grip of Cricket Bat and Stance (Right-hander)

Lay bat face down on ground with handle pointing toward batter.

Pick up bat with both hands together in the middle of the handle.

Position hands so that the first finger and thumb form a "V."

Point the "V" formed by the hands down the bat.

Hold bat firmly with hands close together on handle.

Place dominant hand just below the other hand.

Stand side-on to oncoming ball in the popping crease.

Place feet shoulder-width apart, with knees relaxed and slightly bent.

Keep balanced, weight forward on balls of feet.

Keep the eyes level, chin just above the toes from front on and midway between the toes from side on.

◆ Rest the bottom of the bat lightly against the little toe of the back foot (or place the bat in front of the back foot).

◆ Rest the knuckles of the top hand against the front thigh.

Striking the Ball

◆ Keep head up and still, eyes focused on oncoming ball.

◆ Lift bat high as bowler is about to release the ball.

◆ Coordinate the backlift with the bowler's delivery stride.

◆ Keep the hands in close to the body.

◆ Point the toe of the bat between off stump and second slip.

◆ In backlift position the arms form a number 6.

◆ Square body to the ball and keep head in line with it.

◆ Swing bat down and across to hit the ball well in front of the body.

◆ Transfer nearly all body weight to front foot, lifting rear heel.

◆ Let body weight follow the stroke.

Wicket-keeping

◆ Position directly behind the wickets, knees bent and feet shoulder-width apart.

◆ Keep weight forward on the balls of the feet, ready to react in any direction.

◆ Wear protective gloves which are touching the ground with little fingers together and palms open to the ball, facing the bowler.

◆ Watch the ball right into the gloves, position hands ready to react to the ball.

◆ Keep totally involved in the game, the major focus being the ball!

Player Positions

◆ Fielding team is made up of a wicket-keeper, bowler, mid on, mid off and mid wicket players, covers, point, slips, gully, third man, long on, and fine leg.

◆ The busiest players are the bowlers and the wicket-keepers.

◆ Players close to the bat (mid off, mid on, point, and short leg) are attacking positions and are positioned to take catches that pop up from defensive batting strokes. (Such positions are generally disallowed or discouraged in junior cricket.)

◆ Fielders are placed in positions with those players near the boundary referred to as outfielders.

◆ Two batters from the batting team take up a position at each end of the cricket pitch, standing behind each popping crease and in front of a wicket that consists of three stumps and two bails which sit in grooves atop the adjacent pairs of stumps.

◆ A wicket-keeper positions just behind the wicket stumps.

- A bowler has a cricket ball and may bowl from either side of the wicket with a run-up.
- Put strongest throwers in the outfield.
- Use players who are good at reflex catches in the slips and gully positions.
- Use quick and agile players in the cover and mid-wicket positions.
- Some players will naturally take to wicket-keeping, but also encourage them to develop other skills such as bowling.

CRICKET RULES

Cricket is a bat-and-ball game first played in England, and now played at all levels throughout the world. A formal game of cricket can last anywhere from an afternoon to one day to several days! Rules of the game could be taught as each skill lesson is developed and then recapped in the classroom so that players will develop a better understanding of the game and skills involved. These rules can be modified to the developmentally appropriate ability level of the children so that a positive, enjoyable, and successful experience will be guaranteed. Suggestions to modify the equipment used include the type and size of ball used (such as a whiffle ball, larger tennis balls, soft cricket ball), size and type of cricket bat, the size of the cricket oval, the number of players, the length of play time, and modifications of the rules. Safety must be enforced at all times as the ball can be hit at great speeds and in any direction. Batter must wear protective gear, including shin pads, gloves, and helmet with protective shield; wicket-keepers also wear protective pads covering the shins and webbed gloves designed for catching the ball.

1. **The Playing Area and Player Positions (See Diagram G)**

   Cricket is a bat-and-ball game played on a cricket pitch that is 20 meters/yards in length surrounded by a large oval field. The game consists of two teams of 11 players; one team bats first, while the other team fields. The fielding team is made up of a wicket-keeper, bowler, mid on and mid off players, cover, point, gully, leg slip, 2 slips, third man, and fine leg. Players close to the batter (mid off, mid on, gully, points, and short leg) are attacking positions. Two batters from the batting team take up a position at each end of the cricket pitch, standing behind each popping crease and in front of a wicket which consists of 3 stumps and 2 bails that sit in grooves atop the adjacent pairs of stumps. A wicket-keeper positions just behind the wicket stumps. A bowler has a cricket ball and may bowl from either side of the wicket with a run-up. Batter attempts to hit the bowled ball with a cricket bat which is flat on one side and humped on the other for strength.

2. **The Game Play**

   The bowler of the fielding team puts the ball into play with a straight, overarm, or underarm action thrown along the pitch towards the stumps, so that the ball bounces once. Each bowler bowls an "over" which consists of 6 balls, and then swaps with another bowler who will bowl the next over from the other end of the pitch.

   Each team takes a turn at batting (innings). The two batters on the pitch at any time try to score runs by hitting the ball and then running from one wicket to the opposite wicket. After hitting or attempting to hit the ball, the batters may choose to run or stay as they are.

3. **Scoring**

   The batting team scores a run each time the batters cross safely to the other end and touch the ground behind the popping crease. The fielding team tries to put the batter out until there is only one batter left to take a turn at bat. Four runs are scored automatically without the batters running if the ball is struck into the boundary; six runs are scored automatically if the ball is struck over the boundary on the full. The team scoring more runs after a given number of innings (usually two) is the winner.

4. **Bowling Faults**

    A "no ball" is called by the umpire for an illegal delivery by a bowler if the bowler uses a throwing action instead of the legal straight-arm action and if the bowler oversteps the popping crease with the front foot during bowling. Each "no ball" scores one run for the batting team. Batters cannot be bowled out or caught from a no ball and the bowler must bowl again.

    A "wide" is called if the ball is out of the batter's reach when the batter is in batting stance. Wides score one run each for the batting team and the bowler must bowl again.

5. **Batter and Runner Faults**

    The batter is out if:

    ◆ bowled ball strikes the wicket and knocks over the bails (bowled)

    ◆ ball is caught on the full by a fielder; the batter strikes the wicket with any part of the equipment, body, or clothing in such a way that the bails fall off

    ◆ umpire rules that the bowled ball was not hit with the bat, but part of the batter's body such as the legs (This is called a "lbw" or "leg before wicket.")

    The batter or runner is out if:

    ◆ a fielder (including the wicket-keeper) throws the ball at the batter's or runner's wicket so that the bails fall off while the batter or runner is in front of the popping crease (This is called a "run out.")

The Cricket Field
Diagram G

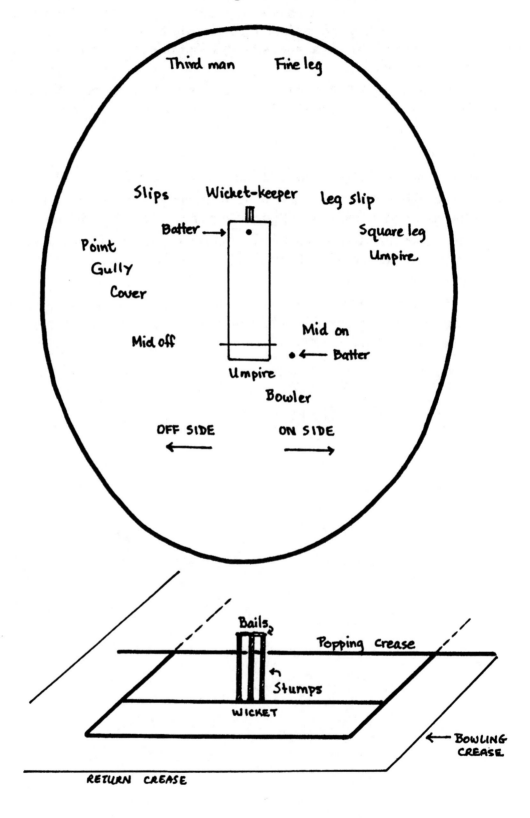

NETBALL PLAY POINTERS

Passing

Allowed to throw the ball in any manner and in any direction to another player.

Allowed to bounce the ball with one or both hands in any direction to another player.

After contacting a ball by using one bounce or bat, or by tipping it in an uncontrolled manner, a player may pass (or direct) it to another player by batting or bouncing it as before.

A ball may not be thrown over a whole third of the court, crossing two transverse lines. (A free pass or throw-in is given to the opposition team at the point where the ball entered the incorrect third.)

Aim pass at a point in space where the receiver will arrive by the time the ball has traveled through the air ("lead pass").

For a long pass, draw arm well back to provide for a long pull forwards and gather speed to produce power.

Release ball with a flick of the wrist, as if fingers are trying to push through the ball.

Exaggerate follow-through to ensure intended direction of flight.

Catching

Keep eyes tracking ball all the way to your hands.

Keep hands in ready position to receive the ball.

Reach and absorb impact of pass by bending elbows.

Look immediately to make the next pass.

Time the catch, making the catch with one or both hands.

Allowed prior to catching the ball to bat or bounce the ball once, or tip the ball in an uncontrolled manner.

Having caught or held the ball, a player may not drop the ball and replay it. "Replay" means the player may neither catch the ball again nor bat/bounce it for another teammate to catch or retrieve.

Footwork

A player making the catch must land on one foot (usually the right foot is chosen for a right-handed player).

A right-foot landing followed by a left-foot landing provides a good base for efficient throwing.

If the landing is on two feet, a player may choose which foot to move.

After completing a catch with just one foot on the ground, a player may step with the other foot in any direction, lift the landing foot, and throw or shoot before this foot is regrounded.

While in possession of the ball, the player may not jump from one foot and land on the same foot (hop); nor may he/she jump from two feet and land back on two, although he/she may land on one.

Goal Shooting

Goals can only be scored from within the goal circle and only a goal shooter or goal attack can attempt to shoot goals. A goal is scored by throwing the ball through the team's ring located in the opposition's end zone. A shooter must be completely within the circle to shoot and may make no contact with the ground outside the circle either during the catching of the ball or while holding it. Shooters may retrieve their own missed shot and shoot again, as long as the ball touches any part of the goal post including the net. Defending player (Goalkeeper) is allowed to lean forward and extend a hand towards the ball.

- Hold ball in both hands and position ball behind the head.
- Keep eyes focused just above and to the back of the ring, not on the defender's hand.
- Keep balance, with one foot slightly ahead of the other, weight evenly distributed on both feet.
- Keep in a vertical body position with arms high in line.
- Release the ball off the fingers in a high arc towards the goal ring.
- Follow-through with both hands in the intended direction of flight.

Player Positions and Responsibilities for Each Position

Netball is played by two teams of 7 players each. Players' movements are restricted on the court according to the position played:

- Goal Shooter (GS) is allowed in areas 1 and 2, and has the main responsibility of shooting goals, has height, and good hands for catching the ball; accurate shooting skills.
- Goal Attack (GA) is allowed in areas 1, 2, and 3, and can also shoot goals and lead the attack.
- Wing Attack (WA) is allowed in areas 2 and 3, and has the responsibility of passing the ball to the shooters.
- Center (C) is allowed in areas 2, 3, and 4, and plays the whole court except for the goal circles, and joins the defensive and attacking sides of his/her team together.
- Wing Defense (WD) is allowed in areas 3 and 4, and defends the wing attacker, playing in the defense and center thirds.
- Goal Defense (GD) is allowed in areas 3, 4, and 5, and defends the goal attacker and plays in the defense and center thirds, including the goal circle.
- Goalkeeper (GK) is allowed in areas 4 and 5, and is the defense third that includes the goal circle.

NETBALL RULES

Netball was created by an American basketball coach attempting to improve the skills of basketball at Luton Teachers College in England. He introduced the sport to many graduating teachers who took this new and exciting game with them as they acquired teaching positions in schools all over England as well as other countries.

Netball is a popular, noncontact ball sport played predominately by thousands of girls and women, either in indoor or outdoor courts in schools, colleges, universities, and clubs in 25 countries throughout the world, particularly in many of the old Commonwealth countries. Today many recreation centers offer mixed netball competition. Since 1963 world netball championships have been held every four years; in 1995 netball became an Olympic sport which further increased its popularity as evidenced by the growing popularity of mixed team and men's netball.

Rules of the game could be taught as each skill lesson is developed and then recapped in the classroom so that players will develop a better understanding of the game and skills involved. These rules can be modified to the developmentally appropriate ability level of the children so that a positive, enjoyable, and successful experience will be guaranteed. Suggestions to modify the equipment used include the type and size of ball used (such as a Nerf™ ball or small/medium playground ball), the size of the court, the number of players, the length of play time, the height of the goal, and modifications of the rules (allow 3 running steps before passing). As a noncontact sport, netball is a relatively safe game to play; but proper court shoes are a must and players need to be taught to stop properly by jump-stopping (author's recommendation) and bending at the knees to absorb the impact. Proper court etiquette should be emphasized at all times.

1. **The Playing Area and Playing Positions (See Diagram H)**

   A regulation netball court is a rectangular play area 30.5 meters (100 feet) in length and goal line 15.25 meters (50 feet) in width, and divided into two goal thirds and one center third. Each end zone has a netball goal positioned just off the center of the goal line in a shooting goal circle. The netball goal is a steel 38-cm (15-inch diameter) ring with an open net, no backboard, and is attached at the top of a 3.05-m (10-foot) high post secured in the ground. The ball is a size 5, made out of leather, rubber, or similar material with a 27–28-inch circumference (about 7 cm).

   Netball is played by two teams of 7 players each. Players' movements are restricted on the court according to the position played: (refer to Diagram H for play areas 1, 2, 3, 4, and 5)

   - Goal Shooter (GS) is allowed in areas 1 and 2.
   - Goal Attack (GA) is allowed in areas 1, 2, and 3.
   - Wing Attack (WA) is allowed in areas 2 and 3.
   - Center (C) is allowed in areas 2, 3, and 4.
   - Wing Defense (WD) is allowed in areas 3 and 4.
   - Goal Defense (GD) is allowed in areas 3, 4, and 5.
   - Goalkeeper (GK) is allowed in areas 4 and 5.

2. **The Game Play**

Netball is a fast game requiring players to have excellent skills and good team work. Play begins at the start of each half of the game and after each goal has been scored with a pass by the center player to a player inside the middle third of the court. A toss of the coin decides which team will get possession of the ball first. Then teams take turns. A regulation game consists of two 30-minute halves or four 15-minute quarters of play with a 3-minute interval between first and second quarter, a 5-minute interval at halftime, and another 3-minute interval between third and fourth quarters. Teams change ends with every quarter.

Throwing the ball through the team's ring located in the opposition's end zone scores a goal. Goals can only be scored from area 1 and only a goal shooter or goal attack can attempt to shoot goals. Shots must only be taken from within the goal circle.

Players move the ball up-court by quick passes or by tapping the ball to a teammate. No player is allowed to run with the ball. Passes may be underhand, overhand, or overhead air passes, or one- or two-handed bounce passes.

A player may catch the ball with one or both hands, and before catching it, may bat or bounce the ball once, or tip the ball in an uncontrolled manner once or more than once (particularly when two opposition players are striving to reach a ball in the air.) Once the player has caught the ball, the player may not drop the ball and replay it (that is, the player may neither catch the ball again, nor bat/bounce the ball for someone else in the team to catch or retrieve).

A player may receive the ball while one or both feet are grounded or jump to catch it and land on one or both feet. After completing a catch with just one foot on the ground, a player may step with the other foot in any direction, lift the landing foot, and throw or shoot before this foot is regrounded. To achieve balance, the less skillful player will step onto the other foot almost immediately. A player may jump from the landing foot onto the other foot and jump again, but must throw the ball or shoot before regrounding either foot.

A player can only hold the ball for three seconds. A defending player must be three feet away from the attacking player with the ball. A ball may not be thrown over a whole third of the court, crossing two transverse lines; otherwise, free pass or throw-in is awarded at the point where the ball entered the incorrect third.

The ball is out-of-bounds if it bounces outside the court or if the player in possession with the ball is in contact with the ground outside the court. The ball is given to the opposition team of the last team to touch the ball from the line. The player taking the pass must place the toe to the line (not on the line) on the umpire's instruction before passing the ball.

3. **Penalties**

Penalties are awarded for:

- ◆ *Obstruction* which occurs when an opposition player attempts to block or guard the player with the ball from a distance of less than one meter.
- ◆ *Contact* which occurs when an opposition player makes contact with the player in possession of the ball or makes contact with the ball while the player is holding it.

◆ *Stepping* which technically occurs if a player walks or runs with the ball or steps again onto the foot that was grounded first when gaining possession of the ball.

◆ *Off-side* which occurs when a player moves on the court outside of that player's designated area.

◆ *Held ball* which occurs when a player in possession of the ball holds the ball for longer than 3 seconds.

The Netball Court
Diagram H

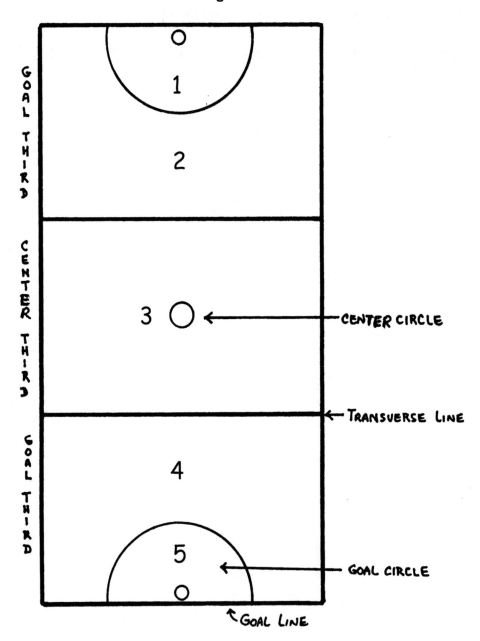

FLAG FOOTBALL PLAY POINTERS

Gripping the Ball

Place the thumb and index finger on the back of the ball.

Spread the other fingers across the seam (laces) of the football.

Use the nonthrowing hand to support the ball on the front inside part.

Stance and Throwing Action

Stand with the foot of the nonthrowing side forward.

Start the throwing action with the throwing arm and hand cocked back slightly behind the head. Nonthrowing hand provides support to the ball almost to this point, then drops away.

Keep eyes focused on the target.

Release ball by throwing flexed elbow forward and snapping wrist downward so that ball spins in a spiral motion to receiver or target.

Follow-through in the intended direction of flight.

Receiving

Make a target with your hands.

Spread fingers wide and point thumbs in toward the body for an above-the-waist catch. Keep little fingers together for a below-the-waist catch.

Relax the hands.

Track the ball with your eyes right into the hands.

Always try to catch the ball with both hands.

Reach for the ball, letting it fall into the cradle of your hands.

As the ball meets the hands, bring the ball, hands, and arms into the body to absorb the force of the throw.

Get ball under control and tuck it into the forearm, covering the tip of the ball with the hand to protect it as you run with the ball.

Center Snap

Grip the ball the same way as for passing.

Spread feet wide apart, bending at the knees.

Look back through the legs to see the quarterback before snapping the ball, but look heads up to face the opposition when actually snapping the ball.

Release the ball with one hand, snapping the wrist.

Extend snapping hand and arm back through the legs into the hands of the quarterback who positions about 5 yards behind the snapper. Non-snapping hand rests on the knee.

Ball should spiral into the quarterback's hands at about chest height.

Lateral Pass (One-hand Underpass)

◆   Grip the ball with the favorite (dominant) hand.

◆   Place the palm of the passing hand under the ball, fingers spread.

◆   Snap the wrist back to make the underhand toss and impart spin.

◆   Ball should spiral as it travels to the receiver.

◆   Pass to the side (laterally) or backwards to a player.

◆   Note that a forward lateral pass beyond the line of scrimmage is illegal.

Pass Running Pattern

Pattern running consists of running and making at least one quick change of direction (or "cut") to get free from a defender and into an open space to receive a pass from the quarterback.

◆   "Cut" by pushing off the inside of the foot opposite to the intended direction of the cut: to cut to the right, push off from the inside of the left foot.

◆   Run at a certain pace, then, bending at the knees and using small steps, make a quick movement to change direction.

◆   Add a head or body fake by a quick movement in one direction to go into the opposite or a different direction.

◆   After making the cut, keep trunk and lower body moving in the intended line of direction, but turn head back to see the quarterback releasing the ball and track the flight of the ball into your hands.

Common Running Plays

◆   *Pitch-out*—quarterback underhand tosses ball to a running back.

◆   *Sweep*—quarterback gives a hand-off to a running back who follows.

◆   *Reverse*—quarterback runs in one direction and hands off a running back traveling in the opposite direction.

Hand-off

◆   *Ball carrier* holds ball in two hands to begin.

◆   As receiver approaches, move ball across to that side with the hand under the ball and the elbow bent.

◆   Hold ball now slightly out from the body.

◆   Hand the ball to the receiver, do not throw.

◆   *Receiver* approaches the ball carrier and raises the arm on the side of the quarterback.

◆   Elbow is bent at right angles at shoulder level, forearm directly in front of body, and palm down.

◆   Bend the other arm's elbow at right angles, position just below the waist, directly in front of the body, with the palm facing up.

◆   Let quarterback hand-place the ball into your hands; don't reach for it.

◆   As exchange takes place, clasp the ball from above with the top hand and from below with the other hand.

Do not stop, but run through the ball as it is handed to you.

Shift ball to the carrying position.

Carrying the Ball

Cradle the ball firmly into the crook of the elbow and your chest, and cover the front tip of the ball with the hand.

Carry the ball against the side away from the defender(s).

Run with head up and into open space; keep alert.

Defending the Receiver

Watch the quarterback for clues to see where the pass will go.

Keep within 3 giant steps of the player you are guarding, but never let the receiver get behind you.

Be alert—ready to react to the receiver's cut.

Try to knock the ball away or intercept the pass to the receiver.

No body contact is allowed until the receiver touches the football, then you can try to pull the flag.

Place-kicking

Slowly approach the ball from about 5–8 yards/meters away.

Plant the nonkicking foot to the side of the ball and about a foot behind it.

Keep eyes focused on the ball right through the kick.

Bend the kicking leg at the knee and straighten as the foot contacts the ball.

Lock angle at contact so that supporting foot and kicking foot are at right angles.

Contact the ball just below the midline.

Follow-through in the intended direction of flight with the kicking leg lifting the kicker off the ground.

Punting

Grip the ball with the laces up and center the ball over the kicking leg.

Place one hand on the back of the ball and the other hand on the front.

Keep eyes focused on the ball through the kick.

Take a 1-2-3 step-and-kick approach: step with nonkicking leg (1), then kicking leg (2), then nonkicking leg (3) and kick.

Drop the ball onto the top of the kicking foot instep.

Point kicking toes down as you kick the ball.

Follow-through with kicking leg in intended direction of flight, keeping hands out for balance.

If ball is punted correctly it will spiral, which will significantly add traveling distance to the ball.

Tackling

In flag football, a defensive player can only make the "tackle" by pulling a flag off the offensive ball carrier.

◆ Keep eyes focused on the flags of the runner.

◆ Keep alert to any head or body fakes and be ready to react.

◆ Stay balanced with weight evenly distributed on the balls of the feet, ready to move in any direction.

◆ Get in good body position to move in quickly and grab the flag.

◆ Remember, no body contact is allowed.

Blocking

Setting the Block

Blocker sets into a three-point stance: one hand and both feet in contact with the ground.

◆ Position feet shoulder-width apart, side-straddled, and weight evenly distributed on the balls of the feet, knees slightly flexed.

◆ Place other arm across the thigh once in set position.

◆ Keep body weight forward on the fingers of the hand resting on the ground.

◆ Keep seat down, head up, and look straight ahead.

Screen Blocking

◆ Blocker simply places her/his body between the ball carrier and the tackler.

◆ Absolutely no body control can occur.

◆ Tackler cannot push blocker out of the way, but must try to go around her/him.

Shoulder Blocking

This is the only body blocking allowed in flag football. A blocker is not allowed to block an opposition player below the knees or on the back, use the hands to grab an opponent, or leave his/her feet to block an opponent.

◆ Place the shoulder against the opposition's shoulder, chest, or mid-section.

◆ Keep in a balanced, forward stride position, knees slightly flexed and body crouched, head up.

◆ Make contact, driving the opponent downfield.

Offensive Positions

Offensive set consists of 8 players: a quarterback, a center (ball snapper), two tackles, two ends, and two running backs.

◆ *Quarterback* calls the plays in the huddle, gives the hiking signal for the ball snapping, and passes or hands-off the ball to the receiver. Also has the option of running with the ball.

◆ *Center* lines up in front of the ball at the line of scrimmage, and on quarterback's signal, hikes or snaps the ball to the quarterback, then sets a shoulder block.

♦   *Tackles* help to protect the quarterback by setting shoulder blocks.

♦   Two *ends* and the *running backs* are all eligible to catch a pass, and any player can run with the ball after it is snapped into play.

Defensive Positions

Defensive set consists of five defensive linemen and three defensive backs (or three defensive linemen and five backs).

♦   *Linemen* are responsible for rushing the quarterback and tackling the ball carrier.

♦   *Defensive backs* are responsible for stopping the sweep, running, and preventing receivers from catching the ball. Usually the fastest defensive backs defend against the long pass.

♦   In one-to-one defense, a *defensive back* guards the receiver wherever he/she runs.

♦   In zone defense, the *defensive backs* guard receivers who come into their zone or area they are defending.

FLAG FOOTBALL RULES

American football as played today was first developed in the late nineteenth century in England and evolved from the games of soccer and rugby. Touch and flag football evolved as modified games to the regulation game of football. Flag football presents a much safer alternative to the method of tackling by simply pulling a flag from a player's flag belt. The skill then becomes to protect or grab the flag when playing the game. Today flag football is played widely by both sexes and coeducationally as a recreational game as well as a more structured league game.

Rules of the game could be taught as each skill lesson is developed and then recapped in the classroom so that players will develop a better understanding of the game and skills involved. These rules can be modified to the developmentally appropriate ability level of the children so that a positive, enjoyable, and successful experience will be guaranteed. Suggestions to modify the game include the type and size of ball used (such as Nerf™ footballs, smaller and lighter footballs), size of the playing field, the number of players on the field, the length of playtime, and modifications of the rules (blocking is not permitted below the waist or in the air). Proper playing etiquette should be emphasized at all times. The playing field needs to be checked carefully to make sure it is free of obstacles that could result in injury.

1. **The Playing Area and Playing Positions (See Diagram I)**

   A flag football field measures 100 yards/meters by 50 yards/meters with a 10-yard/meter by 50-yard/meter end zone area at each end and the rest of the field divided by a center line and two quarter lines into four 20-yard quarters. A 3-yard/meter conversion line is marked off into each quarter field from the center of the inside end zone line. An inbound line running parallel and 15 yards/meters in from each sideline is marked off in broken hash marks.

   A team consists of eight players. Each player wears a flag belt that has two flags attached by Velcro and which can easily be detached. The basic offensive set is made up of a center, two tackles, two ends, two running backs, and a quarterback. The quarterback sets the play and executes the passes to the ends or backs who are all eligible to catch a pass. A defensive set is made up of three defensive linemen and five defensive backs. The linemen are responsible for rushing the quarterback and tackling ball carriers running the ball (but remember, this is only done by snatching the flag of the ball runner!); the defensive backs try to prevent pass receptions and stop the sweep run.

   Regulation playing time consists of two 20-minute halves, with a 5-minute halftime break, or four quarters of 10 minutes. An overtime of 5 minutes will be played if necessary.

2. **The Game Play**

   The objective of the game is to pass or carry the football over the opposition's goal line into the end zone to score while stopping the opposition from doing the same. The ball is put into play to start the game, at the beginning of the second half, and after each score by a place kick (that is, the ball is in a fixed position on a kicking tee) from the kicking team's 20-yard line.

   The player receiving the punt may run with the ball or lateral pass. The ball may not be passed forward. A team then has four consecutive attempts (downs) to try to advance the ball to at least the next zone; otherwise, the opposition takes over possession of the ball at that point on the field. A center player snaps the ball through his/her legs to a quarterback positioned about 5 yards/meters away. The quarterback has the option of passing the ball or running with it. All forward passes must be thrown from behind the line of scrimmage, and all offensive players are eligible to receive a pass.

A team also has the option of punting the ball to the opposition at any time during the four-down sequence. However a team must declare its intention to punt. A team will usually punt after the third attempt when a first-down attempt cannot be made; that is, when the team is unable to move the ball forward to the next zone on the field. The team may decide to "gamble" or attempt to get the fourth down by a passing or running play. If a team is successful in advancing the ball to the next zone, the team then earns a "first down" and receives four more downs to advance the ball into the opposition's next field zone or end zone. The offensive team advances the ball by running with it or passing the ball to another player.

The defensive team stops the ball carrier or receiver of the ball by pulling that player's flag or flags from his/her flag belt. The ball is placed at the downed position which is called the line of scrimmage on the field. Play then continues from this point. "On the line" is considered in the next zone.

A 20-second huddle is allowed by the offensive team before a down is played. The team gathers in a tight circle to listen to the quarterback's play (plan for passing or scoring).

3. **Scoring**

When a team successfully carries or passes the ball into the opposition's end zone, a "touchdown" is scored and counts as 6 points. Immediately following a touchdown the offensive team then gets the opportunity to try to score a 2-point conversion from the 3-yard marker by running the ball into the opposition's end zone over the goal line or a 1-point conversion by kicking the ball into the end zone. A team tackling the opposition ball carrier within that player's own end zone is awarded a safety (1 point). The team scoring the most points at the completion of time wins the game.

4. **Violations**

A ball passed, kicked, or run out-of-bounds on the sidelines is put back into play on the center of the scrimmage line at the point where this occurred.

A forward lateral (one-handed underhand) pass beyond the line of scrimmage is illegal. Blocking below the waist is not allowed. Blockers are not allowed to jump in the air on a block. Blockers are not allowed to extend their elbows away from the body. Ball carriers are not allowed to stiff-arm defenders attempting to pull the ball carrier's flag. The only way a player can be "tackled" is by pulling the ball carrier's or receiver's flag and only that player can be tackled. The noncontact rule for screen blocking is strictly enforced so that players do not collide into each other.

A 5-yard penalty is awarded for:

◆ Off-side before the ball is put into play.

◆ Forward passing from in front of the line of scrimmage.

◆ Failing to declare the intention to punt.

- ◆ Making physical contact with the ball carrier in any way.
- ◆ Insufficient flag showing.

A 15-yard penalty is awarded for:

- ◆ Tackling, tripping, holding, pushing, or roughing an opponent
- ◆ Blocking
- ◆ Unsportsmanlike conduct

The Flag Football Playing Field
Diagram I

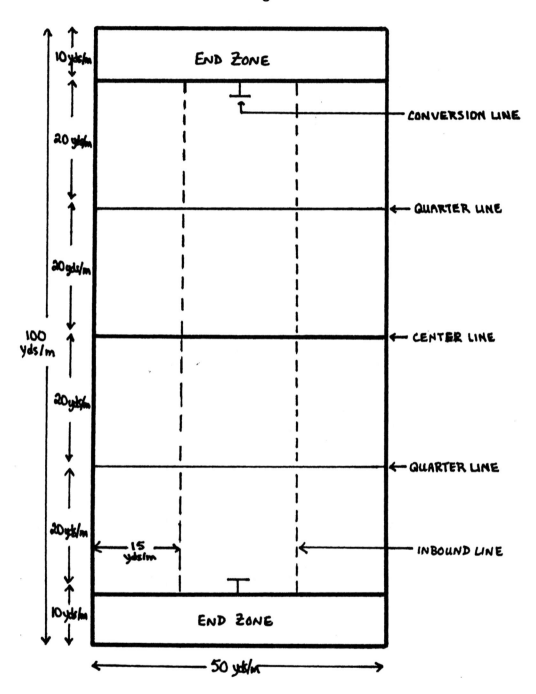

CONVERSION LINE

QUARTER LINE

CENTER LINE

QUARTER LINE

INBOUND LINE

END ZONE

END ZONE

10 yds/m

20 yds/m

20 yds/m

20 yds/m

20 yds/m

10 yds/m

100 yds/m

15 yds/m

50 yds/m

Tournament Draws

ROUND	1	2	3

DRAWS FOR ROUND ROBINS

4 TEAMS

1-2	2-3	4-2
3-4	4-1	1-3

5 TEAMS

1-2	2-3	3-5	4-5	5-2
3-4	5-1	4-2	3-1	1-4
5 bye	4 bye	1 bye	2 bye	3 bye

6 TEAMS

1-2	2-3	3-6	6-2	5-2
3-4	4-5	4-2	5-3	3-1
5-6	6-1	5-1	4-1	4-6

7 TEAMS

1-2	1-3	1-4	1-5	1-6	1-7	2-7
3-4	2-4	2-6	2-3	2-5	3-5	3-6
5-6	5-7	3-7	6-7	4-7	4-6	4-5
7 bye	6 bye	5 bye	4 bye	3 bye	2 bye	1 bye

8 TEAMS

1-2	1-3	1-4	1-5	1-6	1-7	1-8
3-4	2-4	2-6	2-3	2-5	3-5	2-7
5-6	5-7	3-7	6-7	4-7	4-6	3-6
7-8	6-8	5-8	4-8	3-8	2-8	4-5

THE F.I.T.T. PRINCIPLE

F.I.T.T. stands for: "F"—frequency or how often activity is done at the target heart rate; "I"—intensity or how hard we do the activity to maintain and improve cardio-respiratory fitness; "T"—time or how long we are active at the target heart rate; and "T"—what types of activity we do.

> The F.I.T.T. principle states that we need to engage in aerobic type activity at least 3 days and up to 6 days per week; that is, ongoing continuous activity for at least 30 minutes in duration in our target heart rate range.

A variety of activities such as walking, jogging, inline skating, ice skating, swimming and water exercises, cycling, cross-country skiing, hiking, gardening, dancing, rope jumping, canoeing or kayaking or surf skiing, and different sporting activities (basketball, netball, soccer, tennis, and so on) is recommended instead of sticking to just one type of activity. Variety of activity allows different muscle groups to be used without creating an overuse of any one muscle group as well as sustaining interest in pursuing activity on a regular basis.

Aerobic fitness is produced through the efficient working of the heart–lung system to supply fuel or oxygen to the working muscles to sustain activity for a long time. This is called cardiovascular (CV) endurance. Regular aerobic activity helps to reduce the risk of heart disease by building CV fitness, burning off calories to keep body fatness in balance, and developing muscular endurance.

Target Heart Rate

A pulse results from a rush of blood through the arteries after each heartbeat. This pulse can be felt on the radial artery in the wrist or on the carotid artery of the neck. The index finger, middle finger, or both are used to take your pulse. Do not use the thumb because it has a pulse of its own. **Heart rate** (HR) is the number of times the heart will beat in one minute. **Resting heart rate** (RHR) is the number of times the heart beats in a 1-minute count when the body is completely relaxed. **Maximum heart rate** (MHR) is the maximum number of times the heart can beat in 1 minute. MHR is estimated to be 220 minus a person's age in years. For a person to exercise for very long at MHR would be too difficult; it is more beneficial to exercise in the **Target heart rate range** (THR) which is 60% to 80% of the MHR. Exercising in your target heart rate range ("threshold of training") is the minimum amount of exercise necessary to cause improvements in cardio-respiratory fitness. Refer to the following example.

Determining Your Target Heart Rate (THR) Range

To calculate Target Heart Rate Range:

Maximum Heart Rate (MHR): (220 – Age) beats per minute (bpm)

Target Heart Rate (THR): 60% to 80% of MHR

For a 10-second count rate: divide THR number by 6

Example for a 10-year-old:
MHR = (220 – 10) = 210 bpm
THR range = 210 × .6 to 210 × .8
126 to 168 bpm
10-second count: 13 to 17 bpm

Your Turn!

To Find Your Target Heart Rate Range:

Maximum Heart Rate (MHR): (220 – Age) beats per minute (bpm)

MHR = 220 – _____ = _____ bpm
THR range = _____ × .6 to _____ × .8
_____ to _____ bpm
10-second count: _____ to _____ bpm

****

My Fitness Contract (The F.I.T.T. FORMULA):

I need to do aerobic activity at least _____ a week for _____ minutes of continuous activity in my Training Heart Rate Range between _____ and _____.

Date: _____ Signed: _____

****

Monitoring Your Resting Heart Rate

Each morning as you are waking up from your night's sleep, take your Resting Heart Rate (RHR). Plot the number of beats per minute (bpm) on the graph below. Plot your resting heart rate for 10 days.

You can take your RHR at your writs (radial artery) or at your neck (carotid artery).

At the Wrist: To find your radial artery, place 3 middle fingers of one hand on the palm side of the wrist, close to the thumb line. Press gently and listen carefully. Count the number of beats in 15 seconds and multiply by 4 to get the Beats per Minute (BPM).

At the Neck: To find the carotid artery, place 3 middle fingers on the artery located on either side of the neck just below the chin. Never use your thumb because it has a pulse of its own. Press gently and count for 15 seconds, then multiply for 4 to get the RHR.

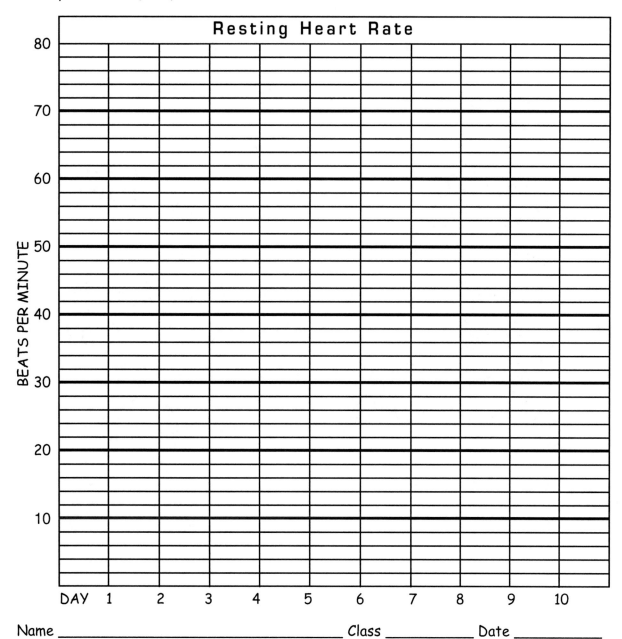

Resting Heart Rate graph with BEATS PER MINUTE on the vertical axis (marked 10, 20, 30, 40, 50, 60, 70, 80) and DAY on the horizontal axis (1 through 10).

Name _____ Class _____ Date _____

Name _____ Class _____ Date _____

Busy Muscles & Busy Bones Worksheet

Over the past few weeks you have been learning the names of the different major muscle groups and the bones of your body, where they are located, what they do, how to warm them up and cool them down properly, and even how to spell and pronounce the names correctly! You have over 600 muscles and over 200 bones! The strongest muscle is your heart muscle which must last you a lifetime; the strongest bone is your jaw bone or mandible.

The body is able to move only as a result of the cooperative actions of skeletal and muscular systems that allow the performance of a whole range of human movement. Muscles can only contract to pull on bone and thus cause movement to occur. Once a muscle has contracted to move a bone, another muscle must contract to return the bone to its original position. For this reason, the muscles tend to work in pairs contracting and relaxing. For example, to bend your arm, the biceps contract while the triceps relax.

Check out the Muscle-Dude and Bone-Dude below:

Muscle-dude   Bone-dude

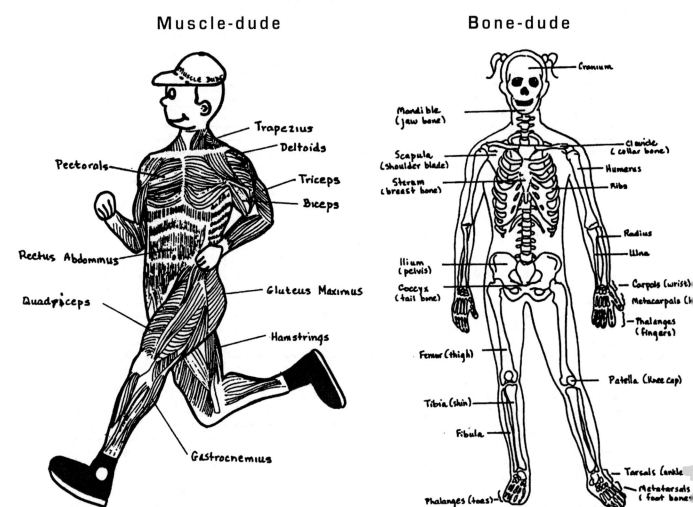

Name _____ Class _____ Date _____

Name the Muscles on the Muscle-dude

Choose the muscles from the list given below and write in the correct place.

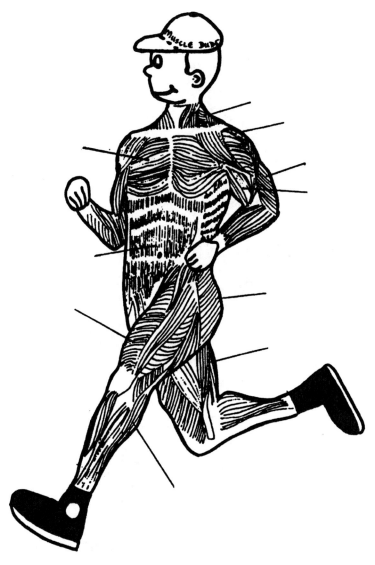

TRAPEZIUS	DELTOIDS	GLUTEUS MAXIMUS
BICEPS	HAMSTRINGS	GASTROCNEMIUS
QUADRICEPS	RECTUS ABDOMINUS	TRICEPS
PECTORALS		

Name _____ Class _____ Date _____

Bone-dude Worksheet

Name the bones on the Bone-Dude. Choose the bones from the list given below and write in the correct place.

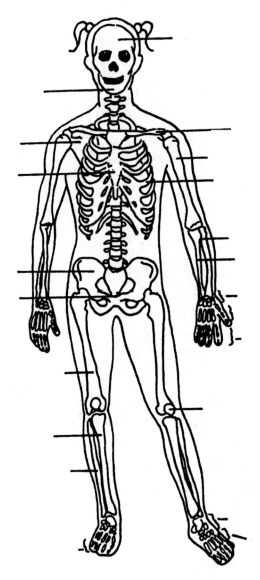

Cranium	Radius	Fibula	Metacarpals
Mandible	Femur	Tarsals	Metatarsals
Scapula	Patella	Clavicle	Ulna
Humerus	Carpals	Phalanges	Tibia
Coccyx	Ribs	Sternum	Ilium

Name _____ Class _____ Date _____

PASSIVE ACTIVITIES

PLAY & LEISURE ACTIVITIES | STRENGTH & FLEXIBILITY

SPORT & RECREATION ACTIVITIES | AEROBIC ACTIVITIES

DAILY ACTIVITIES

How active are you each day?

Fill in your Activity Pyramid with all the different activities you do in one week. Include activities that you do by yourself, with your family, with your friends, with your teammates in the sports that you practice and play, in your Physical Education classes, and in special sports-day events (such as Swimming carnivals, and Track and Field Days), and even household chores!

Pay attention to how much time you spend watching TV, playing computer games, or other quiet activity such as reading a book, playing a musical instrument such as a guitar, or listening to music.

Comments about your activity levels:

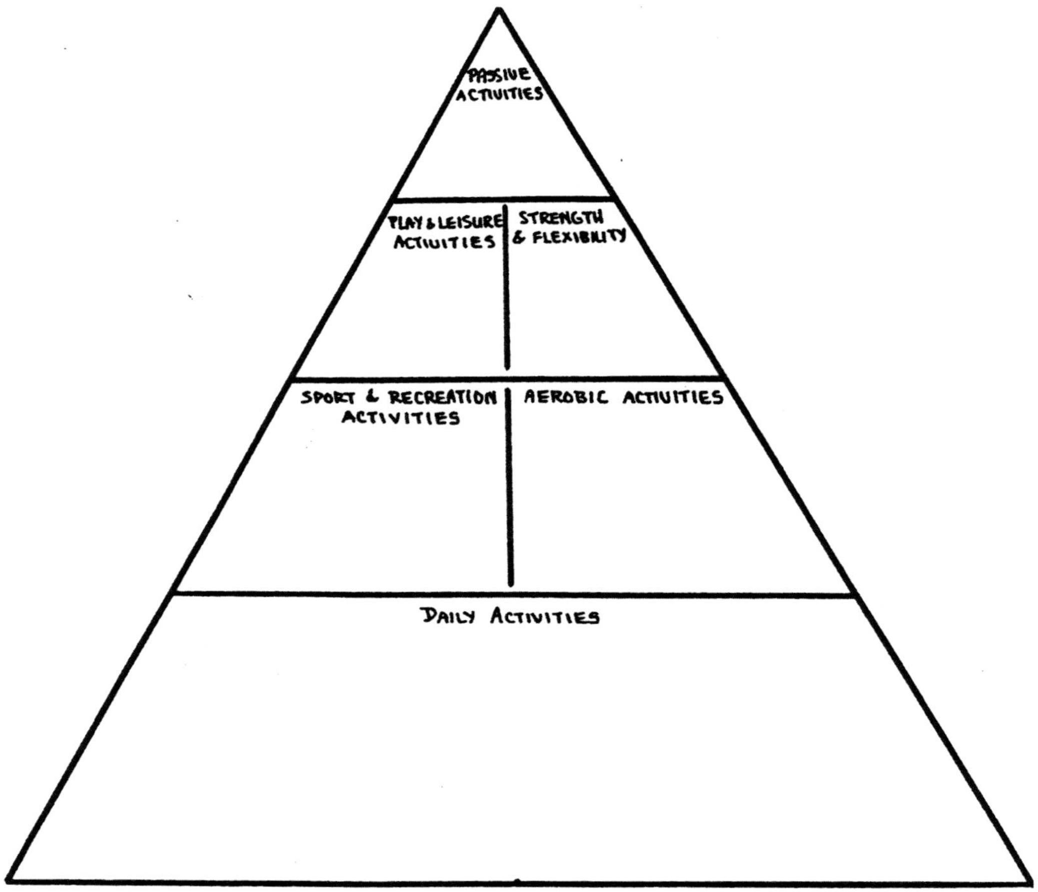

Name _____ Class _____ Date _____

"Math in a Heart Beat" Fitness Activity

Kris has a resting heart rate of 76 bpm. Jordon has a resting heart rate of 56 bpm (beats per minute).

Let's work out the difference in number of heart beats for each over a period of a year. Get your calculator ready—you are going to need it!

Comments:

Kris	Jordan
One Hour:	
76 bpm × 60 minutes = _____/hr	56 bpm × 60 minutes = _____/hr
One Day:	
_____/hr × 24 hrs = _____/day	_____/hr × 24 hours = _____/day
One Week:	
_____/day × 7 days = _____/wk	_____/day × 7 days = _____/wk
One Year:	
_____/wk × 52 = _____/yr	_____/wk × 52 = _____/yr

Difference in Heart Beats per Year:

      Kris's HB/Yr − Jordan's HB/YR =

_____ − _____ = _____ beats per year

_____

_____

_____

_____

_____

Name _____ Class _____ Date _____

Your Aerobic Grids

Power walking, running, biking, swimming, dancing, cross-country skiing, ice skating, inline skating, basketball, soccer, football, netball, tennis, and body-surfing are all good examples of aerobic activities to improve your endurance and build a strong and healthy heart.

After each aerobic activity that you do (and that lasts for a minimum of 15 minutes of continuous activity), color in one of the squares in your aerobic grid. If you continue the activity for 30 minutes, color in two squares, and so on. Your goal is to complete the Aerobic F.I.T.T. grid, then the P.R.I.D.E. grid to the best of your ability within a certain time (to be determined by the teacher)—but have good fun doing so!

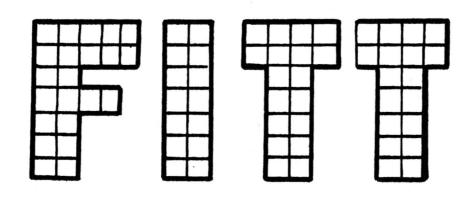

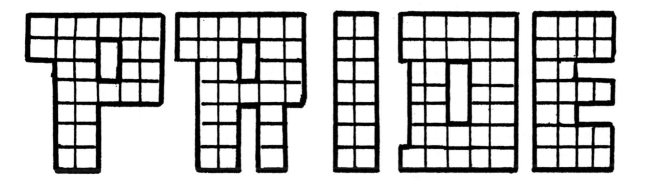

Name _____ Class _____ Date _____

Let's Run Around Australia!

Each team Captain and Co-Captain will monitor their team's efforts. They will be responsible for collecting each member's running sheet for that week and recording the results by shading in the team's "Running Barometer." The Captains use pins to display the distance covered on the team's map and learn about Australia as the class travels from state to state! For example, start from Perth and travel east across the countryside. When you get to Kalgoorlie, study gold mining. As you progress, learn about the deserts, Ayre's Rock at Alice Springs, Barossa Valley, The Blue Mountains, The Great Barrier Reef, Tasmania, and the native animals of Australia. Don't forget to watch out for Kangaroos along the way!

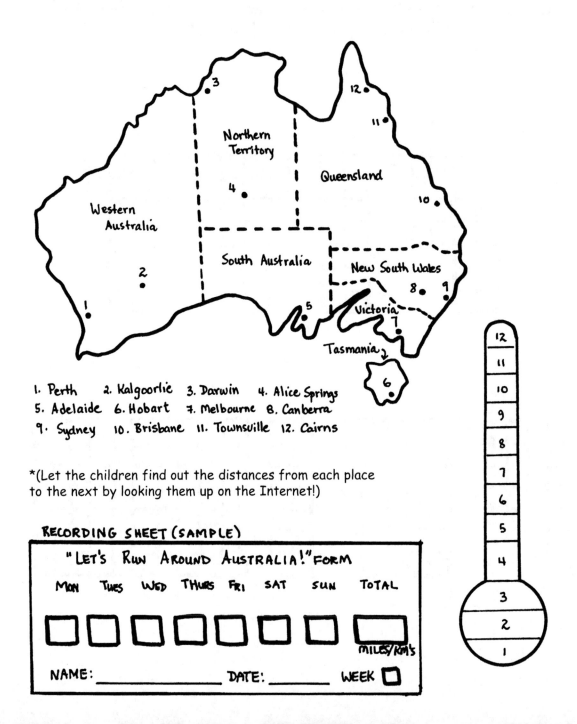

1. Perth   2. Kalgoorlie   3. Darwin   4. Alice Springs
5. Adelaide   6. Hobart   7. Melbourne   8. Canberra
9. Sydney   10. Brisbane   11. Townsville   12. Cairns

*(Let the children find out the distances from each place to the next by looking them up on the Internet!)

RECORDING SHEET (SAMPLE)

"LET'S RUN AROUND AUSTRALIA!" FORM

MON	TUES	WED	THURS	FRI	SAT	SUN	TOTAL
☐	☐	☐	☐	☐	☐	☐	☐

MILES/KM's

NAME: _____   DATE: _____   WEEK ☐

Name _____ Class _____ Date _____

How nutritiously do you eat each day?

Fill in your Nutrition Pyramid with everything you eat and drink each day for one week. Remember to include, if possible, the quantities of each. For example, 5 glasses of water, 3 glasses of milk, 2 medium corn on the cobs, 3 pieces of toast, 2 eggs, 1 bowl of cereal.

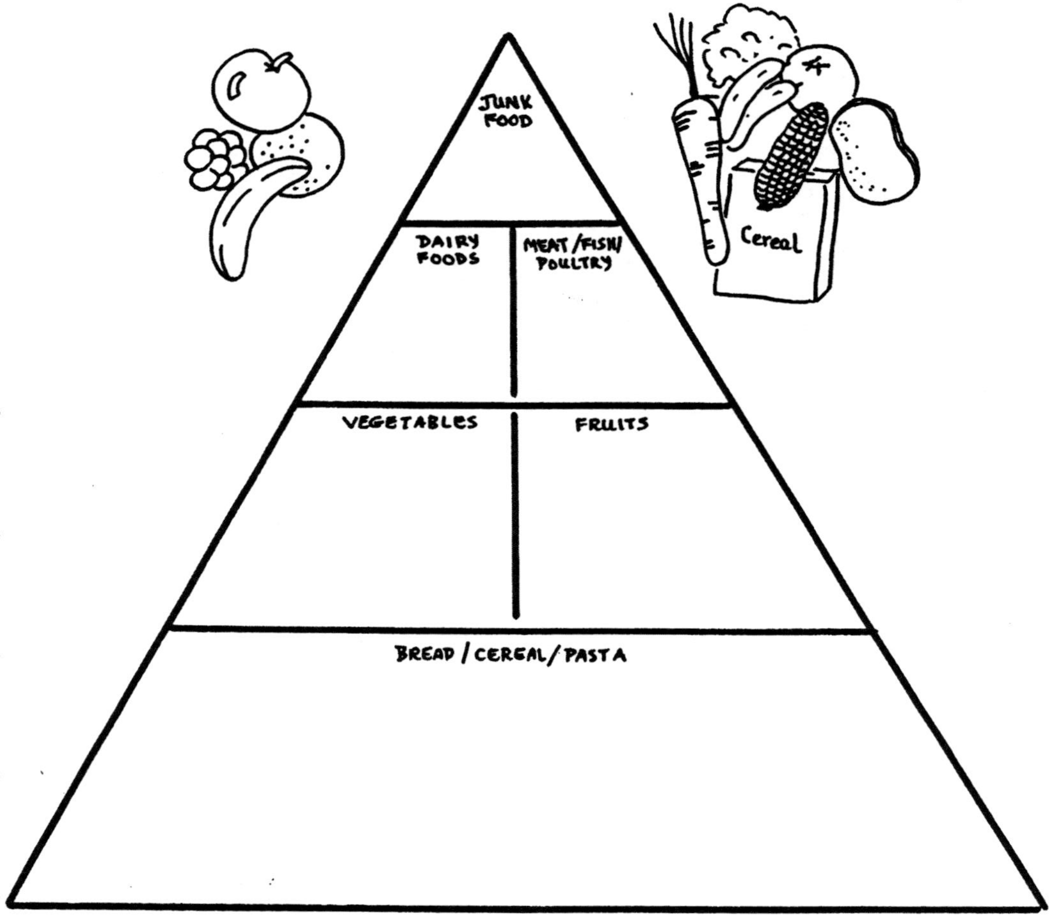

Comments about your eating habits:

JUNK FOOD

DAIRY FOODS

MEAT/FISH/POULTRY

VEGETABLES

FRUITS

BREAD/CEREAL/PASTA

Name _____ Class _____ Date _____

Nutrition Worksheet #1

Compare Max's and Nikki's food eaten for the day.

	Max	**Nikki**
Breakfast:	Didn't eat breakfast	Orange juice Scrambled eggs 1 slice whole wheat toast with no-cholesterol margarine 1% milk (enriched with iron)
Morning Snack:	Doughnut Chocolate milk	Banana Apple juice
Lunch:	Hotdog Potato chips Milkshake	Tuna sandwich on multi-grain bread Carrot sticks Apple Water
Afternoon Snack:	Chocolate bar	Yogurt (blueberry)
Dinner:	Pork chops Mashed potatoes in butter/sour cream Peas Coconut cream pie 8-oz. cola	Pink snapper baked fish Long grain rice Broccoli 1% milk (enriched with iron) Pumpkin pie
Snacks:	Salted peanuts 8-oz. cola	Orange Raisin toast

1. Who ate the healthier menu? Why?

_____

_____

_____

2. What suggestions can you make for improving the nutrient value of the other diet?

_____

_____

_____

Name _____ Class _____ Date _____

Nutrition Worksheet #2

Free Radicals are born by electrically charged atomic particles being released. This is part of the normal chemical process of every living cell. However, external factors, such as exposure to cigarette smoke, radiation, or ozone, can also intensify free radical activity. These free radicals can change the basic structure of cells, leading to chronic diseases and accelerating the aging process.

Antioxidants are the chemical "good guys" that quench or mop-up free radicals and help repair damage to cells. The cells themselves manufacture some antioxidants. Others are found in the nutrients that we eat. The main antioxidants are vitamins C, E, and A (beta carotene).

What did you eat today?
Record everything you ate and drank during the past 24 hours.

Breakfast/Morning Snack:

_____

_____

_____

_____

_____

Lunch Time/Afternoon Snack:

_____

_____

_____

_____

_____

Dinner Time/Evening Snack:

_____

_____

_____

_____

_____

On the back of this sheet, comment about the food you ate and if your day of eating included food from all the Basic Food Groups. Check your Nutrition Pyramid.

FORTUNE COOKIE

Prepare at least twenty Fortune Cookie cards (using 3 × 5 index cards) on which are written aerobic, strength, agility, flexibility, or cooperative tasks. If possible, laminate the cards for durability. In class time have each team create its own set of Fortune Cookie cards. Use as a warming-up activity throughout the year or introduce as a break signal in the lesson.

Teaching Points:

◆   Scatter the cards face down in the center of the play area.

◆   On teacher's signal (locomotor movements such as power walking clockwise, slide stepping counterclockwise, skipping), all players move in a counterclockwise or clockwise direction around the play area.

◆   On signal "Bounce," players bounce lightly in place. Teacher calls out one of the player's names. That player jogs to the center and quickly selects a card. This player reads out the task on the card, teacher repeats the task, and then everyone does the task, then jogs in place until everyone else is finished.

◆   Signal to move is then given, and players again run in a clockwise or counterclockwise direction.

◆   Continue in this way until a warming-up effect is achieved.

Suggestions for Fortune Cookie Tasks:

●   Touch each sideline with right hand, left foot (left hand, right foot).
●   Touch each end line with two hands (two knees).
●   Crab Walk greeting (5 different players).
●   Leap Frog with a partner from one sideline to the other.
●   Thread-the-Needle.
●   Jump up in the air—Sit—Lie Down: repeat 3 times.
●   5 Inchworms.
●   Bucking Broncos.
●   Diagonal Corners—5 push-ups in each one.
●   Rope Jump for 30 seconds.
●   Five-Point Body Balance with partner.
●   Diagonal Corners—7 Knee Hugs in each corner.
●   Periscope Stretch (each leg for 15 seconds).
●   Calf Stretchers (each leg for 15 seconds).
●   Compass (walk hands around feet clockwise, then counterclockwise).
●   Body Circles (3 complete circles—slowly).
●   Breathing (inhale slowing for 5 seconds; exhale slowly for 5 seconds).
●   Step up and down a bench 10 times.
●   Hand-Push (Face-to-Face, Palm-to-Palm).
●   Knee-Box.
●   Make up your own Fortune Cookie task!

'LEAP FROG'

THREAD THE NEEDLE

BUCKING BRONCO

KNEE-BOX

JOKER'S WILD

Using blank 5 × 8 index cards, make up a deck of "exercise" playing cards. Include the "2" through the "Ace" and the "face" cards (King, Queen, and Jack) in each of the four suits (Hearts, Diamonds, Spades, and Clubs). Add four Joker cards which will be the "wild cards." Include aerobic activity, strength, agility, flexibility, and cooperative tasks. Use as a warming-up activity throughout the year or introduce as a "break" signal in the lesson.

Teaching Points:

◆ To start the activity, players jog in place in a home space. One player is selected each time to draw a card.

◆ The card is shown to the other players and the teacher or that player reads out the task to be performed.

◆ Players perform the task, then return to their home to continue to jog in place. Continue until a warming-up effect is achieved.

Suggestions for Joker's Wild Tasks:

King—thirteen quarter jump-turns

Queen—twelve wall push-ups

Jack—eleven sit-ups

10—ten side leg raises, each leg

9—nine bench steps on two different benches

8—eight mountain climbers

7—seven thigh lifts (each leg)

6—six High Ten greetings

5—five agility sideline crossings

4—four "lie down, stand up, jump up"

3—three different stretches (10 seconds each)

2—two-minute rope jumping

Ace—Teacher's Choice (or Player's Choice)

Joker—one speed lap around the play area

Variation:

Poker Dice. One player selects a card while the other player rolls the dice. Add up the number on the dice to determine the number of repetitions to be done for that exercise. For example, "9" (dice rolls a "4" and a "5").

EXERCISE HUNT

This warming-up idea is used to develop fitness, reinforce teams, leadership skills, team interaction, and fair play. An Exercise Hunt can be designed for outdoor or indoor purposes. All activities in the Hunt (including the stretches in the Stretch Tree chart) should have been taught beforehand. Emphasize quality of movement. Emphasize that the Hunt is not a race to see which team can finish first. Observe players in action; make note of leadership shown, quality of movement, team cooperation, and so forth. Join in with each group as you can so that the players can see you involved. At the end of the Hunt provide feedback based on your observations. Have each team design an Exercise Hunt of its own. Check each Hunt to ensure safety and inclusion of fitness activities already taught. Introduce a team's Exercise Hunt as the warming-up activity until each team has had a turn over the next 4–5 weeks.

Prepare a list of fitness activities and photocopy the Exercise Hunt List for each team. Briefly go through the activities and emphasize the quality of the movement. If an indoor hunt, use music as a motivator; if an outdoor hunt, use the existing playground apparatus, and so forth, to do the activities.

Explain that each team can start the Hunt at any point, but they must follow the order until all the activities are completed. Team captain and co-captain are responsible for ensuring that team members stay together. Before a team can move on to the next fitness activity, each team member must have completed the immediate task. When a team completes the Hunt, the team moves to the Stretch Tree which is located in the middle of the play area (or playground area). Players stretch until all the teams have completed the Hunt.

Suggestions for an Outdoor Hunt:

- Touch a tree, a goal post, and a playground apparatus.
- Leap-frog your team a total of 15 leapfrog jumps.
- Move under 5 different playground objects.
- Run once around the perimeter of the school grounds.
- Jump on and off 5 different objects.
- Lean against an immovable object and do 10 push-ups.
- Run from one goal post to the other.
- Ski-jump along the end line of the play area.
- Carefully go up a slide, and slide down it.
- Hand walk across the high bar.

Stretch Tree: (See Station #6, p. 52 for Illustrations)

Pencil Stretch	Periscope Stretch	Finger Stretch	Calf Stretch
Foot Artist	Thigh Stretch	Butterfly Stretch	Side Stretch

Suggestions for an Indoor Hunt:

- Give High Ten's to 10 different players who are not your team members.
- Do 10 Tummy Crunches.
- Puppy Dog Walk from one sideline to the other.
- Jog around the play area with your hands on your head.
- Skip from one diagonal corner to the other corner.
- Chorus Line Stork Stand (hold for at least 10 seconds).
- Touch each end line of play area with one foot and one hand.
- Together sing a well-known rhyme or jingle.
- Jump rope for 30 seconds.
- Do 5 push-ups in each corner.

(See Lesson 6, Warming-up Activities/Games, p. 53.)

JUGGLING SCARVES ACTIVITIES

1. Put your scarf over a knee and grab it in the middle with your first three fingers of your favorite hand, "pincer grip." Wave your scarf through the air as if it was a "ghost."

2. Toss your scarf upwards and let it settle down on a different body part each time. Toss with one hand; then toss with the other hand.

3. Toss your scarf upwards and wait as long as you can to grab it downwards before it touches the floor. Repeat using the other hand.

4. **Traveling Scarves:**
    - Swish your scarf through your legs in a figure-8.
    - Sweep it like a windshield wiper.
    - Twirl it above your head like a helicopter blade.
    - Circle it in front of you like a propeller.
    - Swirl it in a large figure-8 in front of you.
    - Create another way of making your scarf travel.

5. Toss your scarf across your body and let the other hand grab it with a downwards "clawing-like" action.

6. *Challenge:* Start by holding both scarves in one hand, then toss one, toss the other, and keep this pattern going! Repeat with the other hand.

7. Show me what other tasks you can do with your scarf.

8. **Partner Juggling.** At the same time toss your scarves back and forth to each other.

9. **Two Scarves Juggling:**
    - Toss both scarves in the air at the same time, then try to catch them.
    - Try to juggle with 2 scarves by tossing one across the body; then at the peak of the first scarf, toss the second scarf. Grab downwards with the hand on that side. *Cues:* "Toss-toss, grab-grab."

10. **Three Scarves Juggling:**

Hold the middle of first scarf in the pincer grip in one hand; hold the second scarf in the pincer grip of the other hand. Hold the third scarf with the fourth and fifth fingers of the favorite hand. This is the ready position. Now let's try juggling three scarves! Begin with the hand that holds two scarves.

- Toss the first scarf across your body and above the opposite shoulder.
- When this scarf gets to the top of the toss, send the second scarf above the opposite shoulder.
- When the second scarf gets to the top of the toss, throw the third scarf across the body and above the opposite shoulder.
- As a scarf falls downwards, grab with the hand on that side and send it back across to the opposite side.
- Continue this figure-8 pattern, alternating hands and using the cues: "one, two, three" or call out the colors of the scarf (pink, yellow, orange).
- To learn the throwing order, toss the scarves and let them float to the floor, calling out the colors.

Variations:

Windmill Juggling. Toss the scarves as above, but with arm sweeping down and outwards, and then in towards the middle.

Scarf Pirates. Stand with a partner face to face. One partner juggles scarves while the other partner "steals" them one at a time to take over the figure-8 pattern. The trick is to cue in on one color. When it reaches the top, grab it, then the second, and the third.

TINIKLING

This Philippine dance mimes the movements of a long-necked bird as it steps from one rice paddy to another. The traditional folk dance is used to develop excellent eye–foot coordination, improve both rhythm and auditory response, and provide excellent cooperation experience. The sticks consist of two 8–10-foot PVC pipes and 2 crossbars or slide boards (two-by-fours about a yard long) as shown.

Teach the Tinikling Strike Rhythm and Basic Step to music in ³⁄₄ time. Use popular music with a ³⁄₄ beat or the traditional music of the country. Have dancers form groups of 4 and scatter around the dance area. Each group collects two strikers and 2 crossbars. In each group, two dancers kneel at each end of the strikers and rest the poles about 15 inches apart on the crossbars, which are about 7 feet from each other.

1. **Tinikling Rhythm.** On signal "Strike, Tap, Tap!" kneeling dancers slide strikers together along crossbars and strike the poles together; then open strikers apart and lift about 1 inch from the crossbars, and tap twice on the crossbars. Provide ample time for strikers to practice this rhythm sequence. Emphasize that pole strikers stay in kneeling position with their arms extended forward.

2. **Basic Tinikling Step.** Each dancer starts with right side to the poles and practice in turn, to the following footwork pattern using a hopping step:

   "Strike"—hopping step on left foot

   "Tap"—hopping step right foot between strikers

   "Tap"—hopping step left foot between strikers

   "Strike"—hopping step right foot outside strikers to dancer's right

   "Tap"—hopping step left foot between strikers

   "Tap"—hopping step right foot between strikers

   "Strike"—hopping step left foot outside to original position

3. **Straddle-step.** Dancer begins by standing between the two poles. On "Strike," dancer jumps feet apart outside the poles. On "Tap"–"Tap," dancer jumps feet together inside the poles.

4. **Crossover Step.** Dancer uses a crossover step to step in and out of the poles, beginning with right foot outside the poles. Dancer crosses left foot over the right as he/she steps left foot inside; then dancer steps right foot inside.

'Straddle Step'

5. **Rocker-step.** Dancer faces the poles. Choosing any foot, dancer steps in and out (forward and backward) in a rocking action.

6. **Circling Poles.** Dancer positions so that right side is nearer to poles.
   - On "Strike," dancer steps forward on the left foot
   - On "Tap," dancer steps right foot between the poles.

- On "Tap," dancer steps left foot between the poles.
- On "Strike," dancer steps with right foot outside the poles to the right.
- On "Tap–Tap," dancer uses light running steps to about-face so that left side is now nearer the poles.
- On the next "Strike, Tap, Tap" sequence, dancer uses the basic tinikling step to return to starting position.

7. **Partner Tinikling:**

- Two dancers enter and leave toward the same side; enter and leave at opposite end to partner, with right sides to poles.
- Two dancers face each other, join both hands, and perform the basic tinikling step, then join inside hands and move side-by-side.

**7.
PARTNER TINIKLING**

8. **Advanced Tinikling Pole Patterns:**

- **Line Formation:** Space three or more sets of poles about 6 feet apart. Dancers, keeping right side toward the poles throughout this sequence, step their way down the sets, making a circling movement as in the Circling Poles and return down the line in the opposite direction. Dancers do a basic tinikling step, finishing on the right side of the first set of poles. Then use three light running steps to get into position to do another tinikling step at the next two sets of poles. When a dancer gets to the end, he/she circles with three steps to get into position to go up the sets.

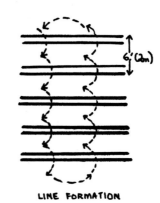

LINE FORMATION

- **Square Formation:** Place four sets of poles in a square formation. Have one dancer stand with right side toward poles on the inside of each set. Each dancer does a tinikling step, crossing to the outside of the square. Then dancer circles with three steps to position for a return tinikling step. Do another tinikling step, returning to the inside of the square. Rotate CCW with three running steps to the next set of poles.

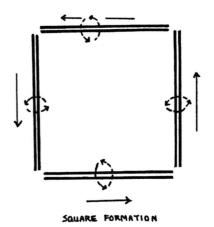

SQUARE FORMATION

Variations:

- Use a 4/4 rhythm and adjust tinikling steps to a "Close-Close," "Tap–Tap" sequence. Basic foot pattern becomes two steps outside poles; two steps inside.
- Also available from sports catalog companies are tinikling sticks filled with plastic pellets so that the sticks sound like maracas, further enhancing rhythm and sensory perception.

BOOMERANG THROWING

Boomerangs have been around for a long time! Mostly associated with the Aborigines, the indigenous people of Australia, the boomerang was used for hunting and many other specialized tasks. However, scientists believe that boomerangs were developed by prehistoric man for hunting purposes. There are basically two types of boomerangs: the returning and non-returning, with the returning boomerangs being the more popular type. Returning boomerangs are used primarily for the sport of boomerang throwing.

Boomerangs are made of wood or plastic and measure from 1 to 6½ feet long and ½ to 5 inches wide. Most boomerangs have a bend in the middle that forms two wings shaped like the wings of an airplane, with each wing being curved on top and flat on the bottom. As the boomerang spins wing over wing in flight, its shape causes lower air pressure above each wing than below it. This difference in pressure is what keeps the boomerang airborne.

Once the thrower learns to correctly throw the returning boomerang, the boomerang will spin forward as it rises and begin a curved path back to the thrower so that the thrower can make the catch without moving from his/her starting position.

Modern-day boomerangs such as the aerobie orbiter (the triangle boomerang) can be purchased from retail sports/toy stores and major sports catalog companies.

Skill Builders

Hand–eye coordination, tracking, catching, overhand throwing, peripheral vision, partner work

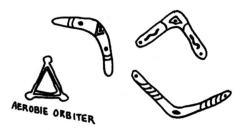

AEROBIE ORBITER

Facility/Equipment Required:

♦   Large oval or grassed area free of obstacles or obstructions

♦   1 boomerang per pair

Teaching Points:

Safety Considerations

♦   Always check the surroundings before throwing the boomerang.

♦   Throw the boomerang in a cleared oval area, well away from other people and any obstructions or obstacles.

♦   Emphasize that everyone stay alert—always watching the path of the boomerang until it lands and keeping on the lookout for any straying boomerangs. If a boomerang does come towards you, quickly try to duck, protecting your head with your arms and hands.

♦   If you throw your boomerang off-line, try to alert anyone in its path.

♦   Do not allow the boomerang to be thrown in strong windy conditions.

Gripping the Boomerang

Grip the end of the boomerang between the thumb and forefinger so that the rounded side is facing you and the flat side is facing out.

The bend of the boomerang should point in the direction of the throw.

Hold the boomerang firmly and cocked back along the arm as far as possible in order to give as much spin as possible.

Throwing the Boomerang (For a right-hander)

Throw overhand—not sidearm.

Throw at the correct tilt angle (angle from the vertical). See diagram.

Try to throw boomerang at a 45-degree angle to the right of the oncoming wind. (Feel the wind on your left cheek.)

Too much tilt angle makes the boomerang fly high and land behind.

Too little tilt angle forces the boomerang to fly lower and land forward.

Aim at a target in the distance.

If the boomerang lands to the left of your target, then throw more to the right of the target and vice versa.

Catching the Boomerang

Catch the boomerang with a two-hand "clapping" position.

Keep fingers relaxed and pointed in the direction of the boomerang's flight.

Track the boomerang all the way into your hands.

Reach and "give" with the elbows to absorb its impact.

Skill Progressions and Games:

1. Demonstrate the grip and throwing position. Emphasize the safety points. Demonstrate the throwing action and catching pointers. Have throwers pantomime this action.

2. Have throwers pair off and each pair collect a boomerang and find a free throwing space. Check for good spacing between pairs. Pairs practice throwing the boomerang from the same point. Practice catching the boomerang with a two-hand clapping position.

3. **Hot-dog Flight.** Who can make the boomerang do the most interesting flight, such as loops and reverse turns?

4. **Hot-dog Catching.** Try to catch the boomerang with one hand; behind the back; under the leg. What other ways can you invent to catch the boomerang?

Boomerang Games

1. **Closest to the Mark.** Each thrower must throw from the same point. The aim is to land the boomerang as close as possible to the throwing point. Play best out of three throws, then challenge someone else.

2. **Airborne.** The object is to keep the boomerang flying through the air for the longest time. Nonthrowing partner keeps track of the "airborne" time using his/her wristwatch. Challenge other throwers.

3. **Round the Pole.** Try to throw the boomerang around a pole such as a flagpole or goal post and catch it. Start about 10 giant steps away from the pole, then gradually move farther away with each successful throw.

Fit-think Idea

Discuss the aero-dynamics of the boomerang and how its shape keeps it airborne.

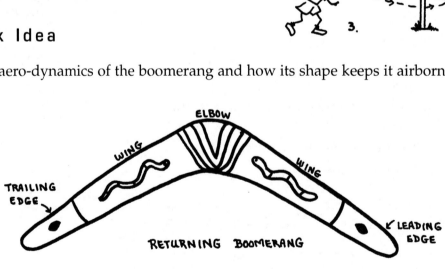

ELBOW

WING

WING

TRAILING EDGE

LEADING EDGE

RETURNING BOOMERANG